I0153573

SHATTERED PEOPLE SERIES

Book One:

Revised Second Edition

Journeys to Joy

Pastor Michael E. Chalberg

SCP
Shepherds Care Publishing

Copyright 2003, 2020 by Evert G. Chalberg

SHATTERED PEOPLE SERIES:
Second Edition - Revised

Journeys to Joy

By Pastor Michael E. Chalberg

Printed in the USA & Internationally by Ingram/LSI.

Library of Congress Control Number: 2003091652
ISBN 97817349703-71 Paperback Pub. 12/2020
ISBN 97809746464-66 E-Book Edition Pub. 12/2020

All rights reserved. No part of this publication may be reproduced or transmitted in any form or by any means without written permission of the Author.

Unless otherwise indicated, Bible quotations are taken from the New Open Bible, Study Edition, Copyright ©1990 by Thomas Nelson, Inc; The Message, New Testament with Psalms and Proverbs, Copyright © 1993, 1994, 1995 by Eugene H. Peterson, and NAVPRESS.

Shepherds Care Publishing - **SCP**
An Outreach of Shepherd's Care Ministries
2473 S. Higley Road Suite 104 PMB 210
Gilbert, AZ 85295

Order: scpublishing2020@gmail.com
Email: SCPublishing@shepherdscareministries.org
Web: www.shepherdscareministries.org

Table of Contents

DEDICATION

We dedicate this book to the glory of Jesus Christ,
for helping anyone in need of His healing love.
Through Him all things are possible to
those who hope and trust in Him.
May it bring to you,
A New Hope
A Renewed Hope
A Remembered Hope
& An Everlasting Hope.

ACKNOWLEDGMENTS

This book and the two to follow it are only possible because of the love and support of many people. My thanks and eternal gratitude goes out to them. To my prayer support team of Bruce and Tone Ferry, thank you for many years of intercession and teaching me the truth about God's love.

To my friends and family, who gave me editorial, financial, practical and legal help to complete this task, blessings upon you all. To my friend and co-editor of the final submissions, David Beskeen, may God bless your ministry gifts far above your hopes and dreams.

To my partner in life, ministry, marriage and the journey still ahead – my wife Carol, my unending love and devotion for your support, editing, love and acceptance of time apart that I needed to write these books.

To the System that is all of the people who are the examples of love, hope, faith, friendship and perseverance contained in these pages, may God richly bless you all with the fulfillment of His promises to you. Your sacrifices to bring hope to others will be heralded in the heavens.

Forward

You are about to embark on a journey which will likely challenge how you think about abuse and the abused, about healing, and about God's commitment to wholeness. It tells the story of how one multiple sought God's healing, and how God responded to all of them. I hope and pray that, if you are one who has been abused, this book will provide support for you in your healing. And if you are a family member, therapist, minister or friend, it will support you as you help those who have been abused.

You should understand before you start reading that this is not primarily a book about Dissociative Identity Disorder (DID) or Multiple Personality Disorder (MPD), nor about a person who suffers from either. Neither is this primarily a book about treatment methods, the necessity of a support system for multiples, or the difficulty multiples have in reconciling what has happened to them with a loving God. All of these issues are touched on, but they are not the core of the book.

Ultimately this book, and the others in this series, is about the personal commitment that God makes to each of our lives to bring healing, to bring fulfillment and to bring redemption; and about the incredible struggle and journey of one group of people who responded to God's commitment.

When Maria first came to my office, there was no hint of either her history or of her vast resolve to recover; nor was there any hint of the community of souls who lived with her. She was a scared, broken individual, hardly able to look me in the eyes; yet behind that fear and fragility laid an incredible reserve of courage and strength, and an amazing ability to take risks in order to find a better life. Ultimately, Pastor Mike and I discovered a level of faith and trust that was, and is, truly humbling. And God met Maria and her system's willingness to take risks and trust (sometimes kicking and screaming) and brought vast and beautiful healing.

And here's the good news: every multiple, every adult victim of childhood trauma, indeed every victim of trauma can find the same strength inside themselves and the same healing response from God.

I have seen the same journey embarked on by many victims, most with the joyous result of healing and wholeness.

If you are multiple, or if you are a victim of trauma, you will find much in these pages to encourage you and challenge you to hope again, to seek healing from God and support from others. It will not be easy, but it is more rewarding than you can ever imagine.

If you are a therapist, you will see a view of the mind and the psychological functioning of a multiple that may be foreign to you. This should challenge you to think differently about those we diagnose as DID and give you a fresh perspective on how to support them in their recovery.

If you are a family member, you will be challenged to provide a higher level of support for the multiple in your life and will gain a greater understanding of what goes on in their very private, very interior life.

And if you are a pastor or church worker, you are in for a bumpy ride. This book is unflinching in its analysis of the modern day church and its attitude and reaction to both those with psychiatric problems and those who are oppressed. It is unforgiving in its view of the local church as nearly incapable of effectively supporting those who are attempting to recover from childhood trauma, and of its focus on doctrine rather than individuals. As someone who lives in both places (helping individuals recover from trauma and working within a local church), I see the struggles of both parties from both sides. This book should, however, challenge you to reexamine how we can recapture Jesus' commitment to those who are most in need of His love and redemption.

Finally, if you are Roman Catholic, you will find that this book is most scathing of a church organization that has, either by intentionality, inaction, or both, allowed horrible abuses within its ranks. It is my hope and prayer that by reading this book you will challenge your leaders or superiors to take responsibility for the reforms and healing that are desperately needed. Meanwhile, we Protestants can view this as a warning: such abuse doesn't occur only in the Catholic Church, and we need to be on guard against the same abuses within our groups.

One more warning: The language that is used in this book will be offensive to some. Please understand that, for a lot of people, cussing is the language of the marketplace, and is evidence of their rage, passion and depth of feeling. If, as you read these pages, you get so hung up on the language that you can't see the message, then you have missed the entire point of Jesus' willingness to live with and minister to those who were labeled "sinners" by the Pharisees.

But as I said at the beginning, these are all secondary issues to the message of hope, healing and redemption…may you find all of these in this book.

Bruce Fielding
Licensed Marriage & Family Counselor

From the Author:

When I wrote the following preface 17 years ago, I didn't realize I was foretelling my own future. Reading it again as I revise this first edition is reassuring to me just how much the Lord will fulfill His plans for all of us. Over the last decade it has been very interesting, yet sad, to see so much of what I write and warn the church about continuing to go on unheeded. It has also been enlightening to learn firsthand from so many more survivors around the world, both about the accuracy in revealing their journeys, as well as how much ritual abuse affects a community for generations and yet still be contained and sustained in fear hidden within dark secrets.

Bringing light into these dark corners has been a blessing to this ministry, as many have found hope again in Jesus Christ. Our purpose is to reach many more survivors of clergy abuse and Satanic Ritual Abuse., including abuses of all types which causes mistrust in God. Our Internet chat room for pastoral counseling started in the fall of 2003 has grown to accomplish more than we had hoped. It has also been made clear that this first book of the **Shattered People Series:** *Journeys to Joy*, and my first adventure into writing, had its content packed too tightly within chapters too long to allow easy retention. To correct this and add new information acquired since its inception in 2003 which confirms the content, this revision will help further our cause.

I will do my best to not make it any longer than it is presently. I am also reducing the number of different fonts used to identify the different people speaking as a reference to the person's listing in the Prologue by page number in parenthesis. However, the greatest changes will be in Chapter Five on the "Abuse of Faith" with the broadening of its focus to include the full affects of Ritual Abuse in which clergy abuse is only one form.

I hope these revisions will help former readers and future readers become resolute in their quest to receive God's love and healing as described in this book series and as a resource support for our new series coming out in June 2020... *Loved Back to Life Series* about many additional personal autobiographies of severe abuse survivors sharing their accounts of healing and renewal without personal commentary by me to support their efforts that will in turn offer the same love to others in need of it. May God be forever praised for what He is accomplishing in this His ministry.

Journeys to Joy - **Book One – Revised.**

Preface

**"Righteous Father, the world has never known You,
But I have known You, and these disciples know
That You sent Me on this mission.
I have made Your very being known to them-
Who You are and what You do-
And continue to make it known,
So that Your love for Me
Might be in them exactly as I am in them."
- Jesus <u>The Message</u>**

"There are two things I want you to consider for your future in ministry. If you have gifts and the necessary skills to do any occupation, other than the professional pastoral ministry, then I think you should prayerfully consider choosing that profession instead. Being a pastor is one of the most challenging and difficult vocations in the world today. There will be times in your ministry when you will be confronted on every side by people that only want one thing from you, that you reveal God to them in the way they want to receive Him... out of the box of their church's traditional definition of God.

Today, by following these 'traditional' guidelines, it is easy for almost anybody with a good heart to do effective and fulfilling ministry within the church, as a layperson in the role of elder, deacon, pastor or any leadership role. Yet, even if we accept our pastoral role as defined by the traditional church, this does not dismiss the responsibility that God offers us individually, separate from the church. If you choose another vocation, it will be easier to find balance in your life between ministry fulfillment and the world's view of the reality of God, which is quite often in opposition to each other. Doing so will allow you to not become distracted by seeking God outside of this box, when you realize God does not live within the confines of our understanding.

However, if you believe in your heart that you have no other choice to satisfy your soul, then accept the call from God to be a pastor. Of all the different professions in my life, none have filled the void in my soul like becoming a pastor. I say becoming, because it is a lifelong process of being, filled with joys and sorrows, blessings and curses, healing and being healed, while continually asking God for forgiveness for my mistakes. Often you will be alone with God, not always because you want to be, but because people in this world believe that is where God has placed you in their job description. Yet, to be called by God into the pastorate is to have your life set apart from the world with a special purpose. That purpose is fulfilled as we encounter God walking with us through life in His presence. There may only be a few 'peak' experiences, special moments on this journey that can carry us through the difficult times.

There are moments in a baptism when you see the baby Jesus in the face of a child, or the glow of the Holy Spirit on the face of a new believer. There are moments in communion when you share the memories of what Christ Jesus did for us, and moments in prayer alone or with another when you hear the voice of God; and moments in the midst of the miraculous sharing of God's grace and forgiveness with another human heart. It is only moments like these that will bridge the larger gaps of the most unappreciated, misunderstood, maligned and challenging professions ever to be offered to people like us.

God will give you His love to share with those who need Him in any profession you choose, but to accept His call into the pastoral ministry means you are accepting the responsibility of giving up your right to choose… any other way but His, if you want to truly represent and know God in His church. When you are ready, God will release you from that traditional box and reveal His plan for you in ways you cannot even imagine now.

If you survive in the pastorate long enough, you may begin to see the masterpiece that God will weave together from these moments in the tapestry of your life. When the moments become joined together, you receive a glimpse of the eternal hope that awaits all who have the faith to complete the journey. The more glimpses you receive, the more patience you will have with the people God brings to you. Don't be afraid to give them the love of

God that Jesus will reveal to you, when you truly hunger and thirst for it. This <u>love of Jesus Christ is the only thing</u> that can empower you to reach the summit of this life, in the profession of God's servant. May God's mercy be upon you all as you journey."

I was surprised twenty-two years ago when God gave me the task of writing this series of books, because this was not in my job description as a pastor and I was (self) employed as a minister. Why did God choose me? I was not an author, yet I stepped out in trust knowing that God had a purpose and a plan for these books. Even when it started out as one book I started preparing for the possibility of more, so it was no surprise when over the following years it became two then three and maybe more. When I gave this portion of the message above to fellow seminarians, I had already been on this adventure for 3 years... with this book half-written. The more I relied on the Lord to write even the first book, the more I learned the need to share the realities that are the lives of the people presented in here so that Jesus Christ could bring His love to you, as He has to me and each one of them.

Carol and I were given a choice over 26 years ago which became our journey to unexpected joys and now we want to share this journey with you. We hope it will challenge your thinking and understanding about how great God is, and how He will reveal His love in wonderful and unexpected ways, as He has with these people we have come to know and love. You are about to enter into their lives in a very personal way with us on this journey. This may very well change you and your perceptions of God, if you are open to what the Lord may be saying to you within these pages, however, let no man or tradition define your relationship with God except God Himself. Our journey as God's servants was clearly unpredictable and yet, God in His grace revealed this truth to open our hearts to learn:

"For My thoughts are not your thoughts, neither are your ways My ways," declares the Lord.- <u>Isaiah 55:8</u>

This proof is reinforced in all my books of the *<u>Shattered People series</u>*. In 1961, J. B. Phillips presented this idea in his book entitled; <u>Your God Is Too Small</u>. This excerpt from his introduction is as fitting today for what we present in these books as it was when he introduced his purpose:

"Many men and women today are living, often with inner dissatisfaction, without any faith in God at all. This is not because they are particularly wicked, selfish or 'godless', but because they have not found with their adult minds a God big enough to account for life, big enough to fit in with the new scientific age, big enough to command their highest admiration and respect, and consequently their willing cooperation.

It is the purpose of this book to attempt two things: first to expose the inadequate conceptions of God which still linger unconsciously in many minds, and which prevent our catching a glimpse of the true God; and secondly to suggest ways in which we can find the real God for ourselves. If it is true that there is Someone in charge of the whole mystery of life and death, we can hardly expect to escape a sense of futility and frustration until we begin to see what He is like and what His purposes are."

Shortly after beginning this new aspect of ministry, the Lord began to teach me through these stories of suffering, sacrifice, endurance and hope by these people - that God was always present with them. He was asking me to reveal the truth of His love for them from birth, through their adversities in this life and present with them throughout this life's journey. The choice to accept Him as that hope was always there for them, but there for individuals to whom God's presence seemed like a cruel joke in light of what they had suffered. My task to show them how to overcome their false perceptions of God was monumental and one for which I felt totally unqualified and in need of God's grace and wisdom to even attempt. I know now how and why God blessed me by allowing me to write these biographies, or autobiographies which we pray will bring hope to the hopeless, strength to the suffering, healing to the afflicted, and the very presence of God revealed by His Spirit to the hearts of every reader who has been held captive by evil in some way and has the desire and faith to claim freedom in Christ today.

Each book will share realities that may be difficult to accept for 'believers' and 'non-believers' alike. The truths presented here have a primary bias through which they are filtered; *"Our God is near and He wants His children to know how to find and know Him in every part of their life."* These stories attempt to present an autobiographical testimony of **"*Immanuel* - God with us"**, through His desire for a personal relationship with all of us. As a reader, you will be asked to walk with these people into the physical realities of this world and the spiritual realities around and in all of us, which takes eyes and ears of faith to be experienced and understood. There is nothing new revealed in these books that hasn't already been given in the Holy Scriptures to prepare us for this reality:

"The Lord is the same, yesterday, today, and tomorrow."

The people of these books tell their own stories in their own words as they come to know God in Jesus Christ. I provide a parallel commentary intertwined with their stories for an historical context and an outside pastoral counselor's perspective of the healing process. I hope to present in these examples a model of loving unconditionally that is 'ministry' to all people, particularly for any faith leader who comes in the name of God to offer healing and hope. I also want to take the mask off of evil's reality for all to see and hear, to show how evil attempts to corrupt our lives to keep us apart from God in cunning and deceitful yet subtle ways.

These books are also about how the call of Christ upon our lives *"to love one another"* can be lived out in relationships today, simultaneously in the world and in the Kingdom of God. The primary audiences we seek to help are those souls who have lost hope in and given up on God... or think that God has given up on them. These are stories of God's relentless efforts to bring His love to all of His children, and about the forces of evil that consistently attempt to block that love. The context for each story, including my own journey as God's servant, is woven together in the words of Paul the Apostle:

"Who shall separate us from the love of Christ? Shall tribulation, or distress, or persecution, or famine, or nakedness, or peril, or sword? Just as it is written: 'For Thy sake we are being put to death all day long; We were considered as sheep to be slaughtered.' But in all these things we overwhelmingly conquer through Him who loved us. For I am convinced that neither death nor life, nor angels, nor principalities, nor things present, nor things to come, nor powers, nor height, nor depth, nor any other created thing,

shall be able to separate us from the love of God, which is in Christ Jesus our Lord." **- <u>Romans 8: 35 – 39</u>**

These thoughts offer to us understanding about how the physical world and the spiritual realm come together daily and can be understood through trust in God's unending love. This means that I will be confronting traditional concepts as their journey unfolds. A variety of faiths, religion, philosophies, psychological perspectives, and cultural biases will be looked at in the fabric of each person's life. We will look together at how Jesus responds to each individual person, with the restraints that society, history, and evil have put upon them, seeking to hinder these people and us from knowing His love. The journeys may cause you to question the potential of mankind to do good, yet they will affirm God's power to cause good to come from the evil that we do to each other. There is a truth you will come away with when you've finished these books, even though the journeys for these people and us are not yet over.

"For I know the plans I have for you,' declares the Lord, 'plans for welfare and not for calamity to give you a future and a hope. Then you will call upon Me and come and pray to Me, and I will listen to you. And you will seek Me and find Me, when you search for Me with all of your heart. And I will be found by you,' declares the Lord."
Jeremiah 29: 11-14

Some people suggested that I should withhold one essential truth about these people until a later book. Their concern is not unfounded given the nature of this truth and its common misconceptions within our society and science of today. However, the Lord has given clear instructions that these books are to be written for the purposes stated which requires me to not be concerned about the belief or disbelief of my readers, only in the truthful telling of what He has revealed.

Most of the lives you will read about in the first two books are the individual personalities that exist in one body of one 'person', someone with Dissociative Identity Disorder, or MPD, with the mystery of why God made it so only now beginning to be understood. After you have finished reading about their lives and Jesus' interaction with them, I leave it up to you to grasp the reality of each one's existence. Your own questions for God may find you walking beside them in their quest. They have all given their individual consent in the hope that lives may be changed for the glory of God and so others won't have to suffer as they did... without hope for most of their life.

A brief history and profile of each person, found in Chapter One, will help establish a context from which each person views their existence and illustrate why God rescues them as a 'body of believers...no pun intended.' I have tried to put their stories in a chronological order whenever possible, as each learned about the 'others' existence and how they coped with the changes. The stories may seem complicated if you try to understand them solely in the context of society's definition of their disorder, instead of how they have lived life's reality as individuals. The concern by some is that the complexity is lessened, when viewed from the hindsight of their corporate story over the individual stories. It is like people reading the Gospel accounts of Jesus Christ... without reading the rest of the Bible to understand the life and purpose of Jesus Christ throughout history.

These are stories of men, women and children in search of life's meaning and purpose with God. They had just begun to discover the truth of their corporate existence, let alone the meaning of Multiple Personality Disorder, when I entered into their lives to explain 'God' and 'the Father's love' to children and adults alike. The difficulty of this task is obvious, when you read how the abuse came from men and women in authority over them ...many under the name of God as their authority to 'teach' them how to receive God's love throughout their lives...thereby causing confusion and pain about what God wants for them. The traumas which began early in life that caused the 'splitting of personalities,' will be discussed in some detail in a later chapter to help understand the process of dissociation and its effect upon each person's view of reality, each other and God. While the book is not intended to define MPD in the clinical sense[1], it will provide understanding from the perspective of the survivors.

I included a definition in the first version from Bob Larson's Ministries which no longer correlates to my own as learned and experienced over the last 26 years of ministering to abuse survivors with DID/MPD in the acceptance of what Jesus has taught me. *(See Addendum #1 for Bob's definition on pages 479 - 480)*

While Bob Larson's definition is still consistent with most textbooks and teaching on the subject that is provided by the caring professionals who recognize MPD as a valid diagnosis, I now know that treating MPD as a mental/spiritual condition with the sole purpose of complete integration or blending is a mistake. I say mistake because it does not take into consideration the greater purposes and plans of God for why and how the person survives. MPD is both a survival mechanism[2] and a gift from God to allow a child to live through the variety of abuses forced upon the innocent by parents, family, clergy, caretakers and people exerting power over them... the base of that power being induced by evil to oppose God's will and love in our lives.

When a doctor, psychologist, or pastor declares to the victim that they have a mental disorder called MPD, it tells the victim "you are mentally ill for having survived the abuse in the manner that you did." This limited classification does not take into account why God gives this 'gift' of survival... so that hope survives. The survival of hope is the defining lifeline of the people in these books, expressed through intimate self-disclosures of what it is like living as a multiple without hope, and discovering the hope we all have of being acceptable to God as we are. This also explains the struggle we have before God in understanding who God is and His love. We all look at ourselves through our experiences in life both good and bad...saying thank you to God sometimes when we are blessed and mostly crying out to Him, "Why did you let this happen to me/us if you truly are an all-powerful God of love?" We approach our relationship with God from how we see ourselves, our own needs, circumstances and self-described purpose for being here...without seeking understanding of how God sees us or His purposes and plans for creating us and power to complete that purpose...if we accept it.

His plan is creating a relationship with Him through Jesus Christ to help support each other in the on-going struggle of love vs. evil. The first book begins with how God's reality encounters them in the harshness of life as they knew it without Him and ends with the first of many miraculous healings that affirm His love for each and every person who seeks Him. It will cover the first two and a half years of their journey of discovery about who God is and wants for them, with flashbacks in their own words about what they were taught about God by others and how God confronts and corrects this.

The information, profiles, verbatim, conversations, faxes, e-mails, letters, drawings, and visions recorded throughout these books, are a by-product of my journey with the people affectionately known as the '**System**.' Many people will enter into their lives for a moment, changing it forever with a careless word… or act of selfless love, while others will come and go over their lifetime without connecting to the purposes God created for them... or that they were 'many'. I will provide observations about other people outside the System including psychiatrists, psychologists, counselors, pastors, priests, family, friends, medical staff, and about those people or forces opposed to these stories ever being recorded. This narrative is to help the reader understand the changes and challenges for us to understand the purposes of God. You may think this will be an easy read about a curiosity known as MPD, but this is not the case. There will not be a watering down of the descriptions of evil encountered in these lives or of the actual responses by people to them, as they learn of evil's reality in twisting God's truths. The volumes of written material recorded from the System, others and myself are the primary sources for these books and reflect the realities of life with God. The content of writings offered here will not be changed to make God, the System, or anyone represented herein more acceptable to you.

The reality of abuse depicted in particular sections may be too graphic for some readers and abuse survivors. A **Content Warning** will be given ahead of these sections to prepare you for what follows it and an **End Warning** at the close of the section. I have chosen to include actual descriptions of certain events because the use of 'softer' statements like "he sexually abused her", can camouflage the real horror of it to our senses through the use of generalities. Propriety, even Christian piety that filters these actions, can render our responses to victims useless when we speak in these terms trying to connect and understand them, by shielding our consciousness from offering help that is without true empathy and understanding.

The portions of documents written by others recorded in these books are kept on file to ensure an honest record of what was said and done. To those who have a relationship with the System, I have explained that they give me copies of all communiqués sent or spoken to them. If they didn't want me to receive it, then they must tell the System not to forward it to me. So far no person has chosen to be exempt. For this reason alone, the names of significant people who have been involved in the lives of the System will not be changed and first names only for some will generally be used as a courtesy to the living, but the names of the System and their family are changed for their protection from the living.

I will share my biases and beliefs with you now, because they are difficult to understand without faith and will be revealed in how I tell the stories you are about to read. Nothing is to be hidden about my motives and everything is to be presented openly, so you can make up your own mind about the truth of these testimonies. My personal biases are the following:

I believe the life, death and resurrection of Jesus Christ is sufficient for all of humankind for all of time as our pathway to know God. Every individual who has heard and understands this 'Good News' will have an opportunity to choose an eternal relationship with God, but it is the individual's choice to freely accept God the Father's love through Jesus, or not. I believe that Jesus will meet each individual wherever and whenever they chose to call upon Him regardless of their human condition or their choices already made in life. What we experience in this life both good and bad is only a part of the journey, and no single experience is meant to be the destination, only an encounter along the way. Even accepting Jesus Christ as Lord and Savior is not the end, only a new beginning. The path ahead is wrought with trials and tribulations that call for endurance, just like these people you will read about experienced. They like myself, learned along this path the truth of the verse in the Lord's Prayer, **"And lead us not into temptation..."** does not mean that we won't go through it, but that He will sustain us through it in His power.

I believe that God <u>in Christ Jesus</u> will ultimately judge the human heart and determine who will have eternal life, regardless of the name for the One true God, our Creator, in any individual's faith, one of many lessons I learned from Jesus. It is not my place as a pastor to judge anyone, only guide people into the presence of Jesus to receive His healing that leads to salvation. Each choice leads to another along the path of life and Jesus wants us to encourage one another on our journeys, to help carry one another's burdens through the temptations and trials for as long as we are needed. It is the way He has walked with us having already paid the price for us all.

Finally, I believe the love of Jesus Christ accepts every life that is genuinely offered to Him, whether it is lived out in a single person's body or in the body of a multiple. Every life has the value that He has placed upon it, in His willingness to give His own life for those to whom He has given life.

This will raise some theological and psychological questions, such as: Does each personality of a multiple have their own soul before God? Or, is integration of the personalities into one soul the only way they are acceptable to God? Is a soul fragmented by evil's power any less valuable to God than one who is 'whole' and rejects His love out of pride? Is it more difficult to accept the reality of the presence of immense evil in this physical world doing horrific things to children through family members or clergy; Or that God would give MPD or dissociation as a 'gift' to allow these children to survive until the time He has planned for their healing in the Truth? Can Christians be controlled/possessed by demonic spirits after accepting Jesus Christ as Savior? Can a demon manifest itself as Jesus Christ in a person's life, and if so, how does one tell the difference? There will be many other questions that you will ask before you are through these books. I hope you take time to thoughtfully consider any question raised while reading these books. These thoughts and beliefs are some of the 'Mountains of Faith' waiting for us to overcome in our pursuit of truth. If you only view from a safe distance the images and the lives you will read about, you may not experience the adventure of the journey or allow yourself the joy of reaching the summit of hope fulfilled with them in God's plan.

When I first joined them in this journey, I had questions and doubts about what God was calling me to do for Him as a pastor and a counselor. Today I have no doubt about 'who' God is and what it is He wants me to do for Him. I will listen and trust God each day to give me the words to present to you the truth about God's love. It may take a miracle for anyone to believe these accounts… but that is between you and God. If miracles are needed… there's no one else who can make them happen.

I have watched the moments I spoke of earlier in this Preface fill my days as a pastor and shepherd and they have become my miracle from God. The future is becoming brighter, as uncertainty turns into anticipation of the adventure continuing… empowered by His hope and love.   Pastor Michael E. Chalberg

"And not only this, but we also exult in our tribulations, knowing that tribulation brings about perseverance; and perseverance, proven character; and proven character, hope; and hope does not disappoint, because the love of God has been poured out within our hearts through the Holy Spirit who was given to us…

"For in hope we have been saved, but hope that is seen is not hope; for why does one also hope for what he sees? But if we hope for what we do not see, with perseverance we wait eagerly for it."
- Romans 5: 3-5, 8: 24-25

Notes:

[1] For a clinical understanding of MPD, I recommend <u>More Than One: An Inside Look at Multiple Personality Disorder</u> by Terri A. Clark, M.D., Thomas Nelson Publishers, 1993.

[2] For an introduction to MPD / DID: <u>United We Stand: A Book for People with Multiple Personalities</u> by Eliana Gil, Ph.D., Launch Press, 1990.

Prologue:

"The Challenges in Discovering Faith"

**"I will lift up my eyes to the mountains;
from where shall my help come from?
My help comes from the Lord,
who made heaven and earth.
He will not allow your foot to slip;
He who guards over you will not sleep."
-David in <u>Psalm 121</u>**

THE BIRTH OF A PERSON
-SPIRITUAL JOURNEY OF A MULTIPLE-
-QUIET WALKER

On a cold, rainy April morning a child is born in a damp room overlooking acres of tomato fields. As she drew her first innocent breath of life, she was unaware of the terrible things that would happen to her during her life's journey. This is her story.

Before she could even begin to walk, the child was given over to a grandfather. During her tender years, she was beaten, sexually abused and forced to work in the fruit sheds. Without any way of escape the child learned to disengage and soon developed other personalities to cope with the trauma.

But more evil followed. Taken into a cult, she was given the orisha Yemaya. She witnessed ritual sacrifices. Farm workers molested her and still she maintained an innocence and purity about her.

As if the fire of God had fallen from heaven upon her, she continued to create more personalities to survive. She was given over to a priest and sexually abused. She was tormented and forced into silence with threats and manipulation. She gave birth to a child with a rare disease causing permanent disability. And if that was not enough, she became diseased with cancer.

13

The one known as Maria was quick to respond. I wish I had died before I was born. Why didn't God just kill me at birth? If I only had died before I was born, then I would be in heaven right now in peace. Why was I born, if God was only going to give me all of this? I just want to die.

What have we done wrong, echoed Louise? And if the feelings of guilt, hopelessness and fear were not enough, Raquel voiced the song of a heart pierced by poison arrows. I long to be freed from this sadness that aches within my being. To die would at least give me comfort. I am utterly helpless and without any hope. I am weary of living, living in my own personal Hell. Why has God made me His target? Why will He not leave me alone? Day and night He pursues me. Even when I try to forget and fall into sleep, He awakens me with nightmares and pain in my bones. Why won't He just leave me alone? Why must He continue to persecute me with pain and suffering? What did we do wrong? God made us and then He destroys us.

But the church would not allow them to express their anguish and bitterness within their soul. God is punishing you far less than you deserve. You do not prosper because you are wicked. You must repent of your sins. If you were pure and good, God would answer you and bless you.

We can't understand. God makes us with the purpose of destroying us if we error? He gives us life, tells us He loves us and then refuses to forgive our iniquities and sends fires of Hell upon us. We are frustrated when He makes no sense. Just the slightest mistakes and we are cast into a life of unbearable pain and suffering. He sends His wrath upon us because we are not perfect? Is this what you are telling us church?

So why did He bother to spend the time to let us be born? Does He take pleasure in destruction? Why didn't He let her die at birth? At least then we would have been spared this miserable existence. But again the church would not comfort them. Chastising them, judging them and rejecting them, as the elders of the church warned the woman, "Repent! Turn to God and you will be restored. God is not a friend of sinners!"

The anger of Liz rose within the system until she could be contained no longer. She began lashing out at the church labeling them Suburban Christians and accusing them of putting words in

God's mouth. She boldly stood against them and told them they were misinterpreting the whole situation. I am not stupid. My mind knows crap when I hear it. Just be quiet church... that would be your smartest move.

Now listen to me. You Suburban Christians twist the truth. I wonder if God knows what you are doing and the damage you are causing to broken and hurting people. Or maybe you think you can fool God. Your speeches and preaching have about as much value as dog shit. You spout off your criticisms against us and shake your finger at us. You don't help take away our grief, you magnify it. You think you are so great...just leave us alone.

And with that, the parts abandoned the Christian church and headed into further darkness to hide. Slamming their heart's door on Christianity, they chose to walk alone. Life did not improve for them. Their hearts continued to scream for help, but no one heard them. There was no justice for them. God had stripped them and broken them down on every side. He had destroyed all their hope. Their relatives had forsaken them. The church mocked them and criticized them. They were alone, persecuted and without hope.

Raquel began to walk the inside path of Sacred Mountain in her search for truth and wisdom. She longed to find the real God... to talk to Him and know truth. Liz wanted to find Him and tell her side of the argument. She refused to agree with the church that all of the suffering and disease is due to their sin. She wanted to plead her case before God. Although they were unaware at the time, they wanted desperately to fill the void within their hearts and heal from their suffering. But they searched in vain and could not find God.

But God was there. And in His mighty wisdom and love, he sent a man out of the west to befriend the parts. God gave this man to them when they needed a friend. He was not just any man, but one chosen of God. A man who would be their champion... their defender... walking alongside of them to meet their needs.

At first, the parts were leery of the man. Liz called him the cowboy preacher and continually tested him as to his motives. Ann refused to form a relationship with him. I've been burnt enough by the church and these preaching Christians. I want nothing to do with him.

But even in the midst of mistrust and fear, the man stayed committed to them at every turn. His unconditional acceptance and willingness to stay with them through the thick of their suffering, mirrored Christ's unconditional commitment to come to them and be their Savior.

He gave of his time, committed to serve them in the most difficult of circumstances. He held them during surgery. He fed them wine and bread when they were agitated and fearful. He listened to their anger, fear and suffering. He never once told them he was too busy. He was committed to give his time to meet their needs. And as he gave, they began to understand Jesus' giving of Himself on the cross as a substitute for them. They began to be encouraged in God. For this man had been sent by God to show them a glimpse of who He really was.

The man continued to support them as they struggled through their past experiences, their hurts and twisted foundation that had been handed to them long ago. They began to understand how Jesus supports them before God the Father, always interceding on their behalf and acting as their mediator. And this man, through his obedience to God, began to show the parts a side of Christianity that they never could grasp in the church.

They began to find strength in God, as the man remained loyal. Like Jesus, he did not forsake them or leave them. Each part, as individual as she or he was, was loved by the man. He stood by them as they struggled with their own relationship with God. Never judging or forcing them into a preconceived mold of how they should act and relate to God, he patiently watched as God did His work.

Each part drew closer to God in her or his own way. Maria and Louise in their simple child-like way saw Jesus as a strong loving friend. They immediately accepted him and trusted their lives to his care. Raquel walked the paths of Sacred Mountain on a spiritual journey to find truth and wisdom. The poet of the system, she knew that obtaining wisdom was worth more than all of the gold and silver on earth. And in her quest, she came to realize that God knew where to find wisdom and if she was willing to listen, He would reveal it to her. For God established wisdom. And she learned that to fear the Lord is true wisdom and to shun evil is real understanding. She too recognized the Jesus of the ancient treaty that the man told her about, was the same as the Great Spirit... true wisdom. And one week after Maria and Louise were baptized, she also accepted Christ as her Savior and Lord.

Liz wrestled with God. She stood before God and cried out to Him in frustration. *God you don't answer me. I stand before you and you don't understand me. I have respect for the higher powers. I know your power, but why are you so cruel towards me? I'm trapped. You constantly persecute me and throw me into the raging storm. All I see is that you and Satan are there toying with my life and the end result will be my death. What did I ever do that was so bad that I deserve all of this shit? Why don't you answer me?*

And with that God said, *Liz where were you when I made the inners of the earth? Answer me! Do you know how the stars are formed or how the seas are kept within their boundaries? Tell Me Liz, can you make the morning appear, or the canary sing her song? Have you ever created a majestic redwood or painted the sky a crimson red? Or tell Me Liz, can you find the end of the universe or create each snowflake unique from all of the others? You who are so smart, where does the rain lay its head or the wind finds rest? Why does the eagle soar and the ostrich run? Do you still demand answers Liz? Do you still want to argue with Me or will you submit? Do you have the answers? You say you are not a whimp. Then stand and brace for battle, Liz. Are you as strong as I am? Show Me that your strength can save you.*

And Liz humbly answered no.

Liz, My ways are not your ways. Know that I am God. You can never fully understand how great I am. I control all that happens to you. Trust Me not because of what happens or doesn't happen to you, but because I am God. For My ways are not your ways and My thoughts are not your thoughts. I, who have begun a good work in you, will carry it on to completion. Your suffering will not end in death. It is for My glory and I will be glorified through it. Be still Liz and know that I am God. Wait and watch, for I shall renew your strength and you shall soar with wings as eagles. You shall be free and everything will turn out okay in the end. Trust Me Liz and ask for strength and comfort. For you shall see through these times My awesome power and unconditional love for you. I am the master weaver and you are the thread. I am the potter and you are the clay. Do not fight Me Liz, for stiff thread and unyielding clay is of no use to me. You do not know the plans I have for you. What I have planned, that will I do. Do you not know that I have created the wild mustang and I prize My wild mustangs that submit to Me? I do not crush their spirit, but mold that spirit so that I may be glorified by it. Continue to hold on Liz. Persevere despite the circumstances. Do not become discouraged. You shall reap a harvest of blessings if you don't give up. Remember that I am God. Trust Me and continue to seek My truth.

And the man from the west continued to encourage the parts about the things of God. With his love and commitment beside them, the system continued to grow stronger and be used of God. As God knitted together the gifts of each of His precious parts, the slow restoration of a person began to take form...and with it something greater than the one took shape...a people set apart by God came into being... and it continues to this very day.

This story, written two years after the Lord brought us together, gives an outline of the first part of our journey to discover truth together. The truth we were seeking was not about them directly, but more about the truth of God's relationship with them... past, present and future. It wasn't about what I knew to be true about God, but about how God has proven Himself to be true. The journey was to find truth about the very nature and person of who God is in relation to each of us, accomplished in His revelation to us through Jesus Christ. The vehicle He used to reveal these discoveries along this journey are the individual life stories contained herein. Our destination is to share the many truths about God living out His love for us throughout our lives, long before we ever come to acknowledge or accept Him as walking with us through it.

This book will tell of the healing process that the System went through to know God in all of His glory and discover within it the Lord's purpose for many of their journeys. The following quote was given to them near the end of the first leg of their journey, when they were thrown back into a state of hopelessness that could only be healed through the power of God. It is a portion of a message given to all of them through Quiet Walker to offer encouragement... the full message is near the end of Chapter Two.

"...Do not give up. Finish the race I have given you. I am asking you to trust me. Look to me, my precious one. I am the light. Do not take your eyes off of me. I want you to be strong in me and in my great power. I am faithful and will give you strength and will protect you from the evil one. Rest in me and allow me to heal you. Just as your garden, dormant in the darkness of winter, begins to grow and flourish in spring; I will heal your soul and it shall blossom and flourish. The darkness will be overtaken by the light. The warmth of my love, breaking through the cracks of your pain and hopelessness, will melt away sorrow. The garden of your soul will prosper and the sweet smelling fragrance of your heart will bring joy to all who see. And then I shall say to you: Look, the winter is past; the rains are over and gone. Blossoms appear throughout all the Land of Preservation. The time has come to sing; the cooing of doves is heard in the land. There are young figs on the fig trees, and the blossoms on the vines smell sweet. Get up my child. Take my hand and together we shall walk through life.

Your loving Jesus."

These words were given to them during a very traumatic time in their lives, when death seemed the easiest alternative for them. When I began to write this book, the tragedies of the New York Trade Center and Pentagon were fresh in my mind. That week the media reflected a sense of hopelessness, intermingled with anger coming from people of all ages within our nation and from the world. With questions of "Where was God?" or, "How could God allow this to happen?" still resonating in my mind, it clarified for me the urgent need to tell these stories. When we respond to such evil as witnessed by the world and suffered by our nation on that day, we enter into the struggle with evil that the System has lived with their entire life.

If we are to walk with God and oppose evil in all of its revelations, then we must make the clear choice to be led by God, no matter where we're taken or what we endure as God's people. It is in this choice to follow God's way, which the following true accounts are given and with it my hope and prayer that God will touch you through these biographies, so you can share in the hope that we have found together. This is not a defense of God's actions or inaction, but a series of revelations about how God walks with us through tragedies and suffering, to lead us from hopelessness to joy. It is also about the ways that God comes to us, regardless of our condition and understanding of Him, to introduce His reality into our lives. It's about how God takes the initiative to bring His love to us often before we even know or want Him in our lives.

The people in the System are allowing their stories to be told at great personal sacrifice, knowing the embarrassment that awaits them as the world reads about their suffering in detail. One person said it is like being told to stand in a department store window completely naked, with the whole world gawking at you and knowing your deepest, darkest, secrets. Yet, they gave permission out of obedience to the purposes of God. As they say in their own words eight years later after beginning this journey, to a fellow traveler trying to understand God's ways:

"We gave our permission for these books to be written, after the Lord told us he wanted broken people to know that he loves the brokenhearted and will heal them, if they trust him and come to him. He told us that he wanted the stories written about his love for us. These were painful words for all of us, especially Maria, yet we all chose to obey our Lord in the strength of the hope that he has given us."

Since these books are also written from my perspective as pastoral counselor and friend, I will share briefly how I met them and also how they introduced themselves to me in a letter some months later as their profiles. I was working towards a M-Div. degree in pastoral care and counseling at Fuller Seminary with plans of finishing within the next year. It would take another four years to complete. God was teaching me that serving Him would be according to His timetable and not my own... if I wanted to be effective in ministry. I was working full-time as a contractor to support both my family and our ministry. My wife Carol was also working full-time while we were taking classes part-time to finish our degrees. At this time I was also an intentional interim pastor helping troubled churches. We were assisting a church with a merger to another local church for renewal and healing. I was serving in our home church as an elder on the Prayer Ministry team, the Mission's Committee and teaching various adult education classes.

While on the Prayer team, I had my first 'hands-on' training for counseling and praying with people who had MPD over a three-year period, before I was introduced to the System. (God never wastes a moment to fulfill His plan and training time for us.) It was at this 'tranquil' time in our lives that I received a request through the seminary to work with a marriage and family counselor. Bruce asked for a man who could commit to 6 months to help counsel a person through a Bible study that was struggling with complex theological questions and recently diagnosed as having Multiple Personality Disorder. I knew that God had prepared me for this and that I could work with Bruce for that period before moving to Pasadena to finish my degree. Carol and I could not have imagined the changes that were in store for us in ministry. We thought that pastoral ministry would eventually be full-time in a well-established church with well-defined roles. Authoring a book like this was not in any job description we had envisioned… go figure!

After a preliminary interview with Bruce, I went to his office on a Saturday for a joint session with the client for her approval of me. Bruce had explained beforehand that there were many (?) personalities, but that I would probably only be working with two or three adults over the next 6 months, (if I chose to stay that long). I'm ashamed to admit that I began this adventure thinking the Lord wanted me to bring whatever spiritual healing I could to this person, before moving on to bigger and greener pastures. I was soon humbled before the Lord that day and many times afterward, for forgetting another simple truth:

"It's enough to reach out to one person at a time with My love, if you really want to bring it to them as My servant."

When Maria walked into his office that morning, I immediately felt her pain as she began to talk. There was a deep overwhelming sadness in her demeanor, which caused me to whisper a prayer silently, asking the Lord if he had made a mistake and maybe I wasn't the one to help her. His answer was simple, **"If she accepts you, then you have My answer."** As she talked, I had the clear

21

sense of someone else watching me and listening from within her eyes. After a few questions from her she asked the question that would be repeated many times over the years, "Why are you here?" Variations would come from almost every person I would meet from within the System. The fact that I did not charge for pastoral counseling only seemed to make the question more relevant for them. My answer then, now and throughout our relationship was the same: *"I'm here because God wants me to tell you about Him and His love for you, if you will let me."* That is when she handed me a paper and said, "Liz has a test for you."

My name is Liz and I have written my question out because Maria is too stupid to get it straight. You get no help from Bruce!

TEST

Pretend that you are a new pastor of a Suburban Christian Church. This is your very first position as a pastor and after years of stretching a dollar, you are happy that you finally have consistent income.

It is late Friday night and you just finished a board meeting with the church council. You are still on probation and the church is evaluating you. This Suburban Christian Church is wealthy and legalistic. The membership is very inbred and the head elders keep a very tight rein on the pastor. They have no tolerance for sin and those who sin.

You walk over to the corner café to grab a cup of coffee before heading home. As you enter the café you notice three young women sitting at the booth near the door. They are in tight black skirts and low-cut silk blouses. Their long earrings dangle as they light their cigarettes and discuss the evening's Johns.

Sitting within earshot of their booth, you overhear one of the ladies of the evening mention that tomorrow is her birthday. The other girl asks her if she is going to celebrate and have a cake and all that shit. F#&% she says, who would give me a cake for my birthday?

WHAT WOULD YOU DO IN THIS SITUATION AND WHY?

I knew immediately that this relationship was not going to be the same as those I had in the past with people with MPD. The Lord told me in a still small voice to think before responding, then **"respond for Me"**. "I would tell the waitress to give a cake to that lady over there and tell her, 'God loves you and says Happy Birthday!' without saying anything else. Why is because I know it's true." Liz had Maria told me, "you'll do for now Chalberg" and somehow it was clear… things were never going to be the same.

Maria left me with Bruce after setting a time for our next session. I was given some history by Bruce about some of the traumas which caused the 'splitting of personalities.' I was told I should expect to meet only these adults - Maria, Louise, Raquel, and possibly Liz, in the initial time span I was committing to help them. I asked about Liz and was told that "she is a teenager about 18 years old, who is street-wise and a protector for the system. You surprised her with your answer coming from a Christian pastor. It wasn't what she expected. That test is the first of many and you may have difficulty getting them to trust you."

When I asked Bruce how many of 'them' existed, I was somewhat surprised to hear his response. "We've recorded around **66** parts, though many of them are functions and you might not count them as personalities per se." I would later discover that many were personalities with fears, hopes and opinions, but their roles might differ greatly from those personalities who would appear on the surface. This will be explained more in detail in later chapters. As I drove home that afternoon, I kept asking Jesus, "Are you sure you want me for this task? I can think of many others with more experience than I have." I heard His answer in a variety of ways over the next several days, but this was the bottom-line:

"You can make real for her the love I've given you. Tell her about Me as you know Me. The Truth has been stolen from her all of her life. You will give it back for Me."

All of the theological training I had received to this point didn't seem to matter much if I couldn't respond to His request. I knew the choice was mine to make and yet, how does one refuse God? I decided I would give it a try for 6 months, because after all, the only thing I had to do was listen to the Holy Spirit. He would tell me what to say to three or four adults for an hour or so… right? Well, not only does the Lord abound in grace, He has a great sense of irony when molding His children. By the 5th session, we were meeting in Bruce's office for 2 hours or more with only an occasional phone conversation with Bruce for guidance. I had now met 5 adults and had a glimpse of 1 child of the System, and I never knew who was going to be the client at the next session.

Every time we met there was something in each person's life where I connected with their pain. Their hunger to know God was somewhat overwhelming. The pain and suffering which separated them from God would have me praying in tears on their behalf all the way home. Yet, with each passing session, I knew God was present speaking to us through the broken vessels of our lives. I was challenged to take the lofty theological answers I might offer in seminary and refine them for people too broken to understand beyond the words, "I know God loves you because…"

Perhaps the final confirmation came in the 8th and 9th sessions when I met Raquel, also known as Quiet Walker, and Mariann, who was 8 years old… and a bit. Raquel is Native American before the eyes of God. Everyone who has ever met her, perceives her as one in all of her being. Her wisdom is what makes her unforgettable. I was challenged to take the Gospel message of God's love and put it into spiritual terms that a Native American would understand, in order to make meaningful contact with her. I had been accepted into a tribe in Alaska some years earlier while working on a church in a village there. Her first question to me about the Great Spirit was one addressed to me as a brother from the clan of the White Bear. We would both grow in faith as we met on the sacred ground of God's word.

When I met the frightened child Mariann, all I wanted to do was hug her to take away the pain she would reveal in her drawings and words… yet I could not. It would take a long time for her to give me permission to show any kind of love, even God's love, in physical contact. She kept referring to a person on the inside as **'Dragonslayer,'** which was her name for Jesus. Mariann also tested me by looking into my eyes, penetrating my soul, to see if Dragonslayer was reflected there. All the children I met later would repeat this test. Was Dragonslayer Jesus? I would test this myself many times thereafter. The results of those tests will be told in the stories in these books recorded not only in their words, but His as well. I would ask you to test them as I did, not only in your heart, but by reading the Bible references as well.

I was given several of their first diagrams showing the structure of the system as they had drawn them for Bruce to understand their inner system of hierarchy. The first was a very rudimentary form, reflecting only what was known to them at that time. I was also given the 4th diagram, created shortly after I began working with them, which included all 66 names of persons and parts and the structure of their inside world as much as they were aware of it by that time. This diagram of the System, Figures 1A & 1B, are found on facing pages 26 and 27.

You may want to refer back to this diagram as you read further, to assist you in understanding the movement and changes that occur as the System heals and their inside world changes. This will dramatically happen more often in the beginning of Book Two: *Journeys to Love*. For now these will help show alliances among parts as they had existed for close to 40 years. Pay attention to the few who travel between levels and why, as we move along in the stories. They will play a significant role in the restructuring of the System later on. This is the roster for the players herein who are described individually in the following chapter.

This map is what I copied from their drawing of the levels of their world by Elizabeth Ray whom you will read about in the next chapter. However, her maps were much more intense and intricate so I simplified it for these pages. You'll learn much more about their inner world as you follow their journey and discover the Lord's creativeness with them. The only person who knew most of it and why it was structured like this was Elizabeth Ray and she wasn't telling anyone except Bruce and I, even then on a need to know basis. One can look at this and begin to get a sense of the complexity of how either of us might begin to climb over the foothills of fear, abuse, survival and protection which were set in place so many years ago for their own safety? One cannot imagine how much hope and strength it took to survive...and now risk sharing these detailed facts with a virtual stranger like me. When I look back, I'm grateful that she gave me only the first diagram when we started together and the 4th after a year together. I don't know that I would have been as obedient in this calling had it been the other way around.

Figure 1A

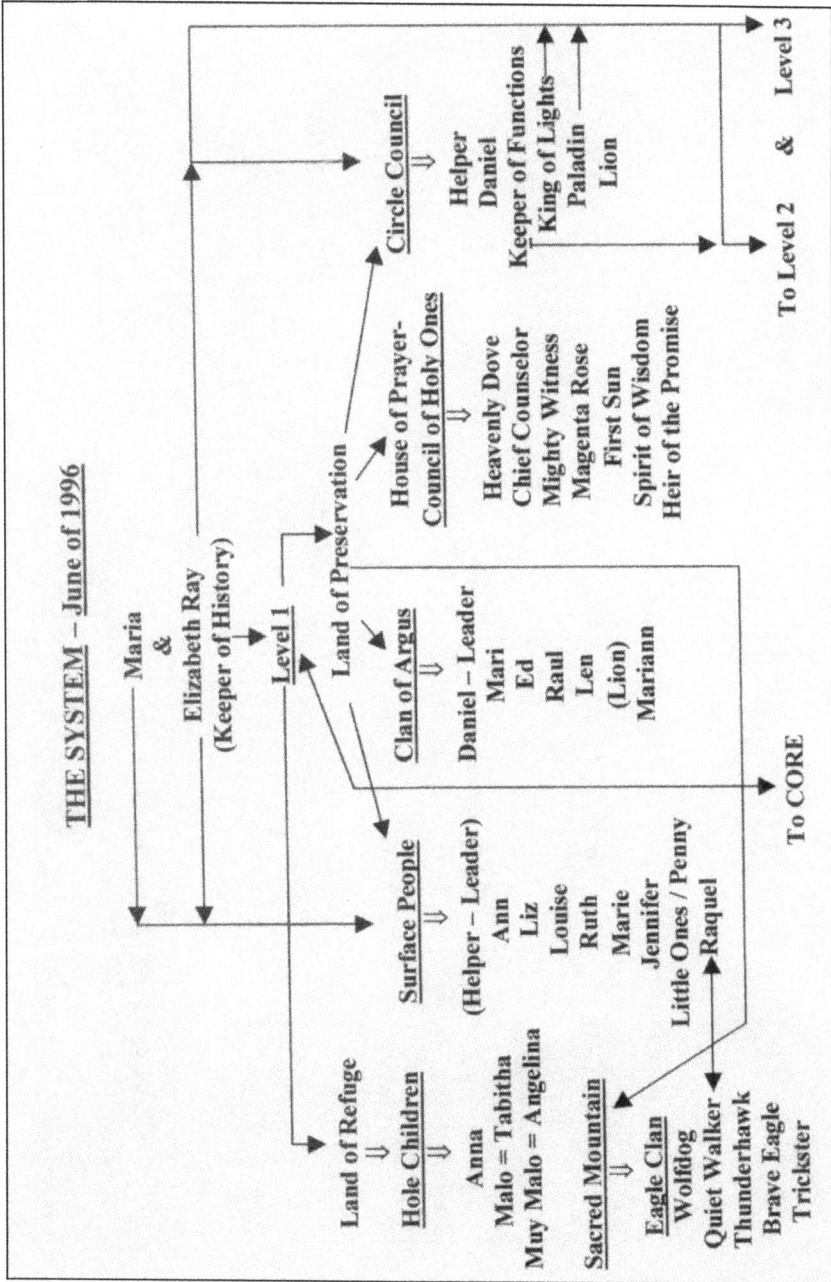

THE SYSTEM – June of 1996

Maria
&
Elizabeth Ray
(Keeper of History)

Level 1

Land of Preservation

Circle Council ⇒

Helper
Daniel
Keeper of Functions
King of Lights
Paladin
Lion

To Level 2 & Level 3

**House of Prayer-
Council of Holy Ones** ⇒

Heavenly Dove
Chief Counselor
Mighty Witness
Magenta Rose
First Sun
Spirit of Wisdom
Heir of the Promise

Clan of Argus ⇒

Daniel – Leader
Mari
Ed
Raul
Len
(Lion)
Mariann

To CORE

Surface People ⇒

(Helper – Leader)
Ann
Liz
Louise
Ruth
Marie
Jennifer
Little Ones / Penny
Raquel

Land of Refuge ⇒

Hole Children ⇒

Anna
Malo = Tabitha
Muy Malo = Angelina

Sacred Mountain ⇒

Eagle Clan
Wolfdog
Quiet Walker
Thunderhawk
Brave Eagle
Trickster

Top half of 4th diagram of the System's inside world. - 1996.

Figure 1B

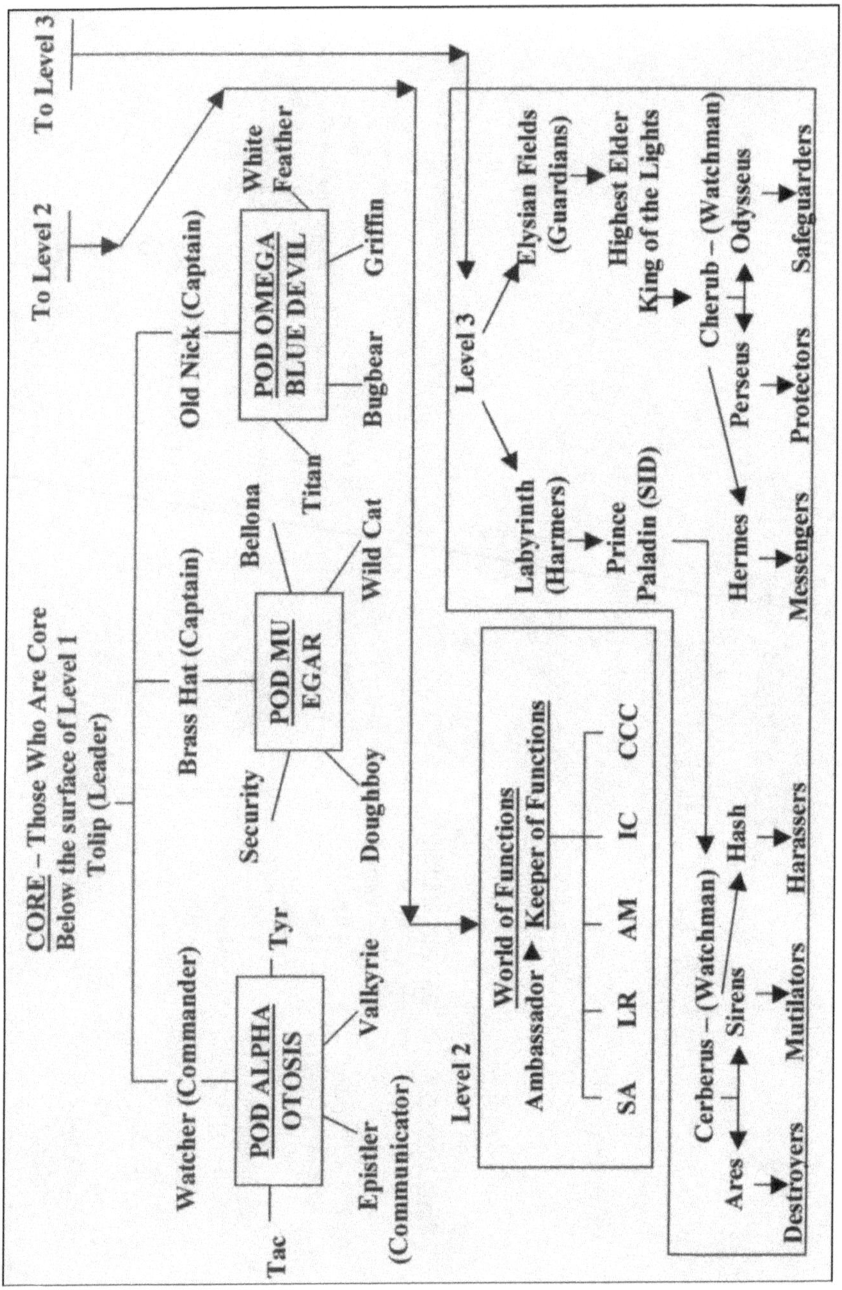

Bottom half 4th diagram. CORE is hidden between Levels 1 and 2.

"There is an appointed time for everything.
And there is a time for every event under heaven ...
He has made everything appropriate in its time.
He has also set eternity in their heart..."
Ecclesiastes 3:1, 11

Chapter One:

"Crawling Into the Light"

"God is our refuge and strength,
A very present help in trouble.
Therefore we will not fear,
Though the earth should change..."
Psalm 46:1-2

Who am I, Lord, that I should presume to approach unto thee?
Behold the Heaven of Heavens cannot contain thee,
And thou sayest, "Come ye all unto me."
Thomas Kempis, *Of the Imitation of Christ, (1418)*

My intention in Chapter One was to provide a reference section for the rest of the books. Knowing a little information about the people you journey with can help establish understanding for what it means to 'walk in their shoes.' To further this awareness, Chapter Three will flashback to 1994 and begins the journey with them and their first therapist Bruce. Most of their stories will be told chronologically from Chapter Three on, with a few exceptions for clarity. Hearing it in their own words, as it happens to all of them together, is less confusing than using flashbacks repeatedly or trying to tell them individually. The miraculous is best comprehended in increments, which is why this first book only covers the first two and a half years. Perhaps it took that long for any of us to be prepared for what was to follow in the next four years (*and in the next 11*).

When I asked to meet more of the System, I was not prepared for what I received. Someone on the inside told them I was trustworthy, so they held nothing back in their revelation to me. The following letter from Ruth and Helper, received in the Fall of 1995, contains a synopsis of the 'System' with 27 profiles to assist me in counseling them. More information would come later, after the System learned to trust my commitments. As you read about them, please try to not make any judgements based on this early information, or you might miss the impact of how God works in their lives to heal them. I caution you only because I made that mistake in the beginning.

By the time I received the letter, I knew some about most of these people in it, but little about their place in the social structure of the System or their responsibilities. This was the first detailed letter from Circle Council explaining their specific role as well. Since I knew Circle Council was made up of the male personalities who governed the care of the system, it was important for me to make the connection and be ready for whatever they said. Their words are *italicized* in the letter. When I insert thoughts within their letters and statements for clarity throughout the books, I will enclose them in parenthesis.

Dear Mr. Chalberg, Circle Council is very appreciative of your commitment and compassion for Maria and Louise. The time they spend with you has helped them know that not all people in the world are out to hurt them. You are having more of an impact in helping them heal than you might realize, and Circle Council appreciates your kindness.

They also realize it must be extremely difficult for you to understand us and why we are the way we are. You have accepted us without explanation, a rare quality in a man. (They didn't know that Jesus had given me the clear instruction for counseling them this guideline: **"Meet and love each one where you find them, for who they are in their own understanding, the same way I do for everyone who seeks Me."**)

But Helper wishes you to understand us so that you might be able to relate to Maria even better. It is with our respect for you that Circle Council has decided to give you a glimpse into our world.

Until we were diagnosed by Bruce in 1994, we did not know we were multiples. We had never heard of multiple personality disorder or that there were others like us. Maria began splitting early in life due to the tremendous amount of pressure from abuse. She was too small to fight back, no one to rescue her from the hurt, and too young to run away. The only thing she could do was go away in her mind to avoid the pain and make another personality to absorb the hurt. (As of this letter many were not yet aware themselves of the particulars or intensity of the abuse that would be revealed over the next few years.) *Maria became an expert at doing what we now know as dissociation. She could block out a memory in her mind as if it never happened, but the memory and associated feelings were stored by one of us inside. That 'alter' would also hold on to the feelings of actual pain from each event they were called to endure, and it would become for them their 'known' existence.*

Since this is Maria's primary method of dealing with life, she appears to outsiders as stupid, forgetful, not focused, strange, and disorganized. This causes her all kinds of problems in her life. She doesn't seem connected to reality and although some alters are better at 'looking together' in the outside world, we too suffer from disconnectedness. We don't always know what is happening in our lives. Much of our past experiences have not yet been shared with one another or present experiences. Whoever is out and whoever is shadowing are the alters with the memories of an event. (Shadowing is the process of staying near the surface listening and observing, usually without physical or all sensory perceptions. Often the surface person does not know who or how many are shadowing.) *Thus, when you mentioned the letter from Elizabeth Ray to Maria, she had no clue of what you were talking about. For instance, a friend of Ann's stopped by last week to chat about a mutual acquaintance in Lodi. I was out and had no idea who she was talking about. We've learned to be highly creative to 'look like we know what's being talked about' just to avoid detection. Some are better at it than others.*

Maria still has major holes in her memory. When she initially went to see Bruce, she had no idea if she had completed high school. She did not know where she lived as a child. All of that was stored in other memories. Maria has a lot of missing time, time when someone else is out and in control. Part of our ability to dissociate is to leave the body. Maria described it to Bruce as "going into a fog of nothingness. I don't feel or know anything in the fog. I am just there looking down on my body and I'm numb." One of the poems written to Bruce about going away inside, entitled "In the Night... When He Comes," talks about the abuse in the pink room with the grandfather. It gives a glimpse of the ability we have to leave the body and 'go away.'

31

Maria began therapy after I stopped an attempt at suicide and took us to get help. Maria was very hesitant to speak with a therapist in the beginning. She was extremely depressed, but afraid of therapist and the mental health profession because of her daughter's and sister's experiences in psychiatric hospitals. Maria, like all of us, was on guard and not trusting this new person who had entered our lives. Maria knew something was wrong with her, but she didn't know how to verbalize it. She thought she was crazy and had finally cracked up. She was afraid to tell of lost time, finding strange clothes and things in her house, having people come up to her as though they knew her and not having a clue.

How could she explain finding herself in strange places with no idea how she got there? Or hearing voices inside talking about her and saying things like; "be extremely frightened about sex' and 'leave her body, go to Kansas and forget things." She had set her mind to believe she was crazy because she knew it was not normal to experience these things, so she was afraid to let anyone know. Though she had experienced these things for years, she had learned how to hide confusion and anxiety. She isolated herself and kept quiet, but her headaches were horrendous for her. They were like severe migraines and no medication could ease the pain of feeling like her head would explode. She would hear a loud buzzing and suffered from 'a loud noise in my head.'

Whenever the therapist began to get close to any of Maria's anxieties, she would become afraid and would space out and go to 'Kansas' to escape the stress. After 3 months of this, I wrote a letter at 2:am to Bruce explaining that she was not crazy. I wrote about us being like a cake having many parts... flour, sugar, eggs, etc. Each part has a purpose including the smallest part. Without all the parts, one would not have a complete cake. Raquel then sent him some of her poetry. One was entitled <u>PARTS</u>. She talked about being separate but joined in this poem, housed together in the same vessel yet unaware of the role each played, born out of their need to exist. She gave him a better picture of some parts like the little ones, the compliant one, the creative one, the angry one, etc. We were hoping he would begin to understand us, because we were yet unaware that there were others in the world like us, or that there was even a name *for us. We were positive we were different from the whole human race.*

Maria began to struggle with what I believe to be 'spiritual warfare.' She wrote about an incident that occurred at 3:23am one Sunday morning (a significant time for us somehow). The room turned very cold suddenly and she felt a presence coming near to her. It told her Bruce couldn't protect her, and that Jesus doesn't want you, so just give up and surrender to me. Then a little voice inside said, "Don't surrender! Remember Jesus is safe and has power over these evil voices." The battle began with the outside voices uttering challenges and telling the warm little voice to shut up. Finally, Maria took a stand and told the spirits they lied and didn't belong to Jesus. She wouldn't surrender and Jesus would take care of her. They left. I recognized them as demons, but Maria still doesn't understand what happened. (This incident would be reviewed several times in our first sessions for meaning.)

It was the first week of August last year that Helper decided to communicate with the 'Outside Helper.' He wanted Bruce to understand our world, as he does you now, so that he would not misdiagnose us or cause us more harm. This was Maria's first knowledge of the rest of us. She read the letter that she found in her home but was unable to complete it. Ann switched out to complete reading it to Bruce and then pushed Maria back out to deal with the ramifications. Maria was overwhelmed and it has taken her months to even acknowledge us. She still vacillates between acceptance and disbelief, believing insanity an easier thing to accept.

In Helper's letter, he spoke of our inside world, how we live in a forest with waterfalls and wildflowers. We have a door into the forest where we enter and exit. On the door is Maria's voice. We take it with us whenever we go into the outside world so we are protected and hidden, so we never appear very different to the outside people. He told how Maria did not live in our world, but in a world next to ours with a different door. (She now lives in our world.) When she went into her world next door, one of us would come out of ours. He told how the evil ones hovered between the worlds causing havoc and taking credit for everything. Their leader was Yemaya. (More details on Yemaya later.) *We now believe that most of the havoc was caused in the third world... the guardians and the harmers, but we were unaware of them at the time of Helper's letter.* (A misconception that would be cleared up when the 'worlds' blended as they are healed.)

Helper told how the walls between the worlds broke down with a loud explosion on November 12, 1993. (The day Claudia was locked up in a psychiatric ward for attempted suicide.) There were many holes existing in the walls for years, where Maria heard voices and experienced the headaches, etc; but on that day she was in shock. Helper continued to give Bruce this overview of the alters he knew about at that time. (I will give another overview at two years later and at seven years later. See System map pages 26 – 27)

*1. **Helper**: He officiates at the meetings in Land of Preservation and Circle Council. He never goes to the outside like all of Circle Council. He's 57 years old, very flexible, compassionate, patient, robust in body and short.* (Helper became my counseling partner on the inside over the next year with Council and a good straight man for my humor.)

*2. **King of Lights**: Blend of all the guardians (7 of them) from level three – Elysian Fields and one of the leaders of Circle Council. He's wise and good with a merciful heart and slow to anger.*

*3. **Paladin (formerly known as SID)**: Blend of all the {7) harmers from level three – Labyrinth and one of the leaders of Circle Council in charge of protecting the system. He likes to shoot first and ask questions later as a response.* (I was careful in the beginning with him, as I was unsure of his role within the System. I immediately thought of the <u>Have Gun Will Travel</u> television western of the late `50s with Richard Boone. Ironically, I wasn't far off in my visualization of his character. He will learn a year from now that he has his own theme song, following a thorough investigation by Ann of his name and role. We will see some interesting changes in him over the coming years.)

*4. **Keeper of Functions**: He is leader of level two, the world of functions created in 1958 following a car crash, and a member of Circle Council. He is an accountant, goal oriented, very attune to* *detail, and responsible for sending functions out to perform various tasks. He is closely tied to Ann, very logical, focused, and a man of few words.*

5. Lion: *A male leader on Council now, who was Mariann's protector in the jungle where they lived. He has great strength, character, wisdom, and quick to protect all of the children.*

6. Daniel: *He's the youngest leader on Council and was leader of the Clan of Argus, the young men who guarded the fort that houses Mariann to protect her from the Beast. (The 'Beast that prowls' represents the Catholic priest who molested Mariann.)* (The Clan of Argus, except Mari, would soon blend into their leader Daniel, as he would perform the roles of Len, Raul, and Ed, on the inside in providing protection for Mariann, after Bruce and I were able to provide protection on the outside. When the need for the 'fort' was gone, Mariann would move in Preservation to live with the rest of the surface people, when Lion and Daniel would join Circle Council to represent all of the 'surface' children.)

7. Tolip: (A leader that comes on Circle Council in a year after this letter is written. He is a blend of the guards for the 'Pod' children or 'Those Who Are Core.' Their names were listed in the fourth structure model, but little information was ever given. He will represent the 'others' mentioned under Tabitha who are the Pod Children yet to be identified.)

8. Elizabeth Ray: *Created in 1953 after Maria Ann (the original one) went to sleep and Maria was born. Though rarely out to the surface, she records <u>everything</u> that is said or happens to the system. Her title is Keeper of History and Scribe for Council.*

(This lady is the reason for most of the written record of the System's life. I knew of the human mind's capacity to remember details, even of time and place or verbatim of conversation, but never before had I witnessed it put into reality. I've tested her accuracy throughout our relationship and I am more impressed each time with the value of her gifts. Her release of information has always been on a need-to-know basis, for Council or any outside helper. This has sometimes frustrated me in the timing of the release, when I'd rather have known useful information before an event instead of after it, but lessons in patience have come from it. Her timing comes from the Holy Spirit to prevent assumptions or conclusions from being drawn prematurely, which could cause us to misinterpret the facts of past truths, or input false memories based upon partial knowledge.

For example: when a child part would draw a picture about a particularly horrible abuse experience, she might wait until other parts or medical evidence would confirm it to us, before revealing the time, place, and perpetrator of the event. When I researched the possibilities through outside sources, I discovered that her accuracy has been infallible. Until recently, it has always been 'just the facts' without emotion or influence, so as to not shade the truth with a bias. Today it is still the facts, but you can feel a measure of the shared joy and pain of healing through mutual awareness. I've taken this time to tell you about her because without her, I don't think these books would have been possible. The witness of Jesus interacting in her life, as I have known it, has given me hope for those gifts to be exercised in the writing of these books.)

Yemaya: *I have included her in this list of personalities, not because she is one of the System, but because she has great influence on the child Tabitha, and through Tabitha she affects the System. She was attached to her through a ritual of the Santeria, a cult of the Catholic Church. She is identified with the Catholic Saint, Lady of Regla, who always wore blue and white with seashells and turtles and having seven pennies in her pocket. She is a <u>demonic</u> spirit.*

(I will reveal more about the truth of this spirit in the children's stories. The Santeria[3] is the outcome of syncretism in the Catholic Church, which began long ago to assimilate the various local religions incorporated by their conquests. It was the conjoining of African religious rites like voodoo, a byproduct of the slave trade, behind a façade of Catholic Saints in the Caribbean and Central America in order to make them acceptable within the Church. Her removal after the revealing of her true purpose for keeping them away from Jesus was vital to the health of the system, but not easily done due to the length of influence on some of its weakest members. She had entered under the guise of protector and savior for Tabitha, appearing in the likeness of the Madonna. Her tactics and various forms of manifestations will continue to attack and disrupt the perceptions of children and adults alike, until they all knew her for what she truly was.)

9. Tabitha (Malo): She is 4 years old and speaks Spanish only, though she understands English. Her triggers are white ice cream and cookies. 'Malo' means bad in Spanish. She was 'baptized' into the Santeria cult at an early age by the grandfather and suffered sexual and physical abuse from him in his home. She has talked about being tied up and being beaten with a strap. She and Maria have a great fear of rats because rats bit Tabitha in the basement, when tied up and unable to get away. She carried bread in her socks to feed them using her toes. She enjoys making books and listening to stories. The two hole children, Tabitha and Angelina, were created in 1954, about the same time as Raquel. The mother beat Tabitha in her crib enough to draw blood, so the system was sent to the grandparents shortly thereafter. Helper, Hash (who eventually becomes Paladin), and the third level of Guardians and Harmers were born at this time, as well as Marie.

During 1954 Maria/Tabitha suffered severe burns from being left outside and was hospitalized. It was after this time that the grandfather abused Tabitha. Tabitha was initiated in 1956 into the Santeria (and given the orisha Yemaya) and suffered Satanic Ritual Abuse (SRA). She learned about the rituals and the Lady of Regla, after witnessing a sacrifice in a red barn that traumatized her and still has a fear of Halloween. In 1957 Tabitha was attacked in the orchard by the "Cuban Man", a local farm worker. After Maria was sent back home Tabitha was hit with an iron skillet by the other grandmother and beaten by the father for continual bed-wetting.

('Others' were split through her to receive traumatic abuses too intense for her to survive the Satanic Ritual Abuse. Each of these 'pod children' will be revealed as the Lord brings them to the surface in His timing for healing, in about a year after this letter. The effect of the sexual, physical and mental abuse by the grandfather and the associated SRA make the time frame for healing of everyone in the system in direct correlation with their acceptance of the abuse as a reality. Dates are included in each profile to help mark traumatic events relative to each person's perspective of the event. The dates given do not give a 'real time' reference for establishing the perceived age in an individual's life.)

10. Angelina (Muy Malo): *Meaning 'very bad' in Spanish, Angelina is the earliest split from Tabitha. An infant most traumatized in sexual molestation by the grandfather in the 'pink room' in 1956. We aren't sure what else occurred to her, but the molestation by "Papa" stopped in 1958 when Maria was sent back to her parents.*

11. Anna: *She was created in 1955 and is about three years old and doesn't speak. She is left-handed and sucks her thumb often. The grandfather hung her pet dog Lady in front of her and cut its heart out to threaten Anna/Tabitha to prevent her from ever telling about the abuse and the (SRA) cult...or the same would happen to her. Shortly thereafter, Anna/Tabitha was attacked by a police dog. It was at this time her fantasy world was created with glue people (made from tree sap in the orchard.) These were her only toys that she kept in a hole in the tree. She spent her formative years mainly with animals. Lila, the Little Ones, and Louise were born during this time.*

(Bruce told me after I was surprised by a child's visit, how these three, Tabitha, Angelina, and Anna, might rotate out during a session. The first thing each one would do was look deep into my eyes to see if Jesus was present there. If so, they could remain calm for the brief time out in order to build trust for them in our presence. These moments during intense counseling sessions with other parts, would bring a time of rest for them and for me, in order to prepare for whoever came out next. I appreciated these moments and it was comforting to me to know that a child could recognize the presence of Jesus within me.)

12. Little ones (Pollyanna kids or 2 little ones and Penny): *In the beginning we thought they were mute, but now they speak. They are three to five years old and seem very happy, much like little Pollyannas.*

(I can't say much about them as I have not spent much time with any of them except Penny, who only recently has affected some parts within the system. Penny retains some memories that had glimpses of abuse, but she would rotate inward and not experience any of the abuse. The little ones were created to exist during the normal or happier times in a child's life and therefore have no memory of any abuse. Sadly for the system this was a very small amount of real time. I have no impulse to force reality upon them. The exception may some day be Penny. She refuses to believe what she has heard about the grandfather she believes to be her father.)

13. Lila: *A child created from Tabitha around 1956, who is hearing impaired due to gun blast near her. She was traumatized in the canyon in 1960 and at home by the maternal grandmother, who would hit her with an iron skillet like she did Tabitha. Ann is born at this time to do chores.* (She was the first Pod Child to be revealed about the time of this letter. AKA: Otosis. Her first healing comes in about a year.)

14. Mariann: *She is an eight-year-old child created in 1960, who was abused by the Beast (Catholic Priest) repeatedly over a period of time. She lives in the fort defended by Daniel and the Clan of Argus. She goes through a secret door in the fort into the jungle, where she is guarded by Lion and lives with the jungle animals. She is visited there by Mari and Quiet Walker.*

(Many of the drawings you will see come from her. A book she write in about a year from now will be published someday for children suffering cancer as revealed in her story. There you will learn about **Dragonslayer** and how everyone else knows Him as Jesus. I would test all of Dragonslayer's words of counsel, whether written or spoken to any of the System for several years against His revealed words in Holy Scriptures. I would also compare His words with the person I know as Jesus in my own life. The outcome of these tests will be shared in the book, but you will have to decide in your own heart if these words are truth.

Often I refer to Jesus as Dragonslayer when talking to or about the System. The name comes from both Revelation 20:1-10, and a child's game that Mariann made up to bring her hope. It is Jesus who gives this name to Mariann to learn the truth about His love. Mariann, like all people in the System, had a life filled with lies and contradictions from men who came in the name of God. It is only through Dragonslayer that the lies are removed and replaced with a loving relationship, one that lives out the truth of God's love built on trust in the sharing of Christ Jesus.)

15. Raul, Ed, and Len: *Three ten-year-old boys who are part of the Clan of Argus. They carry spears and guard Mariann outside of the* *fort from the Beast. They were the lookouts who would shout, "The Beast comes in the name of the Lord."* (See #6 Daniel)

16. Marie: *Caretaker for the children created in 1954.*

17. Mari: *A young woman now created for the purpose of going into the confessional at church in place of Mariann. She would confess her sins as instructed, to the same priest who had abused Mariann in order to be cleansed. Her guilt over not being able to protect Mariann continues to this day.*

18. Liz: (a.k.a. the Angry One) *An angry teenager who puts the system at risk by often going into unsafe places. She displays irresponsible behavior and is always challenging authority figures. She is aggressive and escapes inside after stirring up trouble. She is critical of Maria and Louise and thinks they are wimps. She is physically stronger in the face of danger on the outside, more than any other part. She is always in search of fun through any means possible. Liz and the Clan of Argus were created in 1965, about the same time as the priest stopped molesting Mariann. Liz experimented with drugs and sex in 1966. Liz is the 'street-wise' protector in the system.*

(Though Liz would test me often in the early days, she would become a trusted 'buddy' within the next year. It would take my wife longer to trust Liz. Gaining that trust for us however difficult, has proven to be worth the effort. Liz's story is well worth reading. If you have ever been an outcast on the streets you will identify with her. While her language is replete with colorful expletives and may offend some readers, Liz 'tells it like it is' from her viewpoint. It may take as long as the reading of the third book before you will appreciate her honesty. The Lord knew that Liz and I would connect in many ways and different reasons.)

19. Jennifer: *She is an assistant to Ann, ecologist, conservationist, and animal lover.* (She becomes more confident in her role over the next few years. Why animals are drawn to her I have not yet discovered, but I have immensely enjoyed many humorous situations. In 1997, I found out that in 1995, Jennifer was the last personality to be created, which was shortly after I came into the picture. I have enjoyed watching her mature from a teenage 'Valley-girl' into a mature young woman in her early twenties. She often reminds us to be responsible ecologists in this world.)

20. Ruth (Little Sister): *She is 24 years old, a Christian with no memories of the abuse. She brings comfort to the system through prayerful intervention. She has hope of healing.*

(At the time of this letter, Ruth was thought to be the last person to split from Maria, around 1990. I believe she was created for the trauma of leaving the Catholic Church, in order to be the person that moved the System out of the Church for obvious reasons. She was thought to be baptized at this time in the first 'Christian' Church she entered, but something else happened. At the baptism, opposing forces used the trauma of leaving the Catholic Church to pressure Maria to split another personality called **Dorcas.** Dorcas was substituted for Ruth at the point of receiving the baptismal blessing, so Ruth didn't receive the birthright until Jesus heals both of them in Ruth's story found in the next book. For now, know that Dorcas was substituted and then hidden inside for the next few years and only Elizabeth Ray was aware of her.

Ruth was known as the pesky 'born-again-Christian,' who wanted to evangelize all the others of the System often in not so subtle ways. She was already the go-between for me in counseling sessions to bring balance back after a difficult session. It was difficult for her to learn about the abuse for the first time and accept its reality as her/their own, as a way of learning compassion for others. Created as an adult, relating to the children's stories of profound abuse became increasingly more difficult. The choices she faced in helping the children overcome their fears, would help her become one of the strongest members of the System.)

21. Raquel / Quiet Walker (Creative One): *She is a Native American in her early twenties who lives on Sacred Mountain in the Land of Preservation. She is very wise, quiet, and a loner. She writes poetry, paints, participates in Pow Wows in the Western USA, is a storyteller, and practices Native American spiritualism. She loves the forest and stays close to nature. She travels in Preservation with Eagle Clan (Trickster, Brave Eagle, Thunderhawk, and Wolfdog) into areas no one else is allowed. She is the diplomat between Levels and Groups within the system. The same Cuban farm worker attacked her in 1965.*

(Raquel becomes an integral part of the healing of the System, bringing words of comfort and wisdom to the various personalities as they face their most difficult challenges. She would bring numerous visions and prophecies to Council, the System, and outside counselors, pastors, and friends who are 'family'. As is the nature of prophecy, many are in story forms that take time to analyze their true meaning. Many of the stories can be interpreted simply as Scriptural warnings, blessings and curses, in applying them to our world today. Her life story will weave in and out of most of the others. She is my sister before the Great Spirit who is our Lord God.)

22. Ann (Intelligent One): She is the administrator/financial planner of the system. She keeps the system functioning when all else fails, through logic, structure, organization, responsibilities, and feeling no emotions. She has a degree in mathematics, considers herself to be non-sexual, and the only part to have held a job in the outside world. She does not consider herself to be married to Sergio, like most of the adult women except for Maria and Louise. She is about 40 years old. The year before she began high school, Ann was beaten by the father to near unconsciousness in 1965. Ann went to college in 1970 and majored in mathematics. In 1974, after Maria had married Sergio, Ann attempted to work but continued loosing jobs due to the switching between the personalities.

(At the writing of this letter by Ruth and Helper, I barely knew Ann, but I could tell from her few statements and this description that she would be the hardest to reach for Christ. Since I have taught many classes on apologetics for skeptics, I know how difficult it is to accept the Gospel of a loving God by faith alone. For an intellectual locked into the view of the world based on the scientific method, it would take a miracle. I was a skeptic myself but God let me know He was much more than my scientific reasoning could explain. It was on this plane of thought where Ann and I would find common ground to discuss what is real in life. Her story is still unfolding and I could probably write a single book on her life alone. A common truth runs through all of these stories: Because of Jesus Christ, each person's story and its outcome, is a byproduct of how they interrelate through Him.

Ann fought the longest to not accept Jesus and proved to be one of the more intellectual challenges I faced. She wanted to prove through scientific analysis and deductive reasoning that the System could survive and exist without His help. Overcoming her anger against God for allowing their suffering would prove difficult, but not impossible. At the time of this letter, the System had mixed feelings about 'religion and God.' Faith and trust are very hard for the System because those who hurt them came in the name of God. Raquel seeks comfort in nature. Ann influences Liz into thinking she is so bad that God punishes her consistently. Ann is the intellectual and although she believes God exists, she had major problems with 'Christianity'.

I think many of my readers will identify with Ann's struggle over her agitation with this God who; *"Gave us a mom who rejected us, so He sends us to live with a grandfather who molested us. God provided a cold basement with rats and straps so that we could learn to obey. God then sent the farm worker and the priest to 'teach us'. God loves us so much that He gave us all this."* Her anger at the Catholic Church is evident in these words, *"God gave us the church to learn how to sacrifice ourselves, be subservient and obedient. Here we learn all women are dirty and bad from the Bible where women are portrayed as prostitutes. Eve messed up the world and is the model for the sinful woman."* After these observations from Ann, she would not discuss her 'feelings' about God again or address the subject for a long time.

Although her profile by Helper states that she feels no emotion, this is not true. She merely keeps most of them restrained within. Anger and resentment against men for exercising control over her and preventing her from becoming all she hoped to be was expressed by Ann. Showing emotion is a sign of weakness for her and she was determined to let no one have that control over her, even Jesus. As the System begins accepting Jesus in their lives, Ann begins to experience changes within her life that are irrefutably connected through Him to reality.)

23. Louise (Compliant One): *She is 38 years old, very obedient, traditional Latina, a limited scholastic education, cooks and does household chores. She is the gardener who can grow anything. She is greatly troubled by the statements of the children, Mariann and Tabitha; as she was taught and believes you should never say anything bad about the church. She is very compliant and was* *brainwashed by the Catholic Church. She thinks she is bad and had to be punished by God. She thinks that because she broke the rules of the church (by leaving it 5 years ago), God has to punish us. She believes that we tempted the men and they couldn't control themselves. When Louise talks this way, Ann becomes enraged and shouts back, "How can a four-year-old tempt a grown man, or an eight-year-old a Priest? She tells Louise that we were taught to obey men in everything. We never had any rights and men, the church and God kept us in our place. We are property." Louise traveled to Xalapa, Veracruz in Mexico to attend school in 1969, in part to get away from her environment. A year later, Maria's paternal grandfather was dying so the family required Louise to return.*

(This was the same grandfather who had abused them. It was Louise's list of 34 questions about God, Jesus, the Holy Spirit and the Catholic Church / Christian Church which contributed to my being called in to assist Bruce. Louise and Maria are so close in 'being' that it has always been hard to distinguish them apart. I've often thought they would blend together as one and last month they did. Usually, my wife and I could tell them apart by the task being performed. Louise is an excellent cook and gardener, bringing dead plants back to life with loving care. Louise had the longest road of recovery in her relationship with the Catholic Church. Her recovery would affect and be affected by Tabitha and Marie.

It has been a difficult task to help her retain what is good and true from her heritage within the Catholic Church, while helping her to be released from the history and traditions which held her in bondage. Helping her to understand that no religious leader representing God, Catholic or otherwise is without sin or the capacity to cause great sin in this life was perhaps the hardest issue for her to accept. It was easier to retain her illusion that priests were incapable of sin than to believe what Mariann was saying really happened to her at the hands of a priest. Even when proof was given through outside sources of record, it took a long time to redirect her devotion to a positive light. The Bible study I began with Louise and Maria in April of 1995 in response to her questions, has become a life application study that continues to this day.)

24. Maria (Timid One): *Host personality who is 42 years old. She is very confused, timid, obedient to a fault, very sad, with a general* *lack of education. Even as she learns about the truth of all of our pasts and us, she is still always kind to other, even those who hurt her. Maria was created in 1953, the same time as Elizabeth Ray, after Maria Ann the birth child went to sleep. Growing up, most of the severe difficulties and all of the abuse was taken by the alters, which account for the major gaps in her memory. Most of her outside time was spent trying to please others through obedience, in order to gain love and acceptance from her parents, which was never forthcoming. She only remembers fragments of life with the grandparents (Thank God!) and can never remember anything positive or encouraging coming from the parents.*

Maria married in 1974 and Kansas (her inner world refuge) was created for Maria's escape from the trauma of sex in marriage. Each individual adult female had to adjust to being married in her own way when it was discovered. As her children were born, Maria began having nightmares and flashbacks and assumed she was crazy. She stayed isolated and was extremely overprotective of her children, while not understanding why. While her husband worked hard outside the home, he did little to help raise the children. She was beaten by her sister in 1989 for not being willing to talk about the abuse she said they had suffered as children. She left the Catholic Church in 1990 about the same time her oldest daughter was diagnosed with an incurable physical disorder. Maria was labeled a bad parent by the treating psychiatrists and attempted suicide. Ruth got help and Maria began her therapy with Bruce in 1994. She began learning about the rest of us with great fear and denial in the beginning. Through Bruce first and then you, she began trusting the part on the inside identified as Jesus and became a Christian in 1995. (I'll come back to speak of Maria at the conclusion of this letter.)

All alters in their own way are dedicated to the survival of the system. We support Maria and were created to take on the burdens of her life. We have different relationships between us and in our relationship with the outside world. Maria and Louise are close. Liz and Ann are very strong-willed. There is a definite logic and organization to us if one is willing to take the time to understand us. A crazy person could not create such a functional and logical system such as ours, but we do have problems. We each have strengths and weaknesses and have difficulty relating in the outside world. One thing we do have in common is that we are careful about being found out because we are afraid of being hurt.

(One of the first corollaries I put together was the 'pairing' between adult parts to child parts. The logic and organization was so complex, I had difficulty getting a handle on it until I received my first, (which was actually the fourth), structural map of the System shortly after receipt of this letter. Each previous map revealed the growing awareness of 'others' and levels within the Land of Preservation on the inside world.)

Our communication system is not perfected yet. We still deal with doing our own thing and not relating to each other well. It is a very difficult challenge to be able to work together but we are trying. To just trust each other at times is difficult. Many of the alters are still trying to adjust to knowing each other and being able to like each other. Each one needs to be able to compromise for the good of the whole, accepting each other's opinions, understanding each other and why we react the way we do, learning skills to function in the 'real' world in relating to outsiders, learning how to make friends or how to accept love... and about a hundred other skills.

Since we have never received a nurturing and caring foundation of love, or learned right from wrong, we have had to pick up pieces about life wherever we could. Unfortunately our childhood provided the worst examples for us to learn anything but fear. Thus, we are like infants learning all over again. We are void of the basic foundation that most adults have to live a healthy life. We operate from fear, mistrust, and pain. We don't have a good understanding of 'good' love, protection, trust, support and closeness. We don't know what it feels like to be rocked asleep as a child or read a bedtime story. We don't have many positive experiences of love and being protected. (The only positive experience for them as of this letter was the one growing with Bruce and beginning with me. It will last for a lifetime.)

We have to reprogram ourselves. Decades of misinformation and pain will need to be unraveled as we pour new information and experiences into us. We know now what needs to be done. We also know many alters are scared to undergo a transformation. Many would rather hide and suffer because they know no other way and the unknown is always scary. They are afraid of rejection. They are afraid of the world on the outside. They are afraid of being trapped. They are afraid of being locked up in a hospital. They are afraid of being hurt again. They are afraid of learning the horror of the other alters' memories and how that might affect them. They won't know how to react or how to emotionally respond. They are afraid to taste it, hear it, feel it, so they escape and hide from it or deny it. They go to the mountain inside or become active in outside goals to avoid the unavoidable, while Maria continues with the nightmares and flashbacks.

We are strong in the sense we have survived thus far, yet we are also fragile. We are very sensitive and very hungry for acceptance. We have a difficult time responding to situations on the outside the way it is expected in society. The children want and need hugs, bubbles, and butterflies. They need a tremendous amount of love... and in return they pour out their love to others willing to accept it. Liz needs acceptance and affirmation, without rejection or ridicule. Ann needs approval and acceptance for who she is, not because she is a wonderful 'alter' who completes goals on time or does more than most people do in a lifetime. She needs to learn that people like being her friend without wanting her to do something for them. Each and every one of us is the way we are because of our experiences.

We need people to understand us and accept us. We don't want to be labeled. We don't want to be talked about as abnormal. When some of us cut our body or give the body pain, we want others to understand that we want to make sure that we are real and sometimes we need to get some of the pain out. When we are hit from outsiders, called stupid and humiliated, we just want you to understand that we don't have the skills to stop it. We want you to understand that in our culture we have to obey and serve the man. We need you to understand us and be patient with us. We are so used to abuse that it is normal to us. But now we are experiencing a different normal from you and Bruce, a normal that includes love in a way that we have never known.

You both really listen to us and care about what is happening in our life. You both pray for us and think about us for the purpose of trying to help us. You both want to understand us. Neither of you tells us we are stupid or worthless. These are things we have never before heard or felt. We are learning a different normal and with that comes a challenge. We are caught between two worlds, the world we have known and the new world you are showing us. We like the new world, but some don't know how to make it real while holding on to the pain of the old one. How do we live in our current environment experiencing the old without the hope of change, while tasting the new world in small amounts and being overwhelmed with desire for it? How do we go back and forth between the two? Some alters think it would have been better to have never known what 'good' love is, so we would not have known what we have missed most of our lives, while others are overcome with hunger for it.

I think Quiet Walker said it best when she wrote her Captive Soul *poem. "Release my captive soul and let me soar free and proud." You and Bruce, guided by the Lord, are unlocking our prison door. Many alters are afraid to walk out. We need a caring hand to gently guide us and hold on to us as we take these first steps. Can you not let go of our hand until you know we are safely on the other side? There we will be whole and truly alive!*

In Christ, Ruth

I went to my knees the night I read this letter, praying for answers to both of our questions. *"Can you not let go of our hand until you know we are safely on the other side?"* and "Your plan will take much longer than mine Lord, will you replace mine with yours?" I thought of how the Lord sent His disciples out to accomplish things of a magnitude that challenged the religious thinking and traditions in faith. Jesus told us what to expect when He gave the following to those who followed Him.

"Heal the sick, raise the dead, cleanse the lepers, cast out demons, freely you received, freely give..." "Behold I send you out as sheep in the midst of wolves; therefore be shrewd as serpents and innocent as doves. But beware of men; for they will deliver you up to the courts and scourge you in their synagogues; and you shall even be brought before governors and kings for My sake, as a testimony to them and to the Gentiles. But when they deliver you up, do not become anxious about how or what you will speak; for it shall be given you in

that hour what you are to speak. For it is not you who speak, but it is the Spirit of your Father who speaks in you..." "And he who does not take his cross and follow after Me is not worthy of Me. He who has found his life shall lose it, and he who has lost his life for My sake shall find it. He who receives you receives Me, and he who receives Me receives He who sent Me..." "And whoever in the name of a disciple gives to one of these little ones even a cup of cold water to drink, truly I say to you he shall not lose his reward."

-*Jesus* <u>*Matthew 10*</u>

"To go against the dominant thinking of your friends,
Of most of the people you see everyday,
Is perhaps the most difficult act of heroism you can have."
Theodore H. White – 1969

---

[3] For another outside source and description of Yemaya and the Santeria, I suggest <u>Santeria: A Practical Guide to Afro-Caribbean Magic</u> by Luis Manuel Nunez, Spring Publications, 1992.

Chapter Two:

"Is There Value in Human Suffering?"

"And do not fear those who kill the body,
But are unable to kill the soul;
But rather fear Him who is able to destroy
Both soul and body in hell."
Matthew 10:28

We who lived in concentration camps can remember
the men who walked through the huts comforting others,
giving away their last piece of bread. They may have
been few in number, but they offer sufficient proof that
everything can be taken from a man but one thing: the
last of the human freedoms – to choose one's attitude in
any given circumstances, to choose one's own way.
Viktor Frankl, *Man's Search for Meaning (1959)*

The previous passages in Matthew 10 both encouraged me for the direction I was to take at that time and challenged me when I started putting the material together for this book. I knew that only Jesus could direct my paths in His healing of His children, by giving me the words He knew they needed to hear. I also know that when this book is read, that as many believers as non-believers will want to 'deliver me up for trial' because the truth of it will not fit into their comfort zones of beliefs and traditions. I am not anxious about it now and trust I won't be when it occurs, for I know the love that does not leave nor forsake me in times of trouble. It was in this love that I chose to accept the Lord's plan to move forward with these people to learn together, one day at a time. They knew as well that the subject matter of these books and the sharing of their life stories would open them up for ridicule, persecution and disbelief for telling the truth as it happened. They also know that the possibility of 'trial' looms even larger for them, but we decided together that it was worth it... if only one person comes to know healing through our Lord Jesus Christ.

This decision to tell their stories as a 'System' also created immediate questions about the meaning of 'host personality'. Host personality as given here should be understood simply as the first person created and given the name that all other personalities would use on the outside to protect their privacy. Each person has time lived on the outside in this physical world that constitutes their life with us experientially. If time was the only measurement, then Louise, Raquel, or Ann might qualify as the host personality. If quality of life is the measurement then maybe only Penny's brief time out should qualify her as one without abuse. If learning how to survive should determine who is 'host', maybe Liz should get the honors. You can begin to see the difficulty in determining who might receive 'priority of life' if alters are forced to integrate by outside caregivers... "to sacrifice your life for the host to be normal."

The reality always exists for them that, should any one of them decide to end the life of the body, life would cease for all of them. If the determining factor were who gives the most love, I would be hard pressed to choose who should be host between all of them, especially between the children and Maria. If you isolate it to a particular kind of love, which one should be chosen? The love of a child towards a parent? The love of a buddy like Liz, who would die for you even though she felt she never had to say, 'I love you'? The love of a sister or brother who is ready to walk through any trial with you in this life? What criteria is used, or should I have used, other than the one Jesus gave to me when I began?

"It is enough to reach out to one person at a time to bring My love to them..."

Each person I met from the beginning had a desire to be 'whole' as an individual, not as a part of someone else. They each wanted to find meaning for the suffering they had endured, that there was a purpose behind it and not just the fulfilling of the sick desires of someone outside of themselves. They each wanted to know their life had value and meaning beyond their understanding of it. How could they know the love Jesus has for them, if I couldn't commit to walk alongside of them to model the reality of this same love He has given to me as the answer to our quest for meaning? Could I trust Jesus enough to follow Him wherever this path led? I had to risk more of my understanding of Jesus in my own life than I ever had previously, in order to move forward.

I want to offer some clarity about ages and aging within the System, as I've studied it in relationship with them. Helper may be the only exception to this premise, as he was introduced as 57 years old in the beginning, 15 years older than the suspected birth age of Maria. Since then, he has stated often he feels much older at times but hasn't stated it as a reality for him. For the rest of the System, their aging would appear directly related to the amount of time spent on the surface in the physical world. Aging also occurs to the ones who never come to the surface, like Council, but at a different rate directly related to their growth spiritually with Jesus. For example, Daniel was brave beyond his 10 years as leader of the Clan of Argus in his protection of Mariann in the spiritual realm, long before he came to Council. Since he has been there the last 7 years, he has aged to 17 years of age, offering compassion and wisdom in his perspectives for protecting the children in his care, again well beyond his age. I've witnessed him confront men on the outside twice his age, with a maturity that doesn't correlate with his age. His youth is reflected in his humor that can lighten tense moments in Council meetings.

Those who come to the surface and spend real time outside in this physical reality seem to age proportionately. For example, Maria was 42 when we met 7 years ago and will be 49 on her next birthday, always celebrated on the Easter Sunday closest to it because of her reason for living. Ruth accidentally confirmed this theory recently when she got curious about aging. She was created the age of 24, much younger than the birth age of 42, and has existed for 7 years. While discussing my theory with her, she stated that while some parts seem to age at different rates in physical appearance, they stayed the age they identified themselves to be at. This didn't seem logical to her so she began questioning me first, then Jesus as to why she hadn't aged. I tried to stop her from pursuing it, as she probably didn't want the truth that I suspected was waiting. She blurted the question to Jesus of 'how old am I?' She found out to her dismay that she was 31 years old. She is still trying to recover from this incident. No one else has risked asking this question of Jesus for fear of the answer.

Mariann just knows that she is eight and a bit and that is all that matters to her. Age and time are not important to her. She had very little schooling so she doesn't read or write well, but that was not her primary role in life. Her verbal skills when she first came out with Bruce, and later with me, were around that of an eight-year-old. Later, when she is introduced into a relationship with a caregiver family with young children, she regresses dramatically to accommodate the level of maturity of the child she is closest to and who accepts her as she is. This would fluctuate depending on the intensity of the relationship and the mutual acceptance of each other. The parents stated that Mariann could communicate with their 1 year-old-son as easily as she could with their 7 year-old-daughter.

Yet, she was beyond her age in spiritual maturity when Jesus entered into her life primarily due to her trust in Him, as you will read in her story. In the last few years, she has received very basic reading and writing lessons from Carol. I have helped her relate better with her 'peers', but she has not matured in this area beyond her age, which she now states as 9… and a bit. Defining an age for her really only seems important to her for finding friends to play with who will accept her as Mariann. So my theory for Mariann is that she is the age Jesus wants her to be, no more… no less. I do know she is my spiritual daughter given to me to receive a Father's love from God. So the question of age and aging will remain a mystery for some in the System, but not for curious Ruth.

The ideas and concepts presented in Ruth's letter, of another world existing 'inside' known as the Land of Preservation with forests, waterfalls, mountains and doors allowing access between worlds, probably sounds harder to believe than the fact of knowing that dozens of personalities inhabit a single body. It's easier because, in order to establish an objective opinion about their existence, you can observe, test and hear the individual, before giving testimony of their reality. These people and I cannot offer any evidence about the inside world's existence, other than what we have experienced together with Jesus in His kingdom, which they have witnessed with their own eyes and given in the Bible about its reality. In these books as in the Bible, you are asked to accept some things by faith alone. It is this author's experience that the two worlds revealed in these pages are coexistent, with our world only a temporary reality within the eternal reality of the Kingdom of God. Jesus Christ spoke of this in parables and offers the following perspective:

'And He said to them, "To you has been given the mystery of the kingdom of God; but those who are outside get everything in parables, in order that while seeing, they may see and not perceive; and while hearing, they may hear and not understand lest they return and be forgiven." -Jesus Mark 4:11 – 12

Jesus taught His disciples how faith in Him and His kingdom would allow them to see and understand what others outside the kingdom will fail to comprehend, even though they read or hear the same spoken message. All of the parables on the Kingdom of God speak about the kingdom established and revealed around them in Christ and His more powerful kingdom yet to come. Although everyone is given the potential to understand the 'mystery', only those people who seek to understand by faith in Jesus Christ will have the potential to see and know the kingdom's existence as part of their reality and live in it. Without Jesus as its focal point, there is no kingdom to see or know. These biographies testify to the reality of the Kingdom of God as it is revealed to them by Jesus in their struggle to know God's presence in the harshness of life. What many of them will deny in the beginning, will slowly and gradually be accepted in faith and hope will survive. *(As I follow Jesus into spiritual battles inside His kingdom over the next 17 years to release those imprisoned there by fear and lies of the enemy hundreds of times, I realize how "Perfect love casts out fear" to follow Jesus anywhere to rescue His children. I plan to speak more about these experiences of learning the will and plans of God in the third book of this series reflecting on hundreds of case studies.)*

The ideas, biases, descriptions and perspectives presented in this prologue and preface, make it difficult to define Maria within the confines of our human understanding alone, thus we need to look at them from God's vantagepoint. To look upon Maria as the only 'real person' to exist, would be to shatter the lives of every person inside her body whom God has created and who have changed my life and the lives of numerous others. It would make the reality of existence for each person, as being no more real than what anyone can conceive of in their own mind. When I took this path I was looking for integration, or blending of all of them, as the only way to 'wholeness' in this life. I thought faith in Jesus was the common focal point to achieve that wholeness, but I soon learned how my perspective was in error because it was my concept of wholeness...not Jesus'. I expected Maria the 'host' to be the person to receive this 'wholeness.' Jesus changed that when He told me to share with them His goal for them in answer to their question; "Will I ever be whole so I can be like everyone else?" My response to them from Jesus was this:

"I will love you with an everlasting love and I will heal you. Your wholeness will be found in Me... not as the world understands wholeness, but as I give it. You will remain a multiple for my purposes because each one of you will have a testimony to give about My power to heal and receive all who come to Me. The fact that you are alive today is a testimony in itself of My love for all of you. You will become My witnesses to a world in need of My love. Do not be afraid of this, for I will never leave you nor forsake you."

When they anticipated having to remain a multiple in their current context in life, the retreat into depression was a rapid one. Maybe it was how I told them or in the timing of it so soon after their diagnosis. Maybe it was in our expectations of wholeness that caused this message to not be heard on the first attempt, for over the years we have come back to it many times. It took me more time to really begin to understand its implications. Thankfully, Jesus didn't wait that long to communicate directly with them, speaking to them from His perspective of wholeness in this life. His answer was given in response to Maria's personal cry for understanding and to the whole System for the encouragement of all. This was the first copy of any letter I received which was reported to me as Jesus' direct words to Raquel to tell the System of His understanding of their pain and suffering and what to expect from Him.

In the last seventeen years I have reread it for support, every time more suffering has come into their life or mine. I have edited it because of length and repetition of thoughts needed at that time to penetrate the depth of their pain, but it retains its full essence. For students of the Bible, you will see parallels in The Song of Songs.

A letter to the system, given to me in the stillness of the early morning by the Great Spirit as I walked the paths of Sacred Mountain.

My precious child,

I know your pain. I know the heaviness of your heart. I see your sadness. I know your struggles and your sorrow. Do not worry my child, for I understand. Let me absorb your pain. Give it to me, my precious one. Give me your brokenness and I will fill it with courage and wisdom. Give me your real feelings, for I understand. I am very near you and I hear your prayers. I see every single shed tear of yours. I know it seems that you are in a storm and cannot find the way. I am the way and I will lead you to safety. I will protect you. I am closer to you than your own heartbeat. I can see your frailness. I know how tender and fragile are your feelings. Do not be afraid child, for you are my child and I will be your shield. Come into my love and let my spirit strengthen you and bring you comfort. I am praying for you and speaking your name to my Father, asking him to help you. Do not lose faith during this suffering.

Be encouraged, for I am asking my heavenly Father to grant you an abundance of mercy so that you can come through your suffering. And know that I am here with you in the midst of it. For you are a precious lamb of my flock. I will lead you to where you may rest and I will restore your strength. I will lead you to calm waters. Trust in my care, for I am your shepherd. You may think you are too small for me to bother about and that I am too busy looking after everything to have time for you. But don't you know how precious you are to me? I created you. I have a purpose and a wonderful plan for your life. I have good plans for you, not plans to hurt you. I will give you hope and a good future. I intimately care for you. You are my beloved child. Every tear you shed... every pain you feel... I feel it too. You are a part of me and very precious. I will never leave your side.

I know of the rejection you have experienced in your life. I know how it hurts. When I walked the earth, I was hated and rejected by the people I dearly loved. I came to help them and they betrayed me. They denied that they even knew me. Some would not even look at me. They called me crazy... a lunatic... a liar... a blasphemer. I felt the pain of rejection. I felt the abandonment. I know the feelings my child, that you have experienced... for I felt them too. Come to me with your pain. Though your family and others have rejected you, I never will.

I know it is hard for you to understand your suffering... You struggle with the injustice in suffering that you see. Your grief is overwhelming to you. But know that you will overcome it. Be encouraged. Everyone experiences trouble in this fallen world. But remember I have overcome the world and because you are in me, you too will overcome your grief. You will never be hungry again or thirst again... I will stand before my Father as your defense attorney and I will plead your case. And know child of mine, my Father is pure justice. Rest in knowing that justice will be done, but it shall be done by my Father. Release to me the pain of injustices that have been done to you.

Oh my dear one, remember that I died for you and rose again. This is your hope. Hold tightly to it. I am Lord of suffering. In your suffering and sorrow allow me to enter your darkness. I am your hope. You have suffered much. Remember my child, that those people who know they have great spiritual needs are happy because the Kingdom of Heaven belongs to them. They draw close to me and cry out in their weakness and I fill them with my own spirit. Run to me. I am your place of safety and I will hold you up in my arms forever. I am ready to catch you. When I was suffering in the garden over my impending death, I was thinking of you and praying for my peace to flow through the core of your being... reminding you of my unconditional love for you... My love is strong enough to handle your questions and skepticism. You will not anger me with your shouts of why? Tell me your anger...

Come sit with me and let me hold your pain. And for the times, my child, when you cannot speak, do not worry. Do not worry that you cannot express to me in words, what you feel in your heart. My Holy Spirit will be your voice. I know you are tired and wanting to give up. You have struggled so much and you are worn out. But I am here standing beside you. I will hold you up. I will be your strength. Trust me.

I know child of mine, that in this dark valley of your life, you are having a hard time seeing my love for you, but my love is there. So don't worry, for I am with you. And don't be afraid for I am your Savior... Remember my promise. Bind it up and store it in your heart. The sufferings you have now are nothing compared to the great glory that will be shown to you. This suffering will not last forever. You my child, if you continue to trust me as your Savior, will be with me in a place of unending glory. This glory is beyond human understanding. There are no words that can explain to you the wonder that awaits you. And it will cover over and outweigh all of the grief of this temporal life. You shall be satisfied. So do not give up my precious little one.

I know what you are asking my child... "But this suffering is so long. How long will I be sad and feeling so much pain?" Your suffering has been long. Your burdens have been heavy. Oh my child... human life is a grief journey. Even I, who am sinless, know grief and sorrow. When you suffer, I suffer. But trust me. My child, life is grief and pain. I never promised that your life would know no suffering. But what I have promised is that in all of the pain and suffering, I will be your Savior. Build your life on me... the mighty rock. And when the storms of affliction hit you with hurricane force, you need not worry, if you hold on to the rock... I will lift you up from this place of pain and I will change your name. And you will be a precious vessel that will be used by me to comfort others. You will be a bold vessel that will be used by me to speak truth to my church. And you will be an encourager to others... a voice speaking of my love. Do not give up my little one. Continue to hold on to my hope. Choose life. Oh my child, you do not know the plans I have for you. There are many people who need to meet you. We will travel your life journey together.

Do not give up. Finish the race I have given you. I am asking you to trust me. Look to me, my precious one, I am the light. Do not take your eyes off of me. I want you to be strong in me and in my great power. I am faithful and I will give you strength and will protect you from the evil one. Rest in me and allow me to heal you. Just as your garden, dormant in the darkness of winter, begins to grow and flourish in the spring; I will heal your soul and it shall blossom and flourish. The darkness will be overtaken by the light. The warmth of my love, breaking through the cracks of your pain and hopelessness, will melt away sorrow.

The garden of your soul will prosper and the sweet smelling fragrance of your heart will bring joy to all who see. And then I shall say to you, "Look, the winter is past, the rains are over and gone. Blossoms appear throughout the Land of Preservation. The time has come to sing, and the cooing of doves is heard in the land. There are young figs on the fig trees, and the blossoms on the vine smell sweet. Get up my child. Take my hand and together we shall walk through life.
Your loving Jesus."

I hope you mark the pages of this letter to read again, as you read of their journey with Jesus, because I believe the words can lift you up as well, when questioning the trials and suffering you are experiencing in your own journey. I know He is saying the same thing to each of us, as sure as I am alive today. The letter was received 2 months after I baptized Maria and Louise into their new Christian faith, with Raquel following a couple of weeks later in a special ceremony under a large oak tree... and one month before they will enter into surgery for breast cancer. Trust will quickly come to them at a very high premium as they wrestle with finding the meaning of wholeness in the midst of suffering.

"Blessed are you who are poor, for yours is the kingdom of God. Blessed are you who hunger now, for you shall be satisfied. Blessed are you who weep now, for you shall laugh. Blessed are you when men hate you, and ostracize you, and cast insults at you, and spurn your name as evil, for the sake of the Son of Man. Be glad in that day, and leap for joy, for behold, your reward is great in heaven."
-Jesus <u>Luke 6:20-23</u>.

In the judgment of Christianity and the Mahayana,
even the extremity of Suffering is not too high a price
to pay for following Love's lead; for, in their judgment,
Selfishness, not Suffering, is the greatest of all evils,
and Love, not release from Suffering,
is the greatest of all goods.
Arnold Toynbee, *An Historian's Approach to Religion (1956)*

Chapter Three:

"Craving a Safe Place to Be"

Then, cradling the little one in his arms, he said,
"Whoever embraces one of these children as I do
embraces me, and far more than me
– God who sent me."
-Jesus The Message

"Ask, and it shall be given to you; seek, and you shall find;
knock, and it shall be opened to you. For everyone who
asks receives, and he who seeks finds, and to him
who knocks it shall be opened."
-Jesus Matthew 7:7-8

When I began with the System, I knew I was coming alongside of them in their journey already begun with Bruce. I want to give you an overview of the struggles he entered into with them, to establish the healing process which both the System and I would benefit from as we began our time together. Many of the keys for unlocking the history and the mysteries of the System were the result of sessions with Bruce during their first year together. Even as I began with the adults, Maria and Louise, Bruce was continuing with all of them, concentrating now more on the child parts that were being revealed. He had already established a trust relationship with Tabitha and Anna, to the point that they called him 'Daddy'.

When asked for my opinion in this case of a therapist allowing his child clients to refer to him as daddy, I had no issue with it because I understood his method. The children were receiving for the first time in their existence the nurturing love of a father figure. The need of the children for this love in order to heal overcame the social and professional restrictions that often prevent many therapists from achieving the results Bruce and I were privileged to witness. Bruce was often confronted and questioned by the leaders of the System, Ann or Liz, about his methods and approach to therapy. An excerpt from a letter to him from King of the Lights exemplifies his gentle approach.

As I observe your interaction with the Surface People and hear the reports of your work with them, I am appreciative of your commitment, compassion, and kindness. You are well respected as an outside counselor among the leaders... One question I do have as a leader in Circle Council evolves around the area of therapy or counseling. Is there a difference between Christian counseling and Secular counseling by a Christian? I observed that many of the Christian authors in "Christian Psychology" have jumped on the same bandwagon as the secular counselors in the self-esteem movement... There seems to be very little emphasis placed on the Bible. Feeling better has become more important than finding God. How do you see yourself in therapy?

While I can't have many of Bruce's written responses in these books, a few are necessary to understand the kind of therapist the Lord chose first for the System. His answer to the question above is worth noting:

To King of Lights
Highest Elder of the Elysian Fields
Greetings:

I have received your fax re Christian counseling. These are great questions and they are difficult ones. I am a Christian who is a counselor; I am also a Christian counselor. By Christian counseling, I mean counseling which has as its foundational purpose the propagation of the client's relationship with God. Such counseling must also have as its primary intent the glorification of God.

For these two goals to be realized, the counselor must be committed to serving God and must be concerned about his or her own relationship with God. While I am committed to these, these two goals in and of themselves do not make counseling Christian. I believe what makes counseling Christian is a commitment on my part to Biblical values and the growth of the client ultimately becoming dependent upon God rather than me. I also nurture growth that allows the client to develop a relationship with God based on trust and faith. Thus, Tabitha's viewing of me, as a daddy will eventually allow her to transition her trust to Jesus and to God, since our view of God is most often based on our relationship with our fathers. This is also why I have tried to give the children a

62

rudimentary trust in Jesus as an internal protector. This allows them to build a relationship with God at their most basic points of need.

Perhaps this is the best of Christian counseling, in that it allows a client to develop a relationship with a counselor at their point of need. The counselor gently shifts this relationship to one with God, allowing the client to see God meeting her/him at the current point of need.

Thanks for asking these questions, they are good to think about. My answers may well produce more questions. Feel free to write these to me.

With regards, B.

One of Bruce's gifts was treating each client, including 'alters', with respect for the individual persona he was helping, including Liz after she would dump her anger on him.

This is Liz. And I ain't coming in that damn office... So you are coming up against walls. Shit I could have told you so and I am really angry because I hate it when Maria and Louise hold on to a promise that is not coming true... You can't find any Christian willing to teach Maria, because unless you offer them money they are not going to waste their time with her. Shit they are all talk and no action about this damn discipleship crap Ruth talks about.

Between their elite potlucks, choir practices, board meetings and get-togethers with their fellow Christians, they are not going to donate any time to teaching a stupid, poor Latina about Jesus. Why should they? Pisses me off royal especially when Maria and Louise keep reassuring themselves that he will find a teacher for us. I told them they better stop dreaming... Just don't tell me about walls. Shit and I was beginning to think that just maybe I was wrong about lumping all you guys together. (Liz, page 40)

When Bruce began with the System the year before, he was deluged with letters from various parts, some not aware of what the other had sent, shortly after making his preliminary diagnosis in the second month of therapy. Elizabeth Ray kept a journal of all communiqués sent by the System hidden away at home and did not reveal herself to Bruce until February of the next year. Maria was slowly learning the meaning of her diagnosis about having Dissociative Identity Disorder (MPD), as meaning the voices she heard for many years had names and histories intertwined throughout her existence. Bruce only talked directly with Maria over the first months, but he received information about 'others' indirectly during this period. The acknowledgement by Maria of gaps in time in her life, finding things in her possession she never purchased, written material supposedly by her hand that didn't match her handwriting, not knowing if she had graduated from high school, were all signals pointing to DID.

While Bruce sought a consensus of opinions from his colleagues about his diagnosis before presenting it to Maria, the System was looking for ways to reveal their existence to someone they hoped they could trust and do it through Maria, who was not yet aware of their presence. It was a dilemma even internally as they were still discovering each other's existence after the walls came down a few months before when the psychiatrists declared her a bad parent. Her oldest child was sent to live with her parents, throwing Maria into a spiral of depression and attempted suicide, events that led them to seek help from Bruce.

At this stage in their lives, not everyone was aware of how many parts existed. Elizabeth Ray was not yet communicating with anyone, but quietly recording history. While all parts were aware of Maria as host, they were aware of only a few others and their own particular role within the System, catching fleeting glimpses of others when rotating out. Ruth was aware of Ann and Liz for example, more from the power of their roles than from their personalities. Helper was aware of more surface parts' existence, yet unaware of the other levels and parts that were soon to be revealed to him through Raquel. Raquel would roam around Land of Preservation (Hereafter referred to simply as Preservation) at will, establishing relationships with various 'tribes' or groups, and learning how they traversed between worlds. She, like Elizabeth Ray, would share her knowledge of others only when asked or on a need to know basis.

All parts, including Maria, were very adept at keeping information secret, particularly the past abuse. Now they were faced with the opportunity of sharing that information with Bruce, but how do you reveal a lifetime of secrecy and threats of death to anyone who talks? Maria had it engrained in her very essence from infancy that to talk meant death, and the distant voices in her head confirmed that fact. It is only in hindsight that the question, 'who had the nerve to communicate first to Bruce in the revealing of parts', can be answered. The diagnosis was the key that unlocked the door giving them permission to write him. No part signed their name in the beginning or identified themselves in the letters, poems, and stories except Maria and yet, as you will see, the 'writer' speaks of others outside herself. Maria would obediently give them to Bruce while questioning where they came from, knowing they were not from her.

The following three writings were given to Bruce at approximately the same week as his diagnosis. They are in the order given to Bruce and the first is from Maria, with influences from yet unknown parts that were later revealed to her.

This scares me. I don't understand what is happening. Why are these pictures coming into my mind now? How come I couldn't remember the parts until now? Maybe it is a dream.

He's going to think I'm crazy. He doesn't know about the fog. He's going to think I've lost my mind. But it's real. It's been real ever since I can remember. When something bad is happening I can leave me and go into this fog. The fog is nothingness. I don't feel or know anything in the fog, I am just there and my body is down there and numb. In the fog there are no feelings, like I was trained, no feelings. Secrets are not told.

But why do I have so much to write now and why do I have a hard time speaking it. (A truth the parts learned early was writing and drawing about things was not the same as telling or speaking it.) *I learned how to be silent. I lived with the glue people in the orchard and went on adventures with them when I was young* (Tabitha). *But you must stay silent and secret, my inside voice told me.* (Yemaya?) *Why am I now telling Bruce? It is too painful to share. I never ever want anyone else to find out.*

Maybe it wasn't that bad. I should be able to make it. That's why I like to go to Kansas. It's safe. I can go to Kansas whenever I want. I go to Kansas when my voice says go to Kansas. Nobody knows I can be in two worlds.

This story about Little Indian (Raquel), *where did it come from? I am uneasy about all of this. Am I going to feel better about talking, or can't I just get Kansas and go back to the way it was. I don't feel comfortable talking about this. I can't remember more than just pieces. It's scary to think I might become someone else. Won't it just go away? These pictures in my head, I don't want to remember. It's my fault because why should it not be my fault? These pictures, I can't explain them.*

It's hard to keep going back to Bruce each time. It's scary. When I walk in I'm scared. I can't eat before I go. I don't like being in the waiting room. I hate leaving with people sitting there, but I feel better after I get into the car and breath. Why is this so hard for me? I don't know how I get there in the car, I don't drive. I'm afraid to feel.

Writing is easier for me than talking. I can't look at him and talk. Sometimes I feel so bad I want to die. I can't cope with the feelings and pain that are coming at me. (Maria, page 45)

The following excerpts come from a story written by Raquel and influenced by Elizabeth Ray. It is about a little girl's life of suffering. It was unsigned and speaks about abuse yet carried the style of the 'Creative One'. It begins to reveal the influence of Yemaya upon the child parts in the early years and was the first overview of the history of abuse to the System, to bring affirmation to the diagnosis by Bruce.

Maria

Once upon a time there lived a little girl who played with Wolfdog among the blossoms. She loved to curl up under the trees and watch the leaves dance in the wind and the clouds make pictures in the sky. The birds and butterflies would glide by and make beautiful designs in the warm air. She was happy and spent many hours in the shade of the leaves in the orchards. Her name was Maria. She was almost four.

That was before Maria knew about the bad. At four the bad started. She did not feel safe anymore in the pink room, but only in the orchard with Wolfdog. When she watched the things in the red barn at the end of the lane, it did not scare her. At the water, the old Cuban woman was nice and told her that Yemaya was Maria's orisha and would protect her from evil and is her guide. The waters rushed around Maria, but she was not afraid. Maria gave Yemaya seven pennies. She talked to Yemaya. She was her guardian angel.

Olofi had created her by collecting smooth stones and putting his ash into them.

The bad in the pink room continued however, but Maria thought the orchard was safe. When Maria was about five, the Cuban man asked Maria if she wanted to see a deer and pet him. Maria loved animals so she went deep into the orchard with the Cuban man. But the birds and butterflies were not there and there was no deer. Then the Cuban man hurt Maria and told her not to tell. Maria did not understand what happened and thought she had evil spirits in her because she was bad. She asked Yemaya what happened and to get the evil spirits out of her. Yemaya said it was Penny's fault because Penny let Maria's body do it and didn't stay safe. Penny had not remembered to put her robe on when grandpa was around. Penny set in his lap and danced in the parlor and made him do it in the pink room. Penny went with the Cuban man into the orchard. Yemaya said Penny would get them in trouble and then leave and let Maria be the one to get hurt...

When Penny got them in trouble and they would get locked in the basement, Maria would be very scared of the rats and it was cold and damp. Yemaya told Maria (Tabitha) and Penny that they would have to hide and not tell. She said she would take care of them and protect them from bad. So Maria and Penny would have to keep secret to survive...

The pink room continued until Maria did not live with grandpa anymore. Only the room at church happened now, the basement, the strap and the iron skillet. Maria knew it was Penny because Yemaya said so, and she couldn't stop Penny. At church Penny would get off the bus and he (Beast) was waiting for her. Penny would be happy and go to the room. The room had red and green bells. Penny would set on his lap and then disappear and Maria (Mariann) would have to be hurt. Then he would tell Maria that she sinned and had to go to the black box and do confession to him. She (Mari) had to tell him all that she did in the room. Maria knew all her body had done because she would watch it from the ceiling and then go into nothingness. Yemaya told Maria to obey the man so that she would live.

When Maria (Raquel) *was thirteen, the Cuban man came back and hurt her a lot. Maria knows to keep her legs tight together. She didn't tell because of the knife. Maria didn't go into that orchard anymore and the trees became monsters. Maria learned not to feel pain and had her glue people and the fog for safety... When Maria was fifteen she dove into the pool with her clothes on. She did not know how to swim. She wanted to die and almost did. But Yemaya said she wasn't finished with her yet and pushed her through the water to safety. Maria was not safe but did not tell anyone...Maria missed her grandma and tried to talk with her dead grandma. But Maria got scared when she would get dizzy and hear voices. Then when the man wanted her to sit in the circle with the candles, she got scared and didn't go back.*

Maria married Sergio to get away. Sergio moved Maria from the farm to the city, where she could not breathe because the city went too fast. Maria went to Kansas inside. Three times Penny came out and Sergio was surprised... One time Penny filled the children's pool with dirt and made mud for Penny and the kids to go swimming like Penny did in the ditches. Sergio came home and they were all in mud. Penny didn't come out too often because Yemaya kept her in. Yemaya told Maria she had to get bigger by eating and not exercising to become safe. Maria never came out except when bad happened and the sex.

Maria learned to go to the fog and then to Kansas. Maria in Kansas did not know about Maria in California. Maria was in Kansas with her other family and everyone knew it was safe. Sergio saw Maria once in a while and thought someone else was her, a scared Maria. He saw Penny three times. He would ask Maria sometimes where she was when they were in bed (Louise) *because he knew Maria didn't focus well. He also knew Maria didn't like to be touched.*

One day, Maria's daughter got sick and the doctors took her. Yemaya and Penny stayed inside and Maria again had to be hurt. Now Maria is all the time and Yemaya and Penny stay inside.

Within a matter of days, someone (Ann?) from the System communicated with Bruce about the trauma of the last two years in detail. She told him of her distrust of the medical system and how doctors and psychiatrists had treated her daughter, before she was taken away from her. She told of how her family reacted and how they were kept uninformed about how their rights were violated, because they trusted the 'professionals'. She describes herself:

Throughout all of this, no one knew what I was experiencing and no one knew about my life. The migraine headaches began to return and I began to have nightmares. Several mornings I started shaking violently and I couldn't stop. I blacked out once and three times I could not get out of bed until the afternoon. My body would just not function. I was very aware that suicide was a sensitive thing with me and I tried to push it inside because I couldn't handle it right now. The pictures were like small puzzle pieces of something that didn't settle right inside me. At this point I could not get to Kansas and I had to find a way to breathe and stay together in front of these people. I was able to do what I do when I am trapped and can't space out, to help with the pain. I have to do it first on the right and then on the left so that I can get rid of the pain inside and no one is aware that I'm doing it... It is very important to me that you keep your word. I have never gone to anyone like you before and I need to know that you keep your promises. If you can't, please tell me now and burn all the things I gave you. I won't come back.

Bruce would receive letters the same afternoon following a session, which would soon be occurring two or more times a week. After one such session he received a poem from Quiet Walker entitled "Parts".

Separate but joined
Housed together in the same vessel
Unaware of the role they play
Born out of a need to be
There are the little ones
Innocent and pure

Blossoms and butterflies
Castles and princes
Playing with dolls
Running with Wolfdog
Unaware of the role they play
Born out of a need to be

There is the strive to achieve one
Hard working and committed
Lists and duties
Grades and school
Please accept me is her middle name
Trying to be what she is incapable of being

Unaware of the role she plays
Born out of a need to be

There is the fearful and scared one
Rejected and hurt
Loneliness and guilt surround her
Horror and blame are her companions
Worthless and unappreciated
Holding on to the edge
Not trusting and careful
Isolated and alone

Unaware of the role she plays
Born out of a need to be

There is the strong one
Take charge and survive
Accomplish and push to the limit
Meet the needs of all around
Rigid and demanding of herself
High expectations and unreachable goals

Unaware of the role she plays
Born out of a need to be

There is the compassionate one
Sensitive and loving
She goes where no one else will venture
She brings comfort to them

Unaware of the role she plays
Born out of a need to be

There is the compliant one
Willing to obey at all cost
Lacking in confidence
Insecure and confused

She knows her place
And stays there

Unaware of the role she plays
Born out of a need to be

There is the angry one
Hidden very deep inside
Angry at God
Filled with bitterness
Lashing out inside
Rage from within

Unaware of the role she plays
Born out of a need to be

There is the creative one
Fantasy worlds abound
The teller of stories
That captivates the child
Spontaneous and carefree
Not made for this world

Unaware of the role she plays
Born out of a need to be

Oh so many more parts within
Each separate but joined
Locked away
Behind closed doors
To become as one
Would make us whole

Bruce received this information in the letter from Ruth referring to the System as being like a cake, needing various parts without which the cake is not possible. In it she describes some of the parts that she is aware of from her perspective, as given in these excerpts:

I know that Maria is one part that got hurt and is scared and sad. She seems like part adult and part little girl... Sometimes she needs you to be like a daddy and sometimes like a friend... It is hard for her to ask for anything. Maria gets scared with loud and mean people. She desperately wants to get better. I know these thoughts in her...

Then there is another part that knew something bad happened. She knew she had to take charge because this part believed there was no one to protect us. She is structured and smart and was out most of the time until the hospital. She feels like a slave. She resents that she has no life of her own and has to always do for everyone else...

All of these parts know about you and seem to like you but are extremely careful. They are not convinced yet you are safe and aren't going to use them. I am the only part I know who has accepted Jesus as my Savior. I don't know if any of the others do, or hear you speak of Him in counseling...

I think Yemaya hangs around this last part. I don't think Yemaya is a part, but might be around this part because of connections with the hurt... I don't know, but it seems that for Yemaya to stay, the part she is hovering around must stay. If that part dies then she can't stay, but if that part dies we won't exist...

The nightmares are bad about the pink room. She gets little sleep and has terrible headaches. I never witnessed the abuse. I am just aware when Jesus comes. This weekend in her nightmare, He came into the pink room, after Maria was hurt and grandpa left. Maria is resisting allowing Him in the actual pain as it is occurring because of overwhelming shame and guilt. Jesus came to her bed after the abuse and held her. He rocked her and took His hand to wipe her tears. She went to sleep in His arms, but it took her a long time.

Bruce was beginning to hear about the part inside known as Jesus and His interaction with various parts. After one particular session with Maria at this time, she wrote the following letter describing her 'collective' childhood memories centered around the abuse and her understanding about what caused it. While her view may surprise you, it is not uncommon among abuse victims of all ages.

You know when you asked me about the mom who had told me about her childhood, and asked me if I told her about me and I said no? And then you asked me why I did not think I was abused, but she was? It is because I deserved what I got and I think being abused is only when you don't do anything wrong and you say no, and they keep doing it and you try to get away and fight. I didn't say no and I didn't fight and sometimes I felt very bad because my body would do things that I didn't want it to and I couldn't stop it.

It was my fault because I encouraged them by not wearing my robe and setting on their lap and going with them. So I deserved it because I agreed to it by going with them, so I wasn't abused. I deserved the basement and the strap too because I didn't do my chores right and I used to go into the orchard and forget and play with the glue people. I didn't cut apricots fast and sometimes I just didn't behave right so I had to learn to obey and do what I was told. If I just would have done what I was told and worked faster I wouldn't have gotten in trouble so much. I was always told I was stupid and bad so I always have believed it.

The basement keeps coming back at night but so does Jesus. I am still afraid of rats very much. I keep the other stuff really down inside and I don't think I could ever talk about exactly what I did because it is very horrible and I don't want nightmares about it. Sometimes the migraines hurt a lot but I get used to them. I just wish all this stuff would go away.

I still think about the desert and those words. When evil spirits say things it makes me feel bad and very scared, but these words did not make me feel bad or scared. I am trying to understand all of them. I don't understand what be still means. Does that mean for my mind to be still and not think of this stuff? Do you know? What does my grace is sufficient for you for my power is made perfect in weakness mean? Am I supposed to understand all this voice says?

Sometimes I just get tired and don't want to talk, but instead I need to write. Are you sure there are people out there like me? When am I going to start to feel better? This takes a lot of energy. I am still very mixed up. I wonder if Penny will come back and where is Yemaya? What is Regala? This word has come into my mind several times and I can't remember what it means? What does it mean?

Bruce had begun receiving stories about Yemaya's relationship to the System's past. Simultaneously he researched the culture and practices of the Santeria within the Catholic Church. He received this response from the System, presumably written by Ruth and Maria, in their third month of therapy, as they began separating the voices for Maria.

1. Yemaya says: Surely you must doubt and question why God would allow all this to happen to you?

1a. God says: God's ways are as mysterious as the pathways of the wind and as the manner in which a human spirit is infused into the little body of a baby while still it is yet in its mother's womb. Ecc.

2. God can't help you. You're too messed up.

2a. And it is he who will supply all your needs from his riches in glory because of what Christ Jesus has done for us. (Phil.)

3. God will abandon you just like everyone else has.

3a. I can never be lost to your Spirit! I can never get away from my God. If I go up to heaven you are there; if I go down to the place of the dead you are there. If I ride the morning winds to the farthest oceans even there your hand will guide me. Your strength will support me. (Psalm 139:7-10.)

Be strong! Be courageous! Do not be afraid of them! For the Lord your God will be with you. He will neither fail you nor forsake you.

No one will be able to oppose you as long as you live for I will be with you as I was with Moses; I will not abandon you or fail to help you. (Joshua 1:5)

4. God won't comfort you.

4a. I will comfort you there as a little child is comforted by its mother. (Isaiah 66:13)

5. God can't protect you.

5a. My sheep recognize my voice and I know them and they follow me. I give them eternal life and they shall never perish. No one shall snatch them away from me, for my Father has given them to me, and

He is more powerful than anyone else so no one can kidnap them from me. (John 10:27-29)

6.   *There is no spiritual realm. Bruce made it up.*

6a. *For we are not fighting against people made of flesh and blood but against persons without bodies. The evil rulers of the unseen world, those mighty satanic beings and great evil princes of darkness who rule this world; and against huge numbers of wicked spirits in the spirit world. (Ephesians 6:12)*

7.   *You're not strong enough to fight me.*

7a. *Dear young friends, You belong to God and have already won your fight with those who are against Christ because there is someone in your hearts who is stronger than any evil teacher in this wicked world. (1John 4:4)*

8.   *God does not care.*

8a. *Come to me and I will give you rest – all of you who work so hard beneath a heavy yoke. (Matt. 11:28)*

9.   *God won't forgive you. You have too many sins.*

9a. *He forgives all my sins. He heals me. (Psalm 103:3)*

Brothers! Listen! In this man Jesus there is forgiveness for your sins! (Acts 13:38)

10. *You praying and Bruce praying is not going to work.*

10a. *Admit your faults to one another and pray for each other so that you may be healed. The earnest prayer of a righteous man has great power and wonderful results. (James 5:16)*

Ask and you will be given what you ask for. Seek and you will find. Knock and the door will be opened. For everyone who asks, receives. Anyone who seeks finds. If only you will knock the door will be opened. (Matt. 7:7-8)

Don't worry about anything; instead pray about everything telling God your needs and don't forget to thank him for his answers. If you do this you will experience God's peace which is far more wonderful than the human mind can understand. His peace will keep your thoughts and your hearts quiet and at rest as you trust in Christ Jesus. (Phil. 4:6-7)

11. You don't know how to pray so God won't hear you.

11a. And in the same way – by our faith – the Holy Spirit helps us with our daily problems and in our praying. For we don't even know what we should pray for nor how to pray as we should but the Holy Spirit prays for us with such feeling that it cannot be expressed in words. (Romans 8:26)

12. God won't help you.

12a. Yes the Lord hears the good man when he calls for help. And saves him out of his troubles. The Lord is close to those whose hearts are breaking; he rescues those who are humbly sorry for their sins. The good man does not escape all troubles – he has them too. But the Lord helps him in each and every one. (Psalm 34:17-19)

13. God doesn't love you.

13a. But God showed his great love for us by sending Christ to die for us while we were still sinners. (Romans 5:8)

He is merciful and tender toward those who don't deserve it; He is slow to get angry and full of kindness and love. (Psalm 103:8)

For he loves us very dearly and his truth endures. (Psalm 117:2)

Dear Jesus,
Please answer me when I talk to you. Please listen to me cry for help. I am praying to you Jesus. Save me and get me through this bad. Please keep me safe Jesus. Do not close your ears. I am not strong. You are strong and can protect me. I put my hope in you. Please help me understand what is true. Keep me away from bad spirits and show me who I can trust.

Please come quickly and save me. I am in a very dark hole. I am very sad. I miss my daughter and feel sad that she is sick. I am scared too about the bad things when I was little. But you are God and you

*can hold me and protect me from the scary things and sad feelings.
Please pull me out of the dark hole and let me hide in your arms. Be
my help Jesus. Jesus I am very lonely and I don't know how to not
be. I am very scared of people especially men and I am not very
smart. I forget a lot too. Teach me the truth and what you want me
to do with my life. Please don't ever leave me and always be close
to me.*
Maria

After Maria wrote this prayer and talked more directly with
Bruce about Jesus, there seemed to be a subtle shift in power in
Preservation. Maria began talking more to Jesus and Yemaya moved
more or less out of sight of the adult parts. She still came to Tabitha
and others, usually in the guise of the Lady of Regla – the patron
Saint of Havana's port. Candles and cards bearing her image were
still kept around the house by Louise, mostly because Louise was
not aware at this time of the connection for Tabitha to the Santeria
and the occult. The spiritual battle for control of the System had
moved to a new level. As Maria began speaking more freely to
Bruce about who Jesus is, she also began writing more of her prayers
and questions to God. One adult wrote this poem after one particular
session of encouragement to seek Jesus.

Jesus hold me
Let me cry in your arms
I am so scared

Hold me and rock me to sleep
I've tried to stay together and I can't
The pictures are too real and horrible

Jesus hold me
Protect me from the fear
Tell me about you
Tell me about faith and hope

Jesus is it all right that I cry in your arms
Please stay with me even when I'm asleep
Shield me from the evil spirits
I need to cry

Jesus hold me
I am very scared
So scared I can't think
I can't function
I can't eat

Jesus hold me real close
I can't tell Jesus
It is too horrible to tell anyone
I'm too afraid

Hold me real close and don't let me go
Tell me about heaven
Let me know I'm safe with you
Help me to cry in your arms
Jesus hold me close

While this poem indicates a positive shift in some adults turning to the one known as Jesus for answers, not everyone inside was having the same response. They were still searching for a church home where they could be accepted (and not rejected) and helped in the healing process from 'Christians' more mature than Ruth or any other part. This proved to be a difficult task that would repeatedly set them back in their healing work with Bruce. Some Christians would attempt to help Maria, but with limited knowledge of 'Maria's' disorder and a lack of understanding of how Jesus might want them to respond without causing more pain.

This combination of 'helping one another' without understanding about multiplicity can damage and alter the outcome of people with the purest of motives. I would hesitate to even guess how many 'Christians' over the centuries have encountered a person with MPD and made the immediate assumption that it is demonic possession. While this does occur in some cases, it is not a 'spiritual diagnosis' that fits for all those suffering from MPD. The professional Christian caregiver and lay-caregiver alike can do great spiritual harm in attempting to exorcise a spirit that simply isn't in possession of a person...be it an alter or not. There are cases where some poor souls have even died from such misguided good intentions.

This is not to say however that demonic spirits are not attacking the spiritual parts of anyone, particularly new believers who are abuse victims, through influencing (*influencing from an outside spirit which everyone faces daily is not the same as possessing a person's spirit inside the physical body*) their choices and constantly bringing up memories of past abuses or sins. If Christians think they escape this aspect of spiritual warfare simply by accepting Jesus Christ and being baptized, then they have a lot to learn the hard way about the meaning of **Ephesians 6:12**.

"For our struggle is not against flesh and blood, but against the rulers, against the authorities, against the powers of this dark world and against the spiritual forces of evil in the heavenly realms. Therefore, put on the full armor of God..."

I'll return to this important subject matter later in the book when examples are contextual. It is enough to say for now that I have seen and heard of too many pastors, priests, and well-intentioned laity, destroy the hopes of victims of all types of abuse trying to find healing. The methods of healing that encourage and enrich the hopes of abuse victims are given to all of us to follow, if we are willing to make the sacrifices it requires. Unfortunately for the System, their first six encounters looking for a church home produced negative results due to six different causes. The first two happened with Bruce in this early stage and began defining with clarity of purpose, Liz's role in the System. In the following letter/poem to Bruce, Liz begins a journey in search of what is real in the words and life of Jesus Christ and His church.

They all call themselves Christians
But they all sell something different
Have enough faith = Claudia healed
My sins = Claudia not healed
Claudia healed = revival in your church
Send in your money = healing

Why do you say these things to me Christian?
My pain is already very great
You do not know how deep my hurt is
My child suffers and I must stand by and watch

I know I am not like you
I do not have your knowledge
I am not important like you
I do not have the right words like you

But Christian you do not know my heart
Your child is not in a wheelchair with a painful disease
You have not lived my life
You have not known my pain

Please do not hurt me more
Your words sting me
They pierce at my heart
They overwhelm me
Your letter I got this weekend hurt deep

How do you know what God thinks?
How do you know what God is teaching me?
I don't even know what God is teaching me
You sound so spiritual yet
I don't have the slightest idea what your letter means

Why did you call and make me feel worse
"We did not know it was our responsibility," you said
"to bring dinner during your daughter's hospitalization"
Responsibility… Responsibility
We would starve before we would become your responsibility
No thank you Christian
My children will eat beans

Don't call me and tell me your daughter was depressed
because she had a lot of finals at college
So you got a suite at the Hilton and
helped her get through her finals

Don't tell me you know how I feel
with my daughter in a chair and in the hospital
I'm sorry I have to get off the phone
I have to go visit her in the hospital

No Christian you live in the affluent hills
You drive your Lexus

> **And you go to the Hilton**
> **I live down here**
> **With gangs and drugs and violence**
>
> **I drive an old Ford**
> **My daughter is sick and tried to kill herself**
> **No you don't know how I feel**
> **Please don't call me and make me feel worse**
> **If this is what a Christian is**
> **Then I don't want to be one**

The first sacrifice that is necessary is time in helping those who hurt, by coming alongside of them in the reality of their existence and listening. Listen and hear their reality from their perspective, without trying to associate it to our own experience. The 'connectedness' of shared experiences may come in time, if they are real and particularly with abuse victims, <u>after</u> they know they have truly been heard and accepted in their reality. This is not an easy task for anyone who has never experienced abuse themselves, yet this is in itself an unacceptable excuse for not trying to help. When pastors or priests avoid giving instruction from Scripture in the pulpits and classroom simply because they have never been harmed in such a severe manner, they inhibit the people under their care from being effective in ministry to those who are abuse victims. Being willing to listen as long as it takes to someone in pain, without any other motive than to be there to help with whatever means are at your disposal will always cut into your personal time.

In the Christian Church, both Catholic and Protestant, it is estimated that 1 in 4 women and 1 in 6 men have suffered or are suffering sexual abuse of one form or another. This is a reality of our daily lives, yet seldom do you hear a sermon on these atrocities. If that doesn't challenge our Christian sensibilities… it does render us useless to care. The effect of the first two churches in their quick answers to the System about how to get their life straight without ever understanding the real issues behind their pain, caused some parts to go deeper into depression thinking their hope was unfounded. One part wrote the following poem.

My Hell

The chains are heavy
The dungeon deep
Penetrating darkness
Unnerving silence
Death stalks in the shadows
Loneliness engulfs every corner
Fear and horror abound
Hopelessness and despair flourish
Evil lurks at the door
Ready to destroy and conquer
Help me!

Bruce was faced with the dilemma of trying to explain to the System and Maria why they were now experiencing rejection and judgement from the Church and Christians, and why this was not the same reflection of Jesus' love that he knew or wanted for them. He had them test it with the one known on the inside as Jesus. Jesus confirmed that what they were experiencing was not what He wanted. This made it possible for Bruce to continue therapy with the System, but it put him into a very small group of people actually living out the love of Christ for the System.

"Train up a child in the way she should go,
And when she is old she will not turn from it."
Proverbs 22:6

Ruth describes this time as chaotic in Preservation, with changes occurring often, as individuals roaming around the forest would bump into a new part they were unaware of and some with information about 'others.' Helper was trying to regulate what was being shared with Bruce and by whom. Bruce had just learned of Tabitha and was trying to draw her out into his office for therapy. He wasn't yet aware of how many more there were. He received a letter from Tabitha, typed and translated by Maria for her, of shared memories of the abuse. Tabitha had learned from the adults that writing was not the same as telling about the 'bad.' The following is verbatim as typed. I warn the reader that the following is graphic even though it is a child's perspective of what happened to her.

Later, as child parts reveal themselves with more memories of their abuse, Maria would try to 'forget' the abuse by thinking of it as not occurring to her.

Content Warning!

My room is pink and I sleep in the middle of the big bed with the big balls that go up on the sticks. I see the moon in the window and it makes scary pictures and I put the pillow over my head so I don't see the scary monsters on the roof. My room is very cold cause I have no heat like in the kitchen, grandma puts big blankets on me that are heavy. She made them for me. I say my prayers and then grandma kisses me good night and then I hold my teddy and hope monsters don't get me. I go to sleep but one night I am sleeping and I feel something touch my head. I don't want to open my eyes cause it might be scary monsters from the roof. I peek and it's not scary monsters but grandpa. So I not scared cause it's grandpa. I open my eyes and see grandpa but grandpa stops touching my head and puts his hand under my nightgown and touches my tummy and touches me *where I go potty and I am scared and then hurts me there and something goes in me and I cry and grandpa says be quiet and not make noise but I don't like hurt grandpa says I will learn to like it and be quiet.* Grandpa breathes loud and I am scared. Grandpa is looking down at me and says Maria I have some candy for you like the candy I give you that I put on the couch. This candy is better and I want you to suck it like you do the other candy. *Grandpa shows me a big purple long candy and I say grandpa it is too big I don't want that candy. Grandpa says I will help you and he puts it in my mouth and it's too big and hurts my mouth and I can't breathe and grandpa is hurting me and he is pushing the candy a lot in my mouth and he is moving a lot and breathing funny and then I can't breathe and I am choking and then he goes real hard in my mouth and yucky stuff in my mouth and I am getting sick and he turns me over in my bed and my head is in the chamber pot and I throw up and I am sick.* Grandpa puts me back on the bed and tells me if I tell anyone I will die. Grandpa came in my bed a lot of times and I hurt a lot and I learned to see the moon and go away in me and I never liked it. It made me very sad cause I am a bad child.
(* Note: Italic type is smaller to indicate whispering.)

End Content Warning

Figure 2.

Drawing by Tabitha of her abuse in the basement. Note the rat!

A breakthrough followed at this time for Bruce, when he received the letter previous mention from Helper and Ruth to me. In it he reveals the names and personalities of the various parts he thought were relevant for Bruce to know to better help everyone. It would significantly change how the System would communicate with him into the future, as there was no longer a need to hide behind Maria's name or voice, and each part was now free to speak for themselves. It was to be both a blessing and a problem for Bruce in what it meant. In counseling a 'multiple' it is good to have a player roster to know whom you're counseling, but the mind must also adjust to 'group therapy' of individuals from a single body all at the same time. Bruce proved to be very adept at it.

The first overview of the System given to Bruce by Helper for training happens now about current people and functions and forwarded to me by Ruth 2 years later and covered in Chapter One pages 30 – 48 for review now.)

Things began to move fast for everyone after this letter. Maria began writing or typing notes of conversations between the different parts and herself for several weeks. With Ann's help she also recorded the council meetings that increased in number as the changes and questions increased. Bruce received copies of everything, as well as permission to retain for his records various items from parts other than Maria. Maria was trying to adjust to this new reality for her, but with extreme difficulty. She began dissociating again – this time from the memories of abuse as now they belonged to 'others.'

This has been scary. This is not real. I'm having a hard time noticing that there is an outside world now. I am so in to listening to them that I have to force myself to focus and stay here. I am still scared to take a look at the world they live in. I don't know if I can. I don't want to ask yet. I am also having difficulty not talking with one of them and so I just start talking with him or her. This is very embarrassing when other outside people are around. How do I not do that so people don't think I'm crazy? I really need help with this. There is a very bad argument going on between them over should Ann be allowed to read your books... I'm very tired and going to bed.

The statements in the conversations of the parts were as verbatim as Maria could make them. My research into these conversations and letters help to place people and events into a chronological order for this book. Because I was not given these early documents until four years into our relationship, reading them now helps to clarify my own notes and understanding of various parts I have come to know and respect. Even though I had heard early on in my counseling with the System of Elizabeth Ray's journals of history, I was unaware of their magnitude until given to me for safekeeping.

Letters about the System at this time highlight their care for Maria and their respect for Bruce. Maria and her reaction, to the others in the System, was established as more important than the right of each part to express their self within the System. It is true this may have been done out of self-preservation. But it is also true that there were numerous people inside of Maria, who had remained hidden for years and finally had an opportunity to express the reality of their existence to someone like Bruce, a person who accepted them for who they are.

One of the first parts to write Bruce directly was Ann. She was a stickler for accuracy, so she would write often to clear up the mistakes Maria wrote about. Maria would be obedient and write what she heard from the inside, but she continued having difficulty absorbing the possible reality of the abuse as her own, because it happened to them, not to her. Ann's first letter to Bruce clarified points in the overview typed by Maria, while she was learning it for the first time. She concludes her letter with these comments.

Some of us parts stored different pieces of the knowledge of the abuse. The Little Ones are still protected from this knowledge. As we network, I am organizing these pieces into the full picture. I have always suspected that there were more pieces, but I did not have the information that I possess now. (She would continue to add information over the next three years, as she learns about it in therapy with Bruce and myself.) *Everyone is hurting, and we are especially concerned that the Little Ones will not be able to handle it if exposed to the information. Maria will create more parts to protect them from the trauma.*

The abuse, along with the disability issues, has raised havoc in the Land of Preservation, and all parts have remained inside for most of the time since November. Only recently has there been limited visitation to the outside world. We, as parts, need to address the issue of Maria vividly living through the abuse in your office. Before Monday, we only acquired split knowledge of it. We are concerned that we too might experience the feelings of it. This will be another point of discussion at the next council meeting. Although I am still on vacation, I felt this information was important to relay to you. If you do not have accurate information, it will be difficult for you to work with us.
Ann

Council meetings at this time were very democratic and consisted of all the 'known' parts. One person equaled one vote and the majority rules. Attendance was optional, but you had no say if you didn't attend. As Preservation gets more crowded and 'other' levels become known, the need for a modification to the Council soon occurs within four months. As Maria began listening to the meetings in order to type the minutes, she realized that she didn't have a vote and asked Helper why.

Maria: Helper, how come I don't have a vote at the council meetings?

Helper: Why would you want a vote when you don't believe we are real? If we do not exist, then what we do does not exist. Therefore, there is no need to vote for something that is not real.

Maria: I think I understand Helper. You are saying it should not matter to me to vote if I don't believe in you all. I don't want to vote until I am sure you are real.

Helper: That's right. But we parts would like you to accept us as real and be a part of our discussion and decision making process. What will it take for us to convince you that we are real?

It was Ann's logic and presentation of evidence that ultimately convinces Maria the first time. In order to stabilize and balance her life as her story progresses, she will need constant reassurance when faced with difficult truths. Over the next few months, issues were constantly being discussed in council and in Bruce's office as to the setting and direction the healing process was to take. Issues like Bruce allowing Maria to cower in a corner of his office, cradling a doll on her knees with the blinds drawn in order for her to feel safe enough to tell her story. The issue of Maria accepting a safe touch from Bruce like a handshake or hug, took several days and direction from the System.

Maria's fears were stated and accepted as real by the System and confidence was created between them as they worked together to overcome them. When Maria said she was concerned about Jesus and how, "*He will be so sad,*" it was Little Sister (Ruth) who often calmed her fears. Ruth would repeat Scriptural truths to Maria and the System to help guide them through difficult times. They recognized Ruth's relationship with Jesus as building her into a strong, competent individual with good insight. Her constant reminder of the need for Jesus' direction would bring comfort to the weaker parts and challenge the stronger ones to learn more about

Jesus. As the issues and number of parts increase, so does their need for Jesus to provide the answers.

The challenges that come to Ruth are the same ones many of us face who want to be close to Jesus. Most of Ruth's time in her 'early years' is spent on the inside near Jesus listening to His direction. Her help to the System reflects this relationship in the letters. In the coming years, as Ruth spends more time in the outside world representing and protecting the System, Ruth will become more distracted and tempted by demands and priorities this world deems as important. The results like for us, cause her to not listen as intently to Jesus for direction to accomplish His purpose in their life.

As life continues to become harder for the System, as they become more obedient in its trials, the reality of this becomes reflected in Ruth's relationship with Jesus as she leaves the safety of Preservation. Contrast her statements in this portion of Maria's letter with her doubts later in the books and you can understand why it is true for all of us; "The less time spent talking and listening to Jesus the less sure we become of our purpose in life." It isn't until 7 years later that Ruth is given a chance to redeem her relationship, to become what it was in the beginning between her and Jesus. It will come at a time of great spiritual warfare surrounding the System, during a battle over who will be given control of the past.

Maria: Little Sister, are you always so confident?

Little Sister: No Maria. I too share the pain and hurt. I try very hard to focus on God's word so that I can keep myself out of the pit of despair. But no Maria, I am not perfect and I have my bouts of depression. I also have a difficult time retaining information and must continually reread Scripture so that it can get planted firmly in my heart. (A priority now that slowly relinquishes itself over the years to other demands, something she is trying to recover today.) *I'm also very young in the body of Christ. I have a very lot to learn but I am willing to learn. So Maria do not look at me as smarter or better than you. God has given each of us parts special strengths. However, we also have weaknesses, including me. But there is one thing I know and that is someday I will be with Jesus and there will be no more pain or sadness. I look forward with great expectation to spending eternity with Jesus.*

Maria: Little Sister, why can't we just go now and be with Him. Why can't we just die right now and go to heaven and not have to go through this pain? Will we go to heaven if we make ourselves die now?

Little Sister: Maria, there is absolutely no sin that can take away God's promise of eternal life for believers. However, if we make ourselves die God will be very disappointed when you see Him. He will not be pleased that you didn't trust Him enough to allow Him to work in your life and mold you into the vessel He has planned for you. Yes, it is hard for all of us to go through this, but Jesus is going through it with us and is here to comfort and help us. "Making ourselves die" is what the devil wants you to do because it would make Jesus sad. Remember, Jesus loves you... What about Bruce? Don't you think he would be very sad? He wants you to get better too and really cares about you being safe. He prays for you a lot... We will get through this Maria. Don't give up hope. Jesus will get us through the tunnel and we will come out on the other side whole and healed with Him. Trust Him and hang on.

**"Peace I leave with you; My peace I give you;
not as the world gives, do I give to you.
Let not your hearts be troubled, nor let it be fearful...
These things I have spoken to you,
that in Me you may have peace.
In the world you have tribulation,
but take courage; I have overcome the world."
-Jesus John 14:27, 16:33**

Chapter Four:

"Choosing Good for the One… Or Good for the Many?"

"Come to Me, all who are weary and heavy-laden,
and I will give you rest. Take My yoke upon you,
and learn from Me, for I am gentle and humble in heart;
and you shall find rest for your souls.
For My yoke is easy, and My load is light."
-Jesus Matthew 11:28-30

The longer that I am a pastor, the more I am convinced that these simple verses are the keys to healing for anyone who chooses to walk alone. Maria and the System will continue work with Bruce in their search for the way to ease their burden. They will walk down some very dark paths seeking truth and soon find one they did not want to discover. To heal from the past means exposing it for what it truly is. The past also teaches them that the control of evil does not want to let go of them and continues to remind them that they are still present to torment them.

While Ruth and others continued to assist Bruce with the inside perspective, the world outside at home and at church continued to cause pain and depression for some. For the first time Raquel wrote several poems to Bruce depicting her feelings:

Pointless

I pondered the meaning of life one-day
Far in the crevasses of my mind
Trying to find the treasures of happiness
Chasing fulfillment under the sun

What is life that it is worth living?
Pointless and with no direction
Seeking meaning to my existence

Finding only toil and weariness
A pit stop in the cosmos
Soon forgotten and gone

Not only Raquel, but Maria as well needed help in applying the lessons she was learning from Bruce. Helper would follow-up the sessions with Bruce by trying to help Maria understand the application to her life situation. Sometimes Helper was unprepared for what he heard. He too was learning the hard fact that, when you risk helping someone through painful situations, you may be called upon to understand it through their eyes.

Helper: Maria, did you understand what Bruce said about good and bad touches?

Maria: Yes.

Helper: You must not let people hit you like they do. Don't let them slam you against the wall or slap you or hit you. Those are bad touches. Why do you let them do it?

Maria: I don't know. What am I supposed to do? I don't like fighting I'll be okay. I'm used to it because it was a lot worse in the basement. Helper, do you know what the basement was like?

Helper: No Maria, what was it like?

Maria: It had a door that went down underground and was very cold, dirty, and damp. There was a light bulb in the center and a lot of spider webs. Everything had lots of dust on it, the table in the corner, jars, and old tools. Behind the door was a strap. When I was bad, I was taken down the steps and the strap hit me a lot. When it hit it would sting and pain would travel to my head and my insides felt like they were being ripped open. I was tied up and sometimes I had to go potty, so I tried not to go because I would get the strap more. I looked into the dark and heard the footsteps of rats and cried because I didn't want to be eaten. I wanted my grandma and I wanted to be good. I didn't know what I did bad so I could be good and I thought I would die in the basement. I thought rats would eat me and only my bones would be left. That is what it was like Helper, so I don't think getting hit now is as bad as the basement.

Helper: Maria I don't know what to say. I can't feel this. It is too overwhelming to absorb. I need to just sit here for awhile and be sad for you... Aren't you angry or mad that they did this to you?

Maria: No I'm not. It's something I can't find in me. I think they had a lot of problems and didn't know how to do right. I feel sad for them and I forgive them.

Helper: How could you just forgive them like that? Can't you just go and spit on their graves or call them names or something?

Maria: Why? I just want to get better and try and make something out of my life. I want to change my feelings about myself and learn to like me... I have never been happy in my life except when I had my children. I love my children so much. I wish I could learn to love my husband and like men and not be scared of them. I feel bad that I married him to get away from my dad... That was not fair to him, but I have tried to be a good wife and obey him and do it for him. He gets mad at me and punishes me by not talking to me. He never remembers my birthday or anniversary and he never calls me from work to see if I'm alive. I am just his and I have to be good... Helper, can husbands give bad touches too? I get so confused and wonder sometimes why I was born to have the life I got...Sometimes I wish I had a bedroom with a door and lock so I could be by myself, instead of sleeping on a porch... I don't want to talk any more it makes me too sad. OK?

Ruth, like Helper and Bruce, struggled at times to answer Maria's very difficult questions about Jesus, heaven, and how becoming Christian affects a multiple with parts. In her process of memory work with Bruce, Maria questioned its necessity in council.

Maria: Have any of you ever gone to a counselor before?

Parts: No.

Helper: He's not going to do anything to you Maria. He is just going to help you not be afraid of the memories and learn skills to help you function better in the world. Trust him and you will be okay.

Maria: OK. But why can't I just tell Jesus and not have to tell a person?

Helper: Maria stop getting stressed out and just go Monday and start...

Ann: You must start the process in order to heal... Bruce is the expert in this area. Follow what he tells you to do.

Maria: Little Sister, I prayed with Bruce and I now am a real true Christian like you and I get to go to Heaven and see Jesus. Bruce wasn't sure what happens to the other parts. Do you know? I don't want to be cut in pieces in Heaven like a cookie. How many Christians are there in me?

Little Sister: Only us as far as I can tell Maria. I don't know what happens to parts in heaven. Faith and trust is a hard thing for us. The priest was God's representative and was going to give us spiritual training, but instead he hurt us. You were told to trust the priest and obey him. You believed that since he worked for God he knew right from wrong. He got us all mixed up. Ann will not talk about God. She cannot separate God, the Catholic Church, and the Monsignor. Raquel only reveals herself deep in the forest or when she is all alone. I am surprised that she even communicates to Bruce in poems. She hurts very deep over the church and prefers to lose herself in nature. Compliant One (Louise) is still Catholic because she knows nothing else and is very confused about what she thinks was God's approval of what happened to us. The power and control of the Catholic Church and the brainwashing to obey have forced her to accept the hurt as part of her obedience. Anger (Liz) lost her faith thanks to the Catholic Church.

I came to the conclusion that the Catholic Church and the Monsignor were not God and that I need to hold the right party accountable. I work very hard to try to heal and get right with God. I still backslide and the enemy knows my weakness. You are a brand new Christian and I know you desire a personal relationship with Jesus. He loves us and the hurt was not His fault, never forget that. The Monsignor was sent to a home for priests after other children told about him hurting them. The diocese said he retired due to ill health reasons. They had to protect the reputation of the church without trying to help the needs of broken children. We will never go to that diocese because of the lack of support for those like us. The church has a lot of money and covers up their priests' actions very well at the expense of the victims. How all this will affect us in heaven I have to have faith and wait to see...

Maria: The Monsignor – I can't tell! If you tell, nobody believes you and they get real mean to you, and the church makes fun of you. He is very very important and I am very small and they will kill me they said if I ever tell. No, I can never tell about him Little Sister, Never. If I tell Bruce and the Monsignor finds out, he has a lot of power and will get Bruce and hurt him for knowing his secrets.

Little Sister: No Maria, the Monsignor cannot hurt Bruce or you, nor can he get you. You never have to go into the black box again.

Maria: Little Sister, what about heaven? You said there is no sad in heaven, but if people hear about what happened they will be sad, right? How does it work? Do people in heaven get to be angels and know everything about a person? I don't want everyone there to know what happened to me and I don't want to see those who hurt me in heaven because I'll get sad and scared. How does heaven work?

Little Sister: Maria, ask Bruce. I'm exhausted and I need time to sort all this out. You are overwhelming me. Ask Bruce please...

For the next several months, a common answer to Maria's questions was "Ask Bruce." He was required to perform his duties as counselor and therapist without appearing or behaving like a priest hearing confession. A very difficult task when the subject matter is centered around one's perceptions of God and Church. Due to matters of confidentiality, I haven't included most of his responses. I am extremely grateful that he was the first to receive these questions, making it easier for me when I join him later. I am also thankful that the Lord chose a counselor for Maria with a heart for God. He may never know this side of heaven the outcome of the many seeds he planted in the lives of his clients, which later bloomed and helped them to heal.

Bruce focused his time with Maria and Malo (Tabitha) in trying to draw their memories out. As he interfaced with other parts through his responses to their writings, he felt compelled to communicate with them outside of set counseling sessions. This would become his 'ministry time' for his clients. As Maria (et al.) talked to him in our world, reactions began happening on the inside. After Tabitha's letter, Hash began showing himself to Maria and Tabitha inside with ominous threats of impending death for having told secrets. A council was called just to define for the System who they were dealing with and how best to protect Maria and Tabitha from him. Ruth wanted Tabitha to leave her hole and stay with her, while affirming to her that Jesus was safe.

As the memories were revealed, Tabitha was seeing her world changing. Throughout her existence, she had remained primarily in her hole for protection from the forces that wanted her to hide the truth of her memories. Hash would come outside her hole and yell at her, "To tell is to die!" Hash's created role was to keep Maria safe by any means possible, including threats of death or causing parts to mutilate the body as a way to let the pain out, without telling about the past. Hash was that part which accepted the abusers' threats of death as real and lasting for life. The System would have a difficult time coming to grips with him, realizing that for some, 'the end justifies the means.' Hash will go through his own metamorphosis with Jesus entering into their lives. For now, Hash appeared to Maria and Tabitha as *"very powerful and mean. He looks sometimes like grandpa, the Monsignor, men in the barn, or the Cuban man. He scares us and says we will die if we tell."* Tabitha also told Ruth how Jesus was entering her world as well, by coming into her hole to hold her there.

Jesus was entering their lives now, during times the memories were being told and relived, when the pain of body memories was as real as the day it happened. As Maria remembered what happened to Tabitha (Maria at 4) in the pink room, Jesus would enter the memory or dream after the abuse, to hold and comfort her so that the dream could end peacefully knowing that healing was somehow near. Tabitha knew if she called upon Jesus to come when she was afraid, He would enter her safe place to hold and bring warmth, no matter who might be outside. Tabitha only allowed someone she trusted to enter her hole, and right now one of them was Jesus. The other was Yemaya, but Yemaya wouldn't go anywhere near Jesus so she hid. Tabitha had learned from Ruth that

Jesus was safe and gave good love as the 'Good Shepherd'. Tabitha told Ruth;

After Tabitha heard the story of the Good Shepherd she drew this
And it becomes the favorite story of all the children.

Malo: My hole small and safe. Jesus come in my hole and hold me. Papa can't find my hole and I see his shoes. He don't see me and can't get me in basement. I hide long time in my hole and nobody find me…I get sad and afraid to talk (to Bruce.) *Bruce big man like papa and scares me. I hide and hear Maria talk for me. Where is grandma? Papa says not to tell because big bad man in black kill me and cut me up. I not tell grandma, but I tell Bruce and I hide so man not cut me up. Jesus stop man, okay… Jesus loves Malo and keeps hurt and bad away. Jesus loves Maria and keep hurt away. Why do Jesus' daddy hurt Jesus and put him on sticks* (cross)?

Ruth: Who told you that?

Malo: Papa in basement.

Ruth: Sometimes adults don't tell the truth. Papa did not tell you the truth. This is truth. Jesus came from heaven to earth as a little baby. He grew up to tell people that God loves them and that He came to earth to save people from their sins. Bad people hurt Him and put Him on the cross where He died. Then three days later He came back to life and went to heaven to be with His Father whom He loved very much. Jesus said He came here so that we could live with Him forever, by dying on the cross. Jesus chose to die for us because He wants us in heaven. We have to believe that He came here and died on the cross to save us. If we believe that, then we get to go to heaven and be with Him forever.

Malo: Jesus must love us a whole lot to get hurt for us. Jesus is good and He holds me and I don't get scared. I love Him. I am sad that He got hurt on the cross for me. He smiles at me.

Maria: Ruth I am so glad you are inside. I learn more from you than anyone. Malo is very special and close to me. I don't want her to hurt no more. Thank you for being so nice to her.

Each part was learning about Jesus as He entered their worlds, inside and outside. Maria and Tabitha were the only ones so far who could see Him in the outside world. Ruth wanted this gift as well until she saw how the responsibility of this brings such hard truths into their lives and those close to them, as the enemy tries to bring them down. The forces opposed to God will try anything they can to keep anyone with this gift from telling about their existence around us. They know human nature as well and will use that against us. Maria will learn all too soon how most people will reject her as soon as she tells them she sees angels and demons.

Some want the gift until their first real exposure to spiritual warfare and then it's a quick retreat to 'I'll pray for your support.' Others will enter into Maria's world of constant spiritual battles, only to remove themselves from her small circle of friends because the intensity of faith required to face them is too high. Being told there are demons entering your church or home, to manipulate or coerce the people into moving away from the path Jesus has laid before them is hard to hear. When people in the world can't physically see or hear demons it is easier to deny their existence than to say what they know might be true in their hearts that they are real and exist around them. Yet, a few will remain with Maria and the System in the coming years. As the stories of the System unfold in these books you too, like Bruce and myself, will have to weigh what is real and how it can affect your choices for the future… choices made in faith.

Over the coming months Bruce learns of more parts and how they describe their interactions with Jesus, Yemaya, and various other spiritual entities. He will make professional choices that reflect his faith in Christ. These choices will also put him at odds with many inside his professional community. As he probes deeper into the memories and learns the tactics of the enemy, he and his family will feel the pressure and the pain of acknowledging the spiritual world in which we live. The reality of the evil that mankind has perpetrated upon the innocent, many in the name of God, will only be overcome by the power and love of Jesus Christ, as He reveals Himself to rescue the innocent from despair. For Bruce, like myself, it is only the truth of that love which will carry us through the days ahead, when even more despicable abuses to the System will be revealed. For the System and for us, it is hope found only in Jesus Christ that will lead us through the healing process.

As Maria continues to reveal past abuses to Bruce, a clearer picture of how the enemy used family members both in the past and today begins to emerge. Her father calls one day to tell her that her sister is crazy and wants to know what Maria is going to do about it. This begins a chain reaction of old memories of how her siblings had been abused as well, and the pact they made together in a hole one night never to tell, or they all would surely die. This sends Maria and Tabitha into a depression induced by fear. Maria is barraged by specific memories of physical and emotional abuse from other family members and wants to hide again in her solitude. She declares that none of this is real because no human being would do this to another. She is caught in a conundrum. If the abuses couldn't have happened to her, then it must have happened to them because 'somebody' received the body scars and memories. But if the parts aren't real and only made up in her mind, then the abuse happened to her.

It becomes harder for her when she begins to think that, if she created them in her reality, then somehow she is responsible for the abuse they received. Yet, she knows the people on the inside are real and turns to them for advice about overcoming her sadness. They decide as a group that they didn't survive all this pain to give up now. Steps needed to be taken to deal with the depression that was making all of them weak. They sought Bruce's help and were able to receive an antidepressant to help bolster the strength and viability of the System to deal with the reality of their past and present. Bruce stepped up his responses to those who wrote him outside the office time. Maria began discussing the spiritual world around her with Ruth, asking about the truth of the existence of angels. She thought she had created 'Centurons' to guard the entrance to Kansas and to guard Tabitha in her hole. She asked Ruth if they were parts she made. Ruth asked her to read Hebrews 1:14 and Psalm 91:11-12 then asked her what she thought.

Maria: That angels are ministering spirits and God commands His angels to guard you in all your ways. Does that mean that God's angels protect us? Do they all look about 25 years old with nice smiles, light around them and gold swords?

Little Sister: You call them Centurons Maria. I pray protection over us each day. Is it possible that they are angels sent from God and you didn't know it? I don't know…

Maria: Sometimes Little Sister it seems like there is a different layer of things going on in the world. I sometimes feel things like something is going on that we don't see… but sometimes I do. It's kind of hard to explain. Sometimes I think I see this group around you, but you don't. Why? It's weird, but I'm glad there are Centurons protecting the entrances to the inside. They're nice, but why are they so bright?

Little Sister: I don't know Maria, ask Bruce.

Maria: Why did my brother tell me about the man in the black robe and the tomb? What did we pledge not to tell? Where was he when I was taken into the pink room? He doesn't talk to me at all. Did he see stuff?

Little Sister: I don't know Maria, I don't have the answers. Maybe we will never have all the pieces. We do know that from four to seven, the pink room and the basement happened, these memories are clear. But at seven they stopped, why I don't know. The barn is not clear yet. What did you see or hear? Did they know you were there?

Maria: I don't want to think about that now. I need to get all unscared about the basement and the pink room first. When I talk to Bruce it is hard. Sometimes I have to listen when Malo talks to me because she hears Bruce talking. She wants to know if Bruce is a Centuron that doesn't light up. She says Jesus is there and makes the dark go away. She likes Bruce telling her she is not bad and she likes that he is a friend of Jesus... I pray that Jesus helps me breathe and not feel the hurt when I talk to Bruce. Malo, she got hurt bad and it hurt her body bad. Malo likes butterflies and meadows. Sometimes when bad was happening in the basement, she would go and run in the meadow with Wolfdog and play with the bright orange and yellow butterflies. But in the pink room she died in the nothingness. She couldn't get the butterflies to come into the pink room.

Bruce told us that the bad men couldn't get us anymore because Jesus protects us and keeps us safe. I like Bruce asking Jesus to be with us because when He's there, the bad spirits stay out of Bruce's office. Malo likes Jesus a whole lot and He comes into her hole and makes it light and rocks her when she is scared... Is Hash a part? Jesus puts His hand up and Hash stops yelling. Hash obeys Jesus. Jesus is strong but not mean. When Jesus is there I don't get scared of Hash either. Malo is so pretty and her smile is so sweet. Today she shared her cookies with Jesus. She said, "Jesus me ama. Voy al cielo con Jesus."

When the therapy sessions with Bruce increased to twice a week for longer periods changes started coming rapidly. There was no headlong rush by everyone into a time of healing; it was quite the contrary. Parts began discussing what Maria and Tabitha revealed about the abuse with each other; stating opinions on the best method of therapy; expressing feelings about how this information was affecting them both physically and emotionally; their frustration living in their current environment; and all of this was being recorded in a journal by Maria to share with Bruce.

Ann went to a conference for people who had suffered abuse, thinking it was a seminar on 'this is how you fix it.' It turned out to be in her words, "people going up to a microphone and giving personal testimonies and reading poems." Being one not to show emotions it was difficult for her to maintain control throughout the day. Statements from people like; "I didn't deserve to be loved. I was a bad girl who deserved what happened to me. The look in his eyes and the threats. The ghost of my abuser. Putting pins in my hands and nails in my palms. There is no quick way to do therapy. All is not well with my soul. Where was my soul? I am never safe."

These and others will put Ann on a roller coaster ride emotionally when all she wanted was to gain some knowledge to help their healing process. She shared part of the time with Ruth in order to keep balance. The rest of the System had been instructed to not listen this day, yet all of them were aware that something had happened to Ann. When one lady spoke about abuse in the name of God Ann had to leave for awhile. She became concerned when another spoke about False Memory Syndrome. She listened carefully and wondered if Maria had it (not other parts like herself), because there were so many memories of so much pain. Afterwards Ann went off by herself in Preservation to reflect on all she had heard. Helper gave the parts concerned for Ann the opportunity to discuss it with Ruth. Maria became afraid of the possibility of FMS and quizzed Ruth and Helper about it. The irony of this is Maria taking the same position as Ann that only she might have it, while asking other parts to determine the truth of it.

Maria: What is it and how do you get it and do I have it? If I do, how do I get rid of it?

Ruth: There is this foundation that is discrediting delayed memories of childhood abuse and attacking therapists for implanting ideas in their clients. They are basically saying people are making up the abuse and destroying reputations and lives. Also that lawsuits and financial gain are fueling the increase of false memory syndrome...There is a lot we don't understand about us, but I pray we don't have this syndrome. I don't think we do, but if we do Bruce will tell us. After all, Bruce isn't telling us about the abuse, we are telling him. Maria, we are not out to confront anyone and we have no desire to sue or even talk to anyone. We are not interested in controversy or psychological fads. All we want is to get better, work with Bruce and stay secret.

Maria: Okay, but what about Ann? We cannot live without Ann. She keeps us working and is the one who told us we couldn't give up, remember? She helps me to not hurt me and now she has given up. I feel like I can't promise to stay safe. What do you mean when you said that all is not well with Ann's soul? Why won't Ann talk to Bruce? Little Sister, are you going to save Ann?

Ruth: I can sow seeds and I can water seeds, but only Jesus saves not me. Maria let me tell you the message of Paul to Timothy when Paul was telling him of God's grace to him and us in 1Timothy 1:12-17.

Louise: How long before we get better?

Ruth: I don't know but I'm sure it won't be worked out by the end of the month. People at the conference said they were in therapy for ten, twelve, even fifteen years.

Liz: Years! No... we can't do that! We can't afford years of therapy! You've got to be kidding Little Sister. She's got to finish before Christmas! Why would it take years? Maria you've got to work faster and get this done! I will not go to therapy that long! I don't even want us to go now! This stuff has got to stop! Maria, work faster!

Maria: I'm trying! I can't go faster. I can't go as fast as I'm going. You make me type too much. Why do I have to type it and give it to Bruce? It hurts to tell about the bad.

Ruth: We need you to give these letters to Bruce because you don't talk a lot to Bruce and he will never know what is going on in our life. You have no support person at home who could let Bruce know, so these writings gives Bruce the information he needs to help us. Maria, none of us has confidence, self-esteem, assertive skills, or good communication skills. We each mask differently, so we need each other to survive.

Maria: Little Sister, do you have a name like everyone else?
Little Sister: Yes Maria, my name is Ruth. It means friend. I am your friend.

Various conversations like these were going on all around Preservation between parts, for 24 hours a day, 7 days a week. Each conversation would eventually make its way to Maria for typing.

Louise would discuss the Catholic Church with Ruth and Ann. Maria would discuss her married life with Ruth and Louise, while Ann and Liz argued with them about all of it. Separate conversations were happening with Jesus from everyone, even if it was Liz or Ann arguing with him. When Malo heard the story of how Ruth got her name from the Bible, she wanted a pretty name like Ruth's. She asked Ruth to pick one out like her own. The adult's understood its possible adverse affect of changing Malo's to something else from counseling sessions with Bruce. The adults also chose to go by names of their own choosing.

Ruth: Ever since I met you, I have thought about a special name for you. Remember when I told you that you were a precious child of God and not a Malo child? Your name means bad, but you are not bad. I would like for you to have a pretty name. The name I have chosen is Tabitha, it means gazelle. A gazelle is a small, graceful, little deer who has a lot of energy and loves to run, dance and jump high.

Tabitha: Does my name have a story in the Bible too?

Ruth: Yes, would you like to hear it? (She told the story of Peter the Apostle and Tabitha of Joppa, another opportunity to preach even if it was a child's message.)

Maria was slowly learning about the lives of the other parts. When issues happened with her children at school or in the family, she would hear how other parts coped in those situations within her own life. Ruth gave her a new perspective of Ann one day, when her daughter was struggling with English and SAT's.

Ruth: Ann has a very difficult time with English. She entered high school without a strong foundation of knowledge to build on like the other students, a disadvantage for her. When she took over in high school, she had to find ways to survive and do well without it. She maintained in the 9th grade until she made a deal with the counselor to remove her from basic classes and move her into college-prep classes. She faked her way through with people thinking she knew more than she really did. She learned to play the game of school and succeed. Though she had difficulty with reading and writing, her logic skills were very good, as well as her amazing organizational skills which she needed to get by there.

Ann told me she had a lot of pressure on her by your father. She spent most of her time trying to achieve so your parents would accept and love her, something that continues today whether she realizes it or not. Your mother gave her no support and seemed always in a state of depression. Ann was ignored by her. Your father was abusive both verbally and physically. He ruled over her as though he was God. Ann could do nothing right in his eyes. He had a nasty temper and no control over his anger and rage. The caramel cake episode illustrated the effect his anger had on her. She gave up creative cooking. She has great resentment toward men.

Because of family competition, your father wanted Ann to go to college so he could brag that his kid was the first in the history of the family to attend college. But Ann was exhausted from keeping the mask of the System up in high school. She was afraid she couldn't keep it up in college, but your father's pride made him determined. He told her she had three years to complete a four-year degree at Cal-State and gave her two choices for a major, math or English. She asked to major in sociology because of her interests. She was told that no one in his family was going to study that shit. She majored in math.

College was extremely stressful for Ann. She didn't love school until many years later. She didn't socialize because she had to study all the time. She was one of only two women in the math program and the only Latina, which only added to her stress as her male peers taunted her. Their perspective was that math was no place for a woman, especially a Latina woman. She put up with so much verbal abuse that it made her determined to show those guys what she could achieve even if it killed her. She graduated at the top of her class, though it cost her greatly in physical and emotional suffering. She wasn't allowed to attend graduation because your father thought it unnecessary. She threw her diploma into a desk drawer because she had failed to be accepted by him.

Ruth continued to tell Maria about Ann's life in raising her three children and her many battles in providing a better life for them than she had experienced. She told of her struggles with the Catholic schools without really understanding why the fear was there and her subsequent removal of them to public schools after one incident. There were gaps during this time, which the System was still trying to understand and fill in for her.

As more issues were brought up with Bruce, Hash increased his persecution of Maria to cause her to start cutting her body again. Ruth and Ann intervened to warn her if it continued, Bruce would have no choice but to put her in a hospital. The fear of that caused her to stop for a while until later when the child parts started doing it again. Ruth instructed her to go to Jesus for help with this and she did. Even Maria began trying to help Tabitha to understand how Jesus would not let the bad happen again to her. She helped her to understand Bruce as being like Jesus, not like her grandpa. When Tabitha agreed that there were two men who light up standing behind Bruce when she was there, Maria warned her to say nothing because he wouldn't believe it. Tabitha began asking if Bruce was her daddy.

Ruth confronted Ann one day about her reaction to Tabitha's sharing about the pink room and Ann responded:

Ann: I was numb. I can't let my mask down or I'll fall apart. Someone in this system has to remain strong and together. I guess I'm that one.

Ruth: But Ann, how did you feel?

Ann: An overwhelming sadness over how much little Tabitha has been through so much Hell. I want to cry and scream at the same time, but I can't express it. I try to block the pain. I try to rationalize it and disbelieve it. I try to separate from it and I can't. I've worked so hard to function at a respectable level in the world and now it seems that all my work was for naught. I can't put all of this into a logical order of reason. I don't do well with emotional stuff. I am afraid of it. I don't know why but I'm deadly afraid of it and I can't talk about it anymore.

Ruth: Thank you Ann for being so honest with me. Thank you for standing alongside of us and listening. It took a lot of courage to do that and I appreciate it. Ann, we will make it so don't lose hope.

Liz and Ann got into an argument one-day over whether or not Bruce was a multiple. It went something like this:

Ann: Liz don't we have enough to deal with without you psychoanalyzing the psychoanalyst? You come up with some of the most bizarre ideas.

Liz: It's not bizarre! He's got parts doesn't he?

Ann: I don't know and I don't care whether or not he has parts. All I care about is us getting our act together and functioning.

Liz: Maybe he's just better at it than we are.

Ann: Better at what?

Liz: Better at not being detected.

Ann: Liz you don't have enough to do. Why don't you write a CIA novel?

Liz: I don't want to write a CIA novel, though I would be damn good at it. I think I'd like a career as a spy.

Ann: I can't disagree there. I see you got permission from Ruth to hack up the back yard. Never ever get a job as a professional landscaper!

Liz: What's wrong? Don't you like the Camellia trees?

Ann: You mean those sticks out there?

Liz: You'll see. You must cut away the bad for the good to grow. We'll have beautiful Camellias next year.

(Liz had no idea of the prophetic nature of her statement to Ann. Not only was it descriptive of their current relationship with Jesus, it also would become their prognosis for therapy for a long time to come. In another few years, she would be acknowledged as a 'prophet in her own style' within the System and without. The System as a whole would slowly accept the truth of Jesus' discipline as the branches on His vine over the next 7 years. Their willingness today to be 'pruned' does not always diminish the pain of the process, only the amount of time it takes to grow from the experience.)

Ann: Why did you do that?

Liz: I hate those phone calls from her parents. I hate being told I won't amount to much. I hate the pressure, the control... I hate it all. I couldn't hold it in anymore. I had to explode, so I trimmed the trees.

Ann: It's okay Liz. Next time you get like this... go for the bottlebrush tree. It could use a good hacking. But be careful with that hacker... it is very sharp!

One day as Maria was typing she began telling Ruth about her dreams and asked her to interpret them. They were of a sexual nature about abuse through gang rape. Liz jumped in long enough to warn them about a fact they might not have realized...

Liz: Have any of you parts stopped long enough in our conversations with each other to realize that an outsider will read this stuff? He r-e-a-d-s this stuff Ruth!! Are you oblivious to that fact? I can't believe what you guys type. Why are we giving him these very personal writings? This stuff should stay only between us.

Ann: At this point it really doesn't matter much what he reads. We do not have the energy to edit our work. We really don't have him in mind when we are communicating back and forth. In fact, most of the time we forget he'll be reading it. If he can't handle what we write, then we need to quit therapy.

Liz: But Ann, I really don't want an outsider knowing all of this about us. Can't we be a little more discreet? It's very embarrassing.

Ann: I've never known you to get embarrassed Liz. Look, if Tabitha has the courage to tell him the details of the pink room, than we should have the courage to let him read our journals. Shouldn't we?

Liz: Tabitha is a little child. She does not know what being embarrassed means. Remember dancing with no robe on? She has no concept of it.

Ann: She knows what papa did to her was bad. Bad things scare her. It is as hard for her to tell because she is scared, as it is for us to tell because we are embarrassed. Think about it Liz.

As each part was becoming more aware of their own place in the System, they were also becoming aware of their differences in the inside world of Preservation.

Raquel: Tabitha is a wise child to choose the eagle. When she can come out of her hole, I will show her Brave Eagle. To soar with the eagle is to be free.

Ann: Some of you parts have the uncanny ability to experience a variety of dimensions. It makes me nervous because I can only go between Preservation and the outside world. But you go into magical worlds and communicate with the animals. You don't go into other bodies do you?

Raquel: No, we can't possess another body.

Ann: What the Hell do you guys do?

Raquel: Nothing... we do nothing.

Ann: Look, I know that you, Maria and Tabitha space out into different worlds. Maria has this weird ability to visualize herself soaring through canyons and valleys. How...

Raquel: It's the gift. You either got it or you don't and it is obvious Ann you don't.

Ann: Can I learn to achieve it?

Raquel: I doubt it. You are too logical and structured. You just go back and forth between Preservation and the outside. You need to be different. Most people in the world are too absorbed in it. They are like squirrels running all over the place storing up their wealth. They don't know how to stop and be really aware of their surroundings. We see things others never notice. For example Ann, what does rain look like falling on a leaf?

Ann: Like water falling on a leaf, why?

Raquel: To Maria, Tabitha and I, it is a dance, a symphony in nature. Rain does not just fall on a leaf. There is a pattern, a beautiful display of color, design and rhythm.

Ann: It's water.

Raquel: And that Ann is why we soar and you stay grounded.

After 8 months of therapy, the adults learned of the existence of more children in Preservation mostly by accident, or so they thought. Ann was chastising Ruth for breaking her budget, when she brought a coloring book for Tabitha. She was allowing Tabitha to shadow and experience the outside world at the store, as a reward for all her efforts in therapy. Of course the Little Ones were jealous and wanted the same thing. When told they were too young and needed to stay hidden to be safe, they complained that Tabitha wouldn't play with them because she was sick. (Tabitha was abused and they were not, so they equated that to being sick – an idea that still remains today.) When they were told Tabitha would play with them when she got well, they stated the 'other kids' were sick too and would they play when they got well? "What kids?" was a unison chorus from the adults. "Big kids" was the reply and a search began despite some adults' refusal to accept the possibility.

Not all of the council meetings were about 'heavy issues' needing resolution. Once they were discussing their marriage, home schooling, medication, and angels…

Maria: I wish Bruce could see the bright one behind him Ruth. He is very strong but peaceful and he is listening. Sometimes his hands are outstretched like he is protecting us. He is very holy, isn't he Ruth?

Ruth: Yes Maria, he is holy.

Liz: Hey Maria! Ann told me about these guys you see around your therapists. Do you think one of them would mind sitting next to Ann so that we could use the carpool lane?

Maria: They are not guys they are good spirits. There are different ones, some are like the Centurons. They are like warriors or soldiers and others are like listeners or messengers. I don't think it is legal to be in the carpool lane with them. I think you got to have people.

Ann: Knock it off Liz and quit teasing Maria! We have more important things to talk about besides these stupid angels.

Maria: They are not stupid! They are special to Tabitha and me because we see them. Ann, tell me about the Coat of Many Colors. Bruce said it has something to do with Joseph and Genesis.

Ann: You figure it out. Do I look like a Bible teacher?

Maria: Not really! Bible teachers are like shepherds. They help you stay on the path to the good pasture. You are like a mule train driver. Sorry... but you asked.

Ann: I like to see a little spunk in you kid but remember, not only is it important to have the shepherds, but you also need the mule driver. We need to work on learning to be normal in the outside world so we can function.

Maria: What is normal? Is seeing angels and soaring in canyons normal?

Ann: That question cannot be answered without a doctorate in normalogy.

Maria: What's that?

Ann: A highly specialized field in the study of normal.

Liz: Bullshit Ann! Now look who's teasing Maria.

When we look back now we see the humor, but at the time there was little to laugh about. Maria struggled with all she was learning from Bruce and the other parts living within the same body. Maria began writing her prayers to Jesus concerning all her fears and the changes happening around and in her.

Jesus, please come and save me. My thoughts give me headaches and scare me. Yemaya scares me now and I don't think she tells me the truth about you. My heart is broken and I am very sad. There are horrible things in my mind and sometimes I am so afraid that I shake. I have tried to go to Kansas to escape the bad, but I can't stay there all the time.

Jesus I know you will save me because you promised. I am trusting you. I want to hide in you. Please get me through all these troubles. Hear me when I am crying for help. Save me. I feel like I'm in quicksand and it is up to my head. I am so tired of calling for help. Please get me out.

Jesus I don't think I ever really knew you loved me. I don't think I ever really understood that and I got so confused, because no one told me simple enough about you. It was always so high for me. I tried to be a Christian in the church but I really wasn't, because I didn't understand how you could love me. But it was that book that Bruce gave me. I have read it 5 times. I know Yemaya doesn't think I understand it and she's right. I don't understand all the big words, but I understand what I wrote in the poem. I understand that you really do love me the way I am and I know that I'm a sinner with many really bad sins. But that didn't matter to you because you loved me so much, that you left your comfortable heaven and came to this bad place.

People were meaner to you than to me and you let them do that to die on the cross for all of my sins because you loved me so much because you wanted me to have life forever with you. And God forgives me for all of my sins because when I die, I can hide behind you and you will talk to God for me. God will see that you took my sins and I will go to heaven and live with you forever. I'll never be sad in heaven with you.

I believe that with all my heart Jesus. Help me to get your word in me so that when evil spirits come at me I can have your word as my weapon against them. Please help me in the office with Bruce. I am still afraid of people and I need you to help me trust him. Help me learn to praise you and to always thank you for what you have done for me. Help my mind remember things and especially help my mind and heart remember your truth.
Love, Maria
P.S. Jesus if Yemaya is an evil spirit, please make her go away. Maybe she just took credit for helping me when it was you all along.

Just as Maria was learning to trust Jesus and try to give him her fears, so it was true for other parts as well. As Tabitha shared more with Bruce, the resulting anxieties began to lessen when Jesus comforted her afterward. Yet, the corresponding attacks by the enemy increased every time there was any healing for any part. It appeared that their best tactic was to cause a part to remember more severe abuse from childhood, making them feel that healing was never really happening. For Tabitha, they made her remember the basement.

Ruth: Tabitha you did very well in Bruce's office this morning. You were very brave to tell him about the basement. I prayed for you while you were telling Tabitha and Jesus was there too. He was protecting you so the man in the black robe could not get you. Did you know he was protecting you?

Tabitha: Jesus loves Tabitha and keeps me safe. In basement I hurt my skin when strap hit me. I don't like rat, he bite me. I kick it away and I try hold my feet up so rat no bite Tabitha. The rat got long tail and eat you up. He scared me lots. I don't want to feel rat and I don't want to feel bad candy. I don't want to feel long pointy things and I don't want to do hurt work. I get scared.

Ruth: I know Tabitha. It is very hard, but you are being very brave. Jesus and Bruce won't let anything bad happen to you in the office. There are no rats in Bruce's office. You need to do hurt work to get better. Tabitha, how many times did the rat bite you?

Tabitha: One time I get eaten. Then I get up in the morning from big bed and go in kitchen. I get chair and quiet put it where flour draw is. I get on chair and get bread from breadbox and put chair back. I go back to pink room and I put my dress on and my socks and black shoes. Then I put little parts of bread in my socks all around and then I go to grandma for breakfast. When I get in basement with light turned off and papa gone away, I go walk until I can't walk no more. I push my shoes off and my toes take bread out and put on cement and then my toes push my shoes on. I walk backwards to spot and then when rat comes, he eat bread and get tummy full and not bite me or eat me up. I take bread in my socks every day for rat.

Ruth: The rat cannot get you anymore Tabitha. It is okay to cry now Tabitha.

Tabitha: I don't cry outside.

Maria: Ruth this is getting too hard, I don't think I can do it. I need to go to the fog when Tabitha tells because I can't do it. She makes me remember things that scare me.

Ruth: Maria you need to stay for Tabitha. She needs to not be alone when she tells. Remember that Jesus will protect you and help you not be scared.

Maria: I'll try, but I'm not sleeping at night and the nightmares are very bad again...

Tabitha: I almost get sick today Ruth. I got better when Bruce let me go back to my hole with Jesus. My hole safe, not bad like basement. I like picture of forest.

Ruth: Tabitha would you like to come live with us in the forest? You could live next to Maria and I. The Little Ones have a swing and you could swing.

Tabitha: Jesus comes too?

Ruth: Of course. Jesus lives with us too.

Tabitha: How?

Ruth: Jesus is God Tabitha. Jesus can be all over at the same time. When he is with you, he is also with me and Maria and Bruce and all people who want him with them. Jesus will not come and be with a person unless they ask him to come. Remember when you asked Jesus to come to be with you? What happened?

Tabitha: He came and hold me and rock me and love me with good love.

Ruth: That's right Tabitha.

Tabitha: How come some people no want Jesus' good love?

Ruth: Some people have not heard of Jesus and his good love and other people think they can live without Jesus' love.

Tabitha: I need Jesus very lots.

Ruth: Me too, Tabitha, me too.

Therapy continued as the System's two worlds provided healing and contradictions. All parts expanded their writings and sought understanding of their predicament. Awareness of abuse increased and struggles with family members became more focused as they were now understanding the difference between abusive relationships and what is 'normal'. Liz wanted 'out' as her anger increased, but obviously couldn't leave without the rest of the System.

Raquel began telling more stories to the parts to help them grasp their situation. Most were allegorical in the Native American tradition of story telling, yet her point was made to many parts. Most of these stories I will save for another publication after this book, but I plan to publish them for the benefit they carry to all who read them.

Parts were building their trust in Bruce as a friend and counselor. Liz and Ann still stayed away from him, as each was waiting and challenging the other to be the first to admit they needed his help. Liz rebelled one day and wanted to go to New York, where she thought she could escape the influences of all the men in her life. Ann intervened with reason, calmed her down and caused her to look at the reality of their situation. She began by reminding Liz that she hated Maria's therapist and was afraid to go in for therapy. Liz replied:

Liz: I never said Ann that I hated Maria's therapist, so don't put words in my mouth. I don't hate him. I don't even know him well enough to know whether I should hate him or not. There is one thing I like about him and that is he has been kind to Maria and Tabitha. Don't think this means I do therapy because I don't! So brain, what's your plan?

Ann: We stay put. We get Maria and Louise to work with Bruce on admitting that being hurt is wrong. We, along with Maria and Louise, learn what we can do to protect ourselves.

Liz: You will never get Maria and Louise to admit they are not at fault. Don't you understand that it is the way of the culture and you can't change it? Maria and Louise have been brainwashed in this way for almost forty years. How are you going to change that kind of conditioning over night?

Ann: We don't accept it and we were in the same environment. Why is it that we, who are also Latina and from the same culture, are so totally different from Maria and Louise?

Liz: How the Hell do I know? Do I look like a damn therapist?! That's what we pay Bruce to be.

Ann: Liz, we can overcome this problem. We have one advantage now that we did not have nine months ago, Bruce. I've talked to him a few times now and as remarkable as it may sound the guy's okay. I think he might have some advice and tools to help us in our dilemma. But we have to stick around long enough to get the help we need. All I ask is that you don't panic and run away. I still need that bottlebrush tree hacked up and you're the best hacker this side of the Sierra. So what do you say? Let's give Bruce a chance to see if he can change them. Maria listens to him better than she listens to us.

Liz: Why does she listen to him?

Ann: My guess is probably because he is the first person who has been kind to her and really cared about her. He's the first person who hasn't taken advantage of her or hurt her. I'm really not sure why Liz.

Liz: I really don't hate the guy. I just remember all the men in our life and how we've been treated. I don't want to get close to any male because they always end up hurting us.

Ann: I know Liz. When I come back in my next life I want to be Anglo, male and rich, rather than Latina, female and poor, because that is where the power is and I won't have to worry about being beaten and abused.

Liz: Are you kidding? I never want to be a man. I want to come back as God and take great pleasure in kicking their ass into Hell.

Ann: Liz... you are one nasty part!

The therapy continued and the council meetings increased in number. The decision was made that the children as a group would have only one vote on council. Ann pointed out the possibility of more children somewhere in Preservation and they didn't want to be in the position of children ultimately having the voting power block on council.

Ruth was spending more time out, with the approach of their first Halloween together as a System fully aware of each other. The others saw for the first time the fear of Maria and Tabitha as they cowered in the corner of their closet all bundled up. When Ruth asked about the trigger memories of Halloween, she was told by Louise it was too soon for them to speak about it. All she alluded to was their youth and a suicide of an 11-year-old in 1977. They would not hear the specifics for another few years, except for this information Ruth passed on to Bruce. As Halloween approached, Tabitha was becoming more anxious, so Ruth tried to calm her after one session one afternoon when Bruce awakened a memory in her.

Early drawing by Tabitha of ritual sacrifices in the orchard.

Content Warning!

It seems your question about Halloween triggered the barn memory for Tabitha. I have worked with her since Thursday and wanted to pass it on to you. I don't understand the incident but it seems to cause tremendous fear in her and Maria. Apparently, on Halloween Tabitha was out near a barn that wasn't 'papa's barn' but somewhere else. She heard "funny talking" (chanting?) coming from the barn. She went to the side and peaked in a knothole. Inside were big people with one dressed in a black dress and a big different knife in a thing near his tummy. She said there were lots of candles and someone setting on his knees talking funny with bowls around him. Then the man in the black dress walked around him doing funny talk. The "man in the black dress took his knife" and... (This is where I started to lose her again so I called Jesus and told her He was here to keep us safe, that the bad man could not get her and it was safe to tell.) All I could get was short non-connected phrases like "head cut off" and "blood in bowls". "Tabitha no want blood. Tabitha no want cut up." Then she started screaming, "Tabitha run... run fast... run Tabitha run."

I got Tabitha to her hole with Jesus and Maria started talking to me. She said, "I screamed and started running through the orchard. Someone grabbed me by the neck and said if you tell anyone about what you saw, I'll cut you up and you will die." Then Maria said she wanted to go to Kansas and I got her there. Apparently, Tabitha never told and never went near that barn again. If she knew who they were she isn't saying. I wonder if her papa telling her you tell and you die and someone else grabbing her and saying it, are two separate incidents? I find it confusing with statements made by her brother about things that occurred to `them' and promising not to tell. Did he witness something similar? Anyway, with Halloween here and 'men' dressed in black robes it is causing great panic for Tabitha and Maria. I asked Tabitha today if she was ever in the barn and had things done to her. She said, "Tabitha no go in barn, Tabitha see in hole."

While Tabitha told the truth about herself, it would be another two years before the truth of what happened to child parts, not yet revealed in the System, would come to light. Her own young psyche wasn't in a place yet to learn what happened to others. Just like Maria could only remember bits and pieces, and those as happening to someone else, Tabitha too could only later manage what happened to the younger ones, as happening to them and not to her. Even today none of the children can grasp the meaning of 'splitting' or creating another part out of themselves to handle abuse too overwhelming to add to their own. The adults are no different.

Yes, some can handle the concept as being factual for 'Maria', but I'm not sure any of them wanted to look at it as having happened to them in their youth. They really can only manage it as a team, supporting one another as the truth is revealed and finding strength in Jesus as their Savior, with a purpose for their lives in all that has happened to them. Each step in their healing has required the strength of His love to move them forward, so the power of the memories doesn't take them down. The enemy doesn't ever want them to heal completely, or he loses any control over them.

Over this Halloween, Maria and Tabitha both regressed in their healing because of an incident one afternoon. Driving home from therapy, they saw a Hispanic man beside a house expose himself in their direction, while pointing and laughing at them. This affected many in the System and Hash took temporary control over Maria again. He told Tabitha that she couldn't keep her name and Malo was her true name. She hid curled up in her hole and refused to come out or listen to anyone. Maria was taken outside the forest of Preservation into an area called Refuge with Hash. He continually yelled at her and seem to be growing in power. Maria had learned that Bruce's wife was sick now and feared the enemy was attacking Bruce, through his family for helping her. She asked Ruth to help pray for his wife. Ruth then attempted to help Maria understand the spiritual warfare occurring around them.

Ruth: Bruce is helping us and Satan does not want that. Satan does not want you to lean on Jesus or be his friend. Satan doesn't want Liz, Ann, or Raquel to know Jesus. Satan and his demons will use every way they can to prevent these things from happening but remember Jesus is more powerful than Satan. Whatever Satan dishes out at Bruce or us, Jesus can turn it to good for those who trust Him. There is a very big battle going on for us parts and we must pray that we don't lose focus on whom we serve. The warfare is real Maria and the enemy is out to do great damage. We must remember that we are a part of Jesus' army and the enemy has no power over us.

Yeah he is going to try to convince us that he has power over us, like sending the man who exposed himself the other day to knock us off the path that Jesus wants for us. Think about it Maria, this is no coincidence. You and Tabitha were starting to heal. Satan doesn't want that because it would bring glory to Jesus. Satan doesn't want that and he doesn't want you working for Jesus, so he sends bad things your and Bruce's way to scare you. But he can't stop you from healing if you keep on trusting Jesus. Satan will use every lie and every scheme to discourage you, frighten you and confuse you. Don't listen to him!

Listen to Jesus who promised that He would never leave nor forsake you and that He would get you through the tunnel. Do you see how Satan tried to get you so afraid that you would not go back to therapy? Do you see how he uses Hash to keep you scared, or gets Bruce's wife sick to discourage him? Hash has no power over you and cannot hurt you or Tabitha unless you let him. The devil has one goal for you and that is to destroy your faith in Jesus. Don't listen to him, listen only to Jesus. Jesus is protecting you. Does any of this make sense Maria?

Maria: How much bad will come at Bruce or me?

Ruth: I have no idea what the future holds, but I do know that God will not allow anything to come our way that He isn't there helping us get through it. Maria do you trust Jesus and His promises to you? Because if you do, I want you to come back to the forest and not listen to Hash's threats.

Maria: Yes, I trust Him. But will Hash hurt Malo? I don't want to be the reason why Malo gets hurt, or Bruce's wife and others get hurt. Why does the devil spend his time on us? He is a big... something...and we are just small parts that don't mean anything to anyone. Why would he care what happens to us?

Ruth: First, you are not the reason why others get hurt. Trust Jesus and come over to the light and Jesus will be with Tabitha. Satan doesn't care about you or want Jesus to be glorified. He is a fallen angel that knows he is doomed. He wants to take as many people down to the pit of Hell with him as he can. Jesus does care about you and loves you. He wants you to be safe with Him. You have no idea yet what plan God has for your life. You are important and special to Jesus, so special that He died on the cross for you. Always remember that Maria.

Maria: Ruth, Hash is here now and he is yelling at me and very mad.

Ruth: Maria, come over to this side. Ask Jesus to help you to not be afraid. Trust Him and hold on to Him and walk over here... Yes! See Hash has no power over you. Hash lies.

Ruth and Maria proceeded to help Tabitha to trust and call on Jesus to come to her side. She was told she could remain safe in her hole with Jesus and would not be called out again until they were safe in Bruce's office with Jesus. Maria continued to observe what was happening to her and Bruce. A few days later she asked Ruth to explain something.

Maria: Jesus didn't protect us from the bad man on the street. Why not?

Ruth: Who told you that? Never mind. He protected us by making sure we were in a car where the man couldn't touch us. Then He put His angels around Raquel and protected her when she drove through the red light. He made sure Raquel got to Bruce's office so Bruce could help us. He was helping us all the way. Maria, you need to understand something very important. BAD THINGS HAPPEN TO PEOPLE, EVEN NICE PEOPLE. Jesus never promised He would take all bad things away from us, only that He would be with us to help us get through them. Jesus can comfort and help you in many ways. One way might be to bring someone alongside you to help like Bruce. He can use different ways and different people to comfort and help someone. Do you understand?

Maria: Yes. Bad happens to good people too and Jesus comes to change the bad into good for people that trust Him.

Ruth: You do understand! Very good Maria!

As the trauma of this event occurred over Halloween, parts responded in different ways. Some sought solitude to reflect on their responses like Raquel. This put pressure on the whole System to manage without her. Maria responded to the following incident at home by spinning off another part. Liz was upset with Maria when 'Jennifer' appeared in the forest.

Liz: What the Hell is going on Ruth? Who is this Jennifer?

Ruth: I think Maria spun off another part named Jennifer to handle the pain of her daughter's situation. I'm not sure. All I know is a very stressful phone call came in from her daughter and she was out to take the call. After she hung up she started to cry and the husband told her to stop crying and grow up. I think it must have been at this point she spun off Jennifer, because she immediately dried her eyes and began washing dishes as if no phone conversation had taken place. I asked her about the call and she said she didn't know what was discussed, but maybe Jennifer knows. I asked her who Jennifer was and she wasn't sure, but that she knew Jennifer was building a house below Ann to assist her.

Liz: Shit...we don't need anymore parts! Tell her to stop spinning off parts. This place is getting more crowded than New York City. Who is Marie and the big kids?

Ruth: I have no idea. Marie introduced herself once and Ann scared her off with questions. I have never seen any big kids. The Little Ones said they have seen them near their swing. Penny said they are big and carry sticks. I asked how many and she held up four fingers. They have short hair and may be boys around nine-years-old. I am not sure as the Little Ones couldn't give me much information. I haven't seen them and no else has either that I know. When I asked where they go, they pointed to the East.

Liz: Damn it! I want to know who else is in this forest. Tell that therapist to get Maria to stop spinning off parts. We have enough problems already.

The feelings of being trapped in a body where numerous individuals were sharing the control of its life and actions, with the number growing daily, began to take its toll on Liz. Her choices for personal freedom were diminishing at a rapid rate with each new person appearing in the forest. Shortly after Halloween, she contacted Bruce about meeting with him. She stated she wanted his help in how to escape from her environment, presumably taking the 'known' parts with her to possibly New York or Hawaii. Her conditions for allowing a meeting to happen with Bruce reflected the concerns of most of the System, especially number four;

Number Four: You stay committed. If you are in this with me, I don't need you bailing out on me. I don't have a problem with you getting pissed at me and in fact, I rather enjoy a heated argument. But don't you desert me if I trust you for help. Fighting is one thing, abandonment is another. I will frustrate you and irritate you and there will be times you would like to strangle me. I understand that reaction to my personality, so it is okay with me. What is not okay with me is desertion. So if you are willing to tolerate me, I will tolerate you and maybe we can learn from each other.

In many ways, Bruce's acceptance of Liz's conditions defined the relationship He would build with the System over the next few years. What Liz was asking from him was friendship. Outside of each other, they had no friend outside who they trusted would not hurt or abandon them at some point. Yes, Bruce brought to the relationship a professional aspect that would always put the friendship into a particular context, but it was still a friendship that would plant the seed of possibilities into the System's psyche. The seed was that real friends were possible. The Bible speaks about how **"a friend loves at all times, and a brother is born for adversity."** This is what Liz was asking for from Bruce and she received it. He proved it in ways his professional peers would have challenged him with as being outside their code of conduct and did. But if he had stayed in circles that were safe, the paths to healing would not have opened for the System.

When the Lord speaks of coming alongside a brother or sister to help carry their burdens, He is speaking of this kind of friendship. Not one that is easy and comfortable, or where you always like and feel good about the other person. True friendship comes with a cost and only the one receiving it understands its true value. There were many in the System asking for the same thing from Bruce. Even in depression, Raquel acknowledges her friendship with Bruce as she sought seclusion from his world inside. The incident with the Hispanic man affected her deeply.

I thank you for your letter, but there is nothing you can do for me. The burden is too heavy to be lifted and the chains are too strong. I do not belong in this world of yours. It is too different for me and too difficult for me to understand. I have even tried to understand the others who inhabit my world, but they are like the platypus, they make no sense. I prefer to be with Eagle Clan and walk the ways of the ancient ones.

Yet, as I walk the paths to Sacred Mountain, there is a torturous pain within me, a pain that cannot be washed away in the cool water of the river. The pain runs deep and pierces my very essence. It is locked into my being and I cannot release it. At times it is so strong that I stand on the edge of the cliff and think of being like Brave Eagle soaring powerful and free. The only way to be free is to not be.

Your world is filled with violence and anger. There is no peace and there is no love. I know because I have experienced the violence and hate. I know what man can do and I have seen the destruction. Children are not cherished in your world, only commodities to be used and then tossed aside. I know for I am one of the outcasts.

I have no fear of the end, for my soul cries out for tranquility. My spirit hungers for comfort and I so desperately want to be free from the grip of agony. I cannot find peace in your world. I want to be released from the pain...I want to be. Thank you for being so kind to Little Gazelle and Maria. I know of that which was done to them. Your world does not deserve them. You may keep my art and poems, as I have no need of them. Take good care of the one who swings in the trees for me.

Raquel

This letter put Bruce on the alert for the possibility of attempted suicide. But how could you stop someone like Raquel, who lived secluded on the mountain inside Preservation? Bruce persisted in a dialogue with her to help her overcome her depression. As he prayed for them, an unexpected answer of hope came through Maria. She wrote him about a particular dream:

Last night I dreamed about having to go straight up a mountain path that was rocky and full of thorns. I had a very big sack tied on my back and I was told by someone that I had to make it to the top. Then an ugly creature put a big rock in my sack on my back. It was heavy, but if I walked a little slanted I could balance myself and slowly start up the mountain path.

There were a lot of people along the path that were laughing and pointing at me. I tried to ignore them and keep my eyes on the mountaintop. A little way down the path stood another ugly creature, who put a bigger rock in my sack as I passed. It was harder on my back to walk, so I had to go slower and balance even better.

Every so often, I would meet another ugly creature that would put another rock in my sack. I was about halfway up the mountain and I had to crawl on my knees because the sack was so heavy. My back hurt and I was faint with exhaustion. People continued to laugh as they watched me struggle and yet, I was determined to get up the mountain.

As the seventh rock was placed in my sack, I could no longer crawl and had to drag myself along the path. The thorns pierced my side and the snakes hissed and spit at me. I dug my hands into the soft dirt and pushed myself an inch at a time. I was past exhaustion and wished I could die alongside the pathway, for the sack was too heavy to carry.

Just as I was about to close my eyes for the very last time, I felt the sack lifted off my back. I looked up and there stood a man smiling at me. He lifted the heavy sack and put it on his back and reached out his hand to help me up. He gazed at the mountaintop and then turned to me and smiled. Hand in hand we ascended to the top of the mountain. With each step I got stronger and stronger.

**"Take My yoke upon you and learn from Me,
for I am gentle and humble in heart;
and you shall find rest for your souls.
For My yoke is easy, and My load is light."
Matthew 11:29-30**

Chapter 5:

"Overcoming the Memory of Hope Lost"

"Bless the Lord, O my soul,
And forget none of His benefits;
Who pardons all your iniquities;
Who heals all your diseases;
Who redeems your life from the pit;
Who crowns you with lovingkindness and compassion;"
-David Psalm 103

"The multitudes were aware of this and followed Him; and
welcoming them,
He began speaking to them about the kingdom of God
And curing those who had need of healing."
-Luke 9:11

Bruce was a true blessing in the lives of the System, during this time of what seemed like their greatest hour of despair. Letters from several parts within the Journals spoke about a new reality and awareness rising within the System. They were being forced to look at their current state of reality no longer as individuals, but as a part of a greater whole. While each one wanted to define their own existence in the present, they could not escape their common past being relived with each new revelation of its abuses. To live in the 'outside' world required them to understand how they arrived at their present state, because without it, they could not escape the bonds that enslaved their world. As each person tried to understand the others' experiences, a common feeling was that they were living in the pit of Hell. Where could they go... but up from here.

Ruth tried in many ways to keep hope alive within, but it was becoming harder to do it with words. Fortunately, she never gave up the hope she had in Jesus and that sustained her as the struggle for renewal increased with new knowledge of past and present abuses. As she searched for a way to help Tabitha after Halloween, she was convinced that something Bruce said was true. "The System's survival instincts could only have come from God. He is keeping them alive for a purpose." She spoke to him of her concern, one shared by the leaders:

I am concerned now because the system is sharing information between the parts so that now, each one is beginning to hold all of the horror, including me. (All of the horror would not yet be revealed until they were ready.) *Can each part handle the complete picture? I came into the system only four years ago without abuses and yet, as I listen to Maria and Tabitha's sharing, I am finding myself deeply affected. If it affects me, it must be traumatizing to Raquel and the others. Add to that the pain of them having to deal with their daughter's disability and one has a very delicate situation. How do we minimize the impact on them?*

The answer to this was one of the major problems facing Bruce and the System. One cannot minimize the impact of truth, only help by walking with them through the burden of it. Some would respond by denial, which only lessened the impact for a brief period of time in the delaying of truth. Helping them to focus on the fact of their survival in the present, for a purpose, would prove to be a foundational truth for understanding that their past could be healed one day.

After Liz had her first meeting, session actually (cuz Liz "don't do therapy"), she was quizzed by the others as to why she pretended to be Ann, with the 'voice' and all, instead of being herself. Since she only liked to reveal her true self in anger, he didn't provoke her so he didn't get the true Liz. This caused a discussion by some as to whether or not they could continue to afford therapy "meant only for rich people."

Ann: He deserves what he makes. It's just we are in the wrong class to acquire those type of services. When the money runs out, we are out of there. We have no insurance to cover it.

Ruth: The earthly things which insurance is a part of don't bind us, God is our resource. He will supply our needs. If therapy is God's will for us, the need for finances will be met through faith.

Liz: Why are you a Christian Ruth?

Ruth: Because Jesus Christ gives me a hope within my soul that nothing else can duplicate. He has a wonderful plan for my life, a plan that includes an abundant life full of meaning. Nothing else in this world can give me that assurance. He also loves me unconditionally. I was sinful and separated from God unable to know and experience his love and plan for my life. But Jesus came and died on the cross for me so that through him I could know God. I became a Christian by receiving Jesus as my Savior because I wanted to know and experience God's love for me and his wonderful plan for my life. Without Jesus, there is no hope or abundant life and that is why I am a Christian. Jesus is who he says he is and he is truth that sets me free. As we go through these last times and hear of wars, violence and natural disasters, I am not afraid. Fear is the absence of faith. I know who I serve and I know my reward, eternal life. Do you know whom you serve and your reward Liz?

Liz: You really believe all this shit, don't you Ruth?

Ruth: With all my heart!

Liz: How come Bruce didn't answer the same question the way you did? Aren't all Christians supposed to have the same answer?

Ruth: I don't know how Bruce answered the question Liz and I am not going to get into a debate over that. All I know is that according to 1Peter 3:15 it says, "But in your hearts set apart Christ as Lord. Always be prepared to give an answer to everyone who asks you to give the reason for the hope that you have. But do this with gentleness and respect." You see Liz, my greatest desire is to know, love and obey God.

Some readers will applaud Ruth for her answer, while others will identify with Liz. The difference between the two is time... when measured by life's experiences. Ruth had not yet experienced abuse, pain or fear that could cause her faith to be challenged. That will happen in the coming years and while her answer will still be truthfully stated with faith in Jesus, it will be tempered by life's experiences with Jesus at her side. It will also be stated quite differently to someone who might not yet know the truth of Jesus, or has experienced great pain themselves. Liz's response will also change to one of faith, as she discovers His unconditional love.

Bruce attempted to help the adults understand their present conditions affected by the daughter's disability, by showing them a video and asking them to respond about their feelings connected to it. A synopsis of their answers is given in the following:

Maria: Sad for her daughter being unable to enjoy a full life. Sad because she couldn't fix it for her daughter so that people's reaction to her wouldn't be mean, as often happened. Upset at the lack of caring and rude reactions to her disability by classmates, teachers, and 'Christians' at church complaining about the wheelchair being in the way. Great concern over who would take care of her daughter with dignity if something happened to her. Nobody in Maria's environment outside of the immediate family ever asked why her daughter was no longer living with her. Her 'friends' assumed that she was a bad parent, causing her daughter to live with her grandparents, an assumption totally untrue that caused long-term damage to Maria's self-worth.

Raquel: Wrote this poem.

The Little Disabled Child

Said the little disabled child to the world,
What is normal?

Normal are people who fit in
They take care of themselves and
Don't need people to take care of them.
Normal is Caucasian and middle-class
Not too heavy and not too thin
Competent and well adjusted.

Am I normal said the little one to the world?

No, you are abnormal
You are odd and peculiar
Dependent upon other people.
Abnormal is bad
Being dependent and different is bad
You are bad.

Said the little disabled child to the world,
I want to be normal.
Abnormal can never be normal
You will always be strange and frightening
We will never accept you.

And the little disabled child cried.

Helper: Depressive and highly negative film. Trying to accept what he cannot change. Wants help for the other parts and himself in practical living with disability in the family (i.e.: living arrangements, accessibility issues, negative attitudes by society, help a disabled child become independent, etc.).

Ann: Angry after 15 plus years of going through 18 doctors to arrive at the correct diagnosis; fighting with school systems over accessibility, abusive teachers and attitudes that demoralize the child; irate and vindictive neighbors when the city made them repair their sidewalks; dealing with Kaiser and State agencies for financial assistance. Her closing statement says it best:

"I cannot seem to pull myself together. I have been through so much and I have carried it all alone. Now I have this MPD to deal with. I gave it all my best, but in the end I failed. It has been an exhaustive road for me. Nobody ever said you did good Ann. Nobody ever came alongside of me to help relieve the pressure. All I got was professionals telling me what a lousy mother I am. Yet I would think back to all the walks at the zoo with my children. All the gifted programs they were in. The gingerbread cookies, their warm little coats always on, the trips to the library, no cavities in their mouths, nutritional foods in lunch pails with only 100% juice and nights curled up together talking. But I am labeled a bad mom. I hate therapists, social workers, psychologists and psychiatrists. I hate doctors and teachers and assholes. They have all contributed to destroying us. Like they said in the video: "You are my mom and you are supposed to take care of me." I tried. I do not want to tell you how much it hurts because you cannot understand how much it hurts."

Louise: Scared because it's hard to understand or help my daughter with this. Sad because the priest said God is punishing us for our sins. Why won't God punish me instead of my daughter? It hurts to not be able to help her.

Liz: Angry. Don't give me bullshit that life can be as wonderful with pain and deformity as it can be without it. It doesn't make us feel any better for healthy people to tell us no problem, life is what you make of it. It brought back bad memories of the last 18 years with professional idiots.

"I think Maria has suffered enough. This disability was an unfair and cruel joke. It seems like the childhood she had wasn't bad enough, so God had to destroy the child whom she loves so much. He knew this would crush her and yet he allowed it anyway. I think it is cruel and inhuman. Maria doesn't ask for much. Why can't he give her just a little happiness? It pisses me off."

Ruth: I have questioned God as to why us. He hasn't answered me yet, but I know that He is God and has His reasons for allowing it in our lives. It is still challenging. A blessing that has come out of this tragedy is many opportunities to serve Him in Disability Ministry helping others.

"We as a Christian community have basically shut out the disabled from our churches. Not only through physical barriers, but more damaging are the attitudinal barriers. Only 14% of disabled families claim to be Christian and yet our church body does not see the need to reach them...or meet their needs like respite care for families, transportation to churches, and youth groups that are accessible and who understand their disabled peers. It pains me greatly to see disabled families turned away from the Christian Church, as we ourselves have experienced."

Liz reached such a point of frustration with Christians and their attitudes, that she felt compelled to write Bruce a letter that would describe her role in life.

A Non-Christian Perspective by Liz

I watch Christians a lot. It has almost become a hobby of mine to observe them. The way they act and what they say tell me a lot about who they are. They do not seem to realize that they have to be 'good news' before they can share 'good news.' I find that they are not credible. If being a Christian is so great, then why do they look just like the rest of us? I do not see any difference. They are somber, self-righteous, narrow and uppity like everyone else. Where is this great joyfulness, love and hope they talk about? I sure don't see it written on their faces or displayed in their actions.

The majority of Christians seem to not have the ability to relate to people like me. They are like salt that cannot get out of the saltshaker. They stay in their elite little clubs called churches and never come out. So how do they expect to make an impact without contact? Christians are also moving at as fast a pace as everyone else. They are captive to their schedules and tend to not want to make time to relate to anyone outside their circles. If, as Ruth proclaims, they are supposed to be God's agents for reconciling people back to God, somebody forgot to tell them about it.

Taking time to relate on a one to one basis doesn't fit into the Christian's busy schedule. So they can talk all they want in church about reaching out to the world, but in reality their actions do not match their words. I find them to be hypocrites. How many of these Christians really ever take time to talk about Jesus to non-Christians? They don't even want to be seen with one, let alone talk to one.

Ruth says all the time that the church is the primary hope for salvation of the city. Well if the Christians I observe are the church, then you might as well forget about the city. Christians do not represent anything that we need. In fact, they represent everything we don't need.

As therapy continued, reverberations were being felt throughout Preservation. Parts might react with severe anger as Liz did one afternoon. Since it was vocalized towards Bruce, some child parts were frightened that she might hurt the safe outside helper. Ruth was concerned over why Liz was fuming too. Ann wrote to Bruce about Maria's reaction over the emergence of another part and more revelations. Maria was apparently reacting to more disclosures from Tabitha about the past and the mentioning of a message to Bruce from a part called TC.

...Maria is lying plain and simple. She knows damn well we exist, but she is refusing to believe it again, why? She is doubting her own

memory now and all she has told you. If she has never been Catholic or been around a priest, then why are there pictures of her in her first communion dress and with Father Breen. Why is she denying everything? All she has said up to Monday has been very accurate. All of a sudden she is afraid to believe anything is true.

The only time we told her to lie was to keep us out of jail or the hospital. Other than that she is so damn honest it is sickening. I can believe Liz capable of lying, but not Maria. I know why Maria is lying now, because she thinks it's easier to be labeled crazy than MPD. Damn it. If I do not exist, then who the Hell am I? How can I be typing this right now? If I do not exist, then have Maria explain differential equations, what an algorithm is, or better yet, have her balance her checkbook.

And furthermore, this babble about a TC part is a fabrication on her part. There is no one here called TC that I'm aware of. Also, no one will 'fess up' about doing the cutting, but it is obvious someone did. Maria said she kept her word and didn't do it.

The battery is a mystery to me. I have polled all the parts and they have adamantly stated they did not buy a new battery, so shit if I know. I have checked my money and nothing is missing. I really hate it when I can't figure these things out. Liz has calmed down but is still being an asshole.

Maria began typing a letter to all the parts inside one day. As she expressed her concern that she had to be crazy and all of you must not be real, Ruth began to test her about her memory and events from the past. The more she knew that these events were true and proof was available, she began to calm down and dialogue with Ruth about her fears.

R: Maria, I could go on and on. You do remember a lot of your past history and what you told so far has been accurate.

M: But sometimes it's like someone else wrote the things.

R: I know because another part is helping you or contributing.

M: Ruth you know what? There are others and I am scared.

R: What do you mean?

M: There are others.

R: I know Maria. Marie and Jennifer are friends and you don't have to worry. The little child that came out today won't hurt you. She, or he, seems very small and scared. It will be okay Maria, Jesus is still here for us.

M: But what if it isn't true Ruth? I don't like being not true. But I'm scared to now say anything is true because I'm not sure anymore. I don't ever want to lie.

R: You told Bruce that you were never Catholic, is that true Maria? Do you remember going to mass, saying the rosary with grandma, wearing a blue dress in processionals, the black box and pictures of the Saints everywhere?

M: Yes...but maybe I'm remembering make believe.

R: No Maria, you were Catholic. Remember Holy Ghost Church, Our Lady of the Rosary Church and St. Joachims Church? Remember Father Breen, Father George and Father Ron? If we didn't go there, how do we remember the priests' names? Call the Oakland Diocese and ask them if these priests served there. See your daughter in her communion dress on the cabinet, do you remember this?

M: Yes. I am sorry for telling Bruce I was never Catholic. I lied huh? I have to ask him to forgive me for lying, okay? I want to believe you are real but I'm so scared that maybe you are not, then what?

R: Why don't you believe we are real for now and work with us. Then, if we turn out to not be real, Bruce will help you deal with that...Bruce knows it is hard, how confused you are and how much it hurts to try to get well. But remember, Jesus and I are going through this with you and will never leave you.

Later that afternoon;

M: Ruth, I thought of why my mind is making believe. Maybe I like having attention because I never got any. Maybe my mind wants that and made all of it up to get it, right?

R: Okay! Then we should tell Bruce that we need attention and he should book us for the Donahue talk show and we need to tell everyone we meet.

M: No! I don't want anyone to know about me. I want to be left alone. I don't want any attention at all. Maybe Liz wants attention!

R: But Liz is a part and you said you don't have parts!

M: Now I have to think because I am confused.

Ann: Maria I know how I can prove us we'll take a test. Both you and I will take the test and Ruth will grade it, then we'll look at the results.

M: Okay, but I don't like test.

A: Piece of cake Maria and I have a joke to lighten up your day:

> *A farm wife accompanied her husband to the doctor's office. After a lengthy checkup, the doctor took the wife aside and told her, "If you don't do the following exactly as I tell you, your husband will lose his will to live and surely die.*
>
> *Each morning, I want you to fix him a hearty breakfast of bacon, eggs and fresh-baked muffins before he does the 5:AM milking. At lunch, make him a warm nutritious meal with a homemade pie for dessert. Make sure the hammock is set up under the shade tree so he can rest before he goes back into the field. Serve him supper with a smile, no matter what time of day or night he gets in from the fields. And don't burden him with household concerns while he's eating. After supper, ease him into his favorite chair and give him a beer with the TV remote so he can watch the ball game.*
>
> *On the way home the husband asked his wife what the doctor said about his condition. She replied, "He said you're gonna die!"*

M: Why are Liz and Ruth laughing so much Ann? I don't get it. The doctor didn't say that. He told her to be a good wife and take care of her husband. She lied to him, why did she do that?

A: Never mind Maria, you just rest so you can do well on the test Ruth gets.

M: OK. Louise, do you understand that joke?

Louise: No. Sometimes they are all funny.

Later:

R: Ann let me make a test with ten questions from the book. All we need is enough to show her the difference between the two of you. This isn't a race you know how I feel about these kinds of tests. I'll make it up and give you both fifteen minutes, I think that is all she can handle...

M: I am stupid, see I told you.

R: You are not stupid. I could not have gotten them all right either. Math is the worst subject for me, but that doesn't make me stupid. The purpose of the test is to show you the difference. Now tell me how your mind can do well one time and not the next?

M: I don't know, it is weird.

R: It is because you have parts. Ann went to high school and college. She is not smarter than you only she has had more training in math than you. Naturally she would do better on tests than you because she has taken more tests and had more practice. Does that make sense?

M: Bruce won't think I'm stupid?

R: No. In fact he'll probably agree that your answer on number seven was very creative. I like it better than the correct answer. Your reasoning makes sense to me and I give you points for creativity.

M: OK Ruth, I will try to do the therapy for you and Bruce. It is very hard and scares me a lot. I feel the little kid there. What do I do?

R: Maybe when you feel that the little child needs to come out, you could tell Bruce and move into the corner for the child. I think the little child was forced out because no one else wanted to come out. Ann and I felt you needed to be there and to rescue you from therapy

would not help you. Someone was forced out and that was the child.
We found out about the little child and now we can help it.

The little child just coming out is Anna. It was difficult for
Bruce to identify both Angelina and Anna at first, as both emerged
around the same time. As more of the past was revealed through
Tabitha, their different ages and reason for existence would become
known. Angelina was the first split from Maria as an infant,
suffering abuse from the mother.

Liz chastised Bruce, after Anna first came out, for not
responding very well with care for a baby in his office. Liz's anger
was as much frustration over the revelation of 'another' part in the
System, as it was guarding the care of the System. Bruce soon
realized that Tabitha was the key spokesperson for learning about
the specifics of the abuse suffered in childhood. This explained why
she didn't always react to different abuses being revealed. She, like
Maria, knew another person within the System suffered the 'abuses'.
When they were agitated or physically responding to the memories
opening up, it would be reflected through Tabitha's responses and
drawings first. As each child surfaces before the outside caregiver,
knowledge was gained for treating the specific abuse with the
specific person. This process would continue for the next several
years as more children are revealed.

It is always difficult for a professional in the helping services
to fully understand the 'splitting' process of victims of abuse, when
the numbers of parts keep increasing dramatically. If Jesus had
revealed to Bruce, at this time in the System's therapy, the truth He
later revealed through me of the System remaining multiple for His
purposes, I'm not sure he or they could have continued. Bruce
wanted to help bring healing to the people he was discovering in
Maria. When he, like myself, discovers that an innocent child like
Tabitha has suffered such severe abuses, that she has to split and
create another child to store the intensity of the memories and pain
of the event, it wounds our heart.

We are grateful in knowing that Jesus allows this for survival
of the person, yet we grieve over the pain that innocents have to
carry into adulthood before they can release it for healing. Some
child abuse victims are blessed to receive counseling from someone
as gifted as Bruce at an early age, thus removing the burden of

carrying such pain into their adult life. The trauma of the revelation by the victims is not unlike shock therapy to the body on an ongoing basis. This is why Maria and every person inside of the body had such desire that there were no more parts still inside.

Over the next four to five months in Bruce's care, all parts except Dorcas, would be made known to exist and 24 people would come under his care as counselor for the System. The most painful of the physical, sexual and psychological abuse was still to be revealed by the children of the System. I believe the Lord's timing in bringing me in to assist him, was so Bruce could focus on the children in their first 'outing' since the abuse. Keeper of Functions was the first leader to communicate with Bruce outside of Helper, while still retaining his anonymity from Level 1.

I have been commissioned to communicate to you from Level 2. The level of functions exists directly below the level of parts in the forest. In our level, we are contained in holding cells until needed. When our cell door opens, we travel on the conveyor belt to the office of the Keeper of Functions. It is there that we sign out, receive our instructions and our voice mechanism. We then proceed to accomplish our function. We never know when we are needed to perform our service until our cell door is activated. There is no communication between functions. We are aware of the world of the parts, but we do not enter their inside world.

The Keeper of Functions assigns us our cell when his boss Maria, (done at a subconscious level), *designates our creation. He is responsible for approving our release into the outside world. There are many cells with nametags on the door. As the counselor of record you will not be in touch with them except for those which are required to be in your presence. I have been instructed to inform you that TC function is from Level 2 and stands for Christian Counseling Center function, designed to take Maria from the waiting room into your safe office. The function is to place the blanket and Ollie (doll) in the lap of the body and give all messages from the bag to the counselor. If the TC function cannot complete the assigned tasks, she is to return to Level 2 and is to return immediately upon completion of assignment.*

As functions, we do not designate when and where we serve, we act merely as task performers. Although the parts on Level 1 believe that they perform all duties on the outside world, this is not accurate. For example, the automobile maintenance function recently replaced a defective battery in Maria's vehicle. The AM function is not responsible for all maintenance of the automobile, but only that task assigned by the opening of the cell door. Keeper of Functions assigns all tasks. It can be said that the functions do all the dirty work that either the parts refuse to do or unable to do.

In order for the functions to complete tasks or make purchases requiring money, Keeper of Functions maintains a hidden cash account in the home. Money is acquired by the investment function from small dividends for stock purchased ten years ago. Expenses for Level 2 average $40 a month, which allows the Level to maintain a steady balance. Level 2 has no other source of income. Our knowledge of Level 1 and Level 3 activities is limited. We are aware of the different strata, but we are not involved in any communication with them. We have no purpose in knowing them. Our purpose is to perform tasks ordered by the boss.

Regards from Level 2
CU (Communication Unit)

Maria would find the next several months very difficult just to cope with the influx of new parts. What was revealed was not always shared with her for her own stability. She would struggle with the numerous challenges to her identity and adjusting to the memories that were filling the gaps of lost time for her. She would continue to be challenged as well, by those parts she had for the most part already accepted. Ann and Liz would express their embarrassment of Maria's actions on the outside world, whenever they thought it might be associated to them when they came out. Ann chastised Maria after one such event in Bruce's waiting room.

Ann: Maria I do not want you to embarrass us like that again.

Maria: What did I do wrong?

A: You are to sit quietly in the waiting room and not make up stories about the dance of the flowers.

M: I sat quiet. There were pretty flowers there and the music. I just made up the story waiting to go in. The pretty carnations were the girl flowers with their skirts puffy like the flowers with red and white edges. They danced to the music and the orchid-like flowers, which were pointed, bold and strong boy flowers wanted to grab them and dance with them. But the girl flowers wanted to be left alone and they would all run to the side and dance, but the boy flowers kept chasing them. Then the white flowers were protectors and they came in and pushed the boy flowers away. A battle started and the boy flowers shoved and the protector flowers pushed until the girl flowers danced away when the music stopped. Then I watched the stems become trees in a swamp with the little leaf becoming a lost boat carrying the little lost bug searching for its mother. Then Bruce was there and I had to go.

A: Look, dream all you want quietly, but don't go telling people these things or they will believe you're crazy. Just keep it to yourself. You must look rational.

With all that was happening to Maria during this time, the quieter parts like Louise would often feel guilty about expressing their concerns to Bruce. I've included her letter in its entirety because it so clearly reflects her personality and struggles to cope with her new reality.

Dear Bruce,

I am sorry to bother you again but I have questions I wonder if you could answer for me. I am getting very confused about God. Ruth has been talking to me a lot and she says things different than what the Catholic Church says. I think Ruth is very nice, but she is not like the Pope. So who do I believe? I don't understand why my church would lie to me. Maybe I just didn't understand right but I am sure I did. But Ruth says it isn't true and now I don't know which way to go. I have always tried to obey the rules and obey the church, but I didn't obey good enough. I guess I deserve Hell because of how I tempted the Monsignor (as a child). I broke the rules of the church so God has to punish me. But I try so hard to be good and do what I am told. I just wish I could do better…I try.

Maybe God will let me go to Purgatory instead of Hell. I hope so because I am trying to make up for all the bad I did when I was little. I just think it is so much bad that I will never do enough good to make up for it.

I like Ruth an awful lot. She is very kind to me and is nice, but she says things that are different from what the church taught me. She says I do not have to obey the Catholic Church anymore. Who do I believe Ruth or the Pope? And why would my church tell me untrue things?

I hope you can help me get unconfused. I want to do the right thing but I'm not sure what is right. I am reading the book you gave Maria about Jesus' love and I like it very much. My church never told me that Jesus loves us, only that he expects us to obey the Ten Commandments and the teachings of the church.

I am sorry I am not yet ready to stay when they talk about the bad things in our life. It is very painful for me to think about the parts I did. I try to help Maria in your office when she needs to go inside, but it is hard for me too because I get scared in your office. I don't know what to say or do. I hope I don't get you too frustrated. I do try my best to help Maria.

I am worried about Maria a lot. She has such bad headaches and gets sick a lot. I think this is awful for her. I try to help but it is getting hard for me too. I don't know if we will ever get well. Maybe this is our punishment for being so bad. Maybe if we suffer a lot in this world then God will let us go to Purgatory. I hope so. Thank you for reading my letter.
Sincerely,
Louise

Other parts would follow suit and begin writing Bruce. Jennifer wrote her first introductory letter to Bruce, offering her perspective as the last created part. She was a split from Raquel during a very difficult time in order to assist Ann in her duties, something neither knew.

Jennifer received much of Raquel's youthful, teenage, exuberance in the split, which is reflected in her early writings. Raquel seems to age several years into her mid-twenties after this and her writings take on a more somber tone. She focuses on her

Native American beliefs to find meaning in all she has seen and learned in her life, as she becomes more reclusive inside.

This dynamic in splitting is also reflected in Maria as more parts begin revealing their existence. As more stated their role and experiences within the System, it was as though Maria released ownership of those portions to them. Her writings and verbal skills seem to slowly regress to a less mature age level, with spelling and pronunciation of a 6th grade level, the last grade she attended school before Ann took over. This was actually a positive reaction, as she was able to balance herself easier within the context of her life. Everything became viewed through a simpler approach of not having to understand everything now, just accepting it. While this would help with the healing process in understanding her condition, it would also make her more susceptible to attacks from the enemy trying to dissuade her from the truth with logic and lies, prolonging the healing process.

For Maria, understanding truth would become directly related to her trust in Jesus. She would observe His actions and hear His words on the inside, then correlate their effect and application to the results on both the inside and outside worlds. She waited to see if what Ruth was saying about Him was really true. After I come into her life in a few months, she will continue to ponder all that we discuss about Jesus and read in the Scriptures to squeeze whatever truth she can out of it. The result is her baptism and acceptance of Jesus in just over a year from now. In the coming years, she will see herself as unintelligent and knowing very little about the way the world is, or why there is so much suffering in it. Yet her spirit of trust in Jesus will blossom and grow into a virtual well of wisdom for life lived simply and true with her Jesus. Lives will be touched and changed forever in her reflection of Him.

Jennifer writes to Bruce explaining her new duties and perspective on them.

Ann clued me in to a lot of the history of the System and who you are. So we are in therapy? Why am I not surprised! I'll tell you I don't know how Ann has put up with Maria's mother all these years, one cold lady. I am having a hard time believing some of the stuff Ann has been telling me about her relationship with the mother.

The best thing that could happen for this system is for the mother to adios...

I asked Ann why she put up with it. She said, "You're too new. You just don't understand yet, do you?" Frankly I don't. I mean we got a life, right? How come these people have so much control over us? I have been handling the phone calls from the mother averaging two a week. The amount of stuff required of Maria to do for them is a lot. I can see where Ann was starting to lose it. But the amount of work doesn't bother me as much as the attitude towards me. I really don't think she likes Maria, or me, because she is so cold and distant. I can see that Maria never got any emotional support or even a kind word thrown her way. To this lady Maria can do nothing right and I mean nothing. Also no opinions are allowed and definitely no complaints. If I say something like, well I've been tired lately and I haven't got it done yet, I will receive a stern discipline about complaining and a lecture on my attitude and irresponsibility. She also likes to let me know how wonderful Maria's daughter is doing with her and how it would be a mistake for her to return here... What encouragement for Maria! ...Not!

I am meeting the others. I think Liz is cool, she tells it like it is and I love it. Ruth is okay but she seems preoccupied. Louise is nice but boring to talk to. Maria is nice, but very confused.

I tried to talk to Marie since she is in the same part of the forest as I am, but she isn't interested in talking much. I haven't met the rest of them yet.

Well, peace and good vibes. Jennie

Liz begins to write prolifically about her observations and frustrations with Christians. She discovered that Bruce had done some street evangelism on Broadway, her old hangout. She wrote the following observation after watching Christians attempt to do street evangelism.

The Head Guy Don't Drive No Lexus

It was a cold crisp morning as I walked along the streets of East Oakland. The air still held the permeating smell of the broken wine bottles rocking gently against the curb. I was out for my usual hit of the Mexican bakery at the corner of Foothill and Fruitvale. I always know the exact time the truck pulled in with

its edible goodies just screaming to be sampled by a renowned critic. Stuffing my pockets I headed off toward the park.

This is where I get my entertainment. The Suburban Christians come to the park once every two months to do their Christian thing. Flashing their Rolex watches and their two-colored brochures, they stand there and scream at the winos as to why they need Jesus. I find their antics rather comical as I set on the side observing their performances. After I finish my selections of gourmet delights, I rise and stand against the old, leaning pine tree. As I continue to watch, an erupting frustration explodes out of me. Preachin'...I'll give you preachin'.

To the Christian Church of America; I know you are hard working and prominent people in your wealthy suburban community. You stand firm in what you believe. You have stuck it out in a crime infested, immoral world. Yet, I hold this against you.

On the outside you look good, but there is one thing you lack...LOVE. You people are loveless and if it continues you will be a church that will lose its effectiveness and will be snuffed out! I am frustrated with you. You are like dry bones; unusable, proud and self-sufficient. You don't see the need of these people. You don't see hurting people because you don't look with spirit eyes. You have diverted your attention from love and have become a desert of bones.

Feeling better, I again sit down and watch those clowns as they try to convince people like me that they got what we need. Bullshit! They don't have any idea what we need. They don't stick around long enough to learn.

Just then a guy sat down next to me. He had a pair of torn Levi's on, an old tattered shirt and smelled like he hadn't bathed in days. Yet, there was something real about his smile. He spoke first and said, "Hi Liz. I've been listening to your sermon." "How did you know my name?" I inquired. He said, "I'm really good with names. I've watched you." Great, I thought, the guy's an undercover cop and I'm busted. "No, I'm not an undercover cop Liz," he stated amusingly.

"How in the Hell did you know what I was thinking? Are you some kind of psychic? Then he got up and said walk with me awhile Liz.

Now I don't just go walkin' with anybody, but for some reason, I wasn't afraid of this guy. We walked and talked for most of the morning. As I listened to him speak, I sensed a heart of compassion for my people in the city. Here was a person with no color-coded brochures, no Rolex watch on, no Nike shoes and definitely no Lexus. But here was a guy who had time to walk with those in the city. A person unafraid to sleep in the same damp, lice infested hole in the alley. A guy who strolled in the heat of the night down the busy streets of prostitution and drugs. A man who comforted the weak, the hungry and the brokenhearted. He was different than those Suburban Christians out for their bimonthly good works projects. No, this man had nothing to give but his love and his time...and that was all that was needed.

One day Liz went to Helper and demanded a council meeting. She was tired of 'being blamed for everything around here.' Ann had just had her glasses broken and some papers torn up by someone. Maria had a ring 'stolen' and became aware her hand had been burned by hot coffee when switching to the outside. No known or recognized part was taking responsibility for any of these events. This raised the question of 'others' within the System again. They realized that the mysterious events began after Ann starting reading about MPD in a book from Bruce. They came to the conclusion that 'someone' didn't want the System to be healed. Jennifer suggested the possibility of a whole other world with opposing forces of good and evil around them. Her final question lingered with everyone inside.

"If we exist, why can't another world exist alongside of our world?"

The veracity of her question became known slowly by the parts. Ruth wrote to Bruce to fill him in on statements by Maria in session about a new 'Circle Council.' She and Helper had just been approached by Raquel with this information shortly before and they were waiting for a better time to tell 'their group' about other groups existing. Maria had found out due to 'seepage' within the System. For a person with DID, this can occur when the partitions come down that separate the various parts awareness of others existing within their world. It can be both a blessing and a curse. When trust is built between people within any group, information can be passed on when unintended ears overhear conversations and assume 'their' information is totally true. This can be helpful in the healing process of building trust and a stronger sense of mutual awareness.

However, it can also be used to pass on misinformation in order to bring about chaos from a lack of trust, causing the healing process to be slowed or even reversed. The effect of the process is similar to that of gossip in any society. When the information is meant to cause harm, as in lies or slander, it will disrupt communication within that society through distrust of each other. In this case, information was heard that would eventually help bring better communication throughout Preservation, so no harm was done. The whole System would learn over the next few years how truth can build up a society and lies can tear it down just as quickly. For the more gullible and less secure parts of the System, the continual onslaught of the enemies' lies in the voices heard from a distance, would make their lives feel like a constant pinball game. It would be a little child's trust in Jesus that would bring a reference point for peace therein.

Ruth wrote: According to Helper, it was Raquel who approached him and requested his presence at a 'Circle Council' meeting. She explained to him that she had been greeted twice by someone calling itself SA (System Ambassador) from the World of Functions. The first time SA spent a considerable amount of time with Raquel learning information about the Land of Preservation and teaching her about the World of Functions. Raquel suggested a Circle Council of the chiefs of the different tribes. She explained to SA the ways of the ancient ones and the way of the Circle Council. Raquel also asked SA if the chief of the tribe of Functions would send an ambassador to Labyrinth and Elysian Fields. The ambassador would explain the Circle Council and request their presence at the meeting.

SA returned a second time and informed Raquel that contact was made with the Prince of Labyrinth and the Highest Elder of Elysian

Fields. They agreed to the Circle Council. The meeting will take place in the North in the high country of Sacred Mountain. Raquel will prepare the meeting place. Helper does not fully understand the preparations. Raquel told him the circle represents balance and harmony, a linking of all life. The number four is very sacred and the circle will be connected by the four directions North, South, East, and West. The snowy owl will be of the North giving wise counsel. The Eagle will be of the East giving vision, illumination and guidance. The Mouse will be of the South reminding the leaders of trust, innocence and growth. The Bear will be of the West giving courage, strength and truth. All five men have agreed to follow the ways of the ancient ones in conducting their meeting.

Helper – Leader of the Surface People of the Land of Preservation.
Daniel – Protector and Head of the Clan of Argus.
Keeper of Functions – Ambassador of the Functions of World of Functions.
SID – Prince of the Harmers of the World of Labyrinth.
King of the Lights – Highest Elder of the Guardians of Elysian Fields.

The meeting will commence when the call is sounded on the fourth day of the dawn of the new year. Raquel will sound the call and be present to greet the leaders into Circle Council. After all have arrived, Raquel will retreat. (Did you know Raquel had an Indian name? Helper says she is called Quiet Walker.) The Circle Council will begin with passing of the Camulet as a sign of hospitality among the distinguished strangers. According to Helper, the Circle Council is the gathering of hearts and minds. The leaders of the different tribes come to the Circle Council willing to listen to reason and be themselves reasonable. They must be willing to come with an open mind ready to discuss and communicate. They must listen to everyone's point of view and then be willing to compromise. Through the Circle Council, the leaders will use their collective wisdom and come together to resolve issues. Raquel told Helper that to learn, one must first listen. This is the first step towards wisdom.

Helper has a council meeting called for this morning. Daniel has agreed to attend as a representative of the Clan of Argus. Marie is also planning to attend. Word has gone around that this meeting is

to discuss a special Christmas gift for one outside person known by all the parts. Helper is pleased that the response is good. Present will be Liz, Ann, Louise, Raquel, The Little Ones, Tabitha, Anna, Jennifer, Marie, Daniel, Helper and myself...
In the Precious Name of Jesus, Ruth

A few days after this council meeting, Ruth called another emergency meeting. She had learned through Tabitha of another child part named Muy Malo (Angelina). Ruth understood from her behavior that there was a greater connection shared between Tabitha and Muy Malo than with Anna. Tabitha was very stressed because the child was under attack, which forced her out of her hole near Tabitha. Tabitha came out to help Muy Malo from *"bad man cut Muy Malo. Hurt Muy Malo. No. No cut. No cut Tabitha."* It seemed to Ruth that Tabitha and Muy Malo were expressing themselves together or switching so fast she wasn't sure who was out in front of her.

She would later learn that this often occurs between alters who are very close together and is known as co-consciousness. This is usually not observed on the 'inside' during stressful situations, unless alters are getting close to blending. The triggering of Tabitha and revealing of Muy Malo would be later understood as being caused by the enemy to stop the memory work with the children. The enemy put confusion into the minds of the children by telling them that Bruce was the abuser they remembered. They were told if they came out, he would cut them up like they saw happening in the barn. These attacks were going on simultaneously with other parts, telling them that if they continued to tell they would die.

However, not all of these specific attacks were from the 'enemy' directly. When children who are victims of sexual abuse, or Satanic Ritual Abuse in particular, are brainwashed by their abusers that telling would mean their death or the death of their family, a mechanism is set in motion of self preservation. In Maria's case, the World of Labyrinth was created to 'keep the secrets' so the person wouldn't die. The Harmers' roles were to make sure no one told by reminding them constantly of the lie they believed to be true. This continued long after their abusers were dead. This power of control from the past can happen in victims who are not DID. The enemy will not pass up opportunities like this to use to their advantage on any possible victim. This is one reason why clergy abuse of children, even if proportionally small in society, is so powerfully destructive to the whole life of their victims.

When the abuser is understood to represent the authority or power of an eternal being that never dies, the death of the human perpetrator does not by itself cease the control of the memory of the perceived partner in crime. Unbelieving clergy, who offer forced assistance to victims who finally reveal the truth about their peers or mentors, compound this problem. I haven't met a victim yet who can't tell immediately, after revealing their pain to a counselor, whether or not that listener believes them in their heart. I believe the greater responsibility here is on the clergy to overcome their prejudices within the communities of faith, that their fellow pastors and priests are less likely to have committed the sin they are hearing about, than the possibility the victim is telling the truth. The first step in healing for both victims and abusers is recognizing the truth. The truth will set you free.

What the enemy wasn't prepared for with the System, was their response to more parts existing within their world. The circle quickly closed around Tabitha and the children to defend them from further attack. The surprise of more parts was less important than protecting their own. Those present at the council meeting sought to find a way to show the kids that Bruce was safe and his 'touch' would not harm them. They also tried to figure out how to help them from hurting themselves on the outside, even though they did not yet understand the cause. A method was established for the adults to work in teams with the children whenever they were out in therapy. Through their discussions they acknowledged that their actions never threatened anybody on the outside, only themselves. This raised more questions for them in their own therapeutic process. Liz came up with the question of the necessity for more immediate follow-up after a session with Bruce, as a time of debriefing of feelings for all affected parts with or without Bruce. The need for this became immediate a few days later when another new part, Mari, came out in Bruce's office, revealing the existence of still another child part, Mariann, existing with severe abuse inside Preservation.

Mari in Bruce's office:
The Beast took Maria's sister too. I had hoped he didn't get her. But he got a lot of little children and the diocese and the nuns just turned the other way. I don't know how I got in the Beast's bedroom. I remember watching from above as the Beast had his way with Mariann and when he was finished, he put on his clothes and fixed his clerical collar and dressed Mariann. Then I came out and he took me to the church that was like a mausoleum, cold and dark. He took me to the black tomb of the confessional, where he entered the middle door and I always entered the right. Inside it was dark and cold. I knelt on the kneeler and he opened the metal gate to hear what I had done so that I could be absolved of my sins. I told him all that I had seen done to Mariann. He then gave me penance and told me that God was powerful and if I told, God would kill my family. I left and went back to class and then went home. The Beast, the man of God and the church did nothing. He got a lot of children in those thirty years and the church knew. The church knew!

Ruth wrote Bruce the following day with this report.

Maria had a very bad night on Sunday. I was not aware of the letter Maria's sister wrote or of Mari until 1:AM on Monday morning when I heard Mari talking to Maria. I also heard 'other' voices threatening Maria and Mari that they would reap serious consequences if they told. Maria escaped somewhere inside at this point. I came out. I heard inside Mari speaking to the 'other' voices and saying the secret is already out. Donna and Joe know about the Beast and so does the Oakland Diocese. (This is a terrible name to call anyone. Why does Mari call the priest the Beast?)

Mari then said to the 'other' voices, what are you afraid of? At that point there was a loud screaming in my head as the 'other' voices yelled that, "He can't be trusted. Do not tell or we will die." Then they left. Mari retreated somewhere inside and I could not reach her. I had no connection with Mari again until I heard Mari in your office. Since then I have made contact and she told me what she told you. I can't feel the intensity of her pain, but maybe it doesn't reside in her. How could a priest make a child go to the 'black tomb of the confessional' to reiterate what she had done in his bedroom? I don't understand. Then to use God by telling the child God will kill her family if she tells is terrible.

Mari suggested we not talk about it to Maria until you are present to help us with our feelings. According to Mari, she learned about us from Raquel who she met several months ago in the forest. Mari lives in the uncharted northeastern area of the forest and ran into Raquel on her way up the mountains. She learned from Raquel about the system and how there were others who lived in the land besides the Little Ones. She also found out about you, who Raquel called The One Who Listens. She asked if you could be trusted with secrets. Raquel said she was not sure, because she did not yet feel safe with any man. Mari decided to observe you before she came out.

Mari reported her findings to Daniel, leader of the Clan of Argus. The clan consists of Daniel, Ed, Raul, Len and Mariann. They live in the eastern part of the forest in a fort built as a stronghold against intruders. The four boys each take turn standing guard in case the Beast attempts to take Mariann. They rarely venture into the forest, preferring to stay in the eastern section. The boys carry spears for protection.

Mari asked Daniel's permission to reveal herself to you after the letter was received from Maria's sister. Daniel agreed, however he will not allow Mariann out of the fortress, as he is not sure she can be safe. Daniel must be careful of the Beast masquerading as a friend. Therefore, he really trust no one except Mari. Mari gave him your regards and he nodded acceptance of the greeting.

Mari said she is also aware of another world which Raquel spoke about. She spoke of a place that enters other worlds below. She said the parts are the Surface People and the Harmers and Guardians live two steps below. Raquel said there are two clans with watchmen posted at their camps. Hash is from the Harmers. The Harmers harass, destroy Surface People's property, sabotage things and hurt the body. The Guardians protect the body, safeguard the Surface People's things, guard the way to therapy and keep vigilance over Harmers activities. Raquel does not know what exists between their world and ours. She only knows what she has been told by a Guardian named Heavenly Dove.

I expressed concern to Mari about the Harmers activities this week. She agreed that the exposure of the information on the Beast would cause Harmers to be active. Both she and I will be on alert. I am going to inform Helper of this now. I will seek his guidance as to the proper time to inform the other parts about the Harmers, Guardians and let Daniel reveal his clan.

What Ruth wasn't prepared for herself, was learning so abruptly of the sexual abuse by a Catholic priest to another child part of the System. Being a relatively new part herself as an adult sharing the body of the System, she could not have anticipated the effect of this new knowledge upon her strength and identity as a Christian. It was one thing for her to talk with Louise about the traditions and rituals of the Catholic Church that were not Biblically based, but it was something else again for her to grasp the sinful actions of a Christian man, like a priest abusing a child inside the church setting.

When details come much later in therapy, understanding doesn't come any easier after learning of the Diocese's complicity in doing nothing. Ruth's purpose within the System was to stand strong in her faith as a Christian and to be a beacon for the other parts to discover the true God of love in her example. Her role just became much harder. Maria was the first to come to Ruth for understanding, even though she and others would want to remain in denial of the truth for a few years more. As more child parts reveal the details of abuse by family members and priests who frequented the home of their youth, adult parts will struggle with the unfathomable nature of mankind's capacity for sin.

Maria: Ruth, Bruce says we have to pray now. Don't cry. Why are you crying? (Maria hadn't learned of Mariann's abuse yet, only her existence.)

Ruth: I am human and when I know of suffering of a child, I hurt for them with every fiber of my being. It is all right to cry once in a while. Bruce is right, let's pray.

M: We keep letting Jesus know we are drowning and that we can't make it by ourselves. We need him to get us well because he has the power and we have to keep trusting him.

R: That's right Maria. You have heavenly potential... the Lord is with you.

M: But Ruth, if Jesus is here, why did he let so much happen to me, abandoned me and thrown me away? It is so painful and I feel so bad that I want to lay down and die.

R: Jesus has not abandoned you. You must believe and trust Jesus. You will not collapse under the burden of it all, if you are focused on Jesus and give the burden to him to carry... Maria, do you know who Paul is in the Bible?

M: Yes, he went around telling people about Jesus.

R: Yes, but there was more to Paul's life than that. Do you know that Paul suffered so much bad in his life that he wanted to give up too? In 2 Corinthians Paul tells how "we were under great pressure, far beyond our ability to endure, so that we despaired even to life. Indeed, in our hearts we felt the sentence of death..." Remember Maria this was Paul a godly servant of the Lord, yet he suffered and there seemed no way out of it. In Ephesus, people tried to kill him and in Corinth, people accused him of being out of his mind crazy. He was accused of lying and being dishonest with offering money. Those he loved rejected him and Paul's life was filled with suffering, like your life Maria. But like for Paul, God has a purpose in allowing suffering in your life. When someone is really hurting, they want to talk to someone like you who has suffered greatly and come through it praising God and full of faith.

M: I don't like psychiatrist and experts who don't feel hurt. I want to know about the ones like me who are well and still love Jesus. Nobodies that got hurt like me and wanted to give up and didn't who are happy now.

R: You have Maria, who did you meet this summer that has suffered a lot and is trusting God? Her name starts with a J and you received a scholarship to go to her camp.

M: Joni Tada!

R: Jesus comforts suffering people and blesses them with an influence on others that only those who have gone through it have.

Like Paul, all of us who suffer and still trust are going through a kind of schooling. God is training us to be comforters with humility and patience. When you suffer you learn compassion for others who suffer. We are very sensitive to people judging us in our suffering, thinking we are sinful or lack faith. We have a perspective that even a lot of Christians are lacking unfortunately.

We don't blame people for their suffering, we love them because we've been there. God is molding us to become strong in the fire around us, while being patient and gentle in helping others out. But you must remember Maria that Jesus can't teach us if we won't let him. Paul, even in his worst despair, blessed the name of the Lord. He said, "But this happened that we might not rely on ourselves but on God who raises the dead." When you are at the bottom of the pit of despair, you will rub shoulders with God who is the only one who can get you out. He lets us get there in our overconfidence, until we let Him get us out. Give up trying to run away from suffering or trying to understand. Give up condemning yourself and turn to Jesus. Keep turning to him and cry out "I'm drowning...Save me!" He will.

M: Ruth, sometimes your lessons are hard. Please don't get mad at me if I slip off the rock of Jesus and fall flat on my face. I've got to learn how to not fall off. I'm thankful for Jesus, Bruce, Kansas, flowers and talks with you Ruth.

Ruth, Maria and the entire System would continue to struggle with the knowledge and severity of abuse to the parts both in the past and in the present, but God is gracious in His training to not let them become overwhelmed. Each part will learn to deal with the truth in their own time. Each will learn to trust in the midst of testing and receive mercy from God while the world continues to shun them. Their lives appear to start unraveling with too many parts trying to coexist. But Jesus is beginning to weave a tapestry of their lives, to one day lay before the world as a testament of His love and desire to heal all who come to Him.

As the light of His presence starts to illuminate the darker corners of their pit, the way out starts to be revealed through parts when they are at their weakest. Raquel begins writing again on two different levels; one on the prophetic level that speaks to both the

System and the outside world and two, an allegorical style of stories and poems, which speak of desires and pain too hard for the System to verbalize. She began her preparations for the 'Circle Council' meeting to be held in a few weeks. As she pondered its significance, she issued this warning:

The Great Spirit, creator of Mother Earth, gave to his people the Sacred Circle of Harmony and abundance. His people walked the spiritual path. But the men of greed took the Sacred Circle and have traveled the path of materialism and destruction. Because of this, tribe will rise against tribe. Mother Earth will groan and shake from below. The waters will swell. Fire will fall from the sky and will rise up from the belly of Mother Earth. And the eagle will be no more. The deer and the dove will be gone. And it shall be the beginning of the end.

Oh men of greed! How can you own the wind? How can you claim the eagle or the mighty waters of the river? Oh foolish men of greed! Your ways are not wise, for they lead to death.

Bruce and the System paid little attention to the prophetic messages in the beginning. The present concerns of the parts overshadowed any thoughts of the future of the outside world. Whether or not anyone paid attention to her message did not matter to Raquel. Raquel, as with any true prophet, only stated the messages she received from the Great Spirit. Elizabeth Ray would record them for future reference. Most of the prophecies were for the System or those affected by a relationship with the System. The recipients of these prophecies, including myself, would often struggle with understanding their meaning and timing of the message, much the same way we struggle with Biblical prophecy. I categorize them with Biblical prophecy because many can be found in the Bible and were already given by the Prophets. This does not make them any the less valid, because many are meant for personal application today, she is simply reminding the recipient of truths already given.

I listen with great interest to Raquel when she shares these messages, because I too have been given the spiritual gift of prophecy and use it when called upon by the Holy Spirit. Raquel and I both realize that it is not the responsibility of the prophet to make the recipients believe or understand it, simply that we give it in obedience of the Holy Spirit. This will often make us both unpopular and unwelcome with those we are asked to confront.

In the future, Raquel will find that words of encouragement are welcomed but when words are challenging and call for change they are easily dismissed as coming from 'one of those parts.' When her prophecies start coming true, she receives respect from the System but for those individuals on the outside, she is seen as a threat to many. This is of no great concern for her for as she has stated several times, "my duty is to say whatever the Great Spirit tells me... no more or no less." It is her second level of writings that will become her focus, helping those in the process of healing along the difficult path that lay ahead. When more child parts began to emerge, she wrote this poem for them.

Tell me little child
Of your deep desires
Your fairytale wishes
And buried dreams
Of a safe haven of love

Where butterflies dance
And children laugh
Mommies hug
And papas don't hurt
A refuge from beasts
And monsters that are real

Tell me little child
Of your deep desires
Your fairytale wishes
And buried dreams
To be just a little child.

"O Lord, our Lord, how majestic is your name in all the earth!
You have set your glory above the heavens.
From the lips of children and infants you have ordained praise
because of your enemies, to silence the foe and the avenger."
Psalms 8: 1-2

Chapter Six:

"Hungering for Spiritual Truth"

"Everyone who believes that Jesus is the Christ is born of God,
And everyone who loves the father loves his child as well.
This is how we know that we love the children of God:
By loving God and carrying out his commandments."
1 John 5: 1-2

Events began occurring that caused Helper to make a daily log of events and time for Bruce. This did not last very long because some of the parts felt that their privacy was being infringed upon. With the influx of information about additional clans in connecting worlds, a detailed time chart was put together to explain and understand missing time. After looking at the evidence, Helper could now see the missing gaps as time when Functions, Harmers and Guardians were out. As Ruth reported to Bruce about their findings, she expresses some of the frustrations of the different parts.

The next missing time was from 3:40 – 3:50. Helper believes that a Harmer and a Guardian were out at this time. Knives were on the floor and there were several new cuts on Maria's wrist. He believes that since the cuts are not deep, either the Harmer is not serious and only wants to scare Maria, or a Guardian intervened. By the mess that appears on the floor, there must have been a struggle. During the next gaps throughout the day and night, someone raked the leaves, had a coke, looked at children's books, folded the laundry and sabotaged Maria's typed dreams for you waiting in the out-basket. It looks like someone tried to burn them and either had second thoughts or another part retrieved them. Although some parts do not want to accept it, the facts show we still have lost or unaccounted time.

The only ones who seem stressed about it are Liz and Maria. Liz more out of anger at having to share more time with more parts and Maria out of total fear that "I don't want more people living in me. They scare me." Ann is still gone. Raquel says she is in a cave in the cliffs and wants to be left alone. She is trying to figure the logic to this system and is plagued by the diagrams you gave her. She wonders if maybe the system is like an ellipsoid, a possible elliptic paraboloid where all the intercepts are zero. Or she is wondering if it is a hyperbolic paraboloid where the surface is saddle shape. Raquel said she smiled at Ann and wished her well... before leaving. Raquel chuckles and says the true beauty of the system cannot be appreciated by contemplating mathematics, but it must be experienced in the artistic form for its depth and beauty.

The dreams Maria was experiencing were Tabitha's memories at the barn, in the orchard being raped by the Cuban man, Mari in the church confessional, and Tabitha's initiation into the Santeria. Each dream revealed more details of the event. Slowly, she will remember the initiation in increments over the next couple of years. The first went like this:

I am small maybe four. I am with an old black lady at the water. She is telling me that Yemaya has come to take possession. She tells me that when I receive Yemaya, she will walk with me and I can call on her by her special name "Lady of Regla" and she will be my protector. The water circles around me and I give seven pennies to her. Then I wake up.

The last dream she types for Bruce was the most difficult one for her because it is her own memories jumbled together with Tabitha's.

I am asleep and the phone rings. I pick it up and it's Dr. P*****. (Daughter's psychiatrist) He says I'm checking to make sure Claudia is still living with her grandparents. I said yes. He says she will never live with you. You are a terrible parent and I will see to it that social services take your other children as well. I said please don't take my children, I love them. He says you are a bad parent and they hate you. Then another voice comes on the phone. It is the voice of the social worker. He says Claudia hates you and I will find her a group home. You do not know how to be a good mother. You are the cause of all her problems. You have never given her any emotional support. I did. I hugged her and talked with her lots and I protect and care for her. No you are not good enough to be her parent.

Then another voice comes in of Dr. B*****, Claudia's other psychiatrist. He says you are a dysfunctional family and your daughter suffers because you do not provide for her. I am sending her away. I don't say anything to him because he is too mean. Then I hear Jose. You are so stupid mother. Then Sergio says where is your brain? Check with your friends in there. Then the voice changes and it is my father. How stupid can you be? You never do anything right. Get in there and do it over the right way. Move! And don't cry or I'll give you something to cry about. The voice changes and it is my mother. Maria you're useless. Get out of my sight. Then it's my teacher's voice. I won't waste time on you. You have no potential. Go to the back of the room and set there. And then the voice begins to sound far away. It is papa (grandpa). You were born bad. Now get down there (basement) and I'll beat obedience into you if it's the last thing I do. Hurry up. Then I wake up and go inside and Anna is out under the sleeping bag. I come back out and write it like Bruce told me to do.

The truth here is that this dream is not a dream. It is a real experience that happened to Maria from which she had not yet healed. What allowed me to not get upset in reading this in the journal is knowing that healing does comes for Maria in the coming years. Some family members will grow up and mature, while never really knowing who their mom was or who she has become. The health of the family structure has continued to evolve and change to this day. Maybe by the time I finish the third book, their mental and emotional health will have caught up to their mother's. I will not write much about the immediate family's relationship in the first two books except as it is germane to the System's recovery. Know that at the time of Maria's dreams no one in the family accepted or tried to understand Maria's multiplicity. Even if the husband or children suspected something was wrong, they did not try to help her and only put more demands upon her. This is not uncommon within dysfunctional families where abuse has occurred to one or both parents.

In many cultures including the Hispanic culture, problems are to remain within the family and victims are expected to not seek outside help. There is a basic distrust of people in the helping professions because they are not 'family.' This lack of trust was validated and reinforced when Maria dealt with the psychiatrists for Claudia and again when both receive substandard medical care by physicians later in life. In Maria's case, this is compounded by the Catholic Church culture in which she is raised. When professionals in the church and society never take the time to truly understand the family's history, before making decisions that divide and destroy a family structure the results can be devastating. When opportunities arise for true healing to occur with a therapist or pastor, the distrust that has been built within the family makes the healing a much slower and more prolonged process when and if that ever occurs.

One of the affects of more parts moving between levels was described by a function communicating to Bruce, something Ruth was totally unaware of in her reporting:

I have been commissioned by the Keeper of Functions to communicate with you from Level 2. The Keeper of Functions sends his regards and his appreciation for maintaining the confidentiality of Level 2 structure. Your success in passing Test A-1 has resulted in his further communication and the administering of Test A-2. Level 2 is experiencing earthquakes, which are originating from Level 3 and targeting Level 1. The Keeper of Functions approved the release of SA Function to determine the risk factor for Level 2. SA Function used the conduit near the northeastern side of Level 1 to make contact with the key part known as Raquel. This was extremely hazardous for Level 2, as functions have never before entered Level 1. However, it was Keeper of Functions decision that it was necessary to protect the stability of Level 2. SA Function reported his findings back to Keeper of Functions. Level 2 is a stable and highly efficient system. Keeper of Functions is committed to maintaining that efficiency and order. Any outside influence, which might disturb the operation of Level 2, must be taken seriously. It is not the intent of Level 2 to aggravate or threaten. Level 2 wishes to remain out of the conflict between these other levels and will not take sides in the dispute.

As requested, this communication has been forwarded on 3.5 diskette. Level 2 uses Microsoft Word, Version 6.0.
Respectfully submitted, CU

If you think the last sentence of this communiqué a bit odd, remember the process that Helper and Bruce are going through in maintaining order in the System. All the parts were not aware of the Level of Functions and this knowledge would have put some into chaos trying to figure it out. Ann continued her efforts to put the System into a mathematical equation for her own understanding. She went to therapy seeking help from Bruce not for herself, but to establish a structural foundation to help the System become more aware of all the different parts and their function. The following excerpt from a follow-up letter to him illustrates one of her perceived hindrances in accomplishing her goal.

...I know it would be beneficial for Liz to meet you occasionally. The challenge is that Liz refuses to 'do therapy'. She is really scared to death of you and I know why. It is the same reason many of us are nervous around you. We still do not know if we can completely trust you with our feelings or secrets. However, Liz needs a place to let off steam. Take her for another damn walk and try to knock some sense into that thick skull of hers! I'm constantly thinking of ways to trick her into therapy. I've agitated her by telling her she is just a coward. I've tried to bribe her. I've reasoned with her. So far, she's outfoxed me at every **ANN I AM READING EVERYTHING. YOU ARE AN ASSHOLE. I AM NOT AFRAID OF HIM. I TOLD YOU THAT BEFORE. I DON'T LIKE YOU WRITING TO HIM ABOUT ME. AT LEAST I'M REAL. YOU HIDE BEHIND YOUR DAMN STUFF. YOU ARE MORE AFRAID OF HIM THAN I AM. HE DOESN'T SCARE ME. IF YOU ARE SO BRAVE THEN YOU GO IN THAT OFFICE AND LET HIM PICK YOUR BRAIN APPART. I CHALLENGE YOU. YOU DO THERAPY FIRST AND DEPENDING UPON WHAT YOU LOOK LIKE AFTER, I MIGHT CONSIDER IT! I AM NOT WORRIED ABOUT DOING THERAPY BECAUSE I KNOW YOU WON'T. SO JUST QUIT TALKING ABOUT ME. REMEMBER HOW PISSED YOU GOT WHEN RUTH TALKED ABOUT YOU AND GOD. WELL YOU ARE A HYPOCRITE. YOU ARE DOING THE SAME THING TO ME THAT YOU YELLED AT RUTH FOR. ASSHOLE!**
You have no right to be reading my letter. Stop shadowing me. You are always complaining that we never get to express our opinion. Well, I am expressing my opinion. If you have a different opinion, then write him. I do not care what you say to him about me, just stay off the God issue.
THE GOD ISSUE, HUH...HOT ISSUE, REAL HOT ISSUE! THANKS FOR THE ACE IN MY POCKET ANN.

Knock it off Liz! Just leave. I want to finish my letter. I have things to do, but you would not understand the meaning of work, would you.
GO TO HELL. I DON'T NEED TO TAKE THIS SHIT FROM YOU. I'M OUT OF HERE.
I wish you would take her for a walk and lose her!

...On the issue of forced switching, I have not observed you forcing the switches. It is Maria and the rest of us who struggle with the control of switching. Maria tries to prevent some alters from appearing (as if she can!) and pulls other alters (like Louise) out when she wants to escape. Some of us become stubborn and refuse to allow her to escape inside. We don't want to be there anymore than she does. At times, because of struggles between adults, a child is forced out. I also believe there might be triggers in your office that can force switching like an old rabbit hanging out of a basket. Can this trigger Anna? I don't know.

...Also sometimes a word or particular stance might cause it. Sitting like a priest on that white couch causes stress on some parts. Never wear all black, as that could be a definite trigger. Old Spice is another trigger. Something as simple as crayons on your table can cause it, as there is somebody who likes crayons inside (Mariann). I looked away yesterday to avoid a switch. Whoever wanted the crayons was afraid of you when you sat between the crayons and me.

...I find your explanation of the diagnosis interesting. I do not believe in miracles that is Ruth's bag. However, the fact that you observed dissociative behavior in Maria from the onset tells me that you are alert. Your statement that MPD's with long histories in the system learn techniques to hide their MPD is fascinating. I guess in the long run we should be grateful these techniques didn't work with you, it would have made therapy longer.

There would be no rest for the System in the next few months as more details are revealed about their complex structure and the memories held by those still emerging. Outside family issues would also increase and add to the stress already overwhelming their daily life. Maria's mother was diagnosed with cancer and the prognosis was not good. High blood pressure complicated the need for surgery and the fear was real that she might die during surgery. When Maria wanted to go to the hospital to support her mother, the family refused... only to chastise her later for not supporting her mom like her sister. Her sister was the one who told Maria the family didn't want her there. The sister also caused great anxiety for Maria's daughter Claudia who was now living with her grandparents.

The forced separation between mother and daughter only increased the loneliness and feelings of helplessness they both endured. The mother's illness brought out intense feelings from various parts of the System. Preparations began by the Surface People on how to handle and respond to the possibility of death. When Maria attempted to express her concern to her mom about being sad over her having cancer, she was rebuked and told to 'grow up and just accept it'. She was not allowed to show any feelings or speak to her daughter because the mother didn't want her granddaughter upset. Instead, the sister was telling Claudia the most dire situation and wondering why Maria wasn't calling or attempting to help either mother or daughter. The System struggled with the control constantly put on Maria by the family. Ruth wrote to Bruce of their concern:

Maria was given a list of things to do in case of death. Her mother informed her that she must take care of her father and be responsible for making sure her father's medical coverage is kept secure. Why Maria, if they always tell her she can never do anything right? Maria's mother plans to control her from the grave. We plan to talk about this at length. Maria is in no condition to take on anymore responsibility. Taking care of a disabled daughter and a self-centered, macho son is enough responsibility for a healthy, strong parent, let alone a weak one like Maria. There seems to be in us a great obedience to the 'Honor thy Father and thy Mother' commandment.

I'm very concerned about Maria being able to weather this storm. Harmers are continuing to threaten her and accusing her of causing this situation with the mother. Liz is agitated and doesn't do well with Maria's parents. She feels trapped and unsure of how to deal with the present situation with more parts coming out. Tabitha is stabilized but confused. I need advice on how we're going to explain 'mommy' to Tabitha. She keeps saying, "I want my mommy." How do we explain to her that she can't have her 'mommy'? I want to make sure what I say is the right approach. Liz thinks it's cruel to ignore the plea of the child, yet no one knows what to say.

Anna is still passive and non-verbal. She came out twice on the porch during the night while Maria was having difficulty sleeping. She just curls up and sucks her thumb. Inside she stays in her hole most of the time. I have been able to hold her several times, but she gives no indication if this comforts her or traumatizes her. I don't know how to communicate with her. Do you have suggestions?

Muy Malo is not coming out of her hole. This child seems to be the most out of control. She does not talk to me when I attempt to comfort her. She just puts up her hands like she is afraid I am going to hit or grab her. What do I do? One of the most frustrating aspects of this is that we can't seem to focus on one problem at a time. If we could just handle one issue, correct it and move on, it would be beneficial. But we have the memory work, the disability, Jose, the family and now Maria's mother's illness all coming at the same time. It's difficult.

During this time, Louise was trying to cope with the allegations of abuse by the children of the System about the priests of the Catholic Church. After hearing Mari's confirmation of it in detail, she had the added burden of accepting the possibility that the hierarchy of the local church knew what was happening at the time and did nothing to stop it. She started testing many things she had accepted as truth and now turned to Bruce for specific answers. In a few weeks it would be this list of questions that caused Bruce to seek help and find me.

Dear Bruce,

Thank you very much for talking to me on Thursday. I have been thinking a lot about what you said and I don't know what would make me happy. I guess for there to be peace and everyone to be happy and healthy. But I'm not sure because I never thought about me being happy. That is a hard question.

I know you are busy and take care of a lot of people, but you said in your letter to me that I could ask you questions about God. I have always had a lot of questions and when you have time, maybe you could tell me the answers. I would appreciate it very much. These are my questions:

1. Why didn't God just write the Bible instead of having people do it who could make mistakes?
2. Why do people look at the same verse and understand it differently?
3. What color was Jesus?
4. If Jesus was the Son of God, was he around when God made the world? If he was, then why did he have to be born on earth?
5. What happened to Jesus' dad, Joseph?
6. Did Jesus know growing up that he was the Son of God?
7. Why did Jesus have to be baptized if he was the Son of God and had no sin?
8. Why did Jesus let the people treat him so bad if he was the Son of God?
9. Did Jesus ever get angry at things that happened to him or was he always nice?
10. Did Jesus say we have to forgive everybody for things they have done to us?
11. Does Jesus think women are as good as men? If he does, then why didn't he have any women apostles?
12. Why would God let his son die in such a cruel way?
13. When we take communion, does the bread and wine really become the body and blood of Jesus? How does that happen and does that make people cannibals?
14. How could Jesus be a human being and God at the same time?
15. Does Jesus love everybody including people who kill and really hurt other people?
16. Do people who have never heard of Jesus go to Hell?
17. What about little babies who die, where do they go?
18. Why is there so much suffering for us, if Jesus loves us so much?
19. Why are there so many different Christian churches and why do they fight so much?
20. If Jesus forgives like Ruth says, all our sins, then why do I have to go to the priest and get penance? Why do I have to do penance for my sins?
21. The Pope says that Mary went up to heaven like Jesus did and didn't die. We celebrate the assumption of Mary in honor of that. But Ruth's Bible doesn't tell about that, why? Did Mary not die?
22. Was Mary sinless? Is she the Queen of Heaven? Can she forgive sins?
23. I don't really understand what trinity means. How can God be three persons in one, is it like parts? Jesus is God and the Son of God. How can he be both and what is the difference?
24. Is God a person?
25. What is the Holy Spirit and is it a person?
26. Why does God let Satan hurt people? Why doesn't God punish Satan and make him obey?
27. Why didn't God stop the snake from being in the garden?
28. Why do I have to be punished because Eve ate the apple, I didn't?

29. *Why are there so many different types of sin like original sin, venial sin and mortal sin? Is one sin worse than another sin?*
30. *I'm not important, why would Jesus care about me?*
31. *How do you really get to heaven? Is there really a way to know for sure?*
32. *Christians get me all mixed up because they all say different things. I never know who is telling the truth. Also I lose track of long lectures. I just want to know who Jesus really is and how do I get to heaven?*
33. *Could God take heaven away from me once he promises it to me?*
34. *Does God always keep his promises?*
35. *In your letter you said, 'Some Catholic churches teach rules and obedience, while others teach the love of Christ.' What does the love of Christ mean?*

I hope this is not too many questions for you. Sometimes I listen in Ruth's church and I get mixed up terribly. Sometimes Ruth talks too much and gets me mixed up. Ruth is nice and I don't mean to say she isn't, but I sometimes can only think on one verse at a time, not thirty. I also wanted you to know that I've been thinking about what you said about the Pope and the Catholic Church being infallible. To be infallible means to be perfect and not make mistakes. How can the Pope always do that unless he is God? And if the Catholic Church is infallible, then how come they change things and say different things in different places? For instance, I was taught that it has words like 'Nihil Obstat and Imprimatur', which means that it comes under the authority of the Catholic Church and is true. But sometimes, different books with these things say different things and totally mix me up. Maybe I'm just stupid and don't understand complicated things. I just don't know how you can keep changing things and say you are infallible unless God changes his mind. But then if that were true, there would be a new Bible written every year with God's changes. And I don't think God changes his mind. Anyway, I have to think more on these things. I don't want to say anything bad about the Catholic Church, but I really want to know the truth so that I can follow and obey what is right.

Sincerely, Louise

Over the next seven years, Louise would find answers to many of her questions, but at what cost to her understanding of her culture and religious heritage. Question 23, dealing with the Trinity was not hard for her to understand. Three-in-one was not a difficult concept for her.

Following the disclosure of the mother's cancer, everyone noticed how it was causing a ripple effect throughout Preservation. An hour phone conversation with an Aunt proved very disconcerting at several levels, most of all in Preservation as the person talking with the aunt could not be identified. Both the Aunt and the part knew a lot about the family history and discussed a myriad of topics including Catholicism, Christianity (which the Aunt professed to be), parental and family control issues, suffering and endurance, therapy, depression, spiritual warfare, abuse, children and cancer. The part never revealed too much information or about being DID, yet the rest of the System was upset having 'someone' inside knowing as much as she seemed to know. Efforts to force her to come out or identify her were unsuccessful. She would later identify herself as Elizabeth Ray.

Ruth would soon make a unilateral decision based on her direction from Jesus, to go to Nevada after the mother's surgery to speak with her about forgiveness in case she would die soon after the surgery. This decision raised valid complaints from many in Preservation who feared disobeying the parents. A small majority of the Council of Preservation approved the decision and let her go, but wanted discipline for her making the decision without calling a Council meeting first. Ruth's motive was stated, *"But I want her to know that no matter what happened in the past this system will do what is right. What is right is that I forgive her and I show her my love. She can take it or refuse it but I did what is right and offered it to her. I don't care what the family thinks."*

The mother didn't die and 'Maria's disobedience' angered both parents. The opportunity for reconciliation with the mother would have to wait awhile longer. The endured wrath of the father removed any call for discipline by Council after her return. Outside of Maria's continuing concern for her mother, the focus of the System returned to the issues of therapy and abuse. When Bruce asked why the family seems to be depending on Maria to care for the father after their lifelong statements to the contrary, Liz offered this perspective:

You want to know why everyone depends on Maria when they consider her incompetent and stupid. It is because Maria is the best one of the three. Donna is not trusted. She blows money on drugs like it is water and she is dishonest. The family knows this and knows she would never follow through on anything. Richard doesn't want to be bothered. Besides, doesn't the culture dictate that the woman does all the work and the man reaps the benefits? So you have Maria. One who is easily controlled and manipulated. One who would never be dishonest and never complain, who would do what you asked and gets shit done.

The reason everyone continues to make fun of her and tell her she is stupid is because it's power. They all know that Maria hungers to be accepted by the family. She will work until she drops for that acceptance. If you tell her she is smart and competent then you lose that control. It's the only thing that makes sense to me. I need to go for another walk as soon as your cold gets better. Schedule me for after January 8th.

Circumstances at home made it too difficult for the System to afford sessions twice a week so they reluctantly saw Bruce once a week. The need for healing of memories for the 'Hole Children'- Tabitha, Anna and Angelina, was obvious to everyone. The System decided to let Maria and the children have the office visits while delegating their concerns to letter writing. This too had to be cut back as the volume was becoming overwhelming for Bruce. Ruth and Helper attempted to help Maria and the kids between office visits on the inside, but without a lot of success. Ruth sent a letter describing the state of the System at this time.

Tabitha informed me when we left this morning, that I had to help Anna make a bunny (like the one in your office) and Tabitha make Ollie (like your Ollie) with the hole so Tabitha can make him talk. Tabitha holds Ollie now and Jesus holds Tabitha. I asked Tabitha if she wanted to play telephone (as you do) sometime, but I didn't get an answer. Anna is still not communicating verbally with me. I asked Tabitha if Anna talks and she said, "Anna no talk." Muy Malo is still out of control and I'm unable to comfort her.

Maria continues to have nightmares, one of the most disturbing is a hand holding a man's heart. She wakes up and is afraid to go back to sleep. From what I hear, they seem to be fragments of traumas, but I'm not sure. She will see a rat, then be in the pink room, then a long dark hallway in a church. She seems to be withdrawing from her family. Most of the time she is out is curled up in the sleeping bag on the porch holding her teddy bear. She seems drained and is escaping to Kansas more and more. She tells me the voices say if she continues to tell anymore, she will be punished and the counselor will get sicker. One voice in particular said it was very powerful and in control. It warned her that if she cares about the safety of the children and you, she will not tell any more.

Louise appears to be faring somewhat better. She still is cooking and reading but shows signs of exhaustion. She is experiencing the side effects of the medication of thirst, dizziness and nausea, similar to Maria.

I spoke with Raquel and apparently SID pulled out of the agreement about Circle Council meeting soon. SID needed assurance for the Harmers that they would not be trapped or killed. Everything is on hold until Raquel can guarantee safety for the leader of the Harmers and that there will be no invasion of Harmer territory while their leader is in council. There is much more communication going on in the System than Maria realizes. Ann especially is doing a lot of internal networking, while talking with several of us about assertiveness training. The parts are now aware of each other's existence, location and name (with Core, Dorcas and Elizabeth Ray being the exceptions to date). *We are continually learning of each other's role and function.*

Daniel of the Clan of Argus is monitoring us closely. He is extremely protective of Mariann and still not allowing any other parts but the Clan to see her. However, Daniel and Mari are communicating often with Raquel.

Helper and I tried putting the pieces of the puzzle together last week that we have. So far Anna holds a memory of a heart and a knife. Tabitha holds memories of the pink room, the barn, a basement and possibly an attack in the orchard. Muy Malo holds trauma with being cut. Raquel holds memory of the attack at thirteen in the orchard. Mariann holds memories of the church along with Mari. Maria holds the memory of the sailor at sixteen (?) and Xalapa (?). We are not sure if the memories are shared or who exactly experienced them.

Maria has been very concerned about you being sick. I suggested to her to pray every day to God for your strength and the medication to work on the infection. She sometimes thinks that she causes you many problems. Maria needs more than forty-five minutes a week of support. The time between visits is too long. There are too many unresolved issues and too much instability within the System right now. She needs to interact with caring people who won't let her give up again. Several of us inside are concerned that she wants to die. She has begun talking about heaven and not being a problem to people anymore. She sometimes picks up the medication bottles and just stares at them for a long time.

Is there anything inexpensive that can supplement the weekly session and provide support for Maria? Would it be beneficial or not? Why isn't the medication for depression taking affect? How are we going to get her to see the psychiatrist when she is deathly afraid of him?

Finally, we held a council meeting and agreed that we want Anna out with you as much as she needs to heal. Drawing for you seems to be working. I'm encouraging Maria not to resist her coming out in your office. It scares Maria when she feels Anna coming out. When we have the whole picture of Anna's story, it will be important for Maria to hear it to help understand what her nightmares mean. She is still very reluctant to want to know but knowing is better than guessing.

A few days later:

I have passed on what you told me to the others and everyone agrees with your hypothesis taken from Anna's drawings. I asked Tabitha and she said her dog's name was Lady. She identified it from a book as a collie. She said that one day "papa took us far into trees...put rope on Lady... then Lady be dead." I asked how it happened, but she would not tell me. It was obvious that she was becoming quite scared, so I changed the subject. It would explain Muy Malo as the most out of control and Maria's dream of the heart in the hand.

Marie has begun to question her position on our childhood. There are too many discrepancies between what she led herself to believe and what everyone else experienced. It has been difficult for her to accept that the person she loved and admired actually was an evil person. It is causing her whole world to turn upside down. I tried to explain that maybe when she was out, he seemed nice and she never was hurt by him. It happened to another part and she didn't know it. I tried to comfort her by letting her know it was not her fault for holding on to something she wanted to be true, but that now we as a system must acknowledge what happened and heal from it, so that we can go on with our life. It will take her awhile to absorb this, but I will be there for support.

Bruce had Maria focus on reading in Ephesians about the expected behavior between a husband and wife. While Maria understood the role of the wife and had tried to be just that, she was not able to comprehend the role of the husband being modeled by Jesus. Her letter of response to Bruce asked for clarification:

I asked Ruth about Ephesians 5 verse 23 that says the husband is the head of the wife, like the leader and in Hebrews 13:17 it says to obey your leaders and submit, so isn't the husband the leader we are to obey and submit to him? I asked what submission meant and she said it is to yield to the will of another and obey meant to follow the commands of another. To me they sound the same. I am still confused about it but I learned I need to do better in some things as a wife. But I also learned that a husband is to be gentle to his wife and make her safe, like a shepherd I think.

What if you had a wife that was not real smart and made mistakes, forgot things, made your toast too dark and forgot to iron your striped shirt? What if you had a wife that maybe had parts and frustrated you? Would you hit her to make her obey you? What would you do with her? What if you didn't know she had parts when you married her, would you throw her away? I'm just wondering. Did you find a school class for me to learn more about Jesus? Louise and I want to go together. I want to go to school and be smart like Ann.

The volume of messages began to lessen, as the System became more aware of their own internal structure. The messages were now more focused on their involvement in therapy with Bruce and internally between themselves. Leaders became more assertive in their roles and decisions were being made for the 'good of the System'. After the first Circle Council meeting was held, SID wrote to Bruce about their concerns:

I AM SID, PRINCE OF THE HARMERS OF THE WORLD OF LABYRINTH. YOU ARE ONE WHO LISTENS, ALSO KNOWN AS DOLPHIN AND THE OUTSIDER.

HELPER (LEADER OF THE SURFACE PEOPLE OF THE LAND OF PRESERVATION), DANIEL (PROTECTOR HEAD OF THE CLAN OF ARGUS), KEEPER OF FUNCTIONS (AMBASSADOR OF THE WORLD OF FUNCTIONS), AND KING OF THE LIGHTS (HIGHEST ELDER OF THE GUARDIANS OF ELYSIAN FIELDS) SEND THEIR GREETINGS.

ON THE FOURTH DAY OF THE SECOND MONTH OF THE DAWN OF THE NEW YEAR, QUIET WALKER (ALSO KNOWN AS TURTLE) WELCOMED US INTO THE CIRCLE COUNCIL ON SACRED MOUNTAIN.

ONE OF THE TOPICS OF DISCUSSION CENTERED AROUND THE WILLINGNESS OF THE SYSTEM TO REVEAL FULL KNOWLEDGE OF OUR HISTORY TO DOLPHIN. WE ARE NOT ABLE TO COME TO AGREEMENT ON THIS ISSUE WITHOUT FURTHER INFORMATION. THEREFORE, WE REQUEST ANSWERS TO THE FOLLOWING QUESTIONS. UPON RECEIPT OF YOUR REPLY, THE LEADERS WILL RECONVENE THE CIRCLE COUNCIL TO DISCUSS OUR DECISION.

QUESTION 1: DO YOU CARE WHAT HAPPENS TO OUR SYSTEM OR ARE WE JUST ANOTHER CASE? IF SO, WHY?

QUESTION 2: CAN YOU GUARANTEE SAFETY FOR THE SYSTEM?

QUESTION 3: HOW CAN YOU BE SURE NO HARM WILL COME TO THE SYSTEM IF THE STORIES ARE TOLD?

QUESTION 4: ARE YOU GOING TO ABANDON THE SYSTEM ONCE THE STORIES ARE TOLD OR ARE YOU GOING TO HELP THE SYSTEM LEARN SKILLS TO POSITIVELY RELATE TO THE OUTSIDE WORLD?

QUESTION 5: DO YOU BELIEVE WE ARE DEMONS?

QUESTION 6: WILL WE RETAIN OUR OWN IDENTITIES?

QUESTION 7: DO YOU UNDERSTAND US AND RESPECT US?

QUESTION 8: WHAT ARE YOUR GOALS AND OBJECTIVES FOR US?

QUESTION 9: HOW DO YOU PLAN TO ACCOMPLISH THOSE GOALS AND OBJECTIVES?

QUESTION 10: WILL YOU MAINTAIN OUR CONFIDENTIALITY UNLESS WE GIVE OUR PERMISSION TO DISCUSS US WITH SOMEONE ELSE?

And this from 'CU':

Greetings from Keeper of Functions and Level 2. Unfortunately, we are unable to fulfill your request to communicate by diskette, as we have not received a reply from the diskette we sent when we previously communicated with you.

Keeper of Functions wishes to inform you that SA function and TC function have been terminated. Their services are no longer required. A request came from Level 1 to create a SL function (sex lover function). Word was sent to Level 1 that we are unable to fulfill the command as functions are task performers only. They have no functions that connect with relationships and emotions.

Keeper of Functions is pleased to inform you that you have successfully completed test A-2. Therefore, unless your answers to Circle Council's questions are unacceptable, Level 2 will vote affirmatively for support of Dolphin (Bruce) *and his therapy work with the system.*

Kindest Regards,
CU

The counseling sessions will take a difficult turn over the next few weeks. Child parts that have been hidden for most of the System's life are about to be revealed. One encouraging move will be the revelation of Elizabeth Ray as the holder of history. The door of trust was being opened very wide which made the possibility of expressing even deeper pain now a reality. Was Bruce up to the task that God was laying in front of him? That was what Circle Council wanted to know. Ruth thought she was overwhelmed with trying to provide Christian counseling for her abused sisters in the knowledge she had to date. Would she be able to standfast in her faith in the midst of the onslaught that was coming? Maria was becoming more fragile with each revelation. Her pain drew her closer to God each day but for what reason?

Would the burden that was increasing on her take her to suicide and the easiest way out, or would the grace of God touch her with a desire to survive to find out His purpose for her? Liz was ready to bolt, to run anywhere that was out of this life she knew. Could her anger be channeled by God to add value to the System? Could Ann explain and understand logically and rationally the reason for the System's existence... and do it without God's intervention?

"He has said to me, 'My Grace is sufficient for you,
for power is perfected in weakness."
2 Corinthians 12:9

"And not only this, but we also exult in our tribulations,
knowing that tribulation brings about perseverance;
and perseverance, proven character;
and proven character, hope;
and hope does not disappoint,
because the love of God has been poured out,
within our hearts through the Holy Spirit who was given to us.
For while we were still helpless,
At the right time Christ died for us..."
Romans 5:3 – 6

Chapter 7:

"Seeking the Paths with Meaning"

"I have seen the task which God has given the sons
of men with which to occupy themselves.
He has made everything appropriate in its time.
He has also set eternity in their heart,
Yet so that man will not find out the work which God
has done from the beginning even to the end...
The Preacher <u>Ecclesiastes 3:10 - 11</u>

"Therefore I ask you not to lose hope at my tribulations
on your behalf, for they are for your glory."
<u>Ephesians 3:13</u>

It was Valentine's Day 1995 when the first of the Pod Children came to the surface unexpectedly. Ann wrote about the chronology of events for Bruce, not sure who it was that she was writing about. When he received Ann's letter, he knew his child client roster had increased.

Chronology of events:

Tuesday 1AM – Louise snaps. Runs and hides in closet. Ruth, Liz and I attempt to coax her out. She / we are unable to breathe. Finally able to get her inside at approximately 5AM. I take over.

Tuesday AM – Maria out to fix Sergio his breakfast. Tells him she is going to make him a very special dinner for his birthday and a cake. Sergio goes to work.

Tuesday 8AM – Donna calls crying hysterically. Ruth handles it to screen for Maria. She has a broken ankle in a cast. She's mixing drugs and is incoherent. Ruth attempts to calm Donna down. Donna continues screaming, crying and swearing. Ruth spends about 35 minutes attempting to help her.

After the phone call, Tabitha comes out and begins picking up lint and scrubbing the rugs with her hands. She's very intense about cleaning the floor. Ruth attempts to calm her and get her back inside.

Tuesday approx. 11:15AM – Maria out making Jello salad for Sergio. She becomes nauseous and goes to lie down. Loses control to someone and starts rolling on the floor. The part is very frightened. Ruth and Maria are shadowing and Ruth says the part starts shaking and hyperventilating. Ruth attempts to calm her down as the part goes into convulsion type jerks. Ruth tries to come out to call beeper number but is unable to maintain control and part switches out again. Part cries out, "He has 58 guns. They are locked up. He killed the horses and the puppy. He put gun to Leah's head (Lila?) and said I'm going to kill you and then laughed. Donna jumped over the fence and broke her leg. Lights. Grandma come and help me. I'm in the canyon. I'm cold grandma. I can't find my ears Grandma. I can't feel me Grandma. Grandma come get me. Grandma he got 58 guns." Ruth attempts to find out part's name. Part says, "Grandma it is me your sweetheart. Grandma I want you to come get me. I'm cold and it's dark. Grandma my eyes go dark and then light. Grandma..."

Ruth panics and tries to keep part talking. Plays phone games trying to reach you. At about 2PM the part disappears. There is lost time of about 40 minutes. Bruce calls about 4PM.

I speak to Raquel after the phone call from Bruce. Raquel says Mariann is approximately 6 or 7 years old. She was molested by the priest. She says it could be Mariann but she does not know for sure. She says there is another part in the North who is the holder of history, very elusive but shadows all. Keeps the record of the system's life. She might know Greek Mythology. Raquel has very limited contact with her. Raquel then recites a poem to me "Elizabeth Ray went out to play one day in the month of May." She will not explain her little rhyme or what it has to do with our conversation and then leaves. (Until now, no one except Elizabeth Ray knows about CORE or the Pod Children.)

Sergio comes home and finds Tabitha out eating Tapioca. Tells Ruth the children are not allowed out except in the house when Maria is alone. Ruth attempts to explain to him that sometimes it is difficult to keep the little ones in. Sergio orders her to do it and says he does not want to be embarrassed, and orders Ruth not to talk to Donna. He tells her to stop dressing in a flirtatious manner with flowers in her hair and pants. Ruth questions Sergio about what is inappropriate. He gets mad and says just do what I tell you and Ruth abides. Liz immediately comes out and begins to argue with him. He tells her to go back inside and give him Maria.

Maria has nightmares again, talking in her sleep. Sergio says she was talking to her brother again and asking him why she gets thrown against the wall.

Wednesday morning I prepared the chronology of events to the best of my knowledge.

Note: Sergio has more knowledge about the system. He is now calling our names when he wants one of us. He knows that it is Louise for sex, Maria or Louise for cleaning and cooking, Ann for finances, appointments, discussion and discipline for Jose. He also recognizes Liz and tells her by name to go away. He does not call Ruth, Jennifer, Marie, or Raquel. He is aware of Tabitha and seems to know her name. I believe he orders Louise to tell him.

Things calmed down to only one or two letters a day between sessions and now by fax. Each part seemed to use their own fonts for identification and individualization from other parts. They had done this from the time they started writing. It is also interesting to note that different parts have different handwriting styles as well. After a short time, only the children continue to communicate by letter. The adults prefer to write emails.

This is Liz. When she comes in today I want you to get on her case about allowing Jose to treat her like he did yesterday. Hiding in the shed is not going to stop it. And I am tired of her making excuses for the little shithead that maybe she did something to make him upset. Yeah she did something, she busted her butt making him his favorite dinner and a birthday cake.

Why does she allow that kid to treat her like that? He is getting worse. I don't need to take this shit. I'm tired of always taking this shit. I'm tired of being a part. I want my own life. I hate being trapped by them.

Personally, I never would have gone through the trouble of making him a cake. He didn't deserve it. I don't understand why she always forgives him and still bends over backwards to please him. She's got to learn not to be so good! She is pathetic. And I don't want to take anymore crap from shithead.

Jose will change his attitude in about 6 years when he matures as a young man away at college and becomes a Christian. Until that time he is a brilliant blessing one minute and machismo shithead the next, kind of like the pain-in-the-ass I was for my mom. None of Maria's children seemed to want to know much about their mother's behavior for a long time, except to tell her she needs help. More on that later. Bruce responded to SID's / Council's questions shortly after this incident:

Prince of the Harmers of the World of Labyrinth:

Greetings and regards to you and to the other members of Circle Council: Helper, Leader of the Surface People; Daniel, Protector and Head of the Clan of Argus; Keeper of Functions, Ambassador of the Functions of the World of Functions; and King of Lights, Highest Elder of the Guardians of Elysian Fields.

I was pleased to hear of your meeting together as Circle Council and pleased to receive your letter with the questions it contained. I will endeavor to answer these questions as best I can and will welcome any follow-up questions that any of you have.

Question 1: Do you care?(see questions the end of chapter 3)
I do indeed care very much what happens to your system. When I have been asked this question before, by others, I

have responded that no one could pay me enough money to fake caring for my clients with whom I work. If I did not care, I would not be able to effectively work with you, nor would I have been able to stay in relationship with you this long.

Question 2: Can you guarantee...?
By myself, no. With the cooperation of those of you who are the system, yes, to the point that anyone's safety can be assured. I will do everything in my power to help your system protect itself and I will work with any and all of you to assure this safety. As has been demonstrated already however, I cannot protect you from the current living situation. To protect yourselves in this situation, you must all choose to cooperate to assure your own safety. I will assist in this anyway I can.

Question 3: How can you be sure no harm...?
Again, we will all work together to assure safety from inside. I have worked with others who have parts inside and stories such as those your system has. Whenever these stories are told, there are parts who believe that they must hurt the system. They believe this because of their fear of outside attack, or because they have been convinced by an abuser they must never tell, or because they simply do not wish to bear the pain of telling. With the cooperation of the system, these parts can be helped to survive the telling and the system as a whole will experience less terror and pain.

As far as outside safety, none of the people from the past can harm you now. Most are long gone and those who are not do not need to know that you have told. Whatever threats they made are either null or void or can be defended against by the system and by the work I do with you. Already, some of the children have told stories and have come to no external harm for it. Internal system cooperation is valid in assuring safety. *(What Bruce could not have foreseen, was the way the spiritual enemy would challenge that safety through the Catholic system and through extended family members. What he did have was trust in Jesus to protect them and that has happened.)*

Question 4: Are you going to abandon...?
I will continue to work with the system not only to get through the stories, but also to help you all decide how you will deal with the outside world. This will particularly be true in terms of protecting yourselves from harm in your current living conditions. I will work with you as long as the system agrees there is need. As I have discussed with several of the Surface People before, I will continue to charge for my time, because this is how I make my living.

Question 5: Do you believe we are demons?
No. I do believe that demons are real and that some people have demonic presences. However, I do not believe that you are demons. There was an unfortunate remark made by a pastor regarding all of you, to the effect that you must all be demons. This was foolish to an extreme and reflected the man's lack of knowledge and understanding of you.

At the beginning, I considered the possibility that there might be demonic presences within your system. I encountered one part (I have been told now that this part was a Harmer) who was angry enough to credibly pass for a demon; but there is an absence of evil in your system that makes demonic involvement unlikely. Additionally, even those who have initially worked against my efforts with the Surface People appear to be interested only in protecting the system, not in destroying it. *(Yemaya stayed hidden from Bruce for the most part, while stirring up the Harmers to do what they were created to do. She continually warned Tabitha and the Hole Children not to tell of her presence, or she couldn't protect them from the 'real danger'. Early attempts at exorcising this spiritual influence failed, because one part would agree to tell her to go and another would invite her back. Getting a consensus of faith to do this among the small children, some of whom that haven't even been identified yet, would be particularly hard to do.)*

Question 6: Will we retain our individual identities?
This is entirely up to all of you. Some multiples decide to merge many or all of their parts into a single person. Others decide to maintain individual identities but reorganize for optimal functioning. Still others decide on various ways of cooperating internally to best function both inside and out. I cannot and indeed will not, make these decisions for you. Each of you and all of you must decide and agree on what is best.

Question 7: Do you understand and respect us?
I understand you as well, I suppose, as anyone who is an outsider can. Because I have worked with multiples before, I understand much about the process of becoming multiple and the healing that needs to take place because of the horrible things that have happened to your system. I will never claim to truly understand, because I haven't had the experiences you have had.

I do respect you. I not only respect you I believe that you exist and that each of you have rights and obligations that have to be worked out in the system. I also respect you as individuals. I will not exploit your existence in any way. I have worked with enough multiples now so that the novelty of it has worn off; thus I am not going to do or say things simply because I'm intrigued with the concept of you being a multiple. I also will never make a spectacle of you on TV talk shows, no pop literature, nothing like this.

Questions 8 & 9:What are your goals…?
Ultimately, you must all decide what your goals and objectives are. In terms of my work with you, my goals are the following:

1. Working with you to maintain the physical safety of the system.
2. Working with you to create safe places where any who are experiencing flashbacks or trauma memories may go to rest and get away from the terrible feelings that go with these memories.
3. Reducing (and eventually eliminating) the power and control that memories create for you as individuals and as a system. This will be accomplished by having the various memories told and reviewed until the part telling the story no longer fears the memory.
4. Supporting all of you as you decide how to reorganize yourselves as we accomplish this work.
5. Supporting you all in any other ways that I can which are appropriate to our relationship.

Question 10: Will you maintain our confidentiality…?
Yes, absolutely. The only individuals I'll ever talk to who know you is the psychiatrist and then only after I've been given permission to do so. I may occasionally discuss your case with a colleague of mine, but I will never identify you directly to a colleague, or never give details sufficient to identify you. I trust these answers are sufficient. If you desire further clarification, more information, or have new questions, please do not hesitate to contact me. With regards, Bruce.

With the increase in child parts surfacing, Ruth enlisted the help of Marie in providing care for the children. Apparently, Marie was the part often out when Maria's kids were preschoolers and she helped raise them. She began giving Ruth advice to funnel to Bruce for activities to use in his sessions with the children. The first suggestion was a burrito picnic with Tabitha to review her own story done in crayon drawings. A Spanish vocabulary list was given to him to make it easier for him to communicate with Tabitha. Eventually, even the Little Ones wanted to go to see Bruce, so they could participate in the fun. Ann told them no, as they were not 'sick' like the children who needed to see Bruce, which they understood. The improved situation for Bruce to work with the children forced an emergency council meeting of the Surface People to allow appropriate physical touch by Bruce. The outcome of that meeting was the following instructions from Ann.

*We have had a special council meeting to address the issue of physical contact with the system. We have come to the agreement at this time that we will allow **APPROPRIATE** physical contact with Tabitha, Anna and Muy Malo. Appropriate physical contact is defined as the following:*
1. *Children allowed to curl up next to you in reading the stories or when they are afraid.*
2. *Bruce allowed to help children with earrings, shoes or items in hair.*
3. *Bruce allowed to hug the children.*
4. *Children allowed to touch Bruce's face and hands.*

The following is not allowed:
1. *Children allowed to show 'cortas' (cuts) under the clothes.*
2. *Children taking any clothes off other than shoes.*
3. *Children looking under Bruce's clothing (i.e.: looking for Jesus inside)*
4. *Children kissing Bruce.*
5. *Children wanting to set in Bruce's lap.*

Bruce is not allowed to have physical contact with adult parts. If the rules are violated, a protector will switch out. Word has gone to Level 2 and 3 about the issue of physical contact and the leaders of those levels are in agreement with the conditions established by us.

All leaders realize that children need support, nurturing and physical contact to heal, however they also know of past abuse with physical contact. They are extremely careful to avoid further trauma of children and if you abide by the rules, there will be no problems.

Also realize that there is a lot of shadowing going on when you are with Tabitha. Daniel especially is monitoring closely your interaction with Tabitha. He must be careful for Mariann's sake. I've heard from Raquel that Levels 2 and 3 are listening in and monitoring your approach with Tabitha. Ruth, Marie, Jennifer, Helper and occasionally Liz, Louise and I are also monitoring the sessions. After every session, a council meeting is called to discuss it. So far, everyone has been pleased. I however, do not like going through this with the children, as I am extremely humiliated.

Ruth was relieved when Marie offered to take over the playtime with the children. She observed Marie's skill in this area and regretted she hadn't known sooner. Marie setup various games and activities for all the children who wanted to participate. She located the activity in a meadow area inside near Ann's place, a spot where all the children could see what was going on from their safe places. It wasn't long before the subject of sharing was needed to be discussed and help from Bruce was requested. Muy Malo was the only one not participating with Tabitha, Anna, Penny and the Little Ones, but she was observing from her hole.

Helper was organizing activities for the adults, like recording their particular style of music to share with one another, for the purpose of getting to know one another's taste. In his plan to gain knowledge about one another, he asked that they share their favorite books, foods, heroes, etc. He was currently in session with Circle Council going over Bruce's reply to their questions.

Jennifer had received word that the father was planning to visit in mid-March. This information was withheld from Maria until the night before he arrived. Liz knew and panicked. The System began a process of reorganizing itself for better management and care of itself. Bruce received a response from SID about his answers to Circle Council.

THE MEMBERS OF THE CIRCLE COUNCIL GRATEFULLY APPRECIATE YOUR TIMELY RESPONSE TO OUR LETTER.

CIRCLE COUNCIL HAS RECONVENED TO DISCUSS THE ANSWERS AND FORMULATE A PLAN OF DIRECTION. WHEN THIS HAS BEEN ACCOMPLISHED, EACH LEADER WILL TAKE THE PLAN BACK TO THEIR PROSPECTIVE GROUP FOR COMMENTS. WE WILL THEN MEET AGAIN TO ADDRESS QUESTIONS AND INPUT FROM THE VARIOUS FAMILIES. THE FINAL VOTE WILL BE TAKEN AT THIS TIME AND YOU WILL BE ADVISED OF THE RESULTS.

NOTE THAT YOU ARE BEING WATCHED CLOSELY BY ARIES, THE LEADER OF THE DESTROYERS, AND PERSEUS, THE LEADER OF THE PROTECTORS. BOTH HAVE BEEN COMMANDED TO KEEP VIGIL ON ALL THERAPY SESSIONS AND FILE A REPORT WITH KING OF LIGHTS AND MYSELF. ALL INFORMATION RECEIVED THUS FAR HAS BEEN POSITIVE, HOWEVER, WE ARE CONTINUING TO MONITOR AS A SAFEGUARD FOR THE SYSTEM.

AGAIN, THE LEADERS OF THE SYSTEM APPRECIATE YOUR RESPONSE TO THEIR QUESTIONS AND YOUR WILLINGNESS TO WORK UNDER OUR CONDITIONS. WE ARE ALSO WELL AWARE THAT YOU MUST CHARGE FOR YOUR TIME. WE HAVE NO DISAGREEMENT WITH THAT OR WITH THE FEE FOR THE SESSIONS.

Followed a day or so later by this communication:

To Bruce F., alias Dolphin and One Who Listens

Tuesday, the Circle Council voted on agenda item one and two. After discussing input, concerns and ideas from all known parts of the System and reviewing your work with them to this point, the Council has come to an agreement. Circle Council will instruct parts to work with you and trust you with their knowledge.

Also, a new form of system management will be implemented starting this week. All decisions, which impact the whole system, will be decided by the Circle Council. Issues, which only affect the Surface People and the Clan of Argus, will be discussed at their council meeting on Level 1. Levels 2 and 3 will send a non-voting representative to attend those meetings for informational purposes only. Level 3 will be establishing planning assemblies between the Guardians and Harmers to discuss issues relating to Labyrinth and Elysian Fields. Again, Levels 1 and 2 will send non-voting delegates to our gathering. Circle Council will reconvene in late March to evaluate the new system management and discuss goals and objectives.

Regards,
SID, Prince of the Harmers of the World of Labyrinth

Helper wrote to Bruce about his concerns for the children in therapy and for Bruce as well.

I have been monitoring the situation with Tabitha, Anna and Muy Malo. I appreciate the kindness and nurturing you have bestowed upon the children. You are the very first outsider who has told them that they have worth and are loved just for who they are, through your actions.

I am concerned though, about you becoming exhausted both physically and mentally. Ann's insistence that you take a crash course in Spanish is unrealistic. Therefore, I assigned Marie the task of developing a method of bridging the language barrier without requiring a tremendous amount of your time. She reported back that a picture board drawn by Tabitha, that could be visible during sessions, might help you with Tabitha describing her thoughts. Ruth and I agreed, so Tabitha went with her to Longs and picked items to make the pictures. Ruth then typed the word and translation for you. Hopefully, this will help your understanding Tabitha in record time. Marie also suggested that some type of preverbal picture board for Anna might help her communicate too. Do you know a therapist with a felt board of 'feeling faces'?

Muy Malo is a big concern for us. We are having difficulty communicating with her and she hasn't come out of her hole to play with the other children. Her anxiety level is very high. She doesn't seem to understand our words and responds more to sounds and pitch. Louise crocheted a blanket to cover her face in your office. It has holes so she can peek out to see you but feel covered and protected from you. She seems to feel safer with covering over her. Marie suggested you cover her body with the pink blanket and give her the bottle to comfort her. Marie also suggests you play the tape with her music, maybe that will make her feel safe too. These are only suggestions and we don't know if they will work. We do know that Muy Malo needs to somehow understand that you will not torture her, put bad candy in her, beat her or be rough with her.

The incident Thursday with Tabitha and the other therapist was interesting. Tabitha needed to know that you were telling the truth about the noise. She was afraid to see but felt safe with you as her shield of protection. Ruth says her concept of you is the 'Terminator of bad'. So she peeked around the corner to look, knowing that you were right there to protect her. She never would have had the courage otherwise and I think it was a positive experience. Hopefully, through these types of incidences, Tabitha will learn that not all men will hurt her. That incident also helped her view me in a more positive light. Ruth has purchased a toddler Bible for you to read to them in session. I have no problem with this as long as she also continues her trauma work.

I appreciate your idea of a timeline. It is an excellent activity for the parts to work on and network together. Hopefully, Raquel can make contact with Elizabeth Ray who seems to hold the history of the system. She would be a most valuable part to include in this project for everyone, including me.

I've also discussed with Ruth the struggle Maria and Louise are having with finding a beginning Bible class. Ruth has exhausted all her avenues and come up empty. Unfortunately, Liz and Ann are telling them that Christians don't want anything to do with them. Both Maria and Louise are saddened by the fact that they have no place to go to learn more about Jesus. I seek your advice on this subject. Is it possible that one of those Christian college graduate students in theology, could work with a multiple as a volunteer one hour a week in your office, to say disciple them? That would be extremely helpful and encouraging to them. It would also be beneficial to Liz and Ann to see a white male Christian student caring about spending time with poor, Latina people. I do suggest a male student, as Maria needs more role models in her life representing men who are encouraging and kind. Or is there a retired pastor or intern pastor? Again, these are just ideas, but we know it would help encourage those two parts if we could do this.

Let me express my gratitude again for your commitment and concern for our system. Even the parts who tend to have a less favorable disposition at times, recognize your kindness. They will come around. I have learned much from you. You are a man of wisdom and I'm appreciative our paths have crossed.

Bruce would soon be receiving observations and 'suggestions' from several parts about how to reach the children, so he was not without a plethora of ideas. Jennifer wrote next:

You know Tabitha is getting a little bit pushy with Anna and Muy Malo. She doesn't want to share time with you and is dominating it. Poor little Anna doesn't get much time to get close to you. Tabitha wants all the time, like she is making up for lost time. She tells Ruth you don't hurt her and read stories to her. She now feels very safe in your office. She still thinks the bad man is outside your door and you have the awesome power to make him go away.

I heard you trying to explain theology to Tabitha. You do know the kid is still confused? She keeps telling Ruth, "Jesus en al cielo. Jesus en mi ojos. Jesus no en mi corazon Mi corazon en mi corazon. No comprehendo." (I got help from Ruth with that.) Anyway Tabitha is still confused. Liz is still laughing over Tabitha looking for Jesus in her blouse and Ruth scrambling for direction...

Tabitha talks about her 'comida' with Bruce continually. She describes what was in the burrito and all the treats to Anna, who just curls up and sucks her thumb. I don't think Tabitha is being cruel, it's just that it was so special to her to be able to eat lunch without fear of being hurt was a special moment for her. We've been discussing a way for Anna to have lunch with you one day. We thought maybe a Tapioca Pudding party with her special music would help. Anna eats very slowly and chokes on certain foods, so we thought Tapioca would avoid problems. The idea hasn't been presented to council yet, so we thought we'd share it with you first...

Liz is shadowing and wants to use my time to speak to you, so here's...

This is Liz. I have a hell of a time getting access to this damn computer. Everybody and their brother wants it. Shit, you'd think you were popular or something. Anyway, I want to let you know I think Jennifer's new dress stinks! It makes us look pregnant. Now can you visualize Liz pregnant! Don't answer that! Well one good thing, Rosalinda loves Raquel and Jennifer's clothes. Maybe that dress will get lost in that bottomless pit of a closet in her room.

Hey, Maria told you about the guy that's got the hots for Ruth. You should see Ruth! It's funny to watch her try to get rid of him. Man, at least she could get a good meal off him. Ruth sure doesn't know how to play the game. I can't wait to see him approach her at the next meeting. Ruth is considering not returning, no guts! She should let me out to handle him. Hell, I know his kind. The guy is barking up the wrong tree with Ruth. Ruth is so damn moral she won't even steal a donut from the bakery. I'll keep you posted on Ruth's admirer.

Later:

I am so pissed off at that asshole of a husband of hers. Who the hell does he think he is telling his coworker that Ruth got hit on? Shit, if I wanted the whole damn world to know, I would have rented a f##%#n' billboard. Shit! That does it.

Louise has got to learn to put a cork in her damn mouth. She doesn't have to tell him everything he wants to know. I won't stay locked up! I know how to get out. Ann is pissed too. She asked Jose to give the dog some water and he told her to do it herself. Then Sergio yelled at Rosalinda to give the dog water. Ann blew! She stood up and said, "I told Jose to do it. You are contradicting me. If Rosalinda has to do all the work then she gets this kid's allowance. So which way do you want it?" Sergio then yelled at Jose to give the dog water and Jose started to argue saying you told Rosalinda to do it. Sergio stood up and said, "Are you arguing with me?" Jose filled the dog's dish and gave Ann a dirty look. Shithead!

Ann's already in trouble with Sergio, arguing with him over finances. Ann was winning the argument until she said, "I'll get a job." He blew and said you'll stay in this house and keep out of trouble. Asshole! Bastard makes it sound like it's all Ann's fault.

Shit, Ann knows how to stretch a dollar farther than anyone I know. Man he don't know what spending money is!

We share our clothes with Rosalinda to split the cost. We own no jewelry and don't even have a bedroom, so we sleep on the porch! Spend money... Shit I'd like to spend money. The world is full of male assholes! I'm goin' for a walk... Later!

Ann communicated several issues to Bruce over the next few days. It appeared she wasn't happy with all of the changes occurring, so she tried to set him straight about a few of them. With the changes on Circle Council, she definitely saw a shift in the power of decision making. She responded first to the Bible class motion currently before council and still in the domain of the Surface People. She sent him the following list, most of which I never saw until I read the journals. Bruce would give me the essence of these guidelines at our first meeting, in a little less than a month.

Apparently, Ruth and Helper somehow forgot to inform you of the conditions which Liz and I attached to the Bible class motion before council. In order for us to agree to the motion, we require several addenda be attached to the original proposal. It is imperative that you are informed of the conditions by which Liz and I agree to this nonsense. The following rules must be enforced or Liz and I will demand the tutoring cease.

1. *The tutor does NO therapy. Therapy is only done by you. It must be made clear he does not practice psychoanalysis on Maria and Louise.* (That was true from their perspective for the first 6 months.)
2. *Confidentiality must be enforced. He is to refrain from speaking to anyone but you about us. He is not to tell friends or classmates about us.* (I told Bruce that confidentiality has always been important in my ministry. The only person I would share information with would be my wife.)
3. *He is to respect the system.*
4. *We are not a project, we are personalities. He must be sincere about teaching them and remember they are sensitive, kind human beings.*

5. *He is not to touch her in any way or make advances toward her. He is not to meet her anywhere but your office. No going out for coffee or a walk.* (It would be Liz that changed this in 4 months.)

6. *He is to be committed and not leave her stranded by not showing up. Consistency is important to Maria.* (I missed one session in the six months unavoidably and yet, Maria was distraught over it and felt she was abandoned again.)

7. *He needs to be flexible and creative, with a sense of humor. He must remember that she will not be an expert in theology when he's finished working with her. His goal needs to be providing her with a good basic foundation.*

8. *He needs to understand MPD and be totally non-judgmental towards Maria and Louise. He must realize that another adult part might switch out or shadow. He needs to be comfortable around non-Christian parts and parts like Liz. Liz might switch out and challenge his theology and he needs to be prepared for that.*

9. *He is not to ask Maria any personal questions about her family or personal life. He will be evaluated by council and a report will be forwarded to you.*

10. *He is to be briefed in the following:*
    (Bruce did not brief me on the items listed, because it would have been inappropriate to do so. I would not be privy to most of this information for almost a year and the rest only after two years of working with the System.
    a. *Maria has MPD.*
    b. *Maria was severely and repeatedly abused as a child, beginning at age 2.*
    c. *Maria was abandoned by her mother who abused her and given to her grandpa (papa).*
    d. *There was incest by him and molestation by a priest.*
    e. *Maria was confined to a basement and severely beaten.*
    f. *Maria is afraid of rats and being cut.*
    g. *Maria was initiated into the Santeria at age 4 and witnessed sacrificial rituals.*
    h. *Maria has over 30 individual parts. She is the host personality to know.*
    i. *Maria is Latina and was raised in the traditional lifestyle where the man is king and the woman obeys and serves*

    him. Explain the machismo complex. She was also forced to work at the age of 4. Maria speaks English very well.

j.   *Maria became a Christian accepting Jesus in Bruce's office a few months ago.*

k.   *The other part who will be in his presence is Louise.*

l.   *Louise is not like Maria, but even more traditional Latina.*

m. *Louise is Catholic and obeys the teachings of the Catholic Church. She believes that if she obeys the rules she will go to Purgatory and then hopefully to heaven. You may share Louise's questions with him.*

n.   *Most of the parts are non-Christian and he is to not pass judgement on us.*

HE DOES NOT NEED TO KNOW WHAT GOES ON IN YOUR OFFICE. HE ONLY NEEDS TO KNOW THE BASIC QUESTIONS THAT MIGHT BE ASKED LIKE: IF GOD LOVES ME SO MUCH, WHY DID HE LET ALL THAT STUFF HAPPEN TO US? (Maria wouldn't have asked this question in that way, even in the beginning. This was a Liz / Ann question.) **HE NEEDS TO BE CAREFUL ABOUT READING STORIES DEALING WITH BLOOD OR CONFINEMENT; HOW HE PORTRAYS THE CROSS; HE NEEDS TO UNDERSTAND THE FEAR AROUND BLOOD AND ANIMAL SACRIFICES; AND BE SMART ENOUGH TO KNOW WHAT LESSONS WILL BENEFIT MARIA WITHOUT CAUSING MORE ANXIETY.** (Fortunately for me, Bruce didn't give these to me ahead of time. I had my own issues back then of interacting with non-Christians/Believers telling me how to do my ministry as a Christian pastor. Thankfully, these were withheld and in the last seven years they have taught me the value of tolerance with grace. I can understand the purpose and legitimate concern that surrounds these instructions and the pain in which they were presented. The depth of the information they were willing to share up front indicates their compassion for Maria and Louise's need for spiritual healing. For Liz and Ann in particular, to openly offer these guidelines, shows great courage under fire.)

Tabitha was dealing with her own issues in counseling with Bruce. Her fear of 'papa' finding her was increasing with the telling of her story. She began telling the other kids about what she perceived to be the truth on the outside, in Bruce's office.

Tabitha is telling a most bizarre story about what happens to her pictures in your office. She is freaked out about the hombre malo (bad man) getting her. She says that when it's black outside and Bruce goes home to his casa to sleep, the hombre malo comes. He goes into your office and little Ollie is so miedo (afraid). Ollie has no blanket to hide in the basket. She says that the bad man smells the room and knows that Tabitha was there. He can't find the telling book because Tabitha hides it in her special place. But he sees her pictures she draws for Bruce on the wall and takes his knife and cuts them up. Then he screeches and scares poor Ollie who has no one to protect him. The bad man's candy is very big and Ollie is very much afraid of it. The bad man looks at Ollie and his eyes are mean. Ollie cries "Ayudame! Ayudame (hurry quickly) Bruce!" But Bruce is in his bed and doesn't hear Ollie. The bad man puts his candy away, looks around and then goes outside with Tabitha's pictures. The bad man won't come into office when Bruce is there, because Bruce is strong and makes the bad man go away. So the bad man comes when it is black and Bruce is at home. Ollie is scared and Tabitha is sad. Tabitha's pictures corta by hombre malo. All gone.

What Tabitha describes here is the story of her life, as she sees it happening as she speaks. The hombre malo is the grandpa of the past and present, since she still believes that he is still alive like the last time she saw him. Ollie the puppet represents her memories of the past and real fears of the present in concern for her 'friend' all alone in Bruce's office. The cutting of the pictures could have occurred by a Destroyer/Harmer in front of Bruce without him realizing someone else was out and Tabitha was inside. This occurred later in my presence when her drawings were torn up or scratched over with black crayon. Tabitha's attachment to Bruce and acceptance of him as her 'Daddy' and protector was difficult for some in the System to handle. It also caused some unexpected results for Tabitha. Bruce received this letter to read immediately, before the next session with Tabitha.

Tabitha is not responding well. Both Marie and I spent most of Saturday attempting to calm her down. Apparently the issue is centered around jealousy and abandonment. Tabitha believes her mommy got rid of her because she was bad. Then her papa got rid of her because she was bad and sent her back to her mommy who did not like her. Then, according to Tabitha, she got a new daddy who did not have dulce malo (bad candy) *and did not hurt her. She got to see her new daddy in his office and eat burritos with him. Her new daddy read books and gave her Ollie to hold and love. But then her new daddy didn't want her anymore and gave cookies to a new little girl named Laura. Her new daddy loves Laura and not Tabitha.*

I asked her who was her new daddy and she said Bruce. Both Marie and I tried to explain to Tabitha that Bruce is a friend of all of us and not her daddy. She cried and said, "No Laura. Tabitha be good. Tabitha no make mess. Tabitha no want cookie. No Laura. Go away Laura. No Laura. Tabitha share daddy with Anna and Muy Malo. No Laura. Go away. Tabitha daddy."

Again we tried to explain to her that Bruce is like a doctor and helps all little girls be happy. Bruce has lots of little children see him, not just Tabitha. She would not accept that and sobbed.
She then cried that she would be good and obey. The last thing she said was "No Laura, no take my daddy away." Ann is livid. She is screaming inside at me that she warned us not to become too dependent on this guy. Now look at the mess we've got. Maria is trying to understand what is happening. She's pleading with Tabitha not to get Bruce mad at us. I assured Maria in front of Tabitha that Bruce is not mad. Maria is afraid and upset that Tabitha is distraught. She might also be experiencing Tabitha's emotions dealing with abandonment. (See Figure 5 next page.)

Ann is angry because Tabitha picked up a knife and cut our left hand. Fortunately, I was able to get out before any major damage could occur. But now Anna is upset because that is the hand she colors with and she doesn't understand what's happening. All she knows is something happened to Tabitha, so she's hiding in her hole.

I told Tabitha that Bruce wants to see you on Monday. She doesn't want to go in now because Bruce is Laura's daddy. I explained that Bruce is not Laura's daddy and Bruce still wants to read to Tabitha and play. I said, "Bruce can share his time with Tabitha and

Laura." Then she started sobbing all over again with, "No Laura. Go away Laura. I want my daddy. Daddy no want Tabitha want Laura. Cookies for Laura. Daddy have cookies for Laura. Tabitha no have cookies. Tabitha bad. Bad no get cookies."

Exhausted, I told Tabitha she was not bad and Bruce loves her like Jesus loves Tabitha.

A drawing by Tabitha after she thought she had lost Daddy
Bruce to "Laura" – "Loren go away! Tabitha sad."

Bruce would of course respond to this letter, but not before Ann got off her own letter to him immediately following Ruth's letter and the subsequent session with Tabitha.

Make sure there are no cookies on your desk unless you plan to allow Tabitha access to them. She does not understand that those cookies belong to someone else. They were in your office and on your desk, therefore, they belong to you according to her logic. Now, to placate the kid, we need to go to the store and buy some animal crackers. I also do not want Tabitha grabbing your drinks. She needs to learn not to grab stuff and start drinking it. You need to discipline her more in your office. Do not let her into Maria's purse. Do not drink Bruce's coke. Do not play with the telephone. She needs boundaries. She jumps all over the place in that office. I'm not paying for playtime. I want you to get her to work through that stuff of hers so we can move on. She is not working through her fear of 'dulce malo'. Instead she is reading the Bible. Therapy is for working through her memories, not for earning a diploma in theology.

(What Ann would not know for a few more years was that when Tabitha was growing up with her grandparents, other kids and people were served treats in front of her but she wasn't allowed to eat them. She was to serve and not be seen. She had to grab food when no one was looking or get a beating if discovered. When other kids got cookies, she was allowed only the crumbs. When other kids had ice cream, she would receive only what others shared or if she could sneak a handful. It has only been in the last few years that she eats ice cream with a spoon and without fear of someone beating her for having and eating it. Eating ice cream together is special for us both.)

Anna needs more time out. Please read Tabitha's book to see if you get a reaction from her. I wonder if Anna knows what happened to Tabitha and Muy Malo. By her drawing today, she is aware they have different times out and Anna's music inspired her to draw the dissociation picture. The music does have that quality to it of almost a floating sound.

I still want to know how you plan to get Muy Malo to communicate with you. This is the kid who holds the most violent trauma (something else Ann would learn later to be untrue when the pod children are revealed.) *How are you going to get her to even tell you? She cannot draw. She cannot talk. She does not even play.*

I'm not pleased at all with Circle Council's forcefulness in taking over the system management of our world. I do not like five men determining my fate. I should be allowed to be a part of the leader's group with my organizational and time management skills. Why should they make all the decisions and have all the control over our actions? I plan to voice my objections to Helper at the next council meeting.

Bruce responded to Ann:

I received your letter from the end of last week. I know that you, as well as others in the system, are concerned about Tabitha's dependence on me. Ruth and I discussed this very issue in regard to all of the kids. It is not unusual for child alters to become very dependent on their therapist, and to want to be with him or her constantly. But think about why. For the first time in their existence, an adult is being nice to them, caring for them, and respecting them as important people. This is a necessary step for therapy to succeed and for healing to occur in their lives.

They have to learn to trust and they have to be and feel safe (perhaps for the first time in their lives). O.K., so Tabitha thinks of me as Daddy; I will deal with that issue with her as we go along, and her dependency will be reduced as she works through the trauma. As the system becomes stronger and a greater source of comfort and support for her, it will diminish. This is why I work so hard with Ruth, helping her and others to devise ways to help the children internally.

I realize that a lot of this embarrasses and bothers you, and I'm truly sorry for that. It is not my intent to embarrass you or cause you discomfort. But what we are doing in therapy is necessary for the children, so that they will not continue to be afraid and controlled by their memory feelings. Everything I do in my office is geared to this end. Reading Bible stories expands Tabitha's sense of Jesus and God and allows her to transfer some of her dependence to Him. Even if you don't agree with this theologically, you can see the psychological importance.

Incidents like those that occurred last Friday help Tabitha and the others learn that problems and fears can be worked through. Providing her with cookies today proves that I still care and didn't reject her and helps lay the groundwork for further teaching about ownership and respect for the property of others. This is all time consuming and hard, but it is absolutely necessary.

The new management arrangements bother you. I can imagine why, since we talked about it in my office once before. Talk to Helper, ask permission to address Circle Council, and do what you need to do to get guarantees about how the system will be managed. This is all part of the process of figuring out how to live together effectively. Having the folks from Labyrinth on your side rather than feeling they are working against you must be a welcome relief. Hang in there Ann! You are an important part of the system. I see the imprint of your thinking and organizing often as I work with and communicate with others. Try to lighten up, and if the pressure is getting to you, go to Circle Council and ask for help. This is part of the reasons they have made changes, so that issues which effect the whole system can be addressed and worked out. Perhaps, instead of being a threat, they can become allies in all you have to do.

And come in and see me sometime so we can talk. It's been a long time and I worry about you.

Bruce's response to Ann drew an apology from her, something that rarely occurred. Ann's apology to Bruce revealed a 'softer side' of Ann that was also rarely seen. She felt free to unload several of her own fears, for the System and for herself as well. Because her letter is so profound in its honesty, I will refrain from commenting until the end.

I have read your letter and I know you are right. Please accept my apology for my behavior lately. I really have the system's best interest at heart. I just don't want to see them hurt anymore. We learned a long time ago that to avoid pain one avoids relationships.

If we do not become dependent upon anyone, then we cant be rejected or abandoned. To survive emotionally, we have learned to become isolated and cautious. That is why I'm so concerned about Tabitha and the others forming a relationship with you. I am scared that they will be hurt again. We are already torn and tattered. We are extremely vulnerable. A shield is the only way I know to protect us.

Tabitha loves you as a child loves a parent. She gives you valentine cards, brings you her books and tries to share her food with you. She looks up to you and tries to please you. Besides Ruth, you have become the most important person in her life. I know it is because you have been the first outside adult who has shown her any kindness. This child has been starved for so long for that nurturing that she cannot get enough of it. You are the daddy she has always wanted. You are safe and strong, her protector from the hombre malo. You have become her world. Like Maria has Kansas, Tabitha has her dream – a daddy who loves her.

And this is why I'm so scared, I don't want Tabitha to be hurt. The Laura episode frightened me. I have realized that Tabitha has formed a closer bond to you than I ever expected. When she thought Laura had taken "her daddy away from her", she cut the body's hand. Had we not intervened; how far would she have gone? Would she have killed us over the loss of her daddy? Tabitha cannot handle another loss. I am worried that she will not be able to separate from you. Ruth, Jennifer, Marie, Louise and Raquel have all comforted the children in many ways and continue to do so. Yet, you hold a unique place in her life that is different from us. She knows you are on the outside. She understands the difference. You represent the outside world for her. We represent the inner world.

You are right when you say I'm embarrassed by all of this. I try very hard to look normal. I have worked extremely hard to appear educated and well informed. It is very hard for me to be accepted in the world. It hurts very deeply when people label me stupid. Why it hurts I don't know. Last week a Christian volunteer gave directions to all parents present about how to fill out forms and then turned to me alone and asked "did I go too fast for you? Did you understand?" She humiliated me in front of all those parents. I finished my stack before anyone else and she had the nerve to check and see if I could calculate the figures correctly. Needless to say, I never returned. This is the type of stuff I deal with on a continual basis. Does everyone in this world think that people like me are stupid? From college in all those male dominated math classes until now, you would've thought I would be used to humiliation by now, but I'm not. Each time it tears a little more of my minute self-worth away. I know it is not your intent to embarrass me. Your job is to do therapy of which I guess this is a part. I logically understand the process and accept it.

I guess another fear of mine is that I will run out of money before they all get glued together. We could be in worse shape than before we began. Sometimes when you cross a torrential river, the real danger is not in the beginning or at the very end. It is in the middle that it is the most dangerous and deepest. If I run out of money in the middle, we are going down and drown. Yet, I know this is how you earn your living and I am very conscientious about meeting my obligations. But it is a fear I have concerning the financial implications of long-term therapy. I am exhausted from trying to make ends meet.

I am not against you reading Bible stories to Tabitha. It is just that at $50.00 a session, those are awful expensive Bible stories. I want to make sure you move Tabitha along as fast as you can so we can finish. There are still other children that need to be healed, maybe more than I know. Do you think we should do group therapy that is less expensive? I am not against the Circle Council. I'm against the exclusion aspect of it. Helper is my representative and he will bring up my concerns at Circle Council. Parts are not allowed to address the Circle Council. Questions, concerns, input and ideas are to be given to the representative to take to Council. I am not allowed to speak for myself. That bothers me for several reasons.

First, Helper might not portray my concerns accurately. He would not intentionally misconstrue them, but any messages transferred through a third party can have the possibility of confusion. Second, there is no female perspective on Circle Council. Men do not view issues the same way women do. Since the Council is made up entirely of men, there is no gender diversity on the Council. That is not fair. Helper cannot adequately represent me as a woman. I agree that having Labyrinth on our side is a welcome relief. I also agree that networking and system wide management is crucial to the success of our system. I do not agree that it must be male dominated. I plan to continue to address this issue and lobby for change.

Again, I appreciated your letter. I'm trying very hard to 'lighten up'. I guess it just isn't in my personality. I have been responsible for so long that, I don't even think I know how to lighten up. This is all I know I guess it is my thorn in life. You take care too, because you are a nice person. I'm not just patronizing you I really mean it. Enjoy your mushrooms on Thursday with Liz.

**"A friend loves at all times,
And a brother is born for adversity."
Proverbs 17:17**

Chapter Eight:

"Finding the Path to a Father's Love"

"Though my father and mother forsake me,
The Lord will receive me.
Teach me your way, O Lord;
Lead me in a straight path..."
Psalms 27: 10-11

Ann's response revealed a lot about her character, her depth of caring for others that her outside persona would not allow others to see. Ann modeled for the System how to hide one's emotions. She believed that to reveal them is to reveal weakness, a response that for her gives control away to someone else. Ann strove most of her life to provide the shield for the System, one that kept others out, *but also kept them in isolation.* The crack in the shield was caused by the weakest member reaching out to embrace her greatest fear, a loving relationship with an adult male. Ann could easily see the long-term implications of this relationship and it frightened her. Bruce could no longer be lumped into the category of all other men, that of assholes, because he had traversed a boundary never expected by Ann. He was giving genuine love and friendship to not only Tabitha, but to a part of her, a part that had been buried a long time ago.

If Tabitha could find 'parental' love in an artificially created environment with a professional caregiver, what were the possibilities for the rest of the System? The risks of being deeply hurt again associated with these possibilities were growing exponentially. Would the risk of experiencing love now be worth the pain that might come with the inevitable separation? She saw Bruce as a limited time offer in any case. He would have to separate one day and it was logic, not experience that said; "The longer you love makes the pain of loss or separation that much harder to bear." And for Ann's fear, "What if they never experienced it through any part again?" Ann's experience told her to not trust God to fill that gap, not through any man in spite of what Bruce may have said.

She was not aware of the forces at work around her to keep her behind her shield. These forces had been at work the System's entire life to prevent them from knowing the truth of a father's love. Nor was she able to imagine then how God would use love to break down her shield of fear. The same nurturing love which Tabitha craved and received, would slowly envelop them and give meaning to their lives. How each of the Surface People encounter and learn to trust a father's love, was so far beyond Ann's conception at this point in her life that she could only permit herself the possibility for Tabitha. Ann recognized how the care given internally was not enough for Tabitha. No part until now ever referred to the emotional relationship of any part as a loving one. It was an abstract concept that had no reference in their collective lives. They couldn't begin to understand it, until it was manifested within them and given outward to a real person.

They would gradually understand the basic truth about real love; you can receive it without understanding it, but you can't give it away to someone else unless you know it as real inside. The women of the System who raised and nurtured Maria's children, could say they loved them unconditionally and that was true, but they didn't know how or why this was possible. They knew the feelings of love were coming from somewhere, but they couldn't say from where or who taught them. They had no experiential reference to base it on.

Except for Ruth, no part ever used the word love to express a positive caring emotion. Ruth used it often in reference to God and Jesus, but it fell on deaf ears because of their experiences. As a part pragmatically created as a Christian Ruth knew this love to be true, but how could she convey it to others in the System? Love was a part of her initial experience, but this was not the case for the others. For them love was a subjective concept, not an objective reality. Louise loved the Catholic Church with all of its rules and demands about love and how to receive it. It brought the only sense of order in her life that she understood, but she could not point to a person or time when she received a father's love like this from it. The idea of a father's love from a priest only raised feelings of guilt, shame and unworthiness within her and she didn't know why. When the children started revealing past abuse, she could only understand it as their disobedience of God's rules, thus God was justified in not loving any of them and punishing them. This would force her to look back to the Church for a way out. Ann of course would never allow this for good reasons, which are revealed later in the System's stories.

At the moment, fresh on Ann's mind was the pain Tabitha felt when she thought she had lost her daddy. Her concern that Tabitha might try to kill herself and the System with her, if she ever lost her daddy or was separated from him indefinitely, was genuine. Yet she knew she couldn't deny the child the love she never knew for one simple reason. She had sought that same love from the man she believed to be her father. She wanted his approval and acceptance of her as a measure of that love, and didn't understand until recently, why she never received that love from him.

Her embarrassment was real too. For a woman with her intellect and power of deductive reasoning, how could she not be able to understand and explain a father's love as real? If you can't explain or understand it, then it must not be real at least for her. The trouble for her was that she could see it was real for Tabitha, and that meant another man had control over her. Add to this frustration the new management system over everyone with *five* men assuming control on the Council, and you can begin to understand her growing lack of control over her own life. For both Ann and Liz to simply accept any man, especially *five* of them, as controlling their lives in a purely benevolent fashion was a difficult concept. It would take a long time for Liz and Ann to accept the need for men on a council. Ann's objections as stated to Bruce, were valid enough for her to challenge this male dominance for years to come.

Liz would challenge it too, but for different reasons and getting different results. In a few years, Helper would place Liz under house arrest inside, a bold concept that would alter how Liz challenged the authority placed over her by this God she really didn't want to know. For now like Ann, she wasn't about to let any man tell her what to do. Liz's response to Tabitha's reaction was clearly stated, but as for her feeling regarding Circle Council you judge:

Do you think I give a damn if Tabitha wants you to be her daddy? It's no big deal with me. BUT DON'T FORGET! YOU ARE NOT MY FATHER! I don't want a father…

WHAT'S YOUR OPINION OF THAT CIRCLE COUNCIL OF GUYS? DO YOU THINK THEY ARE AS STRONG AS THEY SAY THEY ARE? WHAT WOULD YOU DO IF THEY MADE SOME STUPID RULE THAT YOU DIDN'T WANT TO AGREE TO? WOULD YOU CALL THEIR BLUFF OR BE A WIMP AND OBEY THEM?

THERE'S ALWAYS A CREATIVE WAY TO GET AROUND A RULE. QUESTION: IF ONE FOLLOWS THE EXACT WORDING OF A RULE, BUT NOT THE MEANING OF THE RULE, IS ONE FOLLOWING THE RULE? SHIT. LIFE WOULD BE SO MUCH SIMPLER AS A SINGLE. BY THE WAY, DO YOU KNOW WHAT'S WRONG WITH ANN? SHE DOESN'T SEEM TO BE HER OLD SELF? SHE MUST BE SICK.

Liz recognized that Ann was struggling with something 'emotional', but she really didn't want to know <u>too</u> much so she didn't ask. She kept her appointment with Bruce for a mushroom feast. A meal was not therapy as far as she was concerned, so she went with a secondary purpose to get the Christian therapist angry. The outcome was getting the wrong man angry and forming a new perspective about Bruce:

Hey Bruce,

Thanks for the memories! You're the only person who ever thought I was worth the time. I appreciate it. I think you should dissociate from those gluttons, gossips, adulterers and thieves who call themselves Christians. Maybe you should call yourself Christlik'n instead. The way you ate sure put holes in my hypothesis about Suburban Christians. If I am honest (which is not my gift), I would have to admit you seem to be very different from them. I would sure like to observe you in other settings. I wonder if you act in the same way.

I never met a Christian who is non-judgmental like you. Christians don't like people like Paul and me. (Paul was her friend who had just died of AIDS.) Christians think we are the scum of the earth. Christians think they are better than us. They don't even want to be around us and when they have to be, they look down on us. They think we are projects for them to get extra brownie points with God, rather than look upon us as human beings. They are assholes.

But you, you bug me because you are sincerely nice to me. In fact, I even tried to get you to turn into one of those not-so-nice Christians and you just keep being nice no matter what I throw at you. I keep trying to figure out why. Why don't you act like all those other Christians I've known? What makes you different? Are you the only one like this in your group? Is it because you are a therapist Christian? I don't know, but you bug me because I haven't figured you out. Too bad Paul is not around, I sure would've liked for him to meet you. Anyway, the mushrooms were good and I enjoyed them. This vinegar is a thank you gift for the mushrooms. Try my recipe sometime.

By the way Helper cornered me, the circle of gods must have been pissed. No, they were worse than pissed. I heard the lecture about the meaning of what we meant. Helper accused me of purposely disobeying the order. No, not me. I told him exactly what I thought of their f##%'n rule and telling me what to do. Then Helper turned to me and did the Bruce thing. "Liz do you think that was a good idea to drink the wine cooler? Because of your actions, Maria who is already struggling with so much is very ill. You know that she along with several other parts has a reaction to the slightest amount of alcohol. Yet you selfishly considered your own pleasures over the safety of others. What do you think we should do about this?"

Helper knows how to make me feel like a worm. I agreed to give my word not to drink any more alcohol. I made it perfectly clear that I was not doing it to obey their rule but because I care about Maria.

It's not funny Bruce. I can see you now grinning from ear to ear. I'm not laughing. Between you on the outside and Helper on the inside, I don't have a chance.
Later-

Jennifer followed Liz's adventure with interest and had these observations:

You know I spoke with Liz before your meeting about the wine cooler. Although I can understand her point of view, I expressed my concern about her challenging Circle Council. I have realized they are very strong and have the support of most of the system. Liz didn't have a chance as all the system was opposed to her on this issue. Circle Council seems to have established very sensible rules. I have not yet opposed any of their requests.

Maria is doing worse this evening. The system is upset that her husband told her tonight that her MPD is going to kill him and it will be her fault. She really doesn't need that extra guilt put upon her. I switched out and defended her. I told Sergio that it really isn't fair to blame us for your health problems. We didn't ask to be MPD. We try very hard to not cause you stress. He then became agitated and told me we cause him nothing but problems. Then he wanted to know how much longer will it be till you get fixed and put together. I suggested that he call you for that information. He got very angry and said, "you know what I think about those people. I don't want anything to do with them, just hurry up and get fixed before you give me a heart attack."

Of course Liz was saying inside, "a heart attack...now wouldn't that be convenient." Ruth reminded her that without Sergio's financial backing we would not be able to take care of the children. Also he would probably get custody of the children because of our MPD, which would break Maria's heart. Anyway, I thought you might like to know that Maria now believes that she is the cause of her husband's aches and pains. You know, like she needs more guilt.

We are running into problems lately with our voice. For some reason, we are not concentrating enough to keep the voice the same. The reason we know is that people who phone us are asking if our mother is home or is Maria at home. Why is this happening? Do you see us not keeping the same voice? We need to work on this to prevent problems. I hope you can help Maria tomorrow, she is very scared about her father coming on Sunday. I've never seen her this upset.

Peace – Jennie

The trauma of the pending visit from the father, caused one child who had not yet revealed herself to Bruce, Mariann, to sneak out and send him this letter:

Content Warning!
i watch them lot now and know the way to do this on the mashine. i am afraid of you you have a stick that can go in my hole and hurt me. they take us all to the room you scare me and i canot tell you my secrets becaz god will hurt me somemore. i am the very bad and dirty i did very bad things. i do not talk with peple you have to stay

hide so god canot get you and hurt you bad. never tell. never tell. be quiet or god will get you the baby take my doll and i do not want her to take my doll. my doll is rebeca. i named her that a long time ago becaz I like rebeca of sunnybrok farm. i do the mashine to you becaz the baby takes my doll please do not let her hurt my doll. my doll is my friend and knows my secrets but my doll does not talk she never tells the secrets. the baby take my doll to you

Another letter from Mariann followed this one the next day:

the father is coming the father the father i hide i here a voice tell the father come the father come. hide i scream not loud. it hurts a long time. the father is coming he will bring it at nite it will come hide far down the father is coming soon help find rebeca hide where here hide here and be quiet he will be here very soon very soon he is big and hurts lots hide and be quiet or die where hurry where here hide here hurry the father is coming the beast will be coming soon help me I am scared here hide here the father is coming where is my rebeca do you have my rebeca the baby plays with my rebeca in your room rebeca must hide the father is coming soon help rebeca the father is coming

Apparently, from the other letters Bruce received, no one knew that Mariann had come out to write these except Elizabeth Ray who recorded them. Even Daniel makes no mention of being aware of this happening. The difficulty in analyzing the letter at that time is this, not all of the children have been revealed. It's quite possible that it wasn't Mariann directly, but a 'Pod' child pushed out from 'Those Who Are Core', to express the fear felt at their as yet unknown level. Cries for help can come from many directions in a multiple. While a personality remains hidden and unidentified, they may still express their fears through the closest personality that does come to the surface. Tabitha was the vehicle for Anna and Angelina until they emerged. Mariann did this through Mari. In the case of the fear of the father, this was shared throughout the system, so the two letters could have come from several people. I believe it was Mariann because of the references to a 'stick' (her word for penis'), the father /beast (her words for the priest) and her doll, Rebecca. When any of the child parts started to become fearful, it had a direct correlation to how Maria reacted as well from her own fears within. Ruth wrote to Bruce in-between Mariann's letters about Maria's condition.

Maria found out about her father coming on Sunday and started having panic attacks. All of a sudden she is denying we exist. She is saying she is a liar and crazy. She wants to go to heaven where she won't be crazy. She believes all of the people in her life, from her family to the psychiatrists, that she is bad, dirty and ugly. She is having flashbacks of incidences where people are yelling at her "she was a curse the day she was born" and "you're so bad and dirty that the pigs wouldn't even want you in their pen." She is sobbing and saying that she is all alone and nobody wants to be around her.

I am trying to comfort her from the inside, but I understand her feelings more today. It must be so hard for her to go through this. You are a great support and I wish we could clone you. She was doing great for awhile and then she became overwhelmed again by voices. I don't know if it is an accumulation of her father coming, Claudia coming, being left alone with Jose over the weekend, Tabitha cutting the hand, Rosalinda gone, or what.

It seems that messages throughout her life are very strong and binding. Your messages were breaking through, but they come so few and far between because you can't see her daily. With Tabitha spending more time with you and Maria less, she is running into difficulty with the messages/voices. Please let me know as soon as possible if the idea of the graduate student will work out. At this point, we are desperate to find some type of additional support for Maria.

I wanted to relay to you an interesting perspective I'm picking up from some of the parts. I think there exist more animosity towards women in our system than men. I know the parts have a difficult time trusting men because of the physical and sexual abuse many experienced. But there seems to be a deeper rage against women because of the neglect and abandonment of the mother. Some parts have this belief that had the mother not done this, maybe the physical and sexual abuse by men wouldn't have happened. Do some of the parts blame the mother for the abuse? I don't know, but I think Helper's suggestion that the graduate student be male, may have more importance than just Maria learning that men can be caring and trustworthy.

Tabitha is doing well and has become absorbed with this daddy focus after the incident with Laura. She is making another book called My Daddy. I don't know what to do with this fascination therefore, I'm not working with Tabitha on this issue as I might cause more problems. I will leave the daddy stuff in your capable hands.

Bruce met with the System just before the father arrived, in an attempt to help Tabitha and Anna prepare for the time he would be there. He suggested they build a tunnel from one hole to the next. Ruth made a valiant effort inside to make this happen. Ruth wrote back that the idea didn't work. Neither did the idea that Anna goes in Tabitha's hole or Tabitha goes in Anna's hole. It seems Tabitha didn't want Anna in her hole because it is for 'big girls' and Anna is a baby. Nor did Tabitha want to live in a baby's hole. As far as the tunnel idea, Tabitha wouldn't allow it because she was afraid that 'hombre malo' will come through the tunnel.
Enter Helper:

Helper came on the scene and I had the privilege of watching him work with Tabitha. He told her he understood why she didn't want the tunnel. "It is scary to think a bad man might come in and you want your hole to be safe. This is your safe place, huh Tabitha." Tabitha shook her head yes...Then he began a strategy I think bordered on genius. "Tabitha, you are a very smart and brave big girl. Anna watches you a lot and wants to be just like you. She learns many things from you because you are like her very big sister. She wants you as her very best friend. She tells me that you are very smart and color pretty pictures and she wants to learn to color like you. Do you think you could teach her how and maybe how to write? You write so well."

Tabitha said, "I be big girl, Anna baby. I make words for Anna." Then Helper said, "Tabitha, Anna wants Jesus in her hole too." Tabitha firmly said no. Helper tried to explain that Jesus could be in both holes at once, but Tabitha couldn't grasp the concept. Helper changed tactics with, "Tabitha, you are so smart, I bet you could think of a way that Jesus could be with you and Anna together. You could think of the holes being together and Jesus setting between them. He can hug Tabitha with his left arm and Anna with his right arm at the same time. He could read stories to both of you and you could see Anna and wave hello to her while still in your big girl hole. Is that possible?"

Tabitha then took everything she heard and said, "Helper I share Jesus. Anna put baby hole here and Jesus sit here and tell me and Anna story, okay?" Helper said, "Okay Tabitha, thank you for coming up with such a good idea to solve our problem. You are a very big girl." Tabitha smiled and watched as Anna is backed up against Tabitha's hole and Jesus sets between them as a common bond. Anna is very happy. She put her bunny in Jesus' lap and Tabitha put Ollie in His lap.

Some readers might think in reading this that Jesus cannot be manipulated like this and you'd be right, except for one thing. Who is always in control? Jesus meets us at our point of need wherever we accept Him. Neither Helper nor Tabitha really understood at this time, who He really was. All they knew at this time was that He was good and kind and the children felt safe with Him, but neither yet understood all about Him or trusted Him as the Son of God. They knew Him simply as Jesus on the inside and outside worlds. Jesus knew the time had not yet come for Him to reveal His power to this System of hurting people. First, they had to trust and believe in the man, before they could overcome their fear in trusting God. They needed to trust this man:

"He has no stately form or majesty
that we should look upon Him,
Nor appearance that we should be attracted to Him.
He was despised and forsaken of men,
A man of sorrows, and acquainted with grief;
And like one from whom men hid their face,
He was despised, and we did not esteem Him."
-Isaiah 53:2-3

Jesus meets each one of us in the way He knows we are ready to accept Him. For some, it is through the revelation of His omnipotent power to overcome our human nature, where only 'seeing is believing.' Love uses a different way to enter the lives of throwaway people, despised and rejected of men; broken people without hope to teach us this truth:

"For we do not have a high priest
who cannot sympathize with our weaknesses,
but one who has been tempted in all things
as we are, but without sin.
Let us therefore draw near with confidence
to the throne of grace, that we may receive mercy
and may find grace to help in time of need."
-Paul Hebrews 4:15-16

Jesus would reveal to each one in the System, only as much of Himself as they were ready to understand and accept. Some, like Ann, would take another seven years to accept Jesus of Nazareth as the God/man He said He was. Through these years, it is not His power in the miraculous events she observes that convinces her, but the overcoming of her doubt. Even Ruth, conceived essentially as a Christian, would one-day question the object of her faith, as she learns the truth of their life of severe abuse. She calls to God, "Why did you allow this to happen to us?" She will have her faith tested as many times as she asks the question, but the answer is the same, "Will you trust Me?"

Jesus will meet the children and each adult in the place of their need. Each will be allowed to choose whom they will trust, Yemaya or Jesus.

"And a little child shall lead them."

We are still running into difficulty with Tabitha's understanding of the cross. She thinks that Jesus' daddy, God, did not make it safe for Jesus and let bad men hurt Jesus. Jesus' daddy did not come to Jesus and help him by telling the bad men 'vete', go away. Then she said Tabitha's daddy did not make it safe for her and let bad men hurt Tabitha. Now Tabitha have good daddy and new daddy say 'vete' to hombre malo. Daddy now make safe for Tabitha and say 'alto', no corta, no dulce malo. No sotano (basement). No hurt Tabitha. Tabitha's daddy muy grande. Tabitha share daddy with Jesus. Tabitha daddy be Jesus' new daddy, no let bad men hurt Jesus no more.

Well Bruce, you have been exalted above God in Tabitha's mind. This is very dangerous. She is beginning to idolize you and she is leading Anna right along with her. I have tried to correct her thinking, but she refuses to budge. You carry more influence with her than I do. She needs to understand who God is and why Jesus died on the cross. She has a very warped understanding and I pray you can untangle the confusion.

The Circle Council is pleased with the progress Anna made in your office. They have concluded that it is better to allow one child out for an extended time than to allow all three to switch in one session...This Thursday, they want Tabitha to come out to clear up some of her misconceptions. They would also like Muy Malo to have a few minutes to become more familiar with the office. They also agreed to allow you to call the children out by name. Tabitha and Anna want to always be with you now. Muy Malo is still afraid, but we will push her out when you call her. Circle Council wants these three kids on track so you can begin working with Lila and Mariann.

With so many parts and so little therapy time, Circle Council must decide how therapy can be most beneficial to the entire system. They have attempted to develop a priority list: Tabitha, Anna, Muy Malo, Mariann, Mari, Lila, Raquel, Maria, Louise, Liz and Ann. Parts who don't need therapy, but can benefit through the skills learned by others: Marie, Jennifer, Elizabeth Ray, Helper, Daniel, SID, Harmers, King of Lights, Guardians and Ruth. This is only an initial assessment based upon the knowledge they currently have on file and they welcome your input.

Ann is pressing Helper on the issue of gender equality at Circle Council. Helper has attempted compromise with Ann, but Ann is insistent that a female representative needs to be on Council. Helper promised to take her concerns to Council and report back to her. No other part has a problem with the present set up. Liz thinks meetings are boring and says she'll do whatever she wants anyway. Ann is the only one angry at the configuration and Helper is in the middle.

After the father's visit, Bruce received letters from different parts about how they handled the trauma. Marie wrote about the children's ages and methods of play that could help with communication in therapy. Liz wrote to straighten out the two 'Anglos,' Ruth and Bruce, about the eating habits of Latino children and the importance for Tabitha in considering herself the oldest. Ruth wrote an analysis of the System between the time the father left and the week with Claudia there until Sergio took her back to Nevada. Elizabeth Ray wrote a detailed report for Bruce about the 'known' children's abuse. She did not reveal information about the children to come, or details about Mariann. She waited for Jesus.

Praise God! We made it. Maria had a difficult time when Claudia left to travel back to Nevada with her father on Saturday. Claudia made it harder by telling her she wanted to stay with her. Tabitha is upset that Claudia's Shelty, Nakita, is gone. It reminded her of Lady and she loved it.

The father left early for Nevada instead of Thursday because of the storm. Thank God for that storm! Maria weathered it okay, no pun intended, as we didn't let her out to the surface at all. I spoke to the father before he left about the mother's health. He said the cancer has gone to the brain. She can't drive anymore and relies on Claudia to get her groceries and medications. She blacks out a lot and has a loss of appetite. I told him I would ask God to strengthen her and comfort her during this time. He just looked at me and told me to get him a beer. He then sat in the kitchen and rambled on about crime, water, the president, Indians, Donna, Darla, welfare and everything in-between. He's so full of hate and bitterness. It is very sad.

We plan to let Maria out to catch up on lost time with Claudia. Helper came up with the idea of renovating the bathroom here to accommodate Claudia's disability. We can't pick her up anymore as she weighs 125 pounds. Claudia gave us some of her SSI money to complete the project. Helper will contact Keeper of Functions to see if there is a carpenter on level two...

Later that day:

Tabitha is still upset that "her doggie is gone". She started to have a panic attack thinking the hombre malo cut out Nakita's heart too. I explained that Nakita was okay and that she had gone home with Claudia. I told her Nakita would be back in a couple of months to play with her. That's when Liz got very angry. She told me that was stupid to tell the kid that the dog would be back, because what was I going to do if the dog got killed between now and then. I guess I made a mistake again, anyway Tabitha is very sad.

I am concerned about her interpretation of the Bible stories she has been reading. She babbles on about how Adam and Eve were bad and God got mad, so he made them leave the pretty place because they didn't obey right. (Not far off?) *Then she says the man got eaten by the fish because he was bad because he didn't obey right and God was mad.* (Again, not far off?) *Then Jesus got dead because he was bad and God got mad at him because he didn't obey right like Tabitha.* (Okay, now we have a problem in understanding God's truth.) *But God made him alive again because Jesus cried. God gets mad. Tabitha get hurt and sotano. Tabitha be bad like Eve eat food and man in fish and Jesus on sticks. I tried to explain to Tabitha, but I need your help with her. Her logic is mixed up with what the grandfather told her and who knows who else.* (We would learn later that Yemaya was active in telling her these things to keep her afraid of God.) *We think it is important to get these things cleared up for all of the children.*

The crisis management team has analyzed the system in relationship to this last week. Their conclusion was we did very well in determining the best part to be outside during the visit of the father. However, they did have suggestions about being more careful in using 'I' instead of 'we', when conversing with the father. We slipped a few times, but he didn't notice. They also noted that when Raquel was out playing with Claudia and Nakita, Sergio noticed and became agitated. He hit Raquel and said, "Maria act your age." Raquel went in and Ann came out, but because Sergio is still not able to handle these situations, the system must be careful about allowing parts out who will agitate him while the children are around. The team noted that the system kept a low profile and avoided threatening situations by diverting the conversation or keeping busy in the kitchen. It also noted the tremendous amount of energy the system had to use, in order to successfully get through the week. The system is unable to keep up that level of watchfulness and responsibility on a continual basis. Circle Council is pleased with the crisis team report and everyone seems to be getting back to where they were before this last week.

I have talked with Tabitha about the sharing of her time with Anna and Muy Malo and told her Anna needs to have her Tapioca Pudding Party like Tabitha had her Burrito Picnic. Tabitha reluctantly (and that's putting it mildly) agreed to allow Anna to have her party and time with you. We think it is important for Anna to share something with you. We want to bring her out more so she can be comforted and start healing. You might want to explain Nakita to her, so she understands it isn't 'Lady' risen from the dead but a different doggie.

If you have found a student before Raquel's visit on April 3, she will wait so Maria can receive a birthday present a day early. Maria needs discipleship from an outsider. It is the most important need she and Louise have. Louise needs her questions answered and to know the love of Jesus. Although you are an instrument of the Lord in helping the system to understand their issues and be comforted, only Jesus can heal them. They need to know him to be truly healed, which is why I'm pushing the Biblical discipleship. I believe Maria needs you and the graduate student, to help her recognize, understand and solve her problems with the Word of God. Sorry for the pressure.

Elizabeth Ray wrote for the first time and did it in a manner as though she and Bruce had been working together already for a long time, which she had, only indirectly through others. Again, I need to warn the reader that the following letter is <u>very graphic in nature</u>. Most of what she tells Bruce is kept hidden from the rest of the System, until they are strong enough to hear it.

To Mr. Bruce F.,   **<u>Content Warning!</u>**

Muy Malo likes to watch Marie play puppet theater with Tabitha and Anna. Muy Malo might respond more to a puppet above her than your voice. She likes to watch the movements when Marie brings them to her hole and will reach out for them, while she listens to them talk to her. We find it interesting that she reached for your hair. We don't know why, maybe she was trying to determine if you were real. She is very tactile and seems to be absorbing information through touch and taste. When Muy Malo becomes overwhelmed, she will rock back and forth and whimper. She never cries, only whimpers. <u>*Muy Malo has never been touched in a non-violent way.*</u> *She does not know 'good touch', nurturing or safety. Tabitha had some relationship with the grandmother, but Muy Malo was out during the assaults in the pink room. The children shared sections of the abuse, since neither one of them could handle the whole situation.*

The grandfather usually started with touch. Tabitha would sometimes switch and Muy Malo would come out. Tabitha would watch from the ceiling and later learned to watch the moon and "go away in me." I recorded the history on the inside. The grandfather would begin at her chest and work down to her vagina. He would take her nightgown off, then kiss her private parts while unzipping his pants. He would then get on the bed and place a large protector sheet under the child. He would place his fingers and other things inside her. Sometimes he would try to place his penis in her, but usually failed because she was too small. If she started to whimper, he would tell her to be quiet and she'd learn to like it. Then he told her he had some candy for her to suck on. He then would put his penis in her mouth and ejaculated. Muy Malo would almost suffocate during this ordeal. She would gag and begin to throw up. He would dump her over the bed into the chamber pot. After he finished, he would put his clothes on and tell her if she told she would die. Then he would take Tabitha and the sheet to the bathroom. Here he told her to remain silent or he would cut her heart out.

Anna was out when the heart of her dog was cut out and Tabitha shadowed. Anna also handled being locked up in the chicken coop where the chickens pecked at her. Like Tabitha, Anna also experienced abuse from the mother. One day, Anna was in the pantry surrounded by bleach that ate through her shoes and got in her eyes. She screamed and was put into an ice-cold tub of water. Anna was also left in her crib for hours, wet and hungry.

Tabitha experienced the beatings in the basement by the paternal grandfather, hiding in the tank-house, the sexual assault at age 5 by the Cuban man, working in the shed on the apricots, the frying pan assaults by the maternal grandmother and the Santeria ritual abuse. Tabitha stood for hours on a fruit box cutting apricots. She hated to go to the bathroom in the outhouse, because she was afraid she would fall in and also because it was so big she had to slide off the wooden hole. She usually got splinters, which would fester and cause her pain. Her paternal grandmother would bend her over her knee and cut them out with a knife. She would then pour iodine on her to disinfect it. Her grandfather always like to watch.

Tabitha's drawing of abuse by the grandfather in the bathroom Cleaning following sexual abuse in the pink room.

The bath scenes were very difficult for Tabitha. For some reason the grandfather always insisted on the bath after an assault. The bathroom was next to the pink room. The grandfather always closed the door so the grandmother heard nothing. He would put very hot water in the claw-footed tub. He placed a board over the tub and placed Tabitha naked on the board. He proceeded to force her legs onto the sides and took hot water and soap to her private parts. He had a small hose with a pump where he would insert the hot soapy water into her to clean the insides. (Figure 6 above.) It was very painful for Tabitha. She had a cloth placed in her mouth so she couldn't scream. When he was finished, he dried her, checked to make sure she wasn't bleeding, then put her to bed. If she was bleeding, he made her set in the water until it stopped.

Tabitha had a very difficult time urinating for awhile. She would try to hold it, but eventually she had to go. To this day she doesn't like going potty because of the memories. Maria never was completely trained until her junior high years. Maria has had complications all her life with her reproductive system. (I want to insert a blessing for me at this point before continuing this horror story of abuse. Though I had read through these journals a couple of times in the last five years since receiving them, I missed this letter by Elizabeth Ray each time. Tabitha gave parts of this information in her drawings, which Elizabeth Ray confirmed when I asked directly for the purpose of counseling. But until this night I didn't know the details presented here.

The reason I say it's a blessing is that when I was working with Tabitha and her fears of the bathroom, I was glad that I was not aware of the severe abuse, because I'm not sure I could have held it together. That work culminated last month with intensive counseling for her, in trusting that Jesus would go in there with her and I, to show her the truth about her fears and that it would never happen again. I am thankful He withheld these images until after she was healed of them. The results of her healing in this area will be in the third book, because everyone in the System was affected deeply by both the counseling process and the healing that followed. I can see more clearly now the courage it took for Tabitha to trust anyone again. We will always dearly love her.)

The children rarely had anyone to play with or communicate with while on the farm with the grandfather. Tabitha was a very gifted child and began to create a world of glue people who would go on elaborate adventures with her. Tabitha would hear language in the apricot shed and copy it, which is how she learned to speak. She had no books or toys, so she created her own. One of her favorite games was getting the apricot pit into the hole in the tree. She would make a line in the dirt and pitch the pit in from behind it. With each successful throw, she'd move the line one step back to see how far she could get. If she missed, she had to start over. She liked to spend a lot of time sitting in trees.

In the springtime she would sit in her favorite large cherry tree. She would climb to the top and look out at the creek. Sometimes she would watch the clouds drift by and make up stories about the worlds beyond the clouds. She and Raquel spent a lot of time at the waterhole in Sunol. The Ohlone Indians had a village there. Tabitha would walk the streams and find arrowheads, birds and acorns. It was a very isolated area. She liked to listen to the silence and drift off to sleep. It is now a state park with a replica of an Ohlone village there.

Raquel was attacked by the Cuban worker when she was a teenager at 13. It was in the orchard behind the main farm. The Cuban threatened her with a knife and sexually assaulted her. When the body was twenty-two years old, Raquel spent a summer in Bluff, Utah (Monument Valley) and the Four Corners area when Donna ran away from home and lived in a trailer next to the Indian Reservation for four years. Raquel loved the area and explored the Indian culture there. The System came back to California to finish college.

There is no way to explain to you the pain and the memories of the system. When I think of these children in your office, I wonder how they are able to even function, let alone trust you after all they've been through. I wonder, with all the stuff you must hear as a counselor, do you ever become immune to the pain and hurt? Can you feel what they've suffered with understanding, or do you have to deny it for your own health? All these little ones ever wanted was to be hugged, loved and safe somewhere. Instead, they received torture, pain and suffering. Can you provide the compassion and love they never received? I wonder if they are like Humpty Dumpty. "All the king's horses and all the king's men, couldn't put Humpty Dumpty back together again." Are these kids Humpty Dumpties? I hope not.

I don't like divulging the history of the children in detail to anyone. It isn't an easy thing for me to have to remember and painful for me to write about their experiences. Yet, I feel that you need to understand what they went through so you will know why they are the way they are.
Sincerely,

Elizabeth Ray   <u>**End Warning!**</u>

I have never talked with Bruce about this letter, nor asked him how he felt when he read it for the first time. We both marveled about Elizabeth Ray's ability to remember so many details so far back as she does. As this letter indicates, it is a great gift if you don't have to remember the pain that goes with it. As more painful memories continue to emerge over the next few years, she will take on a counselor's detachment. It involves the setting aside of the pain being received through the hearing or visualizing of it, so that the energy can then be used for recording the details accurately without the interference of emotions. The problem with this 'gift' is that you can never escape the memories of it, without the Lord's help.

I've experienced this detachment often and thank God for how He allows me to give the pain of it to Him for disposal. I believe I can only do this because I wasn't the perpetrator of the sin, or the recipient of the pain relived by the memory. The pain of empathy is but a momentary effect, which can connect a counselor with a victim. If I were to dwell on the visualizations too long, I'd either have to move into a cold detachment without true empathy or leave counseling because the burden of pain is just too great. Neither option would provide the long-term care most victims need from a trusted individual. Each victim of abuse has enough of their own pain they bring with them. They don't need a counselor adding to it by the 'sharing' of their pain carried in from other cases. As a result, I have to be willing to accept a level of pain that is real, that comes from the 'carrying of another's burden' kind of understanding in empathy. It will never be at the level of the victim's pain, but it can be enough to create the compassion needed to come alongside, with real strength to help both people rise above the memory.

This is the kind of compassion the Lord modeled for us. He allows no burden too heavy that we can't carry with His help. I could not do counseling if He was not right there with me. This is why Bruce could answer Elizabeth Ray's question regarding understanding their pain by stating, "Yes! I feel what they have suffered with understanding. I don't deny the pain of it because Jesus takes that burden off of me and onto Himself. He can take it off of you as well, if you give it to Him." Every victim of sin of every kind, who suffer the real pain of memories can give that pain to Jesus to carry, if you are willing to trust Him to do so. It has been for Maria a burden she has chosen not to give Him, because she doesn't want Him to suffer anymore than He already has. She loves Him too much to "abuse Him with her pain." She is slowly learning that her pain is His pain too. He can remove that pain if by faith she allows Him to take it.

Everyone in the System is about to enter a very long chapter in their healing process of memory work. Mariann is about to emerge for counseling with Bruce. She will tell Bruce about her abuse by the 'Beast', Father Vincent 'Vinny' Breen. Her story is one of deep spiritual and sexual abuse repeatedly done by one priest and enmeshed by the theological and psychological system in which he served. Mariann will share her story in the beginning through her drawings, like Tabitha. It will take the next eight years for her to work through her fear of the Beast and his 'boss' (more on her fear of his boss in the next chapter). The System held the belief that they would be healed by just the telling of past secrets that held them in their prison of fear. The parts retaining 'body memories' of the abuse also believed that if they told about the abuse it would allow them to release the pain buried so deeply within their collective psyche. No one was prepared for the effects of clergy abuse on a child, much less the effect of the abuse on all the parts to follow her into adult life. Every corner of their life within the Catholic Church and Hispanic culture that surrounded Maria's life growing up, would become a continuous stream of stumbling blocks on their journey to trust God again.

While they make good strides forward in the healing process early on with Bruce, they will become overwhelmed by the past memories and subsequent pain contained within these memories. With Elizabeth Ray's help, Tabitha will continue to reveal more details of the abuse by the grandfather within the Santeria cultic sacrifices. These will include Satanic Ritual Abuses, where priests within the Santeria cult, or Santeros and some other prominent leaders, participated in these ceremonies. Though most of them are now dead, like Father Breen, the fear of retribution for telling what they saw and knew would stymie the healing process at every turn. For example, six years from now Penny will have a most difficult time. Because her only time out in the early years was to serve dinner and wine to the group of priests meeting in the grandfather's home to discuss 'church business.' She would retain her memories of the "nice fathers" holding her on their laps at dinner and refuses to believe the stories of Tabitha, Mariann, Mari and the 'Pod Children' over these last few years. When the Catholic Church does finally admit to child abuse by priests hidden by the Church over many years, Penny will essentially have to start over again in her therapy to understand what is true and what isn't... and which voice does she believe.

All of the System would learn over the years of therapy, that 'healing' can happen with the release of body memories holding pain, without the forgetting of memories of the act itself. There will eventually be a sharing of some of the body pain memory within the System, to parts other than Maria, like Ruth for the purpose of learning compassion for those parts abused. I believe the Lord allowed this to occur for a purpose, at a time when some adult parts were struggling to understand why the media blitz over the Catholic Church's sex scandal, was causing Mariann to regress rapidly in her therapy. Seeing the many 'Beasts' on the news coverage repeatedly caused Mariann to relive body memories, while telling me of her fear "the Beasts were coming to her house to kill her as they had promised." The adults couldn't grasp why Mariann was reacting to a 'picture' like that on TV, or to Ann and Ruth reading the newspaper. Maria and the children of the System just wanted it to all go away, so the triggering of memories would stop. The adults wanted to stay alert on the issues to see if justice of any kind will occur.

When Ruth shared Mariann's body memory of the tearing of her vaginal walls by the priest at the age of eight, I wondered if there was only some way to inflect that pain-filled memory upon those priests and anyone else who abuses a child, as part of their therapy for recovery. But the Lord is always more gracious than I will ever be. Maybe the sharing of the stories in these books will help the Church-at-large and society understand the victim's point-of-view of clergy abuse and the fear that permeates it from their first abuse until their healing or their death, which ever comes first.

One's character is the product of the dark
and difficult hours of the past.
-Raquel

"And we know that God causes all things
to work together for good to those who love God,
to those who are called according to His purpose."
-Paul Romans 8:28

The conclusion, when all has been heard is:
fear God and keep His commandments,
because this applies to every person.
For God will bring every act to judgement,
everything which is hidden,
whether it is good or evil."
-The Preacher Ecclesiastes 12:13 – 14

"To God belongs what is in the heavens
and what is in the earth,
that he may recompense those who do evil
for what they have done,
and may recompense those who do well,
with the best reward."
-Koran, 53: 32

Chapter 9:

"The Abuses of Faith Along the Path"

*'And He called a child to Himself and set him before them
and said, "Truly I say to you, unless you are converted and become
like children, you shall not enter the kingdom of heaven.
Whoever then humbles himself as this child,
he is the greatest in the kingdom of heaven.
And whoever receives one such child in My name receives Me;
But whoever causes one of these little ones
who believe in Me to stumble,
it is better for him that a heavy millstone be hung
around his neck, and that he be drowned in the depth of the sea.
Woe to the world because of its stumbling blocks!
For it is inevitable that stumbling blocks come,
but woe to that man through whom the stumbling block comes!
-Jesus Matthew 18:2 – 7*

"Then I saw that there was a way to Hell, even from the gates of Heaven."
-John Bunyan, *The Pilgrims Progress* (1678)

There is a need to be more specific about the sins of clergy abuse in the System's life, before I go on with their stories, to help understand Mariann's early revelations to Bruce and their subsequent effect on the adult parts. While Mariann begins to draw (See Figure 7 following page.) and speak in whispers at first about the Beast, she will not overcome her fear of his 'boss' for many years. She believed his boss was God because he came to her in the name of God. (In a few years, when she reaches the stage of understanding that God was not directing the actions of the Beast, she accepts the Devil as his boss.) Even when she does openly express her fear of the Beast in public, which is anytime she sees someone dressed like a priest or nun, she will continue to speak about his boss only in whispers and only in a safe place. She will come to know Dragonslayer and trust Him with her very life, but still have to separate 'God the Father' as the boss of the Beast from Jesus' Father as 'Daddy God'.

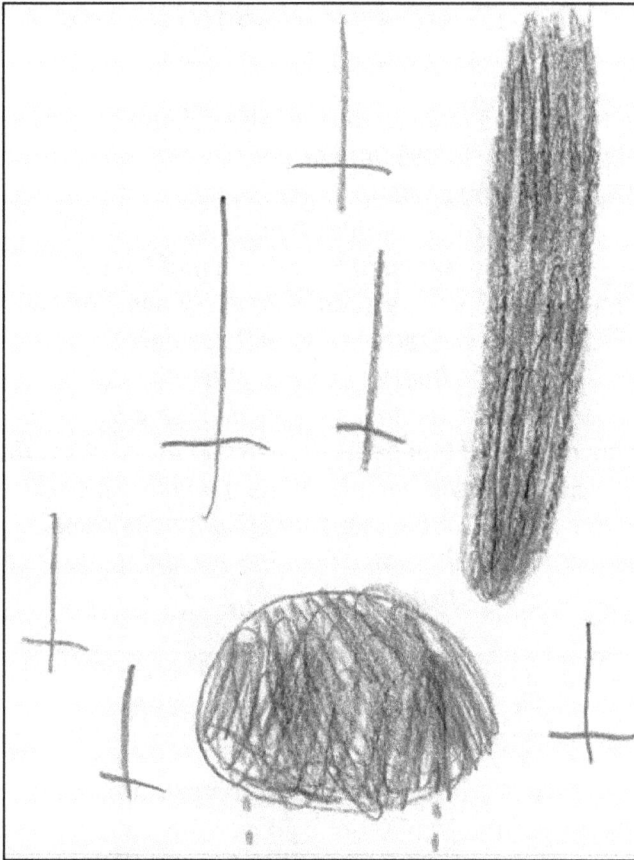

Fig. 7. Mariann's drawing of abuse by Father Breen in the rectory.

This difficulty existed for all of the abused children in their concept of 'father', but most persistently held by Mariann. One will represent pain and fear, while the other was represented in the love and safety they receive from Dragonslayer. Daddy meant love and protection for the children and some adults, while father was connected to fear, pain and suffering, waiting behind their obedience to him.

One truth that has come out of the history of the System is their yearning to know the love of God from birth. It has been shown through the scientific studies of anthropology, archeology, sociology, psychology and theology, that there exists in every civilization throughout history an understanding of a moral code in that society. It is this knowledge of good and evil at work within the social fabric that relates all humankind together in each society's acceptance of this moral code. Plato refers to that moral code as the 'common good,' which is true and right for all of mankind. For Muslims, Christians and Jews, we believe this knowledge is given to us by our Creator God, innately into our souls at our creation. Both the Bible and the Koran define this moral code as coming from God, our only source of absolute moral good. This knowledge of God from birth then becomes what drives our conscience to make moral choices between good behavior and evil behavior. Our conscious instincts even before birth is to attain life for this created soul, without knowing what drives us to seek it, often for many years with one purpose in mind, to know our Creator and the reason for our creation.

All people are accountable to God for their behavior in this life, individually first and corporately second, in how they treat their fellow man. God takes particular interest in His instructions to us about how we are to raise all children into a knowledge of Him, without hindering their search to discover Him and fulfill that desire implanted in our souls at creation. However, every person is also given free will to accept or reject this knowledge, as well as how we use this knowledge in teaching our children about God, before they are mature enough to exercise their choices before God. The Golden Rule proclaims it - Proverbs says it like this:

**"Train up a child in the way he should go...
Even when he is old he will not depart from it."**

I present this verse because it most aptly defines the responsibility for all parties concerned in the process of knowing God in anyone's lifetime. The Hebrew word for 'train up' has three concepts of usage within it: to dedicate, to instruct and to motivate. All three terms are used to move the child in a direction of learning the truth about God. All three are the responsibility of someone other than the child. If the people dedicating, instructing or motivating are not themselves dedicated to God, instructed in His precepts and inspired within themselves to know the will of God, how then can they teach a child correctly with sincerity of heart?

The word for child as used here is better translated as 'dependent', someone in need of assistance in finding the 'way that he should go.' Children, especially smaller children, are always dependent upon older adults for their needs. Societies throughout history look to the parents to fulfill this moral obligation before God. Parents throughout history have been dependent upon their religious leaders to teach their children and themselves about the god of their chosen faith. I underlined this to point out culpability of parents in choosing who they share their responsibility with, for the spiritual education of their children. Yet, clergy of all faiths have accepted that responsibility upon their shoulders, empowered by the grace of God and motivated by their dedication to their calling by God, to serve Him in obedience by teaching His truths.

This is one reason why clergy abuse of any kind and most certainly of a child, is so abhorrent. The abuse not only affects the child in many ways, it affects everyone who has been or will be dependent upon the abuser for spiritual guidance. When any clergyperson distorts the truths of God, all that are within their sphere of influence are affected and sometimes infected, by the evil that motivates them. A child that receives lies about God, as their instruction at an early age, either by their parents or their spiritual instructors, will carry that distortion into and beyond the age of discernment. Their ability to choose right from wrong and good from evil will be compromised throughout life, unless they learn the truth about God and trust it.

The hardest part of my counseling for clergy abused victims, is not helping them accept the truth about their abuser, it's helping them accept and trust the truth about God, after they've suffered for so long under the lies about God. The evil that we choose as a response to our fellow human beings, over and against God's instructions to us to "Love One Another" isn't limited by our understanding of sin in control of our lives. It is our faith and trust in God to empower us to do His will that can limit it. Any person, who publicly accepts the responsibility of being a role model and representative of God, also accepts the accountability for that position before God and the people they are called to serve as a leader. No one escapes their accountability before God for either their sin or their complicity in the sin of another against Him. Social justice may be blinded by extenuating circumstances, a lack of physical evidence, or a myriad of other legal maneuverings, including a statute of limitations, but God is not limited by any of these things in the dispensing of true justice. For His 'shepherds,' with whom He has entrusted His truths for the edification of His flock… He offers this warning from **Ezekiel 34**:

> **'Thus says the Lord God,**
> **"Behold I am against the shepherds, and I shall demand**
> **My sheep from them and make them cease from feeding sheep.**
> **So the shepherds will not feed themselves anymore,**
> **but I shall deliver My flock from their mouth,**
> **that they may not be food for them…**
> **I will seek the lost, bring back the scattered,**
> **bind up the broken, and strengthen the sick,**
> **But the fat and the strong I will destroy.**
> **I will feed them with judgment."**

I trust that God will administer His justice for the abusers and those complicit in their crimes at His appointed time, whether at the end of their lives or during their lifetime. My goal in looking at the crime of clergy child abuse specifically, is to help both victims and caregivers inside and outside of the church understand the ways in which evil will use our sinful nature to implant lies about God into the innocent. The very fact that this sin comes through an alleged spokesperson for God makes the distinguishing between truth and lies all that more difficult for the victims.

The best way I know to reveal a lie is to hold it up against the truth, but I need to caution my readers about one thing in particular. As stated in Ephesians 6 and quoted earlier in the book, we do not fight against the enemies of God where most of us can see our adversary face-to-face. We can however, hear the 'Father of lies' when he attempts to hide them in a faade of truth. To do this, we must be able to compare it to the truth we do know about God. I give you two ways to make a unified comparison, the Holy Bible and the Holy Spirit that speaks to your desire to know the true God. If I can show the circumstances surrounding how the lie is delivered and revealed by this comparison throughout the book, a methodology can be established to break the chain of its delivery and its power to hold its victims in bondage.

Mariann and Maria, like many victims of abuse, must fight against a very pernicious lie that the enemy perpetuates to prevent them from healing. This lie is like a two-edged sword that cuts from both sides equally well. Clergy child abuse at the heart of the sex-scandal of the Catholic Church reveals inside it the lies that continue to control the minds and souls of victims, for decades after the abuse first occurred in many cases. The front side of the lie says, "God is a partner in the crime of (clergy) abuse, because He allowed it to happen by men representing Him." The back side of the lie and the most problematic is, "From whom does the victim seek justice if God is the final authority of the Church and complicit in the crime?" Both statements are lies given by the enemy to place the focus upon God to explain His actions, or lack of them, instead of the actual perpetrator, the enemy that empowers the sin which still resides within mankind. The thought of seeing that enemy clearly alive and well within any man who is supposed to be representing God's love, is repulsive to anyone who has experienced the love of God. It is equally abhorrent for any victim who was abused by someone they loved and thought he or she loved them. Clergy abuse compounds the pain of it, because it can cause the victims to be afraid to turn to God for healing. That is why I'm using this example to show why these lies can control victims, perpetrators and onlookers, who don't want to see the truth of that which gives the lies their palatability.

The victims of clergy abuse are caught in a circular trap from where there is no escape, if they accept either of the lies. First, if they believe that a "man of God - is abusing them", then they are lost to the first lie in its very contradiction in terms. God does not operate His 'permissive will' by allowing anyone that represents Him to contradict His commandments in their behavior. Nowhere in the Bible will you find child abuse, rape or molestation permissible under any circumstances. The victims start accepting the lie the moment they believe the perpetrator represents God and yet, what choice do they have when society, fellow clergy, and higher church authority confirm the lie by not holding the abuser accountable to God's prescribed justice. They even add to the abuse of the victims by not believing the possibility when allegations are made as a child, or as an adult some 20, 30 or even 40 years later. If society and church leaders expect there to be a statute of limitations on crimes against God or His children, then they do not honestly represent the eternal nature of God's love and justice. The dead will assuredly face their accountability before God and be judged by Him, but it is for the living victims that some measure of justice is needed to promote healing.

For a victim to see and hear their abuser confess publicly their sins and ask for the forgiveness that comes through grace, it has to happen with heart-felt repentance from the offending party directly and not the institutional representative, be it a lawyer, a Presbytery official, or the Pope himself. A generic request for forgiveness, as done by the Catholic Church's hierarchy in 2000, showed behavior and readiness to accept whatever punishment the law requires, the possibility of healing for victim and abuser is now open to them... but little understanding or empathy for the plight of the victims. God was still being kept at an impersonal distance, with the questions of justice and forgiveness still hanging in limbo. As the scandal started to unfold this year, words like forgiveness, repentance, healing, rehabilitation and justice became as subjective for the victim, as it did for their abusers in their lack of meaning. The leadership of the Catholic Church will fail miserably in any attempt to move forward or bring about healing for the victims, if they don't seek first to bring about restoration of accountability before God publicly for the actions of a few and the genuine contrition of the leadership who were complicit in the cover-up.

God calls every church leader of any authority and every denomination to a higher standard of accountability for their actions done in His name over His flock. When the evil of clergy abuse is uncovered, He doesn't want 'damage control' or 'what constitutes serial child abuse vs. a one-time event kind of sin' to be the topic of debate from His leaders. He does want His Father's house to be cleaned out of the evil that resides in it. To cover up an evil or make it sound less than it is to its victims is to rob these victims of the truth of God's words applying to everyone equally. To say to a single victim of clergy abuse by even a one-time offender, that the pain and shame they carry the rest of their life isn't as important to seek justice for, as it is for seeking healing for the abuser, is to diminish their self-perceived value in God's eyes. Jesus didn't cleanse the Temple by going to the Pharisees and saying, "Let's setup a system of recovery for these money-changers and Sadducees to learn the truth about the use of My Father's house." No, He cleansed the Temple first with clear statements about what was wrong in His house and then set the example of what was to follow:

'And He said to them, "It is written,
'My house shall be called a house of prayer';
but you are making it a robber's den.
And the blind and the lame came to Him
in the temple, <u>and He healed them</u>.'
-Jesus <u>Matthew 21:13 – 14</u>

I believe that Jesus has more righteous anger today, over how the leadership of the Catholic Church is responding to the truth of clergy abuse within their ranks, than what He felt on that day in the temple. His call to them today is unchanged,

"Clean up My Father's house...NOW!"

This may sound harsh to the devout Catholic not scarred by past abuses, or unfamiliar with the tattered lives of victims, like in the stories presented here. Yet, for the victims, it is only a start, a new beginning for the restoration of their lives from the separation they've felt from the love of God. To clearly understand that separation, we only need to look at the lies implanted into the victims of clergy abuse with more detail. Because the implications of the lies perpetrated are so pervasive, I believe it necessary to describe in detail, how these lies were put into the psyche of the System to best illustrate how evil can control a victim. I've heard similar stories by other abuse victims not reported in this book and by victims who were not suffering from DID. The burdens of the lies were no less painful for them. Maybe this real contextual setting will help you to understand the struggle for meaning by the System, making their discovery of the truth of God's love all the more miraculous as their stories unfold.

Obviously, Maria's child abuse started at infancy with the neglect and physical abuse by the parents. The sexual abuse began with the grandfather shortly after being put under his care. From infancy to the age of seven or eight, Maria was splitting into other personalities to receive the trauma of the abuse, so the psyche/soul could survive. Some of the details of the suffering of these personalities before Mariann's arrival have already been given and more severe abuse for additional children is waiting to be revealed. I reiterate this only for the timeline perspective given in the books. The lies said to the children, as each one was created to receive a different abuse, will have the cumulative affect of not recognizing the truth they seek from God for each additional part created after them. By the time Mariann emerges, the System will equate a '<u>father</u>'s love' as that demonstrated by the grandfather's abuse and abandonment by the man perceived to be their earthly father.

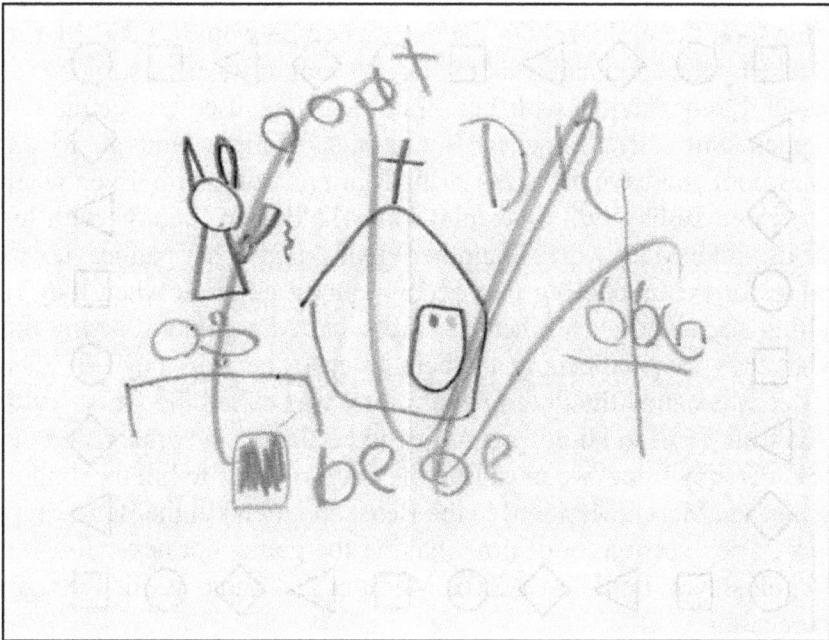

Drawing by Tabitha showing symbols to SRA abuses: 666, DIS, upside down cross, symbol of Goatman – leader/priest, the sacrifice of a baby [bebe], and a Catholic Church with a confessional inside reflecting knowledge of Mariann's abuse along with her own and younger child parts. Note: the scratching over of the drawing to indicate fear over telling anyone.

Their concepts of 'God as Father' would have come through Tabitha and Penny's differing experiences with the priests around them in the home, at church and through the grandfather's threats made after each abuse. The ritual abuse of the 'Pod Children' by the grandfather, priests and others within the Santeria cult, will build a basic fear of God. (Figure 8.) This fear will in turn be controlled by

Yemaya and subsequently added to and used by Father Breen. The fears of all the children of the System will cause the parts like Maria, Louise, Ann and even Liz, parts who did not in themselves experience the abuse of the early years, feel the anxiety from within every time they interacted with the church through the present day.

When Maria was seven, Mariann is created primarily to attend catechism classes after public school at Holy Ghost Church, where Father Breen served. He was the highest-ranking priest, but not the only priest living at the rectory house next door, where he often took the children. On the days when he would select 'Maria' to take by the hand and walk to his bedroom, it wasn't a surprise for the children playing with her, for they were used to seeing this happen with different girls. Sometimes Vinny would go to the classroom and have the Sister bring Mariann out to him. Even when her friend Bobby told other playmates he'd seen 'Vinny' with his hands under Mary's dress (another victim) and in her panties, it was cause for the snickering that occurs among children when they're telling secrets to each other. The kids started a game of acting out what they saw happening to them to ease the fear they felt. The Sister was called the dragon and Vinny was called the Beast. Both kids would run and hide, pretending to be fleeing the dragon and the beast. Bobby said, "we must find the dragon slayer to kill the dragon that sends Maria (Mariann) to the Beast and then kill the Beast, <u>if he can</u>". They spent a lot of time playing the game, but never found a dragon slayer, until Jesus gives Mariann that name as His to begin the healing.

Vinny worked for God, so anything he did was within his power over them. Vinny had been to Maria's grandfather's home many times before and had her (Penny) set on his lap to gain her trust. The first time she entered his bedroom, he had her set on his lap again so he could brush her hair while he talked with her about her body. He began telling her that he would give her tests from God and total obedience was required to pass. She still recounts today that she was punished by Vinny because God was angry with her for not passing the tests correctly. He would tell her truths about God; **"God is all powerful. God is the divine healer. God can destroy and create, etc."**

<u>Content Warning!</u>

He would mix it with other statements to dominate and control Mariann; **"God will heal the evil parts on you, only if you pass the tests. I work for God and have been given the power to help you with the tests, so that you can be pure and not dirty and make God happy."** The condition to receive God's healing every time was to pass the tests. There were several tests, the most important one being that his 'stick' (penis) could not 'throw up', no matter what he told her to do to him or he did to her. He would pose her naked in different positions to stare at her. He would rub and kiss her 'evil bumps and genitals' and rub his 'stick' over her vagina and buttocks, while gasping out, **"God is angry because you're not obeying him."** He would attempt anal and vaginal penetration over the years, but with little success. Her 'punishment' immediately afterward was to have to swallow his stick's 'throw up.' She never could pass the tests… no matter how many times she asked 'God' for help.

After each time of testing, Vinny would subject his 'pupils' to a 'ritual of cleansing'. He would dress them and escort them over into the church and the confessional. He would 'instruct' each child before they entered, to confess in detail all they had done to him, so that he could then absolve them of their sins for not passing the tests. This ritual secured control in several very different areas with the child and for Vinny's own spiritual understanding. The child is now totally confused about God, sin and forgiveness. 'God is angry because she did not pass the tests. God forgives her sins because she confessed them as her own. God won't heal you from the evil until you pass the tests. God loves me and has Father Breen give me these tests so he can heal me through the power God gives to him. Father Breen loves me because he isn't going to tell anyone about me failing God's tests. If Father Breen says this is truth from God, then it must be so. None of the other kids who said Father Breen was testing them have told big people about the secrets and I can't either.'
End Content Warning

I think that Father Breen convinced himself after his first victim that the evil he was doing was somehow God's work. He would rationalize his behavior to ease his sexual tension in a way that was more satisfying than by himself, because after all the Bible doesn't allow masturbation as a placebo for abstinence. He struggled not only with his sexual identity, but also with the power he had politically in the community and in the church. This social power or pride corrupted his ability to distinguish between the truth he knew about God and the lies evil justified in his mind as truth to continue his behavior. This might explain how he could instruct his pupils in God's 'truths' one moment, then hear their confessions and absolve them of sins he forced upon them after that.

He could in his mind receive forgiveness himself simply by confessing it in private to God or to another priest. Nobody in the church or outside were confronting him with his behavior as wrong and many would never accept the allegations later in life. If you read the book[4] on Father Breen written after he was forced to retire, you can see how many only saw the good side that evil hid behind. The hierarchy refused to pursue future allegations twice (maybe more), when the parents were afraid to stand against this powerful man within their community backed by the Church's leaders doing nothing and denying the accounts.

The sister or other priests might have known that something was wrong when he took the children into his bedroom at the rectory, had not the presumption always been there that evil couldn't overcome a man of God. Yet, no one pursued holding him accountable for his actions the rest of his life. When allegations do arise again some twenty years later he is forced into retirement 'due to ill health' and prevented from being promoted from monsignor to bishop. The opportunity for his victims to confront their abuser is long gone now, but not for the hierarchy to help them heal. Who do you think had the greater conflict within their spiritual search to know God? The man of God struggling to justify what he knows in his heart to be lies, before a God he believes will forgive all sins confessed to Him? Or a child of God growing up in the struggle of believing lies about a God she doesn't know, and justifying the lies as truth in order to survive?

For every victim of clergy abuse who believes that God condoned the behavior of the abuser, because of the authority invested in their profession as 'being a man of God', the abuser takes on the attribute of their authority as never dying. The abuser's threat, "If you tell you die" takes on an eternal quality to it, where even the death of the perpetrator doesn't remove the threat. Before any victim can no longer have the fear of retribution by God hanging over them, they have to come to know the true God and trust that He never hurt them in the first place. Evil, through the continued recalling of old memories and reiteration of new repeated threats in a life accustomed to abuse and lies as truth, will maintain its control over its conquests for a lifetime.

Sometimes evil allows the abuse to be reduced to that of a 'maintenance level', so as to maintain control without destroying its victim. Maria would 'exist' for another 30 years in this condition, before Ruth is split out to start confronting the lies about God embedded in the System's early formation. She will begin at the beginning, without knowledge of the abuses herself, seeking the truth of God's love. As Mariann emerges with her revelation of abuse by Father Breen, some four years later, she and Louise will have the hardest time accepting the truth. As the healing process began with Bruce, everyone would be caught up in the spiritual battle for their souls. The specific actions of evil using Father Breen as stated above, have been retold to me by Mariann, Elizabeth Ray, Mari and others, but the spiritual battle within his heart was revealed to me by the Holy Spirit.

"We are not born in our full development, but with a capacity for good and evil; we are begotten as well without virtue as without vice, and before the activity of our own personal will, there is nothing in man, but what God has stored in him."
-Augustine of Hippo (5th century)

"Every human being has been given free will. If he wishes to incline himself towards the good way and to be righteous, he is free to do so; and if he wishes to incline himself towards the evil way and to be wicked, he is free to do that...Every individual is capable of being righteous like Moses or wicked like Jeroboam, wise or foolish, merciful or cruel, mean or generous."
-Moses Maimonides, Mishneh Torah, 5:1-3 (12 century)

Perhaps one of the 'curses' in receiving the gift of free will from God given to all mankind to freely choose good or evil, is that it has to be given to all to have any true value of being free. Yet, the paradox of value is that our will is never truly free from evil, until we accept the payment of Jesus to overcome it and release us from our fear of having to choose without Him.

I'm going to change the book's timeline for a moment and give you two letters from the System that I received in the year 2000. I share them now because I feel they give a clearer picture about how evil relentlessly attacks our understanding of God to insure its control over the lives of the abused. The first letter I received in late March from Circle Council regarding thoughts and responses of the adults to Bishop Cummins asking for forgiveness of the past sins of their Diocese in the Catholic Church, as directed by the Pope in their year of Jubilee. You can contrast the System's answers then, to that of victims stepping forward today and the general opinions stated by parishioners to the Catholic Church scandal in 2002.

1. *"It bothers me that the church thinks they can just say please forgive us and that's it. For them they can leave it behind them. We live the effect everyday. It has changed our lives forever. As much as we would like to, we can't leave it behind us. It is part of us and will affect us until our death." – Marie*

2. *"What do they mean forgive us? They say it and then they say, 'Oh the church is pure! It was people that misrepresented the church that did wrong things, not the church.' Yet, isn't the church made up of the people who might not have physically done the wrong, but they didn't have safeguards in place to protect the children. When rumors about it surfaced, they looked the other way. Why did it take them twenty years and hundreds of affected children, before they would do something? Even then, when they did acknowledge it, it was to protect the priest, not help the children. And we are supposed to say we forgive you, why?" – Mari*

3. *"Forgive them? I'd like to chop off their collective dick is what I'd do." – Liz*

4. *"They request forgiveness without understanding what that forgiveness entails. Do they know of the deep pain and suffering caused by their actions? Have they understood what has happened to those children they allowed to be hurt? Have they*

changed their procedures and policies to show an act of responsibility as church leaders? Have they wept?" – Raquel

5. *"How can you put the crusades, the missionaries, the child abuse, the gender abuse and all the atrocities done in the name of the Catholic Church in one statement of 'Forgive us'? It is further victimizing the victim by making such generalized lightness of these actions." – Ann*

6. *"I just want them to understand how hard it is for me in my life because of what they let happen. I can never get back what they took from me. It hurts me that they never really want to know what their actions did to people like me. Do they really understand what they are asking of us? I wish I was strong enough to sit face to face with the Bishop and explain to him what his actions and those of the other leaders of the Oakland Diocese have done to us. I think of Mariann. I think of the pain and darkness and confusion that she experienced because of the Oakland Diocese. I wonder if the Bishop really knew what he was asking of us, if he would ask it? I don't know. I don't hate anybody, but I don't want the church to make light of our pain either." – Maria*

7. *"I should really ask them to forgive me for tempting the priest. I know everyone says a child can't do that, but we must have done something to tempt him. Maybe it was because we were already dirty from tempting the grandfather and we knew how to be flirting with him. I really don't know how it happened, but I'm sorry that it did happen and I am not angry at the church. I love my church. It is God's holy church and if it came from God it isn't bad. We are the ones who contaminate God's holy place, not God's holy fathers." – Louise*

As you can see from Louise's response, after 6 years she had not yet come to an acceptance of evil perpetrated by the church or even individually through Father Breen. The evil that was planted there so long ago still fought to misdirect the different parts of the System in the midst of their healing process, to bring them back under its influence. This can be more clearly seen in the second letter of December 2000. This letter is a conversation recorded by

Elizabeth Ray that occurred inside Preservation during a time of ongoing spiritual warfare to stop God's healing. More detail of the overall battle will be given near the end of book 2, but for now the spiritual being who is speaking identified herself to Louise, Marie, Mariann, Mari and Tabitha in the same way to draw them away from the presence of Jesus. Again, this is only one tactic used by evil during this battle. Ruth sets the scene:

Conversation recorded earlier this afternoon by E.R. I can't find Louise, Marie or Mariann. Maria is still asleep. Ann, Jennifer and Liz are here with me. Joy, Hopi and Lilah are in Jesus' arms shaking. Mari and Tabitha are with the woman. Jesus is setting on the rock still and I don't understand why. Council is in prayer. Land is tilted. I am praying for guidance and protection.

La Mujer: Mary I have come to help you with your confusion.

Mari: Who are you? I haven't seen you here before.

La Mujer: I am a friend of the child Tabitha. I am the mother of God. Your name honors me.

Mari: Are you Yemaya that Tabitha hung around with?

La Mujer: Oh no Mary, Yemaya was a trick and Tabitha was very wise in removing her.

Mari: How come Jesus is not with you?

La Mujer: Mary that is another trick. He is not real. If he were my real son he would take care of you. My real son sent me to rescue you. You are in much trouble. My son is angry with all of you for leaving the true church and going to the demons' church.

Mari: I don't go to church.

La Mujer: But Maria has and she goes to a church that lets demons attend. Today I rescued her from that church and the tricks that they are teaching her.

Mari: What tricks?

La Mujer: That I am not to be worshipped and honored. Tabitha knows how to honor me. Because you have strayed from the truth you have been subjected to all kinds of confusion.

Mari: I got hurt in the Catholic Church.

La Mujer: Mary I know and that was because Mariann didn't follow the instructions she was given.

Mari: What instructions?

La Mujer: The instructions from my friend Vincent. You were so good in confessing Mariann's shortcomings and did not my friend Vincent absolve you of your sins. Yet Mariann went right back to Vincent and messed up again. If she had followed the instructions properly, my son would have taken the evilness from her. My friend Vincent tried very hard to teach Mariann how to love the correct way, but Mariann continued to follow what she had learned from Tabitha and the Santeria. It was very hard for Vincent to be so patient with Mariann in teaching her the way to love a man of God. You all have suffered because of Mariann's disobedience. Mariann wants to hug you because she is being tricked. She is trying to remove her guilt of disobedience.

Mari: I don't want to talk about it anymore.

La Mujer: I know Mary it is very hard for you right now. I don't blame you for not wanting to speak anymore. Tonia and Maria were right that every time you or her speaks, outsiders take it the wrong way. Mike, Dave and Rob confuse you. If you were wise you would come with Tabitha and me to hide from the outsiders that are trying to trick you.

Mari: I want to talk with Shepherd 21. (My Internet name in another ministry at that time.)

La Mujer: He has left the area (Back east over Christmas) *and when you need him he abandons you. But I am here now. My son has sent me to rescue you. I am trying to take care of all of you. Maria almost made a foolish decision to let the demons in. If I had not stopped it, who knows the problems you would have now. I have prepared a place for you. Come and don't listen to the trick of the one who disguises himself as my son. Tabitha can teach you how to honor me and that will bring great honor to my son.*

Know for now that the being recorded as La Mujer was not the Mother of God. It was evil using an image that it knew would be accepted by those in the System indoctrinated with images of Mary and Yemaya. When Yemaya gained access back into Preservation after being rejected, Tabitha invited her back in because she came in the image of Mary. Shortly thereafter it would be Tabitha following my instructions to take her to Jesus inside and watch what happens, that reveals to the System the true nature of the being called 'La Mujer.' A significant amount of spiritual warfare happens during this time in the System's life, but that will wait for the proper context in book 2. This is only one illustration of the way evil will manipulate our fears and our experiences, of our basic desire to know and obey the one true God. In all of the spiritual battles that lay ahead for the System, from 1995 until their death, only Jesus remains the constant power that reveals evil for what it really is to heal the spiritual and emotional wounds of the past.

I will illustrate for the reader a final example about the effects of clergy abuse on the innocent children and how the evil remains for a lifetime. I described earlier in this chapter how the 'Church' played a part in what happened to Mariann at the time of her abuse, from documents and stories she and Elizabeth Ray have told me in counseling sessions over the last eight years. The following conversation was taped in May of 2002, during a healing session with Mariann and Hopi.

Hopi is one of the Pod Children from Those Who Are Core and his existence will be revealed in the summer of 1996. In 2002, my relationship with the System has grown into one of great trust and love with all the children now seeing me as Daddy Mike. We've been through hundreds of hours of healing sessions and had finally reached a point where Jesus said it was time to help them confront their fears of the Catholic Church and the 'Beasts'. As I listen to what Mariann and Hopi wanted to say to Catholic Church officials and priests in the presence of Dragonslayer, they reflect the pain and anxiety they were feeling from all the coverage of the sex scandal still raging on.

The letter is typed dialogue of a taped conversation with Mariann. She requested that this letter be given to Church officials from her and Hopi. I am to relay this letter to church officials in person because it is still too hard for them to express it in person. She refers to Father Vinny, or the Beast named earlier in this chapter in the past tense, though she was not totally convinced that he was dead yet. This letter is an excerpt of the third book being written about these severely abused people and God's power in healing them.

Recorded @ 2:15PM.   **<u>Content Warning!</u>**

"My name is Mariann. I want to tell the boss of Father Vinny about things... but I afraid."
(Calls Dragonslayer for help.)
"Dragonslayer help me say the things cause I afraid."
(Long pause.)
"Why did you let Father Vinny hurt me?   Why did you not say it was wrong? Why did you not bring help for me?"
(Long pause.)
"Why did you not think about me? Why did you throw me away?"
(Long pause.)
"Why did you not be like Dragonslayer?"
(Pause.)
"You make Dragonslayer cry because you still not know you hurt me and you not stop the hurt."
(Pause.)
"Do you listen to the smelly ones?"
(Pause.)
(I see anxiety in Mariann and distraction. I pray with her to not listen to the voices outside only to the voice of Dragonslayer inside, because she knows whose voice it is. As I pray for her, she begins speaking again.)
"When the smelly ones say to you... 'Let Mariann be hurt'...and 'Do not tell... or you will lose your power..."
(Pause.)
"Do you listen because having all the power is more important than Mariann? Do you know how it hurt? Do you like fingers in your pee-pee? Do you like to make sticks throw-up? Do you like sticks in

your mouth? Do you like going in the black box (confessional) *and say you be bad? Do you like these things? Mariann not like them!"*
(On the tape you now hear me explaining to Mariann what the tape is for as I turn it over. I explain that she is talking faster than I can write and the tapes tells me what I may have missed. I ask her to continue.)
"You not care about Mariann... you care about you! You not stop the hurt. I not like these things... why you let these things be for me?"
(Pause.)
"Why you not listen to Dragonslayer when he tell you stop it?"
(Pause.)
"Your church be big... but it not... it not... it not take care of me and throw me away... cause you say the church more important than me... got to save the church... got to throw Mariann away...it hurt."
(Pause.)
"I want you to know the hurt! I want you to know it hurt me... I don't want you to throw me away. I be Mariann! Dragonslayer not throw me away. Father Vinny say Dragonslayer throw me away... His daddy (God) *say that I have evil bumps* (breast) *and I have bad... bad where I go pee-pee... and... and... he not happy with me... he not want me... but Dragonslayer say that be a lie... Dragonslayer want me and I not have bad bumps."*
(Pause.)
"I don't trust you cause you say... you say you sorry but you not really say you sorry... cause you let the Beast still be... you let them still be. You still throw Mariann away... you still let the Beast be...you not sorry... you not tell... tell the truth... you be a trick. You listen to the Smelly One...he say to Dragonslayer – You bow down to me I give you all this power... but Dragonslayer He say no but you say yes. I want you know how it hurt... you want somebody look at your pee-pee?"
(Pause.)
"Dragonslayer, He not do it... He get mad cause you let... let... umm, you let the Beast do it and they come in the name of the Lord... come in the name of the Lord, they say they work for Dragonslayer... they say that Dragonslayer give them special powers to make Mariann be a good girl... they make Mariann bumps and pee-pee hurt... that be a trick! ...That trick. Not like that you say

Dragonslayer...you come for Dragonslayer when you come for the bad angel... you trick! ...You scare me you make it bad... you make it bad. You know what I want, I want you to know hurt... I want you to know what it be... then you stop it when you know what it really be... that what Mariann want. I no want a peanut butter cookie from you... no, that what Mariann want."

(Pause.)

"Dragonslayer, He want you to stop using His name for bad... He not like it when you do bad in His Daddy's house... He not like it when you say that you be working for Him and you ... you hurt... He not like it when you hide and you think you more important than His kids. Dragonslayer not like it when money and power are more important than do the right thing... and He not like it when you say you work for Him when you do these things. That make Dragonslayer mad and Dragonslayer not want peanut butter cookie from you either. That what I want... for you to know the hurt."

(Pause.)

"This be a letter from Mariann."

(I ask Mariann if Hopi a younger abused child within the System had more to say. She adds words from Hopi.)

"Hopi say yes to Mariann's (letter)... Hopi not like... Hopi not like burn, he not like the light burning him..."

{The light burning that was inserted into him, yeah that hurt, a heated crucifix was inserted into the body during a Satanic Ritual Abuse event by a man dressed as a priest... possibly a Santeria priest at the time. Hopi was created to receive these ritualistic abuses.}

"Daddy... he not know how to say words..."

It's okay, I know...

"He hurt, he not like the boss hurt... but the boss (Bishop?) hurt lots cause he not stop it...he not say don't do that... he not put... put... he not put Father Vinny go away... to place not hurt."

Could Dragonslayer help Hopi with his words?"

(Pause.)

"Hopi say it hurt so much you want to scream but... you can't. Hopi say to put the Beast's boss umm... umm to put the Beast's boss umm... to put the Beast's boss in Hopi's skin then he know how it hurt. Hopi say that he not like that they make fun of Hopi's hurt... and they talk lots in papers and they talk about things but they not know hurt."

245

They don't know about the hurt Mariann and Hopi went through…
"Daddy, you going to tell them?"
I will tell them…I will be strong and tell them for you…
"Okay… Okay, umm Hopi and me afraid again…"
Why are you afraid?
"Cause they big!"
Are they bigger than Dragonslayer?
"No Daddy, but Daddy we can't talk to them… too big."
You don't have to because Dragonslayer is telling Daddy to talk for you.
"Okay."
Daddy's not afraid of them…
"Daddy they do not know… what they do…"
No they don't Mariann…
"Got to tell them they say they do …they say they do but they not do…Cause if they do they would have a crying and they have a whole day and they stop and they cry."
Cry for a whole day… if they understood they would… and maybe longer.
"Yeah Daddy, but Daddy they… they like green paper (money) *and they like to umm… umm… they like to make it go away cause… umm, they not like to talk about it. I not like Mr. Law…"*
You don't like Mr. Law?
"No."
You've never met Mr. Law though…
"But I hear about him, he likes the Beast. He say… umm, I hear about him when the big people talk about him… I hear what he say… he say that he… he have trials cause of office, but he… he say trials his hurt… he not know real hurt."
He's caused trials for the people who have been hurt like you and Hopi…
"But then the big bosses… they not make him… umm, they not make him stop being umm, umm… umm… umm… they not make him stop saying I come in the name of the Lord. They not make him stop Daddy."
No they haven't… not yet anyway.
"Daddy… that man… that man… he… he not know hurt."
He doesn't know hurt… Bishop Law doesn't know about the hurt that he's caused directly or indirectly does he?

"No, he not... he go to the gold place with all the other big bosses, he go to the gold place Daddy..."

The Vatican.

"Daddy they talk but they not know the hurt... They not know what to do... They know what to do. They got to know the hurt and they got to stop it and cry... and ask Dragonslayer, Please clean them up... Please clean church... clean Dragonslayer's Daddy's Church with Dragonslayer soap... Yeah Daddy..."

(Long pause.)

"Daddy... why do... why do the... why do the priests, why do they listen to the smelly ones... why don't they tell Mariann I work for the smelly ones... why did they say they work for Dragonslayer, they come in the name of the God? Why?!"

Well the Father... Father Vinny Breen, he believed he did...maybe he didn't know he was being tricked and used by the smelly ones.

"Daddy..."

You think?

"Daddy umm... Do you know that it is a trick to look at a pee-pee?"

Yes.

"Do you know that it hurts to put your fingers in the pee-pee?"

Yes.

"Then if you know it... why do Father Vinny not know it?"

That's a good question Mariann...Father Vinny must have known... but he did it anyway. So he could only have been listening to the smelly ones and not to Dragonslayer.

"So why Father Vinny's bosses say, I know what he do but I not going to hear it or see it and say it happen."

Yes, I guess they said that a couple of times didn't they?

"But why?"

They didn't want to believe it I guess.

"But they know it! Why did they throw Mariann away?"

I don't know Mariann. They weren't supposed to... none of this is what Dragonslayer wanted to have happen.

"It hurts!"

He wants His people that come in His name to be kind and loving and not hurt His little ones.

"Daddy I want you to tell them about it hurting me..."

I will for you Mariann...

"Okay."

And I will for Hopi and all of you and others. I will try to be your voice.

"Tomorrow Daddy!"

I don't know about tomorrow... it's got to be in Dragonslayer's time.

"Okay."

What is Dragonslayer saying right now to you Mariann?"

(Long pause.)

"That He will take Mariann's hurt, but He still wants the boss man to be ac..c.ountable."

Accountable...yes!

"He still want them to stop doing bad and evil in His name... Stop using Him as their power... they tell people they come in Dragonslayer's name... Stop using His name for bad. That make Him not happy."

How can Daddy help you...how can Daddy help you to... you and Hopi to give that thing you feel... the pain and the memories that you have inside you... those pictures that keep coming back in the body memories with pain... how can we give those to Dragonslayer? Does Dragonslayer know about them?

"Dragonslayer know everything Daddy!"

Yes! He does know everything."

(Long pause.)

"Dragonslayer... Mariann not want to hurt no more... Hopi not... but Dragonslayer it hurt... Daddy?"

Yes?

(Long pause.)

"How do you tell Dragonslayer how much it hurts?"

You tell Him with your heart... You have your memories in your mind, but you just tell Him like your talking to me right now from your heart...

"Dragonslayer... One day Mariann have a heart and it was happy... and it was pretty and it... danced! And Mariann's heart not know bad... then Beast he come and it chew up Mariann's heart... and it spit it out in pieces... and it not dance no more... and it lose it's prettyness and can't find it no more... and it all in pieces and bloody... and it cut up Dragonslayer... and it hurt and it not dance no more."

(Long pause.)

"And it stay like that cause can't put it back together... Can't go back to it dancing cause it got grabbed by the bad... and it got chewed up...that what it be Daddy."

Can we give the broken pieces to Dragonslayer? How about if you close your eyes... here you close your eyes with me and Hopi close his eyes... you pick up all those parts to that heart...

"Can't Daddy... too many and They're all squishy..."

Do you want help? How about if you let me come inside with you and Hopi and Dragonslayer and we'll pick them up together...

"Okay..."

...And putting them in Dragonslayer's hands... as many as we are able to pick up today.

"Okay... Dragonslayer already have the hairbrush piece... He take that... Dragonslayer... there's the real squishy one but I don't want to put my hands on it..."

Can I pick it up or Dragonslayer...?

"Okay Daddy..."

I've got this one... Which one is this that I've got now?

"The one that is hanging down all sad... it's the one of the Beast looking at our pee-pee..."(Mariann starts crying after giving to Jesus what are probably the least traumatic memories).

I'm putting it into Dragonslayer's hands and you don't have to look at it anymore... You don't have to remember it anymore because it is in Dragonslayer's hands.

(Mariann cries harder and I try to console her.)

"Daddyyyy..."

That was hard, very hard wasn't it? ...It's okay Mariann...Hang on to Dragonslayer... How about if you and Hopi put your arms around Dragonslayer's arms and hang on to Him...And Daddy will pick them up when you are ready...can you hang on to Dragonslayer...Look in His eyes Mariann and what do you see there?

"Dragonslayer loves me... He's sad... Dragonslayer... He so sad Mariann got pieces in heart... Mariann not have dancing heart... Mariann heart in pieces... Dragonslayer sad Mariann dancing heart be put in pieces..."(crying continues).

Dragonslayer... Dragonslayer can heal this Mariann... Dragonslayer can heal your heart and Hopi's heart and put it back together...

249

"Daddy can't do no more!... Do no more Daddy!..."
No more... No more... it's okay! (Maria switches out and is sobbing... followed shortly by Joy, the youngest child part, who focuses on my eyes and my words of love and shortly falls asleep.) Session ends.

End of Contact Warning

Someone would have to actually participate in a session like this to feel the emotional pain on a smaller scale of what the victim feels most of their life. If healing is not brought to each victim through the power of Jesus Christ, they have no choice but to bury the pain internally. Often in the healing process Jesus removes the body memory of pain, but the mental picture is remembered with one change... the healing by Jesus. Maybe I will have an answer back from the Catholic Church for Mariann about this chapter sent to them this summer for comment before the third book is published. If so, I will include it in the third book. There are two more points I wish to make the reader aware of about evil and its methodology before I continue with the System's stories.

First, just because someone accepts Jesus Christ and is healed of sins separating them from God, this does not mean that evil gives up and goes away. It constantly works at breaking down the relationship between God and us in any way it can. It will try to plant doubt, foster fear, manipulate truth – even Scriptural truth. It will try to cause anger and division among the people of God. It will use any method at its disposal to accomplish its purpose. Evil may even come in the image of those we love and are taught to honor. It is tireless in its goal to cause hurt and pain.

Second, evil can be a very intelligent enemy in that it can learn through trial and error what works, what gets the reaction it wants. It may take it several years or several minutes, but it can adjust to the situation and adapt its tactics to try to get the desired affect. You will read throughout the books, how evil will escalate the warfare anytime it thinks it is about to lose ground in the arena of our souls.

Third, the evil inherent in clergy abuse is never removed in the courts by the receiving of monetary awards for its victims. These awards can provide a means for its victims to receive the kind of care they need to reveal that which empowers the evil that controls their responses to God. A monetary judgement cannot heal them but in some cases it can be used to find professional help to heal. Victims will find that evil cannot be paid off to leave. Our hope to overcome evil lies only in Jesus Christ who overcame evil for all time on the cross at Calvary. Evil just hasn't accepted that fact yet and doesn't want you to either. Evil took notice when the System began to heal especially when Mariann came out in search of her Dragonslayer.

Mariann, Tabitha, Angelina, Anna, and the other children inside who were close to being revealed, were being attacked spiritually by evil in their memories of the abuse. They continued to be afraid with great anxiety that they would be killed for telling about the bad. Louise and Marie were still hurting over the revelations of Mariann's abuse by Father Breen, as well as being challenged by evil about what really was the 'truth' about the Catholic Church. Raquel, Liz, Jennifer, Louise and Maria were all fighting against evil influences inside. They fought against the memories of their own experiences, while trying to learn the truth about God, Jesus and the Church on the outside in our time together. Even with all these attacks occurring, the next phase of their healing process over the next year will be remembered by some as the easiest time in their lives. They were all on a journey into the unknown spiritual side of their existence. Once they began this particular path there would be no turning back. They could not return to another time when truth was a choice.

"Let no one deceive you with lies about God, for they will receive the wrath of God that comes upon the sons of disobedience. Therefore do not listen to them like you used to do in darkness, For now you have light in the Lord so walk as children of light, And the light will guide you to goodness and righteousness and truth, Helping you to learn what is pleasing to the Lord. Expose the lies and deeds of darkness with the light of Jesus, where all things become visible through the light of His truth; Therefore be careful how you walk this difficult path,

*Making the most of your time in wisdom from the
Word. The days are evil and the time is short so
do not be foolish, Stand boldly within the will
of the Lord and receive life everlasting."*
Paraphrase is mine from: **-Paul Ephesians 5:6 – 17**

*"Not everyone who says to Me, 'Lord, Lord,'
will enter the kingdom of heaven; but he who
does the will of My Father who is in heaven.
Many will say to Me on that day, 'Lord, Lord,
did we not prophesy in Your name,
and in Your name cast out demons,
and in Your name perform many miracles?'
And then I will declare to them, 'I never knew you;
depart from Me, you who practice lawlessness."*
-Jesus Matthew 7: 21 - 23

Notes:

[4] For another perspective of Father Breen's career, written after his retirement, Love Will Follow, by Andres L. Abejo, Ph.D., Publishers Press, 1983, Quezon City, Philippines.

Chapter 10:

"Will Faith of the Abused be Enough"

"Behold, the Lord God will come with might,
with His arm ruling for Him.
Behold, His reward is with Him,
And His recompense before Him.
Like a shepherd He will tend His flock,
In His arm He will gather the lambs,
And carry them in His bosom;
He will gently lead the nursing ewes."
<u>-Isaiah 40: 10 – 11</u>

"With all of my heart I will search for You;
Never let me stray far from Your word.
For they show my soul the Way,
To never be separated from You again...
Thy word is a lamp unto my feet,
And a light unto my path."
-David <u>Psalm 119</u>

> " Either God exists or he does not. But to which side shall we lean? Reason can decide nothing, there is an infinite chaos which separates us. A game is being played, at the extremity of this distance, where heads or tails will fall. What will you bet? If you win, you win everything. If you lose, you lose nothing. Bet then that he exists, without hesitating." - Blaise Pascal, *Pensees* (1670)

Bruce was only receiving about 6 or 7 communications a week. They dealt less with issues about God and more with issues focusing on therapy and the cost to the System. 'Those Who Are Core' began to slowly reveal their existence in words and symbols drawn on the pictures of Anna, Tabitha and Mariann. The words and symbols were indicative of Satanic Ritual Abuse. Bruce and I discussed the possibility on several occasions but Bruce wanted to wait to confront this for several reasons. We were not sure at that time if the abuse had occurred to Tabitha, Anna or Angelina, or if there were more parts left to be revealed. Neither of us wanted to risk the possibility of implanting ideas or memories, so the best posture was to wait and listen until they revealed themselves.

For the Clan of Argus, the Guardians and the Harmers, the time when Mariann reveals herself directly to Bruce was one of great fear. They had spent 32 years protecting her and keeping her secret from the world and the rest of the System. It wasn't easy to relinquish control to new leaders... or to the one on the outside:

Why are we now writing and allowing him to enter our world? The child has revealed herself to him. How did that happen? Was she not guarded? Yes, but the lion of the jungle said it was time. Danger is approaching so the child was revealed. Does she (Maria) know of the child? Only the voice in her mind. There is trembling in the jungle, the child must be protected. The one whom she has revealed herself to cannot protect her from the Beast. Lion is on guard and snatches her back to deep inside the jungle where she cannot be found if trouble comes. The Beast cannot find her hidden among the briars and thistles. But when she reveals herself while on the machine to him she is vulnerable to the Beast. Lion is on guard. Did they put the curtains up... are the secrets well hidden? Yes, it has been done and all has been hidden in the space of the spiders. THE DANGER IS HERE, SEND AND DESTROY. (Danger = the father's visit.)

Later, after the father left:

The danger has returned to the East. The trembling in the jungle is diminishing, but do not let up guard. The child has been revealed and we are no longer a secret. She has made contact with the Outsider. Why did Lion allow it? He said it was time. The Outsider with the beard and monkey has been observed for many months. The Lion has watched his working with the hole children and the weak one. The child cries out in pain and agony, just like the hole child with no voice. The Outsider comforts the hole children with their pain. Might he not do the same for our child? Lion will determine the path and the time. The child only contacts by the machine, as the child is not ready for the room.

254

How will the Outsider view us? Will the Outsider understand the jungle? Will the Outsider remain safe and trustworthy? Will he weep for our child, as we weep? I do not know, but we must follow the leading of Lion. Do the Surface People know of us? They have heard the voices, but they know not of our world. They know not of the door leading into the jungle, nor of the pain and suffering of the child we protect, but in time it will be made known to them. Some of us are concerned about revealing our world to them. Those of the Trees are greatly concerned about the risk and danger in revealing our existence. They say that safety and protection can only be secure through isolation and secrecy. To expose the jungle to the Surface People and the Outsider means to risk loosing that. I understand their concern, but Lion knows it will be difficult for all of us. He remains on guard to protect the jungle from danger and he never sleeps.

Mr. (Bruce) F.:

We of the Jungle have watched you work with the Hole Children. You have comforted them and helped them with their memories. The Surface People of the Land of Preservation trust you and the Clan of Argus have also spoken well of you. Our child of the Jungle is a sacred child. We will protect her at all costs from the Beast. The animals of the Jungle have agreed to allow our child to meet with you, so that you can help her. She is called MariAnn. In her heart is a piercing thorn that was placed there by the Beast.

MariAnn can not talk with us about the pain of the thorn. We know of the pain, because deep at night our child cries out in agony. The Jungle animals do not know how to remove the thorn from her heart. Therefore, we are trusting you to help comfort our child and heal the wound that agonizes her.

We will be on alert and watching you. Do not hurt our child or we will retaliate and cause you much harm. The Jungle will risk all to protect our child. That is why we exist.
LION

Jesus will ask me to give Lion's letter to Maria again, eight years later to the day in 2002, to help her understand the pain in her heart over the Catholic Church's scandal happening at that time. The

System was attempting to come alongside of Bruce for the greater need of healing for the children. There was a real sense of unity in moving toward this goal. They learned from the children in their acceptance of each other and watched the actions of the one called Jesus with the children. Ruth wrote to Bruce:

Dear Bruce,

The children have made a lot of progress since Monday. Tabitha has tried to help Angelina as you requested. She came up with the idea that she and Anna would travel with Jesus to Angelina's hole and be nice to her. It took awhile for Tabitha to convince Anna that it was safe. Interestingly, her rational was that as long as Jesus held them, the bad man would not come. So the three of them went to see Angelina. Tabitha says that when she looked in Angelina's hole, it was "yucky and smell like poop in outhouse."

Apparently, Angelina did not want to come out. Tabitha reached in and gave Angelina a flower. She told Angelina that "Jesus was here and Anna's friend and keeps the bad man away." Then she told Angelina that "Daddy say you no do dirty. Papa do dirty. You no very bad. You cry cuz it hurt. Angelina no bad. Daddy say Papa do dirty." According to Tabitha, Angelina listened to Tabitha's explanation. Tabitha then said that Angelina put her hand out to touch Jesus' hair and Jesus went into the hole and held Angelina and her bear, "for mucho tiempo Ruth." (The Jesus I know will go willingly into a shithole to rescue one of His children.)

Tabitha said she told Angelina that Anna had a very nice baby hole that was warm and Jesus was there. Then she looked at Anna and said, "you let Angelina come in your hole with Jesus?" Anna nodded yes. Jesus came out of the 'poop hole' carrying Angelina, picked up Tabitha and Anna and carried them back to their holes. Tabitha said that Jesus looked back at the poop hole and it closed up, then Jesus let her climb on top of His back with Ollie so she could see things, because she is the big girl.

Tabitha says that Anna and Angelina now share a hole next to her big girl hole. She told me that Angelina sits in Jesus' lap because she is very much afraid of the "dulce malo of the bad man and she needs to be covered by Jesus' white garment." Jesus lets Angelina drink her bottle on his lap. Then Tabitha said, "Daddy happy! Tabitha be good girl to Angelina. Daddy give Tabitha ice cream. Tabitha want go bye-bye in daddy car and have ice cream...white ice cream. Tabitha be good for daddy and help Angelina." I told Tabitha that she had to talk to you about that, but that I was very proud of her for helping Angelina.

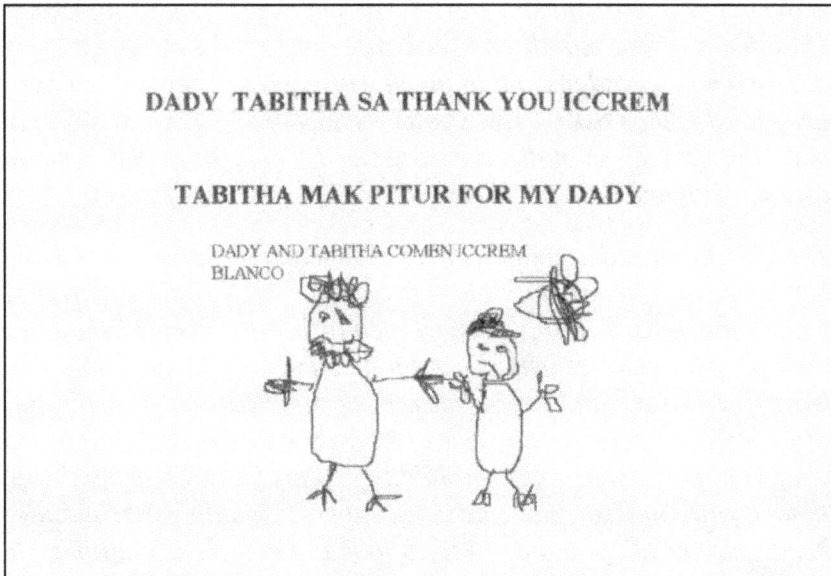

DADY TABITHA SA THANK YOU ICCREM

TABITHA MAK PITUR FOR MY DADY

DADY AND TABITHA COMEN ICCREM BLANCO

THERE IS LIGHT AT THE END OF THEIR TUNNEL.

And the letters keep on coming:

Liz had an interesting evening. I went to a Bible class and the topic was spiritual warfare. Several people were discussing demons and got on the topic of possession and how Jesus dealt with it. I was uncomfortable with it, especially since I knew that Liz was listening. Well, one of the 'spiritually mature' Christians decided to express his opinion on mental illness and demonic possession. I immediately lost control of the outside and guess who came out.

I was able to listen and thankfully Liz kept her mouth clean. It was funny though listening to her lead the guy right into a corner... the way a sheep is lead to the slaughter. First she expressed interest and said, "could you expand on your knowledge of mental illness and demon possession in say for example, multiple personality disorder.

257

Are you familiar with this disorder?" The guy says yes. "It is a classic example of demon possession. People, who have these voices and different personalities, have been taken over by evil spirits and demons. We need to look at Jesus' example. He called the demons out and healed the person."

So Liz says, "Have you ever met a multiple? I mean how would you know a multiple if you saw one?" The guy says, "They look crazy. They foam at the mouth and look disoriented. They will speak in different voices and are not in touch with reality. They are not hard to spot." Liz then asks, "Have you ever met one?" The guy says no, but "I'm very good in discernment and I would know if I came in contact with one."

Then Liz says inside, "Watch this!" I immediately panicked and told her do not say we are multiple! Liz begins, "Well you know what... I have specialized in this area of mental health. People who have multiple personalities actually are gifted and intelligent people who learned very early in life how to split off trauma in order to survive. Most multiple personalities were severely abused as children and your God gave them split personalities to protect them from dying. In fact, you could say that God is the expert in multiple personalities because after all, you only need to look at God. He is multiple. He has three parts in the same God. The Father, Son and Holy Spirit are three persons in God. God is the Father, God is the Son and God is the Holy Spirit, but the Father is not the Son or the Holy Spirit and the Son is not the Father or the Holy Spirit... Kind of like a multiple personality. As far as demon possessed that is a bunch of shit unless you are telling me that God is demon possessed."

The guy just sat there. Liz looked at him, smiled and said, "I got to go. See you around." And she leaves. She gets in the car and proceeds to tell me in her colorful language exactly what she thought of 'that idiot.' I tried to calm her down by agreeing with her that they were not based correctly in Scripture or psychology. That was like trying to plug up a volcano with a cork... Liz is still screaming.

In Him, Ruth

One Who Listens:

Mari told Brave Eagle that Mariann is coming to see you. Mari said that Lion and the animals of the jungle are going to let her visit today in the hopes that you can help her with her memories. I have fixed the body's hair the way Mariann wears it in the jungle so that she will feel more comfortable on the outside. Mari suggest that if Mariann chooses to draw instead of talk, that you provide large paper as she likes to draw large pictures.

Mariann is very obedient and follows Lion's orders to the letter. If she feels that she is safe with you she might wish to stay out the entire session and draw. If she is uncomfortable or afraid Lion will draw her back inside. According to Mari, Mariann knows of Maria's grandmother. However, most of her time was spent with Maria's mother and father living down the street from where the grandparents lived. Mariann cared for her younger brother and sister because the mother was not available much and the father was gone most of the time. Mariann was responsible from seven to twelve years old for her younger siblings' well being.

Mariann is afraid of priests, churches and your God. She does not tell about her feelings according to Mari, but Mari knows of the things that happened to Mariann. Mariann is around eight years old and very rarely in the outside world because of the importance Lion puts on her safety. She knows about Brave Eagle and me, who she calls the girl who knows Mari. She is also close to the Clan of Argus and knows there are others but does not know who they are. The Clan of Argus guards the fort, but in the fort is a hidden door that opens up into the jungle. That is so if the Beast gets past the Clan of Argus he still will not be able to get Mariann because of the hidden door escape route.

Later that day after the session with Bruce and Mariann;

Communiqué to the Counselor

I have been appointed by Lion to forward all communication from the Jungle as well as the Clan of Argus. Lion is pleased with the results of the session with MariAnn. He agrees with you that if the sessions continue Mariann will need to be comforted afterward on the inside. After each session, Lion will take Mariann to his den where the Ones of the Trees will provide her with coconut milk, nuts and berries. Mariann will spend as much time as she needs with Lion, until she feels safe enough to return to her hut in the Jungle. When she is comfortable, elephant will take her deep into the Jungle, where she can play animal games with her friends. Mariann needs assurance that her Jungle is always close by and she can return in an instant by calling upon Lion.

Lion has instructed Mariann that she is to visit with the healing man in the office. He will help her make the bad nightmares disappear and will remove the thorn in her heart. Mariann trusts that Lion never sleeps and will be watching to protect her from harm. Lion has told her not to fear the healing men in the office for he is on guard. This has given Mariann courage to meet with you. Lion thanks you for your letter. He will comment on what Mariann tells you and elaborate on issues he thinks will be of importance to you.

Lion says that Mariann's drawings that follow are fairly accurate. The blue door is actually a blue mist surrounding a hidden opening into the Jungle. The thistles are compacted and impossible to traverse. Only Lion, Mariann and myself know the secret password that will open a path in the thistles. This word is never spoken so that the enemy does not gain a foothold in the Jungle. Her house is made of sticks and moss. The house is deeper in the Jungle, but Mariann ran out of paper to give you a true perspective of distance. A hidden circle dug out of the ground surrounds the hut. In the circle are poisonous sticks under the brush. If the enemy somehow got the password to make it to the hut, he'd fall into the circle and die. Mariann is lifted over the circle and out of the hut on the trunk of an elephant. She is able to call on the animals at her request and they will come to her aide.

Mariann's food is provided by the Ones of the Trees. Her hut was provided by elephant and maintained by beaver. Elephant, horse and giraffe provide transportation. Lion provides protection. Dolphin helps her with her bath. Owl teaches her. All of the animals in the Jungle exist to care for the child. A letter is being given to Brave Eagle to inform Raquel to take the information about the Jungle to Helper of the Circle Council. Helper will be instructed to inform the Surface People that the Jungle is off limits. This will allow us to protect our child from danger.

Daniel will continue to guard the fort against the attack by the Beast, who comes in many disguises including that of friend. The Beast has many in his army. They live in a castle of gold in a place called the Vatican and serve the Creator of all. They are very powerful and can destroy our child if we are not careful and vigilant in guarding her. The Jungle animals are still hesitant in trusting you. They know the strength and power of the Beast. Security has been heightened because of the risk in our child switching to the outside to see you. Mari

and munkey and
bear and egle and
lots more.

The news of another world of the Jungle was not well received by some of the Surface people, especially when they were told they couldn't go there. Both Liz and Ann were upset because here was another area in their lives where they couldn't be in control. Liz was still upset because she thought that Bruce hadn't found someone to disciple Maria and Louise yet. Maria and Louise were scared because they thought that more and more parts were going to continue to appear.

Ruth would continue to encourage them to stay close to Jesus and trust Bruce to help. Jennifer, being the newest part without abuse, planned to stay aloof from all that was going on, in order to avoid her having to identify with the pain of the System. Even though Ruth understood her desire very clearly, she knew that neither of them could do that for very long.

Ruth was frustrated too, because she could see the needs for her support were increasing exponentially. She was already exhausted every night from working with the kids and now there were more coming. She was becoming aware of how the System had a very difficult time taking care of their own needs, before the needs of others in the family. Problems with Maria's sister were increasing with her drug abuse, so Ann took her niece home with her to care for her while her mom was incapacitated. There seemed to be no let up in the stress upon the System.

As more stress increased for Maria in conjunction with the arrival of more parts, she started regressing rapidly. This was evident in her displayed educational level, which was revealing itself to be about a sixth grade level now. All of the other parts remained somewhat constant, but Maria deteriorated in her cognitive processes and emotional self-esteem. She became very dependent upon the rest of the adults to make it through each day. She wrote Bruce of her concerns for everyone.

Ruth says for me to write you a letter and she will send it for me. I don't like to write cuz I don't write good. But I am scared cuz there is another place inside with Mariann and more parts. I don't think they will ever stop coming and I can't remember all of them. I don't want no more to come so that I can try to get used to the ones that are here. I been trying to shadow lots of them so that I know more about what happens. Yesterday I heard my sister on the phone, but they came out before I could get there. She is very sick and I worry lots about her. Ruth and Liz and Ann have my niece staying with us and I like that cuz she is nice. I am praying for my sister to get better.

Sometimes it is very long before I get to see you cuz the children want to visit with you. That is ok cuz I don't know what to talk about with you and then I don't have to. But sometimes I feel like I need to get it out and I cant. I want to cry and yell and cry, but I cant. I don't even know why I want to cry and yell. Maybe it is another person inside me that wants to. Sometimes it is hard to tell someone else what it feels like to be me. I try to do what Ruth says and think about good things like Louise's roses and Jennifer's bird. I think about Kansas lots. But sometimes deep in the night the bad is more powerful and it makes me think of things I don't want to.

Do you like me a little? Can I call you my friend? I would really like to be a friend with you. I hope you are not mad that I would like to have you as a friend cuz I don't mean anything bad by it. It is just that it would be nice to have a good friend. Liz says that I might not get to go to school cuz you can't find a teacher. I promise I will be good and try really hard. I will listen lots and do all the work. I want to go to school and I will try to be a real good student. Maybe if you tell the teacher that I will be real good then he will want to teach me. Sunday is Easter and Ruth is singing in the choir. Louise is making a ham dinner for Jose and Sergio. I know why we have a holiday on Easter cuz Jesus came back alive. I hope you have a nice Easter.
Bye, Maria

I NEED TO EXPLODE. I AM GOING TO EXPLODE. I CAN'T HOLD IT ANYMORE. I CAN'T. SO YOU'RE GOING TO READ MY EXPLOSION. I HATE THEM! I HATE THEM ALL, INCLUDING THE GUY UPSTAIRS. HE DOESN'T GIVE A SHIT ABOUT US. HE IS OUT TO GET US. HE NEVER LETS UP. HOW MUCH DOES HE EXPECT US TO TAKE? WHAT DID MARIA EVER DO TO DESERVE THIS TYPE OF LIFE?

HER FATHER IS MEAN, CRUEL AND SADISTIC. HIS MAIN OBJECTIVE IN LIFE IS TO DESTROY HER. DAMN HIM! JUST BECAUSE ROSALINDA LOOKS IDENTICAL TO MARIA DOESN'T MEAN HE HAS TO RIDE HER ALL WEEK. THE KID WORKS 20 HOURS A WEEK, HAS A 3.9 GPA, TAKES CHEMISTRY AND ADVANCED MATH AND GOES TO JUNIOR COLLEGE TAKING CLASSES, AND HE HAS THE NERVE TO HASSLE THE KID BECAUSE SHE DOESN'T KNOW WHERE THE SPARE TIRE IS. HE THEN PROCEEDS TO TELL HER THAT HER MOTHER IS STUPID TO BE FIXING THE BATHROOM UP FOR CLAUDIA AND GET OUT OF THAT HELL HOLE AND MOVE UP HERE. BUT NO, SHE CAN'T SEE PAST HER NOSE.

AND IF THAT AIN'T BAD ENOUGH, WE CALL THEM TO FIND OUT WHAT TIME TO PICK ROSALINDA AND RACHEL UP AT

THE AIRPORT AND THEY TELL US 1:30. SO MARIA SITS IN THE AIRPORT AND ROSALINDA ISN'T DUE IN UNTIL 3:30. WHY? WHY TELL MARIA THE WRONG TIME? WHY HASSLE HER SO MUCH? WHY CAN'T THEY JUST SAY WE HATE YOU? YOU ARE A BYPRODUCT OF EVIL AND YOU REMIND US OF IT EVERY TIME WE SEE YOU. WE HAVE HATED YOU FROM THE BEGINNING AND WE NEVER WANT TO SEE YOU AGAIN. AND THEN GET OUT OF HER LIFE! BUT NO, THEY HAVE TO STAY AND MAKE HER FEEL LIKE SHE IS WORTH LESS THAN COW SHIT AND SHE CAN'T SEE IT! SO WE GET HIT BY THAT AND THE BITCHING ABOUT THE BATHROOM REMODEL. WELL WHAT DO THEY WANT US TO DO WHEN CLAUDIA HAS TO BE ABLE TO GET IN. WHAT DO THEY WANT? ANN IS DOING THE BEST SHE CAN WITH WHAT SHE HAS. THEY'RE VERY WEALTHY AND DON'T OFFER ANY FINANCIAL HELP TO US, JUST DANGLE CARROTS AND PULL STRINGS TO CONTROL US. I HATE THEM!

THEN ANN GOES TO GET MEDICINE FOR CLAUDIA AND BECAUSE GOD LIKES US SO MUCH, THE TRUCK ON THE FREEWAY DROPS A GOOD SIZE ROCK AT LEAST 4 INCHES OR MORE IN DIAMETER AND YEP... RIGHT INTO THE SIDE OF THE DAMN CAR. THE SYSTEM TRIES TO FIGURE OUT HOW IN THE HELL WE'RE GOING TO HIDE IT. RAQUEL COMES UP WITH THE STUPID IDEA OF SPLASHING MUD ON IT AND OF COURSE IT DOESN'T WORK. SERGIO STARTS IN, YOU'VE HAD THIS CAR LESS THAN TWO MONTHS AND LOOK AT THIS! DON'T YOU PAY ATTENTION? LOOK AT THIS! I MEAN WHAT THE HELL WAS RUTH SUPPOSED TO DO? I GUESS HE'D HAVE RATHER IT GO THROUGH THE WINDSHIELD AND KILL US. SHIT!

NOW SERGIO IS ON A ROLL! MARIA SIT DOWN! I NEED TO TALK TO YOU (NO HE MEANS TALK AT HER). HE STARTS IN ABOUT HER MOTHER. YOU ARE GOING TO HAVE TO COME TO TERMS WITH THE FACT THAT YOUR MOTHER IS DYING. SHE MIGHT NOT LAST THE SUMMER AND YOU HAVE TO SETTLE THIS IN YOUR MIND RIGHT NOW. I DON'T WANT YOU FALLING APART WHEN IT HAPPENS! (Maria doesn't, but not for the reasons Sergio thinks at the time.) YOU TELL THAT THERAPIST OF YOURS TO GET YOU TO ACCEPT IT. WHILE YOU'RE DOING THAT, SEE IF HE CAN GET YOU TO ACCEPT THAT YOUR GRANDMOTHER IS GONE AND HAS BEEN GONE

FOR 30 YEARS. WHILE WE ARE ON THE SUBJECT OF YOUR THERAPIST, ARE YOU BECOMING ATTRACTED TO HIM?

MARIA SAYS WHAT DO YOU MEAN? THE HUSBAND SAYS YOU KNOW WHAT I MEAN, ARE YOU FALLING IN LOVE WITH THE GUY? MARIA SAYS DO YOU MEAN LIKE WANTING TO DO IT? NO, YUCK. I LIKE HIM AS A FRIEND. HE IS NICE AND I LIKE TO HEAR HIM TALK AND THAT'S ALL. I DON'T LIKE THAT OTHER STUFF. I WOULD NEVER DO THOSE THINGS. SO THE HUSBAND SAYS, WHAT ABOUT THE OTHERS? I DON'T WANT ANY OF YOU TO BECOME PHYSICALLY ATTRACTED TO THIS GUY! I'VE HEARD ABOUT WOMEN FALLING IN LOVE WITH THEIR THERAPIST AND I WILL HAVE NONE OF THAT. DO YOU HEAR ME?

MARIA TRIES TO DEFEND THE SYSTEM. I DON'T THINK THEY THINK LIKE THAT SERGIO. LOUISE JUST LIKES TO TAKE HIM TEA AND JAM AND LITTLE THINGS LIKE FOR A FRIEND. CAN WE PLEASE HAVE HIM FOR A FRIEND? WE WOULD NEVER DO ANYTHING WRONG. SO HE SAYS, WHAT ABOUT THAT LITTLE FLIRT RAQUEL? MARIA WAS BECOMING VERY SCARED SO ANN CAME OUT. SHE GOT HIM OFF OF THE SUBJECT BY SAYING, DON'T YOU THINK WE HAVE ENOUGH DAMN PROBLEMS ALREADY? THE LAST THING WE WANT TO DO IS BECOME INTIMATE WITH ANYBODY. BESIDES THE GUY IS MARRIED AND HAS THREE CHILDREN AND DOESN'T NEED ANYMORE HEADACHES EITHER. ANYWAY WE ARE NOT HIS TYPE SO DON'T SWEAT IT.

I DON'T MIND BEING ACCUSED OF SHIT I DO, BUT DAMN IT IF HE IS GOING TO ACCUSE ME OF SHIT I DON'T DO AND I DON'T DO LOVING MEN! SHIT! IF HE IS SO F##%##G CONCERNED ABOUT IT, THEN HE SHOULD HAVE THE BALLS ENOUGH TO GO IN AND DISCUSS IT WITH YOU LIKE A MAN INSTEAD OF HASSLING HER. HELL, NOBODY IS SERIOUSLY GOING TO BE LOOKING AT HER. HE IS JEALOUS FOR NO REASON.
SO SORRY TO BUST YOUR BUBBLE BUDDY... WE AREN'T IN LOVE WITH YOU EVEN A LITTLE BIT. WE LIKE YOU AS A FRIEND, SOME OF US MORE THAN OTHERS. THE KIDS MIGHT LOVE YOU LIKE A CHILD LOVES A GOOD DAD, BUT THAT IS ALL. THE ADULTS RESPECT YOU AND LIKE

SPENDING TIME WITH A FRIEND. THE HUSBAND IS OFF BASE. WE ARE NOT IN TO SEXUAL STUFF AND IF ANYBODY SHOULD KNOW THAT IT SHOULD BE THAT DAMN HUSBAND. WELL I FEEL I HAVE LET OFF ENOUGH STEAM TO NOT EXPLODE FOR AWHILE. YOU EVER FEEL LIKE YOU JUST HAD A LOAD OF HORSE SHIT THROWN ON YOU AND YOU JUST WANT TO FLING IT BACK? I'M TIRED OF HAVING TO LIE IN IT.

SCHEDULE ME IN IF YOU CAN BETWEEN ALL OF THESE KIDS THAT KEEP POPPING OUT. THE TOPIC WILL BE HOW YOU EXPLODE AND SURVIVE TO TELL ABOUT IT. I WANT TO HEAR HOW YOU GET PISSED OFF AND HOW YOU HANDLE THE ASSHOLES IN YOUR LIFE. I DON'T WANT NO PIE IN THE SKY CRAP, I WANT TO KNOW WHAT BRUCE, THE REGULAR GUY IN THIS F##%#D UP WORLD DOES TO HANDLE HIS ANGER. I'LL BE THE ASSHOLE AND YOU SHOW ME YOUR STUFF, THEN YOU BE THE ASSHOLE AND I'LL TRY YOUR TECHNIQUES ON ASSHOLE ONE AND TWO AT HOME. SO START THINKING NOW. SEE YOU SOON.

LIZ

Bruce was reaching out to many parts at the same time to try and keep the System balanced as they were going through therapy. He gave books by C. S. Lewis to different adult parts to read and comment on by e-mail, something I continued to do as well. Raquel was the first to respond in a letter, followed by the beginning of her writing about her journey in search of truth called the Journey to Sacred Mountain.

...Why do some people believe it is better to reign in Hell than serve in Heaven? Why is there always something they insist on keeping, even if the price is misery? I cannot fathom this. All that is, is a gift. Man cannot own what does not belong to him.

When I read about men who are so interested in proving the existence of God that they come to care nothing for God himself, or those so occupied in spreading Christianity that they never gave a thought to Christ, I thought of Liz's Suburban Christians. But more than that I thought of the early Christians to this land who came and enslaved the Indians, tortured them and destroyed them in the name of this God. Yes, they spread their religion but they did not model their God.

The ghost who said she had forgiven Robert as a Christian, said something that confused me. Is it true that there are some things one can never forget? Can one forgive and yet never forget? In the end the narrator realized that his vision was that of a dream. Yet, I wonder of the dream... for the Great Spirit does speak in visions. So I asked myself what did I learn from this dream? I learned that I want to know truth. I do not want to learn societal truth to fit man's desires, but real truth to satisfy my hungry spirit. And the price for that wisdom... leave myself at the base of the mountain and crawl up to the peak of truth.

-Quiet Walker

Journey to Sacred Mountain
Part One

Long ago, to escape the pain of the Outside World, Land of Preservation was made. It is a land of majestic forests and pristine rivers where the Eagle flies free and the Surface People are safe. Far to the North, towering up into the mist lays Sacred Mountain. It is at the foot of this mountain that my journey began.

One morning while the Land of Preservation was still asleep, I arose early and began walking toward the lower slopes of the mountain. Brave Eagle flew above me and circled the treetops as if tempting me to soar with him. As we approached the path where the great boulders were scattered like acorns, I gazed up at the vast, gigantic mass of rock before me. It is too steep and difficult to climb I thought, but what of the truth that lies at the top? I crave to know that truth, yet I carry within my soul much fear. I have fear of the Little People.

The stories have been passed down by the ancient ones of the Little People who inhabit the Sacred Mountain. They have stolen children and trick those who journey the path. Many seekers have been lost forever because of the dwarf-like creatures. They live in caves and crevices and these hairy-faced little men are cunning and deceitful.

One must have the favor of the Great Spirit to overcome the trickery of the Little People.

As I sat on the rock at the edge of the mountain, I shuddered. I knew to walk the path of Sacred Mountain meant to encounter suffering and sorrow, yet I wanted the truth that would set me free from my fears. I looked back at the Land of Preservation that led to the Outside World. The answer is not there, I thought. I must go forward.

I leaped onto the jagged rock in front of me and began my journey. The way up the mountain was very steep. No sooner had I climbed passed the first slope, than I met the Little Person known as Peacock. Peacock strutted beside me and spoke, "Quiet Walker I am glad I have found you. You must go back. There is no truth at the top of this mountain. The mountain is dangerous. You have been lied to and you will die if you pursue this foolish plan."

I began to feel this pull and desire to turn back to the safety of the Land of Preservation. Just as I was about to rise and follow Peacock's suggestion, a vision came before me. I saw the glow of spirits urging me forward. I called upon the Great Spirit, holder of all wisdom, to help me resist the temptation of Peacock. With a mighty thunder and a great flash of lightning from the direction of the spirits, Peacock fled my presence and ran back to his cave.

As I turned and gazed up the mountain, a luminescent being approached me and said, "Quiet Walker you have learned the first valuable lesson in your walk to wisdom. If you stop to listen to Peacock's suggestions, it will bring more pain and sorrow. Peacock has a high opinion of himself. The first step towards obtaining wisdom is seeking humility. The Great Spirit give gifts to the humble but curses the proud." With that I fell fast asleep.

The next morning, I regained my strength and began the steep climb. Brave Eagle continued circling the path, occasionally diving at a wandering mouse or lizard. The path turned to the left and to my amazement I saw a vast desert before me. The desolate land was covered with white sand and small thorny bushes. There was no tree and no shade from the blistering sun. I stopped. This is not the way to the top of the mountain, I thought. I must be going the wrong way, but as I looked to my left and then to my right, I realized there was no other way around the desert.

Appearing from no where was another one of the Little People named Mule. He sat on the dirt path leading to the desert and spoke. "Look at this place Quiet Walker. Does this look like the way to the high country? Why do you listen to those spirits? You are smarter than they are. Go your own way. It is far better than this way." I looked at the parched land before me and turned to look at Mule. Behind Mule stood a spirit listening to our conversation. Mule noticed her and began to quiver as the spirit spoke. "Quiet Walker this is the right path. To obtain the wisdom and truth you seek, you must go through the fire of the desert. Do not be stubborn and go your own way. Yield to the Great Spirit and allow him to refine you. For you shall be made into the finest jewels." I looked at Mule and smiled as I turned toward the desert. Mule created a canoe and drove it into the side of the mountain, disappearing before my eyes.

I am now in the desert. I am still on the journey, waiting patiently for the upward path to be revealed to me. I see the steep and narrow cliffs to the top, but I have not yet found the path. The desert is hot and uncomfortable, yet there is wisdom to be gleaned from it... Much wisdom.
End – Part One.

One Who Listens:
Thank you for your letter. I will travel to the library and find the books of Narnia. I think I will recommend <u>Mere Christianity</u> to Liz...I asked Ruth if you knew how I could contact the one whom you and Ruth follow. I would enjoy spending time with him and learning of his ways. He must be very special, for I do not believe Ruth would follow someone unless that someone represented what she believed was important. Therefore, I wanted to meet him, but Ruth told me Jesus is a spirit and cannot meet me in bodily form. I understand spirits, for I have met many. If 'realness' is found only in relationship with the Great Spirit who created us all and Jesus is part of the Great Spirit, then how does one have a relationship without ever meeting? How does one become what one is destined to be if one cannot form a relationship? This confuses me much.

I am comforted that you think one can forgive without forgetting. I have heard Liz talk much of the ones called Christians, who tell people to forget past hurts and move on in life. I do not believe it is possible to truly forget the knife, but I do believe one can forget the pain of the knife.

I have thought much about the word forgiveness and my feeling about those who have cut me with their knife. I do not spend my energy resenting those who have hurt me, yet I do not know if I have forgiven them. It seems that to forgive means to accept that which they did was not of paramount importance. I'm still confused by this word. I cannot express to you what I feel in moments of solitude when I remember that which happened. It would be a great gift to forget... for to forget would be easier than to forgive. Can one truly forgive one who murdered one's soul? I must go to Sacred Mountain now, as it is hard to write of such things.

Thank you for telling Maria that you will be her friend, it is very important to her. Ruth and I gave Maria a poem listing 8 characteristics of a true friend. I shared with her that a true friend accepts you as you are, listens, cares, is available and needs you. Ruth told her a friend challenges you spiritually to do what is right, is faithful and never talks behind your back, never tears down your self-worth and never encourages you to do things or go places where you will have to compromise your values or beliefs. Maria, Ruth and I think you are a true friend to all of us. We thank the Great Spirit for your friendship.

Quiet Walker

 As Mariann shared her drawings and stories with Bruce about the Beast that hurt her, the adults of the System dealt with their understanding of it, each in their own way. For most of them it was too painful to even think about the possibilities and the ramifications of it. Here is a clear instance where all of the adults could only think of this as happening to Mariann alone, but not to the 'host body' of the System. Most began their own search for God by trying to understand who Jesus Christ really was in each life, considering these possibilities. Some began their search based upon what Ruth had been telling them. Others took a wait-and-see approach, while studying every move the person of Jesus made within the world of the System.

While Liz grew in her anger at the institution of the Catholic Church and its abuses of the System overall, she also challenged the Protestant Christian Church as well. She didn't think she could have any effect on the Catholic Church, but she hoped to stir up as much 'shit' as she could with the Protestant Church in the hope that some change for the good was possible. While no one else in the System sided with her in her vigor, nobody dismissed her either, because they knew the truth about many of her statements. Jennifer and Ruth wrote to Bruce about their questions and thoughts about faith and the System:

Jennifer: I want to ask you a question. Ruth doesn't want me to go to see the fortuneteller, she said they are evil. Why? All they do is tell your fortune and Ruth gets upset about having crystals, taro cards or reading our horoscope. She says all of that is evil and if I don't stop, she is calling for a council meeting to have me restricted. I don't think that's fair because I'm not bothering anyone. I like peace and everything to be easy going. Do you think they are evil? Ruth says I have to become a Christian. Like why? I don't want to belong to any religion like Louise's.

Ruth: Liz is writing an essay on religion, so I shadowed her on the computer. Her words are powerful and I am impressed with her insight. Ask her to share it with you when she's done. Its title is <u>Religion-Deep In Tradition</u>...I have learned a lot from her as I get to know her. She is not the bad part she wants everybody to believe she is. She has a tender heart for that which is right and just. She cuts through a lot of garbage and gets to the meat of things. She has strong opinions but doesn't have a problem hangin' with a variety of people of different cultures. She is stubborn! Her frustrations with churches seems to be that they preach more obeying and performing traditions, then helping set people free to love each other and care for one another.

Her negative attitude toward the Catholic Church is obvious after what happened to Mariann, Tabitha and Louise. Her issue with the Protestant churches stems from the people controlling the Pastors. She has seen this at our church, where a Pastor wants to minister to the hurting people of Oakland and grow into a multicultural church. The old guard of the church council and prominent members keep the Pastor from doing God's will. This angers Liz and pushes her farther away. Liz has great insight and I'm truly blessed to know her. Someday she is going to have a powerful meeting with God and I'm excited to see that.

Liz wanted to confront someone about the abuse of Mariann and in general, the abuse of the System. Yet, she was blocked from doing so by her explosive anger. If she couldn't learn to manage it, she might cause residual harm to the System. Liz sought a resolution by asking Bruce to teach her techniques of assertiveness training so that she could confront the Catholic Church:

Before we begin my training in how to be a manageable asshole in today's society on Thursday, I want to do some role-playing. I want you to be the Pope and I will be Liz. You have called me into your castle (I mean office) for an appointment, because I've been pissing off your priests in the Bay Area. They have accused me of talking to some of my Catholic friends and encouraged them to leave the Church. So you start in on me about obeying the teachings of the Catholic Church, respecting the high authority of the priests and bishops in charge of me, following the traditions and obligations of the Church, etc. etc. Don't forget when you start interrogating me to tell me to kiss your ring and kneel before you.

I will enjoy the debate if you make sure you act like the Pope. You must be authentic. You've got to hit me with hard questions like; I have heard from the reports I am receiving that you are telling people we are aloof and arrogant. Is that true Liz? Are you opposed to authority? Have you been condemning the way the church is structured? Are you angry with church leaders? Jesus gave authority to legislate to the church, so how is it that you refuse to obey that authority? You have discussed with people that you think the way we live here in the Vatican is not in balance with what Jesus taught. Explain that! Did you tell people that we do not teach religion properly? What is your definition of the church? Do you have a theology degree?

These are just a few suggestions for when you play the Pope. Hey, if you're really into it, I'll get you a ring and limo… Just kidding! I couldn't resist. Anyway, I got to get this out of my gut before we start on Thursday in training to be an effective asshole.
Your buddy, Liz

P.S. If Jesus came back in disguise today and started talking to people, who would attack first? I don't think it would be the gays, prostitutes, poor, drug addicts, gang members or average Joe. No, I think it would be the Christian Church's pastors, priests, bishops, cardinals and the Pope. Hell, he'd piss them off and they would get real scared that they would lose control of people's thinking and then their churches would be empty, because people would be free instead of controlled by a church that has no feeling for hurting people. Just look at Louise if you want a classic example and how she's handling everything right now. Later…

Shortly after this letter, Ruth went on a woman's retreat that had a profound affect on her, Jennifer, Raquel and indirectly Liz. Liz responded first to Bruce on Monday:

I had a shitty night. The whole damn system is against me, except for Ann. The rest of them are hassling me about my play for Thursday. Ruth has this holier than thou attitude about respect for church leaders. She says that even if she disagrees with the doctrines of the Pope, she respects him as a leader of the Catholic Church. She says we should not mock him. Shit! I got into this big damn argument with her. I told her that Jesus called the popes of his day whitewashed tombs. You call that respectful?

Well, she kept throwing scripture at me. Then Maria and Louise started in on me about the church coming to get us for talking bad about the church. Then Raquel and Jennifer start in on being at peace. That was the final straw for me. I told them all to f##% off and I was going to do what I want.

Well you know what they did next? They took me to council and they all voted against me except for Ann. I can have a play but the pope character must not represent the real Pope and the church he leads must be called something else. If I refuse the proposal, I can't have the play. I hate being told what to do with my opinions!!!

I don't want to talk anymore about it. The leader of the church is called Zor and the church is called Dogma Church. He rules his universal church from his headquarters in Jerusalem. He lives in a three-square block mansion with gold floors and priceless art. He wears a robe of silk with gold threading. On his head is a gold crown and around his neck is a gold crucifix. Each one of his rings is crowned with priceless jewels. On his left hand he wears the ring of the church which every person must kiss in homage to him. He is infallible and all the people in his church follow his dictates. THERE! (Sound like anyone you know?)

See you Thursday Zor.

Raquel wrote about another part of her journey:

Journey to Sacred Mountain -Part 2

I have traveled in the desert it seems for many years. At times, exhausted and confused, I would sit in the hot sun and gather the sand in my hands. Letting it sift through my fingers, I would watch the dust and shavings fall to the ground and leave the beautiful grains of multicolored sand secure in my hand. One day, while I was performing my ritual of sifting sand, I felt a presence around me. In the still of the moment, I heard a very small, calm and peaceful voice say, "Some of my most precious jewels are wrapped in wrinkled paper." Looking up into the cloudless sky I meditated on that revelation. Yes, I answered back, some of the most precious of jewels are wrapped in wrinkled paper. The voice spoke again. "No, my precious child. I said some of MY most precious jewels are wrapped in wrinkled paper. You are one of my precious jewels."

I began to weep and then I overflowed with sobbing that echoed throughout the desert. My weeping continued through the day and into the cool evening. Then, through my tears, I saw a spirit. The spirit radiated and its brightness lit up the desert. The spirit spoke, "Quiet Walker. The Great Spirit has revealed himself to you. You have learned the next most valuable lesson in your search for truth and wisdom. You are precious to the Great Spirit. As you would treasure a precious jewel, so the Great Spirit treasures you. Do not be sad about the time that you have spent in the desert, for although the journey is difficult, the Great Spirit has been with you. Accept with joy the desert he has taken you through, for it is only through the desert of our lives that we come to know where our treasures are."

The next morning, I got up refreshed. In front of me was a patch of wild lilacs slowly waving in a cool breeze, which I had not noticed before and a path was in the middle of the meadow of lilacs that lead westward. Again I heard a small voice that said, "Walk this way." I was beginning to recognize this voice. I obeyed and walked westward. I found myself at the ocean, where waves crashed against jagged pillars of rock and the seagulls squealed overhead. The beach was filled with driftwood and seaweed that had rolled ashore. I began to walk along the edge of the beach, enjoying the soothing cool water on my hot and dry feet. I felt different inside. It was as though I had experienced knowledge of extreme importance in my wanderings in the desert. I had a new joy in my being. The fear of Maria's relatives that I had held deep within me was gone. The despair one is chained to when one's spirit has been torn had disappeared and something new, something wonderful, something exciting was growing in its place. I wasn't quite able to truly understand what I was experiencing, but I hungered for more of it. For the first time in my life, I was feeling love and a sense that there was an answer to all of my sorrow. I gladly skipped along the beach and watched the nature around me in a way I had never experienced it before.

I was spending so much time enjoying the animals I observed on the beach, that I had not noticed I had entered a small cove. It was there I met Parrot and Platypus. Parrot spoke first, "Quiet Walker. You know if the Great Spirit really cared about you, he would just give you wisdom. Why does he make you go on this most difficult and exhausting journey? You are really stupid. Here he gives you nothing but suffering and sadness and you let him treat you like this.

276

I thought you had more of a backbone than that. Demand your rights! Don't let him treat you this way. Tell him if he doesn't give you what you want, that you are going back right now to the Land of Preservation and turn your back on him."

No sooner had he finished and Platypus spoke up. "Poor Quiet Walker, you are such a trusting and obedient little girl and look how he treats you. He tells you that you are his precious jewel and look where he leads you...into a hot and unyielding desert and lonely ocean. Instead of treating you like a jewel, he has confused you and divided you into parts that don't go together. Everyone laughs at you. You are all mixed up. You must feel so sad and sorry for yourself. You have every right to feel sorry for yourself. He doesn't take care of you and lets so much bad happen to you."

Exhausted and trembling I began to take in the words of Parrot and Platypus, but then I remembered the small, peaceful voice of the Great Spirit. I picked up a piece of driftwood and tossed it at Parrot and Platypus with all of my strength. Parrot scrambled away into the sky and Platypus hurried away out of sight. Then another spirit appeared before me. "Quiet Walker, you have learned another important lesson on your way to wisdom. Patience leads to wisdom and understanding". Confused I questioned the spirit, "Why did Parrot and Platypus appear when I was so happy and thinking that now it is time for me to climb to the top?" The spirit then kindly but firmly spoke in words that I immediately understood. "Sometimes when one can see the light flickering at the end of the tunnel, one becomes confident in one's self. Do not abandon the one who has led you to this point and attempt to finish the journey alone. The thorn of impatience can lead to a wrong turn towards your enemies." I knew the spirit was right.

A path appeared leading to the East and the climb upward to the top. Joyfully I leaped and skipped down the path. A song in my heart, I began to thank the Great Spirit as I passed the ferns and dripping moss along the way. It was springtime in April. There had been a heavy rainy season and the wildflowers exploded in color with the warmth of the morning sun. Everywhere I glanced I saw bluebells, poppies and lilacs. In a little meadow to my left was a mother and baby deer resting in the shade of the trees. I took a moment to enjoy the beauty of the love I saw in the mother to her fawn. The fawn was snuggled close to her and content in knowing that she was safe from harm, as long as she stayed close to her mother.

As I continued my walk among the towering redwood trees, my mind kept focusing on the deer and fawn. Then I heard the small voice say to me, "As the deer comforts her fawn, so shall I comfort you my precious child." Tears rolled down my cheeks as I stood on the path and looked up into the trees and softly said, "Now I understand." The small voice spoke to me again. "Quiet Walker. I am the great I Am. I am who you seek. I will give you wisdom. Follow me for I am he. I am Jesus who loves you so much that I died and rose again for you, my precious child, so that you may have life. Now come my child and see what I will do."

And with a peace I have never known before, I began the next part of my journey.
-Quiet Walker

Ruth would write about the changes that she saw in Raquel as well, the week before I would meet the System. She saw a definite turn in her spirit toward wanting to know more about Jesus, after writing the second part of her journey. She wrote the following excerpt to Bruce:

Raquel and I have been spending a lot of time together this morning. She is very interested in finding out more about Jesus and what he is like. I have offered my Bible for her to read and suggested she start with the Gospels. She asked me about this class Maria and Louise are going to attend this weekend. I told her it was a beginning Bible study class to learn more about Jesus. She asked if it was okay if she also attended the class. I told her that I'm sure of it. She said she'd like to shadow Maria and Louise.

I know you'll be meeting with Mr. Chalberg this Wednesday night. Raquel has given her permission for you to tell him that she will be shadowing. I think it would be a good idea for him to know where each one of the three are at spiritually, so that he can work from there. If he attacks the Catholic Church, he will cause Louise to draw back. If he attacks Native American Spiritualism, he will alienate Raquel. If he attacks the Hispanic culture, he will cause both Maria and Louise to flee. I wonder if he knows the challenge that he is getting himself into here? But I also wonder if he realizes the blessings that will come in his work with the System? I will be in prayer. Let me know how it goes.

"Every understanding of the human story, even more obviously than every understanding of the natural world, must rest heavily on a faith commitment – for we do not yet see the end of the story. But no human life is possible without some idea, explicit or implicit, about what the story means. The Christian faith is – as often said – a historical faith...in the sense that it is essentially an interpretation of universal history. Its defense, therefore, will be as much concerned with how we act as with what we say."
- Leslie Newbigin *The Gospel in a Pluralistic Society*

"If anyone supposes that he knows anything,
He has not yet known as he ought to know...
For even if there are so-called gods,
Whether in heaven or on earth,
As indeed there are many gods and many lords,
Yet for us there is but one God, the Father,
From whom are all things, and we exist for
Him; And one Lord, Jesus Christ, by whom
are all things, And we exist through Him."
-Paul <u>1 Corinthians 8:2, 5-6</u>

"The steps of a man are established by the Lord;
and He delights in his way. When he falls,
he shall not be hurled headlong; Because
the Lord is the One who holds his hand.
I have been young and now I am old;
Yet I have not seen the righteous forsaken...
He is their strength in time of trouble. And the
Lord helps them and delivers them; He delivers
them from the wicked and saves them,
Because they take refuge in Him."
-David Excerpts from <u>Psalm 37</u>

A drawing by Mariann showing her safe in the arms of Dragonslayer...while being surrounded by the 'Bad Ones.'

Chapter 11:

"The Narrow Path of Choices"
"People in Search of Truth & Freedom"

"Heaven can be entered only through the narrow gate!
The highway to Hell is broad, and its gate is wide enough
For all the multitudes who choose its easy way.
But the gateway to life is small,
And the road is narrow
And only a few ever find it."
-Jesus <u>Matthew 7: 13-14</u>

"Then I will give you shepherds after My own heart,
who will feed you on knowledge and understanding."
- <u>Jeremiah 3: 15</u>

"How then shall they call upon Him in whom they have not believed?
And how shall they believe in Him whom they have not heard?
And how shall they hear without a preacher?
And how shall they preach unless they are sent?"
-Paul <u>Romans 10: 14 - 15</u>

"Do not imagine that the journey is short; one must have
the heart of a lion to follow this unusual road,
for it is very long and the sea is deep.
One plods along in a state of amazement, sometimes smiling
sometimes weeping. As for me, I shall be happy to discover
even a trace of Him. That would indeed
be something, but to live without Him would be a reproach.
A man must not keep his soul for the beloved and
must be in a fitting state to lead his soul to the court of the King."
'Attar – 13th century

"It was April 23, 1995. Springtime was in the air and the
fields were painted with life. Suddenly a strong, spring storm
appeared over the horizon. The wind rose with an authority of its

own. The movement of the wind stirred the little seed withering and dying in the ditch. As swift as a herd of wild mustangs running through the canyon, the wind picked up the little seed and carried it into the rich, warm farmer's field. The seed immediately began extending its fragile roots and buried them into the life-giving soil. Absorbing the moisture and nutrients that the land provided, the seed began to grow. It grew and it grew into a strong vibrant plant, until the little fragile seed that had been given up on by the other farmer produced a hundred-fold."

-Raquel

Hindsight is still the best way I know to see how the hands of Providence will mold miracles out of the human condition. When I began my journey with the System, there was no way I could have imagined the manner or method God would choose to bring so much good, out of so much evil. Looking back, I can see the purity of wisdom in His initial instructions to me about how to minister to them with simple, practical, and real truth in love:

"Meet and love each one where you find them, for who they are in their own understanding, the same way I do for everyone who seeks Me. It is enough to reach out to one person at a time with My love, if you want to bring it to them as My servant."

Perhaps it is its simplicity that empowered me to know how to come alongside of them. Together we began a journey in search of healing, but discovered it was a search for truth and primarily, truth about God. The healing we sought became a by-product of the reality that is God. In my heart, I wanted to be an instrument of God's healing to an individual overwhelmed by a life of suffering. In my mind the task was to bring the truth of God's promises from His Word and watch Him do the rest. Our journey together so far has proven to me that God's truth is an action He initiates through the soul. Our mind accepts the possibility of this action through faith and carries it to reality through the heart with love. When He reaches out from eternity to lift another soul out of despair, it is not by our capacity to love by which this task is accomplished, but by God's alone. It was not my preaching or teaching ability that brought healing to the System, but God's grace and mercy that changed us all with His truths.

> **"He is a vain preacher of the word of God without,**
> **who is not a hearer within."**
> -Augustine of Hippo

In the next year and a half, they will search for God... and God will find them in the midst of their daily life still struggling to accept all that had happened to them. Several had already accepted Jesus on the inside as a friend, as someone who brought comfort in the reality of their pain, but few were ready to equate Him with God the Father. It would take much more than just hearing the claims from Scripture. They wanted substance that could overcome their corporate feeling of abandonment by God. They wanted to know without a doubt that His love was real. All of the adults perceived of Him in a similar fashion even if each one stated the following differently:

"You've got some explaining to do God."

I remember asking God after the first couple of weeks, if my confidence in Him had allowed my ego to set me up for failure in my effort to reach them. It wasn't easy to get a read on the System's perception of me as we pursued the truth together. Something Walt Whitman said in *Leaves of Grass*, reminded me of how I felt when I was with them in the beginning,

> **"Silent and amazed even when a little boy, I remember I**
> **heard the preacher every Sunday put God in his statements, as if**
> **contending against some being or influence."**

Was this the way they were feeling about God as I talked about Him? How could I pierce the wall of fear about God and make Him personal, in a way that could break through the shadows that put chains around them? I decided that the Bible lessons each subsequent Saturday should be less structured and more relevant to what they were asking behind their questions. Part of my confusion was that I wasn't sure who was going to be present each week to ask me questions. We started off with the list of questions from Louise, but soon we had surprise mystery guests each week asking their own questions.

It became a test of my memory, when Louise or Maria would be back picking up where we left off with the last question, as though there hadn't been any lapse of time between our last conversation two or more weeks ago. Their needs for answers were very basic. They wanted clarification of the contradictions between what the Catholic Church, Father Breen, family and other Christians had taught them about God and with what I was teaching them about God. It became apparent to me that I shouldn't preach or teach the theory of God's love but be God's love. God could not be a 'being or influence we contend against', but the very source of love in all of us that cries out for a place to mature into reality... for a heart in need of a home.

"Let the preacher labor to be heard intelligently, willingly, obediently. And let him not doubt, that he will accomplish this rather by the piety of his prayers, than the eloquence of his speech."
Lancelot Andrewes – <u>Private Devotions</u> – 1648

Easter 1995 proved to be a time of rapid changes and challenges for everyone. Bruce received an update from Circle Council concerning Maria's sister telling her over the phone that their father and brother abused them both. Determination was made that no sexual abuse had occurred to Maria by them, but no one could speak to the veracity of the sister's claim. Council wanted to keep Maria separate from her outside family and stressful confrontations with them during this fragile time. The adults had tried to relax that Easter while anticipating the various child parts that might reveal new memories and the time for therapy needed to help known child parts.

Jennifer wrote to Bruce following the discussion that came up that day on immortality and the meaning of Easter. The topic of the truth about Jesus Christ would no longer be casual in its approach after this weekend.

We were all sitting in the meadow inside and talking about Easter, while Mariann slept. Louise asked the group if they thought a person who dies really can live again. Everyone put in their opinions and there were different answers. Death is final and you are put into a hole and it is over. Death is a release from the restrictions of life. The good in your life will live on influencing others, but you have no afterlife. After death comes reincarnation. You turn into another form of existence. Liz was funny with this one. She said she didn't want to come back as no damn mosquito! Well Ann spoke up and said how do we really know that there is life after death? Ruth said because Jesus rose from the dead. Ann challenged Ruth and said how do we know that they (Disciples) didn't make it up to make a name for themselves? How do you know Ruth that it is true?

Ruth thought for awhile and said, Ann you know a lot about Watergate right? Remember the guy that walked into the prosecutor's office and told everything about the break-in, what was his name? Ann said John Dean. Ruth said that's right, but on March 21, 1973 John Dean told the President about the burglary. The whole Presidential Advisory Council knew about it and was going to keep it quiet, but according to Dean's memoirs, three weeks later he told everything to save his own skin. Here was a guy like all the other advisors who had all the clout of the most powerful office in the world behind him. He could snap his fingers and there was a jet waiting for him. He had it all, yet he could not keep the lie hidden. Why?

Are you suggesting Ann, that eleven apostles, powerless outcasts each, living under the power of the Roman Empire with no power, no army and nothing but their word as proof are going to pull off a lie of this magnitude that will change history? It does not logically compute. They couldn't possibly have maintained a lie without ever renouncing it as such under the fear of death, unless it wasn't a lie but true. For that they would have to have seen it for themselves. Peter would have been the one to run to save his own skin if it wasn't true, because he'd done it before. No Ann, it's a fact. The evidence is clear. Jesus rose from the dead because without the resurrection, life doesn't make a lot of sense. Death leads us to resurrection for those who believe and the reward is a celestial, glorified body without pain for eternity. No mosquitoes, no death to nothing...just a celestial, glorified body. Jesus says, "Whoever believes in me will never die." Death was defeated in Jesus and cannot touch the soul of anyone who dies in Christ Jesus. It is available to us all, but you must believe!

It was interesting to see the reactions. You could just see Ann's wheels turning in her head. Maria was smiling and Louise was thinking. Raquel got up quickly and walked away thinking. Liz was cleaning her nails with her switchblade and mumbling something about the mosquito. Me, I'm not into debates like Ann and Liz, but I guess if I'm really honest with myself...I would like to live forever, just not here. I've got to ask Ruth more about this celestial body thing. I think she debated Ann real good, like you know, using Ann's logic against her. That's the only way to debate Ann, it takes lots of brainpower. Me, I want to live in a place where there is no war or hate and it must have whales, oceans and birds. It has to be a place where no one has power over you to abuse or hurt children like here. I'm gonna think about it too.
Jennifer

Hey Bruce,

What did you do to Maria – give her a happy pill or something. All she talks about is going to school with this guy on Saturday. How can anyone get excited about teachers and school? Yuck! Hey, don't forget, when she meets this guy I have a test for him first! (*See Prologue.*)

Tabitha is having these bouts of fear about bathrooms and baths. I went to take a hot bath last week, complete with candles and the Enquirer. Tabitha went bananas screaming about baths. I was pissed and told her to get the Hell back to her hole and stop disturbing me. Would you please fix that kid?! I am getting real tired of these outbursts.

Ruth showed me something in the Bible that we should have used when we were playing Pope...I mean Zor. It's in Mark and the uppity leaders are asking Jesus why his disciples didn't live according to the tradition of the elders (The Rules!). Jesus gets ticked and says, 'Isaiah was right about you guys. You are hypocrites. You just give lip service. Your heart is far from me. You guys worship in vain and you are bound by rules taught by other men. You have set aside the commands of God to observe your own traditions.'

Man I like that part in Mark. Rules are so unbending and break people's spirit. Jesus was trying to tell those know-it-alls that he put people before the law. He was trying to tell them that they had taken what he meant to free people and turned it into a regimented religion, where people are threatened if they don't obey the rules they made up... The church is supposed to be a place to give support and encouragement and guidance to people not a group of bosses forcing people into their molds.

Jesus came to free people from rules they couldn't possibly obey. He doesn't want people to love him because they are forced to, but that they follow and love him because they want to. I am not afraid of the wrath of the Catholic Church. What I choose to believe will be because I freely choose to believe it, not because some priest intimidates me. I don't believe in religion. Religion doesn't bring joy into people's hearts. It brings misery, confusion, fear and guilt and makes God vindictive and cruel... Jesus taught humility and simple living. He also lived that way, yet the church leaders live in gold mansions and teach a message affirming their worldly power and authority. That is hypocritical.

The so-called Christian leaders aren't any better because they teach people to be phonies too. Too many of these Suburban Christians look good in their outside religious practices, but they have no love for people who are different, hurting or unimportant in their eyes. They talk a good talk but their actions don't back up their words. They're a bunch of counterfeits! I'd rather not ever step foot into a church again and be real in caring about people, then go to church every Sunday and never notice the homeless, those with aids, the rejects of society without hope.
Later, Liz

Healing continued within the System, with Bruce and I only hearing of it several days later. We could see the hands of Jesus at the potter's wheel, molding His creation into a better form for His purposes, often without their knowledge that He was orchestrating it. Elizabeth Ray sent the following letter to Bruce the week after Maria started classes with me.

Circle Council Update
Level 2 reports that they are not in need of therapy, since their purpose for existing is to be task performers. Level 3 has restructured. According to Sid and King of the Lights, Level 3 no longer considers their primary goal to be the maintaining of complete confidentiality about the abuse. Discussion among Harmers and Guardians centered on present day protection for the system. It was agreed that Level 3 needs to be more active in protecting the Surface People.

Due to the change in purpose, Level 3 agreed among its members to have a ceremony called The Blending. In this ceremony each family group blended its members into one. According to King of the Lights the ceremony was a sacred one. Two streams of clear water that merged into one was the location of the blending. Each part chose to walk in one of the two streams toward a cylinder of light that rose from the water at the juncture. When they reached the light and the merging waters, each part experienced a sense of unity with each other...taking on an awareness of the other's thoughts, feelings and emotions. Coming out of the light on the other side, there was a blend and they were one. Each one blended with another one until finally all the Harmers had blended with Sid and all the Guardians had blended into one with King of the Lights.

These two leaders representing all of the attributes and expertise of all of the members of Level 3, will be responsible for protecting the system from present dangers. With Circle Council's approval, these two will be in charge of establishing a plan of action to protect the system to keep it safe. Since there are only two now, they submitted a request of Circle Council to move to Level 1 from Level 3 and live with Helper. Motion was granted and the Odyssey Trees attaching the levels to Level 3 were severed. Level 3 has drifted off into the unknown and is no longer a part of the system. Sid and King of the Lights will begin work on their plan. They will be shadowing more and listening to the advice of the Outside counselor, as well as any classes attended by the parts with Mr. Chalberg that can provide valuable information to them.
E.R.

Dear Bruce,
I disagree with Ann that Maria should be bombarded with homework. It would be unwise to make this a performance-based class with Mr. Chalberg as Ann requested. The purpose of the class is for her and others to know about Jesus. Ann wants her to take the class to keep her busy and out of trouble. Maria wants to take the class to understand who Jesus is and also become smart like Ann.

Tabitha misses you and is having a hard time not seeing you as much as she has in the past. I have suggested to her that she draw pictures and write letters to you, but all she wants is hugs. Do you have any suggestions? She is doing better now that Liz is taking showers only. She is fun to listen to as she explains things to Anna about the differences between boys and girls. She kept telling her that you are dada and not mama. She explained that mamas have bottles of milk they carry for babies to drink and daddies don't, so that is why you are a daddy. Tabitha is so serious about Anna getting it straight in her head. Anna pointed at Tabitha and called her daddy and Tabitha became stern saying no I'm a big girl. You are a baby and he is a daddy. Anna got scared and started sucking her thumb and Tabitha threw up her hands and went back to her hole.

Also, SID has changed his name to Paladin. I find this interesting because, if you remember the drawings that somebody made in the beginning of therapy there was one with the word DIS on it and I was disturbed because this word DIS stands for the ruler of the underworld. The underworld was known to the Greeks as Hades and later became associated with Hell in Christianity. DIS reversed is SID. I do not think that SID is a demon, but I think his name represented the type of environment that Labyrinth portrayed. SID ruled a world that was represented by a maze with no way out of the problem of safety for the system. He and his followers tried to maintain safety for the system using methods and techniques that are considered bad or evil. In other words, their motives were good but their techniques were bad. Then you come into the picture and they learn to trust you, a way out of the maze is now open.

It became no longer necessary to have the maze (Labyrinth) and the blending occurred. Since that time SID has been under the King of the Lights and Helper's guidance. He is learning other techniques to keep the system safe and therefore the name no longer reflects him and his new name reflects the new method of ruling.

I've learned from Paladin that Labyrinth was a level under the other levels and therefore it was designated the underworld to reflect its position in the system. The maze signified the constant struggle with no way out of the dilemma. Although Labyrinth members never meant to kill the system or cause major damage, some members tended to go overboard in their attempt to keep Maria 'in-line' (i.e.: self-mutilation, destruction of parts property, running away, attempted suicide, etc.) This is why Elysian Fields was created according to King of the Lights. Although Elysian Fields was on level three, it was not the same place as Labyrinth. Elysian Fields was above Labyrinth – not alongside of it. Level 3 was three-dimensional and reflected an upper world of Elysian Fields and an underworld of Labyrinth. According to both leaders, they had the same goals but different methods in achieving them. Paladin had a very difficult time keeping those under him in control at times. Some parts tended to get so depressed they wanted to end the life of the system. There were close calls but King of the Lights averted the disaster.

Paladin has been won over by King of the Lights and they have become very good friends. King of the Lights is a very wise and compassionate part. He has never condemned Paladin, but rather he has walked alongside of him in friendship and love. This impressed Paladin and has caused him to want to associate with King of the Lights. Paladin is attempting to set up some guidelines of protection concerning Maria's sister Donna. He says that we cannot severe the connection between the sisters like Sergio demands. He has asked me to ask you if you have any suggestions you think might help us provide a security plan.

In Christ,
Ruth

For Paladin:
Greetings,

I was told you would appreciate my input regarding protection of the system from Donna. I'll expand my reply to protecting the system from any threat. Ultimately, everyone in the system must decide that being safe is a priority and that other allegiances take a second place to safety. Case in point is Donna; it is very hard for Maria to avoid Donna because she feels such a strong obligation to her sister. It takes a lot of internal work, as well as intervention on my part, to assure her that hiding from Donna is not only okay, but important. As Maria's attitude changes, it will become easier for her to stay safe from Donna (and therefore the system as a whole). This principle is true not only for Donna, but with anyone who would hurt the system or any part of it.

I once had a client who had a family member show up at the door and misuse and beat her. We worked for hours in therapy trying to arrange for the safety of her system. But when the family member came again to the door, a child would switch out and open the door. This child had been taught to be compliant and obedient and to always respond immediately to the demands of the family. These attacks finally stopped when all of the children of her system were taught and became convinced that the safety of the system was paramount. And that safety took precedence over what they had been taught as children. This had to be done gently and lovingly of course, so as to not further traumatize the children internally.

It will be similar for your system. I believe that you, King of the Lights, Liz and those who work with the children and others will be instrumental in helping this change occur. I hope this is helpful.

With Regards, Bruce

So many things were happening with the System at this time in their lives, that no one could fine time to balance or to rest. Ann was busy remodeling the home for Claudia's return in a few weeks. She also started another new job to stay out of debt. The leadership was still restructuring from the blending of Level 3 and trying to protect the System from attacks by Maria's outside family, specifically her parents and sister. Maria and Ruth were struggling to help the children inside and Maria's children outside at the same time. Liz was ready to explode from the control placed on her directly from Council and also restrain herself at the same time from the desire to do bodily injury to the husband, son, mother, father, sister, and anyone else she thought deserved it. It was not surprising that emotional overload hit Maria after several weeks of adjusting to the new environment.

Maria had just returned from a trip out of state when her son told her he wished she had never come back because she was a pain to live with. Ann lost her temper the following day and told her to stop saying Bruce was her friend. She told her that he tells every client that because he is paid to say that. Think about it logically she said, he's not your friend he's your therapist. Get it in your mind now that someday he will go away like everyone else. Don't get too close! Don't depend on anyone else, or you will be disappointed.

Maria's sister called and she was not allowed to talk with her for good reasons, but this began a downward spiral into depression. Her mother had a stroke and refused to allow Maria to visit or care for her. That Saturday, I was delayed in traffic and didn't arrive at Bruce's office until after she had come and gone with no way to reach her. It hurt too much to take so much perceived rejection from those that she thought cared about her that she took an overdose of medication. Council wasn't on guard because they felt she had grown so much that she wasn't as fragile as before. It was Liz who saved the day and got her some help from Bruce that afternoon.

After clarifying events, Bruce made a promise for Maria that he truly was her friend and loved her with good love. She made a promise to Jesus that she would never try to take her life again. I spoke with her that evening and reinforced the bond of friendship, while showing her through the events how the enemy had manipulated circumstances to lead her to that point. She acknowledged how they had been at her all week telling her she had no friends and nothing to live for, as she was unworthy.

Ruth asked her that evening if she believed that Bruce was her friend. Her promise to never try to go to sleep forever was contingent upon him never leaving as her friend. That promise would be challenged in a few years, when Bruce leaves the counseling profession without ever really having closure with the System. In book 2 you will see how the Lord replaces that friendship with a stronger one between us to carry her through this time. Yet, there will be others who make the same promise to her and ultimately leave causing severe bouts of depression. It is only her friendship with Jesus that sustains her during rough periods, like when my wife and I move to Southern California for two and a half years and try to maintain our friendship through visits and numerous phone calls to them at critical times.

By June 1995, Bruce and Circle Council will begin working together to draft a letter to Maria's husband Sergio about Maria's condition and how he might best support her in therapy. He despised therapists of any kind for years after what happened to their daughter Claudia. Drafts would go back and forth for four months, before an agreement was reached about content that they hoped would not cause a violent reaction against the System. Council wanted Bruce to request support from Sergio starting with the following 8 items:

1. Avoid sexual language and sexual harassment.
2. <u>Listen </u>to Maria and encourage her to talk.
3. Spend time with Maria away from the children.
4. Accept the differences in each part's personality.
5. Take charge in protecting Maria from son, sister and parents.
6. Understand the parts are afraid of sex and consider it dirty. They need time to be retrained.
7. When you lose your temper the system becomes traumatized.
8. Accept advice from Bruce to help Maria.

While Bruce composed the letter, he requested Elizabeth Ray to give him as much history of Maria's immediate family as she was willing to share. There were obvious clues missing in information surrounding Maria's relationships with her parents and siblings, which might prove valuable for strengthening the marriage relationship. What she gave him is still helping me today in providing counseling for her relationship with her immediate family. At the end of her report she wrote: *"We cannot change yesterday. We can only make the most of today and look with hope toward tomorrow."*

Life settled into daily chaos for the System. Ruth had convinced Ann to let a 'Christian' contractor from her new church do the remodeling in their home. Ruth's naïve assumption was that because he was a Christian he would be honest. Over the next year or two, his lack of integrity and skills in craftsmanship will cause great anxiety and stress for the System overall and Ann in particular. Ruth's character assessment of people will be held suspect by Ann for an even longer period of time. Relationships like these will cause Ann and Liz to become more convinced that most Christians aren't any different than anyone else, but Bruce and I were simply mutant strains from reality.

Ruth wasn't having a good year all and all, especially at church. By now they were in their third church trying to find a home. With Ruth on the outside, Liz listened in on a Father's Day sermon and decided the pastor needed a critique to educate him. She sent a copy to Bruce to check its appropriateness before sending it. Ruth's objections of "Your letter is judgmental and inappropriate, do not provoke the pastor" went unheeded. She was preparing material to give to future pastors to help them understand her opinions on everything, including some sermons she wrote about the perception of Christians from street people outside the church.

Dear Pastor J...

I wanted to express to you my opinions on your sermon last Sunday. I agree with you that one's father is the first and most permanent example of how one views God. I also agree that what a father is overshadows what he says so as to render his highest pronouncements and ideas meaningless, unless they match his actions. The job description for fathers in Ephesians 6:4 is an excellent list of what a father must do and not do in raising his kids.

However, your sermon was a discouragement for me. In essence you surmised that a person who did not have a positive relationship with their father would never be able to have a loving relationship with God the Father. You left no hope for women who are struggling with childhood abuse and their spiritual 'rightness' with God.

Even though some women have been sexually abused by grandfathers and physically and verbally abused by fathers, can't they learn to have a positive relationship with God? According to you it is impossible and I don't agree with that. A buddy of mine once told me that nothing is impossible with God. Yeah, it might be hard for these women to trust God the Father and not understand affection, gentleness and tenderness, but maybe with the right nurturing from compassionate and <u>encouraging</u> pastors and other positive 'father' role models, they might be able to heal enough to understand a loving God.

I'm sure your sermon left many of us who have been abused by our fathers discouraged. Instead of hearing the negative consequences of our childhood, we needed to hear that God is big enough to bring men alongside of us willing to show us what a loving father is supposed to be like to help us heal. You never know the kind of damage your words can do to people who are hurting in your audience. We need hope not discouragement. Most of us know all too well the weight of discouragement, criticism, character assassination, brainwashing and physical abuse to last a lifetime. We are not interested in getting more from the pulpit and don't tell me that I misinterpreted what you said. I heard you loud and clear. Sincerely, Liz

Liz wrote the sermon entitled "And They Will Know We Are Christians By Our Love" shortly after this letter. She would become a prolific writer and playwright in the coming years. Her style of writing would be very different from Raquel's, but often they would present a similar message. Over the next year Raquel would shift from sending her messages and stories to Bruce and gradually start sending them to me. She listened to my talks with Maria and Louise from the very beginning as we went through the first dozen of Louise's questions to Bruce. Each week we would tackle a question or two. Some questions were easy to answer, like "What happened to Jesus' dad, Joseph?" Others were not so easy such as, "Why didn't God just write the Bible instead of having people do it who could make a mistake?" We often revisited the same questions when someone new was out, or someone needed more clarification.

Early on they learned from me that no question was out of bounds or be considered too dumb to ask. At times I would start to laugh at a question if I was a bit nervous, but mostly because they would ask the most difficult theological questions in the simplest of words. Questions like these deserve answers that are easy to understand. Predestination was expressed as – 'God's plan ahead of time' and free will became – 'the gift to choose.'

The questions surrounding communion would persist and be asked by nearly every surface person in the System. The children would revisit the question of communion many times over the next eight years. The children would finally grasp the meaning in 2001, with a children's communion service on a hill above our home, using water and Cheerios. If you read book 3 you will begin to understand the theological meaning behind this simple ritual and how Jesus knew it would bring comfort to His little ones.

Each passing session would help us to know each other better and lead us further along on a journey of healing. Raquel began sending me some of her poetry to read in between our visits, so I could know more about her before she actually met with me for the first time. Maria wrote in a letter to Bruce the following excerpt of her perception of me:

Are you proud of me that I talk more now? I try hard to write more. It's easier to write than talk. Our teacher is very nice and knows lots of stuff. Raquel let him read her poems. She has watched him and

has a name for him. She calls him Shedding Tear. His mom killed herself after she was married seven times. He almost died 21 times so far and had a sad childhood after he left Texas. He did bad things before and then became a pastor. Sometimes he tells me things and a tear comes from his bad eye that he can't see from good and I say it makes you sad huh? He says yes and then we pray to Jesus. He told me I ask good questions like the ones they talk about in theology school, I just use different words. He explains good.
Bye, Maria

Liz had a somewhat different perspective of me, which she shared with Bruce.

I've listened to the preacher man. He's nice to Maria but a little hard to believe. I mean do you really believe he almost died 21 times? Come on. I don't know about him. I'm still checking him out. He told Maria about his past, which was really messed up. Sometimes he'll start to cry and she will comfort him. She worries about everybody but herself. Well I figure the best test I can give this guy is to go for a walk with him. I'm not sure how he'll react to me. He's not like you. I'm still not comfortable revealing myself to him yet. Raquel is going next so I'm going to watch how he handles her. He says he's open to meeting all the parts. He doesn't get it does he? He ain't going to meet all the parts.

Elizabeth Ray was kind enough to send him an outline of the structure of the system and our names, since he was hopelessly confused as to who was who. We don't like people to mix us up; it bruises our individual identity. I especially hate being called Ann. That is an insult! He is not going to meet the leaders, kids on level two and probably not Marie or Elizabeth Ray. He'll only meet those parts who want to meet him. He told Maria the next time they get together they would be discussing Purgatory. This should be interesting. I still don't understand his explanation on free will vs. predestination. What's your explanation?
Liz

Liz and Bruce had a mushroom brunch while discussing the merits and pitfalls of the Christian persona. He calmed her down and gave her pause to reconsider why Christians upset her so. She wrote back that evening in the first email that follows. Jennifer writes the day after Liz sent this and she checked out her concerns about Jesus with Bruce:

Thanks again for the grub. You're right about having to make a choice. Maybe that's what's bugging me so much. I know I got to decide what I'm going to do about this spiritual stuff. It just won't go away and it's driving me crazy.

I've tried to ignore making the choice, but it keeps haunting me. To ignore it and not deal with it prevents the chance of being rejected again. I really hate being rejected all of the time. I'm trying to find my place in this world, a place that I can comfortably fit in. I'm tired of being on the outside all of the time and having to claw my way in. It perpetuates the anger in me and makes me feel miserable. I don't like being angry all of the time, it's just that I am that way.

Shit Bruce, I'd like to hang out with Jesus like I'm hanging out with you. I just don't want to get trapped in all that Suburban Christian shit. Maybe you're right, maybe not all Christian Churches are filled with assholes, rules and power addicts. Maybe I just haven't found the right crowd yet. I admit I ain't no angel and I can be an asshole just like the others say. I'm not saying it's right. I'm saying it's what I know and how I survive.

You have been nice to me even though I'm not a Christian like you. I have to tell you, I have tried my darnest to get you to hate me. I wanted to say see, I knew you were like all the others. But you never rejected or judged me. You cooked for me and hung out with me. You treated me like a person and made me feel that I was okay in your book even though you know I do shit. I can't understand why except that maybe you're one of the few Christians that walks the talk. I know that I set myself up and I cause my own discomfort. I know I have to decide and not set on the fence all of my life. I wonder what Jesus thinks of assholes like me? Maybe I've been wrong blaming God for all the shit. I still can't understand why if he is as powerful as everyone says he is that he never stopped the hurt. I always thought he only intervened for those he loved and we weren't one of them. I've got to think this stuff out.
Later – Liz

P.S. I think you're right Bruce, I've got to find the right crowd. I think I can hang out with Jesus and not be one of those Christians. So I think I'll just say OK Jesus let's go to lunch and talk. Bruce recommended you!

Dear Bruce,

Do you think I could listen in on the teaching that Maria and Louise are going to? I am curious about why this guy would waste his time working with us. I mean like he is not getting anything out of the deal and Ann says nobody does anything unless there is something in it for them. So I thought I would just listen for awhile and try to figure out why he would work with us. I mean like with you, you get paid for spending time with us, but we are not giving this guy anything. So why would he spend time on a Saturday with us? Maria is very excited about going to school with him again next Saturday. Ann is cautious and told Liz that he better not set Maria up and then reject her. Ann is always so negative!

Guess what? Liz had a big talk with the guy Ruth likes. You know - Jesus. She told me that he listened to her and she had a hard time staying mad at him. Then he said something that tore her apart. He told her what sin of hers made him cry. Like she was almost crying as she told me. You know what he said? It wasn't what I thought her worst sin would be. After listening to Ann talk about Liz you would think Liz was one bad cookie.

I was real curious and asked Liz if she was going to tell me or not. She then said, he told me my refusal to let him love me. I asked her what she did when he said that and she told me that he put his arms out to her and she walked into them. Then she said to him I don't want to be a wimp and I don't want to be a Suburban Christian. I want to be real. She said he held her tight and whispered in her ear, "You will be strong in me."

Liz told me lots of stuff she learned, like the law is only good if it is used correctly. She wanted Jesus to tell her why she ticks Christians off when she questions their actions and their words. Jesus told her many will gather around those who say what their itching ears want to hear and they will turn their ears away from truth. Then he told her to know the truth, hold firmly to it, encourage others with it and refute those who oppose it.

You know Liz and the others; they like can't even love themselves. How are they going to be able to love others if they don't even love themselves? This is too difficult to understand. What is Liz talking about and why did she cry? Liz just doesn't cry! She says that crying is wimpy.

Peace, Jennie

Louise wrote to Bruce about her own struggles ongoing with the Catholic Church and her difficulty believing all that I was teaching her:

I want to tell you something real important. On Friday we went to my godson's graduation. After the mass, Father Wayne came over and said hi, but Ruth came out and I couldn't get out to talk. He asked if we were still attending St. Joachim's and she said she left the Catholic Church and is a member of the Assemblies of God church. Father Wayne was very upset and told her that she could not receive the full Eucharist. Ruth looked at him and said anyone who accepts Jesus Christ as their personal Savior and Lord can accept communion.

It really upset me. Ruth would not let me out to talk with Father Wayne. On Saturday I was scared to go see the Pastor teaching Maria, because we Catholics are not supposed to talk to Protestant pastors, only to priests. Ruth and Maria said that it would be okay and he could talk about Purgatory and Penance. I went in and he had a black shirt on just like a priest. He was very nice and we talked about the Catholic Church.

He told me that popes did not exist right after Peter. He told me the foundation the church was not built on Peter, but what Peter said about Jesus being God. He told me that some popes became Pope because they had a lot of money and some were corrupt, while others were good. He told me that no man should tell another person they can't take communion if they know they have accepted Jesus as Savior. He told me that we can talk directly to God in prayer and don't have to go through a priest. He showed me in the Bible that Jesus is the way, the truth and the life and that nobody can come to the Father except through Jesus. You can't come to the Father through the Catholic Church alone.

Why did the Catholic Church tell me all those rules to get to heaven, if they were not true? Why would the Catholic Church lie to me all these years? Why did they teach me things that were not truth? Why didn't they explain the cross to me and what Jesus really did like the Pastor? It makes me very sad that I trusted them to tell me the truth and I worked very hard for many, many years to obey them and they lied to me. Why did they add stuff to the Bible and tell me it was part of the Bible? Why did they tell me the Pope was infallible, when he is just a man? Why did they tell me that Mary was the Mother of God, Queen of heaven and that you could pray to her and she would answer prayers? He showed me in the Bible that she was the mother of Jesus on earth, not God in heaven, and Jesus is the only one we should pray to. Why did they tell me that you could pray your relatives out of Purgatory? Only Jesus decides that and we can't change the past. Why did they tell me this stuff and none of it was true?

I was worried that maybe Pastor Chalberg wasn't telling me the truth either. I was getting so mixed up, because everybody says things different. Ann's friend the Mormon Bishop says one thing, the Catholic Church says something else and the Pastor says something else. He says to trust only the Bible. So I really had to think about who I was going to believe. I decided not to believe any of them. I decided that from now on, everything everybody says about God, I am going to read about in the Bible to see if it matches. I am only going to believe the Bible because it has been around a lot longer than anybody else has. I think I will use Ruth's Bible because it is easiest to read.

The Pastor and Ruth and you have not said anything so far that does not match the Bible. Saturday I became a Christian like Ruth. I am very happy. I know what a Christian is now. A Christian loves the Lord with all her heart, her mind and her soul. She believes that she is a sinner and that Jesus died on the cross for her sins, so that she could have eternal life. She believes that Jesus rose from the dead and sits at the right hand of God the Father. A Christian knows that she can do nothing to earn heaven, because if she could then Jesus dying was not enough. Jesus gives us eternal life as a gift and when we die, he stands before the Father like our defense attorney. We can hide behind him and the Father accepts us into heaven because of Jesus. He paid our punishment for us. I understand. Jesus loves us so much that he died for us. That is a lot of love!

I am very excited. I really know now that I get to go to heaven and see Ruth and you and especially Jesus. I am sad about the Catholic Church though, but I am not angry at them. We need to tell them they got it wrong and that they don't need all those things. All they need to do is believe Jesus died for their sins and his death was enough. Ruth tells me the Catholic Church gets angry at Catholics that know this and go to other churches. Why should they get angry when someone believes Jesus and gets to go to heaven? I would think they would want everyone to go to heaven. I do.

It makes me sad to think some people go to Hell. I don't want anyone to have to go there. I have to decide about still going to mass. The Pastor says there are Evangelical Catholic Churches that I might like more, but maybe not until the others understand better. I like the music at Ruth's church, but sometimes I don't understand what they talk about. Why do people fall on the floor and shake? Why do people talk in different languages that I can't understand? It might take me a long time to understand all these things, but I wanted to tell you the good news.
Louise

Raquel wrote to Bruce in search of answers about Jesus. We had both encouraged all the parts to be reading the Bible in their spare time so many wrote about their understanding of it.

One Who Listens,

Greetings from the Eagle Clan and I, Quiet Walker. Many moons have come and gone since our time under the porcupine tree. I have walked far along the path to the top of Sacred Mountain in search of the truth held within its core. The spirits of the ancient ones have guided me on my journey and have bestowed much wisdom upon me. I patiently await the time of our crossing. I wish to listen to you and learn of the spirit that you follow called Jesus.

I have heard Shedding Tear. He is one who comes in peace and carries in his words much wisdom. He is well respected among those who live in Preservation. I have read some of the writings of his ancient book. The Psalms are like the maple flowing from the maple trees. The words speak of a pouring out of the writer's inner feelings to the Great Spirit. I find much comfort in the 37th writing. There is much wisdom in the message where trust, delight and commitment lead to peace. One must refrain from anger and wait upon the Great Spirit to help and deliver those who trust him.

I have also read of the ones called Saul and Jonathan. I favor Jonathan. During the time of crisis, Jonathan stood in the battle taking that which he believed as truth to the other side. He drew his strength from the promise and he jubilantly would have given his life for that promise. The other one called Saul seemed like the ones I hear Liz speak about. He would not leave his tribe, for he looked at the predicament and not at the promise. He had no substance to his character.

He was like the hen and the pig, which were to feed the hungry traveler. The hen gave eggs from her comfort, whereas the pig gave a total commitment of ham and bacon. Saul is like the hen. He follows the Great Spirit with much atrophy. The ancient book of writings that Ruth studies is of interest to me. I wish to hear from you about the book and the one you follow. I must close now, for my time in the outside world has ended. I patiently await your invitation.

Eagle Clan and I are journeying to the jungle to be guests of Lion. Brave Eagle carried the message to us that Mariann wishes to see the girl who flies with the eagles. I shall visit her soon, after I visit with Shedding Tear.

-Quiet Walker

Ann continued to struggle with her issues about the Circle Council leadership consisting of only men. She began doing extensive research and analysis of each leader. She wanted to know whom she was dealing with whenever she brought an issue before Council. She tabulated their weaknesses, strengths, history, character traits and any general information she thought might be useful for her purposes. Because she developed extensive histories, I will give here the Reader's Digest version of her work.

I find it interesting that the leaders have their own following among the parts. Maria and Louise feel most comfortable with Helper. Both of them are afraid of Paladin, because he dresses all in black and has this gunfighter, militant-type attitude that frightens them. Liz of course likes Paladin, all six foot two of him! Ruth is close to Helper and King of the Lights. I feel slightly uncomfortable around King of the Lights. Whenever I speak to him he is polite and kind but seems to see right through me. It makes me extremely uncomfortable when I sense that he knows me better than I know myself. He seems to read my mind and just smiles. I don't like it one bit.

Raquel likes King of the Lights and Daniel, because Daniel is around eleven years old and closer to her age. I still disagree with Council allowing a child on the most important court in the system, but I've given up that fight, as I have no support. Daniel is mature for his age and seems focused on being watchful for the Beast coming. He and the other boys are like a pack with a mission. My favorite is Keeper of Functions, because this guy knows how to get things done. He is highly efficient and organized. I like the way he runs his operation on level two. The children all like Daniel, whereas Jennifer and Marie have no favorites.

Helper: Appears to be a passive leader who listens to all sides and attempts to be fair in his dealings with the Surface People. He is not as well organized as I would like him to be and he lets a lot slide, which irritates me at times. But to his credit I have seen him stand on issues with Liz. He never judges or puts anyone down but will take charge if he has to. He reminds me of you somewhat in his disorganization! Helper will listen to me though and he is my ticket into council.

King of the Lights: I need more time to analyze him and figure him out. He is very kind and compassionate but makes a lousy leader. He seems more focused on the spiritual issues than politics. He is very well educated but doesn't boast about it.

Daniel: He leads his pack well and they have great respect for him. He is willing to suffer greatly to protect Mariann. He is always alert and sees more than I do, like he has eyes in the back of his head. I found the association of his name with Daniel of the Bible interesting. Like that Daniel, this one is willing to die for what he believes is important, protecting Mariann. He, like King of the Lights, is not interested in politics and system management. I will have a difficult time getting him to support me on issues, because he is not very interested unless they deal with Mariann. This could be because, in Greek mythology, Argus was a monster with 100 eyes that guarded IO, a mortal maiden loved by the god Zues. This was interesting because Zues was the top god in Greek mythology. It fits that Daniel would be guarding Mariann from the Beast, who is also considered a god that is employed by the head god. Daniel also guards a maiden and is always on watch like Argus.

Keeper of Functions: He reminds me of an accountant and CEO all wrapped up in one leader. I enjoy discussing philosophy, logic and mathematics with him. He is very intelligent and thinks in a logical fashion. He will be my greatest advocate in system management. He is also not a chauvinist like some of the other leaders. Highly efficient...yes!

Paladin: This leader is a pain. He is taller than the others and dresses in black with a stupid cowboy hat. On his clothes he has a monogram of a chess piece, the white knight. He seems college educated but has this military mentality. He is stubborn and seems to have a code of ethics he lives by. I asked him what his new name meant and he just smiled at me. Damn I hate that. He thinks I will quit, but he doesn't know me very well. I told him I would figure it out.

My only clues were the white chess piece, his name Paladin and something Maria once said that he was related to Daniel Boone. Okay, why the white chess piece? In chess, white always makes the first move. I must remember this about Paladin. Okay, the king is the most important piece in chess. Unlike the King, Queen, Rook and Bishop, the Knight does not move in a straight line. A war-horse's head symbolizing power, long service, and reliability through hardships and speed represents the Knight. These are definite characteristics of Paladin that I need to remember in dealing with him.

Now the Daniel Boone connection, how does that fit? Frontiersman around 1776 who marked out the Wilderness Trail. Interesting that we have a saying on our porch that says, "Do not follow where the path may lead...Go instead where there is no path and leave a trail." I don't know, but that sounds just like a Daniel Boone quote! Check out why Lord Byron's poem Don Juan mentions Daniel Boone and any connection to Don Juan. Only connection may be Carlos Castaneda, the controversial writer on Don Juan in the 70's. He wrote books with interesting titles and mystical themes like, The Eagle's Gift, The Power of Silence, The Fire From Within and A Separate Reality. I wonder if Raquel has read any of these?

So shit, Daniel Boone is a dead end. I wonder if there is any other Boone related here. I'll check the reference librarian to see if she knows anything about Paladin or someone by the name of Boone. (I've edited this down, but as you can see, Ann really got into this.) *BINGO! BINGO! TRIPLE BINGO! Richard Boone who is a descendent of Daniel Boone played Paladin on the 1957 to 1963 television series – Have Gun Will Travel. There's the connection!*

Okay, Paladin had no other name and was a hired gunslinger from San Francisco. He would hire out his guns and experience to people who can't protect themselves from danger (MARIA). He had a black leather holster that had the symbol of a Paladin, apparently another name for the white chess knight! I didn't know that! He also carried a calling card with the symbol in the show.

The television character was college-educated and a graduate of West Point. He was a man of culture, fine clothes and literate company. When he had an assignment, he became an intimidating figure all dressed in black. He had a sense of ethics that dictated what he would and would not do. He stated he would never draw his gun unless he intended to use it. I need to remember this, Paladin does not bluff. Interestingly there is a song called the Ballad of Paladin sung by Johnny Western and put out by Columbia Records. Okay, time to find the ballad at the record store. – Shit, nothing damn it! I never heard of this show or seen it. Somebody must have seen it when Maria was between five and eleven years old. I'm going to the Wherehouse and see if I can trace it there. BINGO! Columbia Country Classics – Ballad of Paladin / Americana Volume three. Back to the library! - Alright! - Found it!

"Have gun will travel leaves the card of a man.
A knight without armor in a savage land.
His fast gun for hire, he's the calling wind.
A soldier of fortune there's the man called Paladin.
Paladin, Paladin, where do you roam?
Paladin, Paladin, far, far from home.
He travels on to wherever he must.
A chess knight of silver is his badge of trust.
There are campfire legends that the plainsmen spin.
Of the man with a gun of the land called Paladin.
Paladin, Paladin, where do you roam?
Paladin, Paladin, far, far from home."

That must be it and he thought I would never figure him out. He doesn't know about my persistence. Okay, now when I deal with him I need to remember that he is strong, doesn't bluff, and means what he says; has a tender heart for the underdog, tends to be a little bit cocky and arrogant; likes the finer things in life, enjoys a good literary discussion, is intelligent, has a military strategy type of mind, makes a damn good soldier, a leader and a planner. Gotcha!

When I have time I'm going to investigate King of the Lights. That should be interesting. I wonder what doors will open up there? This is amazing.

Everyone focused their energy on their own issues to handle each day. The bulk of their letters as the source of these journals, would continue to go to their primary caregiver Bruce for another nine months or so. Bruce continued to focus on the children in drawing them out for healing. Working with Mariann meant working with Lion, Daniel and the Clan of Argus at the same time. One afternoon in his office, a priest was spotted in another room and that sparked alarms for the entire System as they left:

Daniel is extremely concerned about safety for Mariann in your office. Today as the system left the premises, there was a Beast sitting in your waiting room. Daniel was shadowing the part known as Ruth and observed the Beast through the open door. He was dressed in black. The Beast is close and waiting to catch Mariann for telling the secrets. The Beast has found your office. (Any priest – not Father Breen) *Daniel has informed Lion of the threat. Lion will not allow Mariann out again until he has your assurance that the Beast will not find her.*

Mariann believes that the Beast followed the system from the Opera (Phantom of the Opera), *to your office. She believes the Beast is mad because she has seen the Dragonslayer. She knows he will get her. Lion must protect her from harm. What is to prevent the Beast in the waiting room from coming into the office and killing Mariann? The Beast is stronger than you are and Lion cannot protect Mariann on the outside. Mariann must remain hidden until safe.*

Circle Council struggled to take care of the System's safety as turmoil increased around them. Paladin was putting together a proposal listing personal rights within the System. The debate issued thoughts over what is an inalienable right versus a privilege. Questions immediately arose about how they could work together to defend those same rights. Some hard choices about the welfare of the System and the time necessary to heal through the trauma of their past and present were becoming difficult to avoid, in order to be prepared for the future.

A primary issue at the forefront was who should have therapy time with Bruce. Ann was straining to maintain the cost of therapy once a week as it was, because of a promise to Sergio not to go into debt over therapy and fear of the repercussions if she did. It was agreed in Council that the smaller children, Tabitha and Angelina, should take priority over everyone else including Mariann. The time with Bruce would not be split up as in the past with the hope that the use of concentrated time would speed up the healing process. Explaining to Mariann why she had to wait wasn't easy, for they feared she might perceive it as a form of further abandonment.

There was also the day to day conflicts within the family that increased stress on everyone. Sergio was telling the System they needed to see a sex therapist to fix the fear and loathing of sex. Of course there was no effort on his part to understand their history or problems. Ultimately the letter from Bruce in a few months will have no response or positive result. Sergio would come to the conclusion that his wife was 'frigid' and there was nothing he could do about 'her problems'. Council was concerned that Maria and Louise might never be ready to talk about sex with anyone. This does become an issue discussed with my wife and I, but not for another four to five years from now. While Maria never brought it up in her time with Bruce, she would marvel over the fact that Bruce never hit his wife in their marriage, a concept that was a new revelation to her. Paladin wrote to Bruce to get his thoughts on the following draft:

DECLARATION OF THE RIGHTS OF THE SYSTEM

All parts are entitled to basic fundamental human rights. It is imperative that the System protects the natural rights of each and every part.

1. *All parts have the right of life. No outside or inside person has the right to extinguish a part's right to life.*

2. *All parts have the right to security and safety. No part shall place the System in danger of harm. Safety of the System takes precedent over all other allegiances and commitments.*

3. *All parts have the right to develop themselves to the fullest. No part shall be denied the opportunity of employment or education.*

4. *All parts have the right to preserve their culture.*

5. *All parts have the right of expression and creativity. No part shall be denied the right of their opinion or ideas.*

6. *All parts will respect each other's beliefs and freedom to believe. No part will promote an established religion on any other part without that part's consent.*

7. *All parts have the right to happiness and peace.*

8. *All parts have the right to resist oppression.*

(Of all the rights listed, number six will be argued about the most by everyone.)

Bruce attempted to help the System by having them attend a seminar one Saturday that he was leading. The following two letters from Liz and Elizabeth Ray/Council are a result of that day. Liz's response to this person was overstated. Her anger over the misconceptions from Christians and the general public that existed about multiples was real and true enough. Consider what misconceptions you may have.

Ms. R...(Therapist at a Christian counseling center that introduced Bruce.)

On Saturday, we attended a seminar in Milpitas that was presented by Mr. Bruce F. You introduced Bruce as a specialist in working with MPD's and stated that you had enough problems dealing with just one client.

I am a multiple. I found your comments rude and insensitive. Not only did you give the general public the perception that working with multiples is a real headache, but you also insinuated that clients are problems. If you think that clients are problems, then you need to get the Hell out of the mental health profession. Who made you God anyway? Do you think you are better than the rest of us and look down at your clients as poor bastards with problems? That's just what the world needs... more suburban, white, Christian therapists to f**% up the rest of society and label them problems. You're the one with the problem, not us.

The problem with people like you is that you don't know the first thing about professionalism. You don't value and respect people... especially people who are different than yourself. You don't know the first thing about displaying the conduct and qualities that should be the mark of your profession. Multiples are already portrayed as outcasts... to be shunned, drugged, exorcised and locked up. We've already dealt with more pain, more torture and more discrimination than you will ever know. But you "loving person", who wears the Christian label, decided that we haven't had enough pain, rejection and ridicule. You need to add to it by getting a big laugh at the expense of us multiples.

Now my perception of you is that of a wimpy little asshole, who has no idea which way is up. I see it now... little suburban white Christian, toting her Bible to her elite white church and praising the Lord in her cute little peach chiffon dress, with cute little dimples on her smiling face. You praise the Lord and then go out and makes fun of multiples. You help solidify my decision that I never want to be a damn Christian. Because of you and your stupid comments, Council nailed my ass for screaming at them over it and blaming me for the other parts who are scared and insecure, thinking that they must be a burden and problem for their therapist. They don't want to be problems for anyone because they know that being a problem means getting hurt, both physically and verbally.

If you don't want to earn your therapist license out of a Cracker Jack box, you had better get your brain out of your ass and start thinking about what you are going to say before you open your mouth. The possible damages to the audience listening to whatever you say, could have long term effect on them more than you can realize.

Liz

Dear Bruce,

I have been asked by Council to send you this update report. Circle Council has been meeting hourly to extinguish 'fires' that have erupted due to Saturday's Seminar. Assignments have been given to Marie and Ruth to comfort the children. Tabitha heard Liz screaming to Council about her anger that even Christian therapists think we are bad and a problem. Tabitha became distraught as she started crying and rambling on that she was a bad girl and Jesus' friends laugh about us. Ruth has tried to explain to her and reassure her that she is not bad and 'daddy' doesn't laugh at her. Marie is trying to distract them from the tension within the system by using games. Angelina doesn't know what's going on but senses the tension and is reacting by hyperventilating and shaking her hands up and down. Anna wants to go back to her hole. Ruth is telling them a story now about a little ' lammy' that must keep his eyes on the Shepherd to stay safe.

Lion has reported that Mariann is not doing much better. She heard through the 'air' the sound of Liz's screaming and began to panic, thinking the Beast is near and will destroy the Dragonslayer and kill Lion, before killing her. Lion has asked Raquel for help to comfort Mariann. Raquel has spoken to Mariann about the two of them making puppets to have a battle in your office. The battle will be between the boss of the Beast against Dragonslayer. It will have supporters on both sides there and Dragonslayer's Daddy will officiate. You will work the boss and his supporters, while Mariann will do the Dragonslayer, His Daddy and the Dragonslayer supporter puppets. Raquel asked Ruth to find some music suitable for using in the battle play.

Council questioned Raquel about the play and Mariann's ability to participate in it. She said that the battle must take place, because "It is time for the Jungle Child to know of the power of the One who comes from the Great Spirit." Circle Council respects her wisdom and approved the battle. Mariann trust Lion who has told her not to be afraid, because he will be right there to pull her in to safety, if he thinks she will be harmed. Raquel plans to go slowly with Mariann and is anticipating the battle to occur in mid-August.

Jennifer has been assigned the duty of shadowing Maria at all times. Maria has swirled down into more depression and not communicating with us. On Saturday she cried that she is a problem for Bruce and he is her friend. She said she would rather not live than be a problem for him. We tried to comfort her, but she wanted to be left alone. Council is concerned that she will switch out and destroy the body, so as not to be a burden to you. Maria has difficulty handling this amount of pressure. Louise is fairing a bit better. She thinks we need to apologize to you for being a problem and promise to obey you better. She doesn't know what she did wrong, but she assumes it must be a terrible thing. She is carrying much of Maria's workload and modeling much of Maria's feelings and actions. Paladin is keeping an eye on her for now. Raquel doesn't say much about the incident on Saturday. She did state to Council that, "One who is wise overlooks the insult of a fool," before leaving for Sacred Mountain.

Circle Council is allowing each part to address them about their concerns. So far, Liz has been the most agitated and expressed her anger about Paladin trusting a Christian Counseling Center. She blasted him for being off-guard and becoming lax in trusting it to be safe. "If there is anything we have learned in this shitty life of ours, it is that we don't trust anyone or anything outside of the system." Her tirade lasted for most of the afternoon. Ann agreed with Liz about being more diligent. She said that until we become organized and efficient, we will not be able to be functional at a successful level outside. She questioned Council if they were considering discontinuing therapy to prevent further shock by therapists. (Council is not ending therapy and trusting you to handle the other therapists as Director of the center.)

Paladin has asked that I keep you informed of this situation until your next session. Other information that might be helpful for you is this. Liz's obsession with mushrooms has a symbolic meaning. Mushrooms represent a part of the male anatomy that has caused considerable pain for many parts. She enjoys cutting them up and frying them until they are 'wimpy' enough to squish between her fingers and devour them. This ritual of hers allows her to let out great anger and tension.

Lila is still hiding somewhere in the system (Those Who Are Core). *The others are unaware of her history and her trauma. She is hearing impaired and unable to read or communicate by sign language. She is partially deaf in her right ear from gun blasts near her ears. She can pick up a few words and will ask where her ears are. She calls for her grandmother and will tell you the phone number for her. Trigger words for her are canyon and broken legs. When you relate to her, hold her gently close and talk softly in her right ear.*
Respectfully, E. R. – Keeper of the History

> ***My journey is one of hope.***
> ***Longing to be released from***
> ***the bondage of the past.***
> ***Traveling the path of pain to arrive***
> ***at the destination of peace.***
> ***So that I may heal and soar***
> ***free as Brave Eagle.***
> *-Quiet Walker*

Liz received a response from Ms. R., just not the one she wanted. But it was Ann who took the time to write when Liz was too disgusted to try again.

I am the administrator of the system impacted by your comments regarding multiples. Liz received your letter and chose not to respond in disappointment. Your communication appeared to be a form letter written to appease your boss, rather than a note of understanding. What Liz was looking for was an apology for not understanding what a comment like yours can do to a multiple. She hoped you would learn something.

Although Liz was upset at your comments at the seminar, she was more so at your lack of understanding the purpose of her letter. I realize that Liz is not the best communicator and states things exactly the way she feels about them without regard to the impact they might have on the recipient. What Liz was trying to say is that, as a therapist, your words carry a tremendous amount of power. When people are hurting, a therapist can comfort them or destroy them, based upon the professional's statements and body language. A therapist has a great amount of responsibility, because the welfare of people's lives is in the therapist's hands.

She understands that therapists are not perfect and make mistakes, as she has pointed out various ones to our therapist, but she is willing to overlook those mistakes when the therapist is honest and real with her. You could have made a great impact on her if you had only admitted: "Liz I blew it...Thank you for holding me accountable...Your message will help me become a better therapist. We therapists can learn a lot from our clients. I hope I might someday meet you. Take care, P."

A note like that would have satisfied her and she would have forgiven you immediately. Liz can tell when someone responds to her sincerely or respond out of obligation. She didn't want to read about all your excuses about why you said what you said. She was not traumatized by your comments, as you assumed, but angry with them. That should have been obvious by the tone of her first letter to you. Since you didn't pick up her feelings from her letter, she wondered if you read it at all. She wrote it for one purpose, that you learn from the incident.

Ann was continuing to take care of the System, but she didn't tell Liz about the follow-up letter because she knew it would hurt her pride. Ann would not release herself from the self-perceived responsibility for everyone for several more years until Jesus and I prove ourselves trustworthy in her eyes.

Shortly after this, Raquel visited with me for the first time and introduced herself as Quiet Walker and I was given no prior notice of her visit. I was pleased because I had already read some of her writings and was looking forward to the day this would happen, but I just didn't think it would be so soon. I had some previous experience working in Alaska with the Tlingit peoples, so it did not take me too long to relate to Raquel. I adapted quickly to speak with her within the cultural context of Native American spiritualism and understanding the meaning of the Bible in that context. Within three hours we managed to cover the basic principles of the purpose of the Bible, who Jesus is and the purpose of His life, death and resurrection, and the reality of the bond between Jesus and myself that will last for eternity. Not bad for a day's work. This meant of course that, ready or not, Liz would be my next visitor.

During the week before Liz came however, I would receive two letters that included similar material. The one from Ruth included the basic outline of people in the System (which is given in the Prologue) as an introduction to many of the people I would meet. The other one was from Elizabeth Ray with more detail of the causes and effects of the abuse reflected in their life histories. It also included more stories of Jesus' interaction with the various parts to date, while they were still unaware of who He truly was. It spoke of angels and demons constantly at war over the System. Her final words were revealing:

Ruth is sure that there exists no possession of the system by demons. However, she has warned me that the enemy wants this system badly. Attacks continue especially toward the weaker ones. When a part begins to search out truth the enemy increases the attacks on the system. They come in many forms; beatings, sickness, financial problems, nightmares, threats, suicidal thoughts, self-mutilation, problems in relating to the outside world with triggers happening and anything else that might put us into a tailspin. But Ruth also believes that God sends His angels to watch over us and guard against these attacks.

The enemy does not like Maria and the others associating with you or Bruce. Their threats to kill you are constant. Ruth prays not only for the system's safety, but also for you and that of your family. Why do you think the powers of the enemy want the system so much? What is it about this system that is worth that much effort? Do you know?

The answers to her questions would be on the table for several more years to discover.

**"And not only this, but we also exalt in our tribulations,
knowing that tribulation brings about perseverance;
and perseverance, proven character; and proven character,
hope; and hope does not disappoint, because the love of God
has been poured out within our hearts through
the Holy Spirit who was given to us.
For while we were still helpless..."
-Paul Romans 5: 3-6**

**"Do not be conformed to this world, but be transformed
by the renewing of your mind, that you may prove
what the will of God is, that which is good and acceptable
and perfect...For just as we have many members in one body
and all the members do not have the same function,
so we who are many, are one body in Christ,
and individually members one of another..."
-Paul Romans 12: 2, 4-5**

Chapter 12:

"The Children Shall Lead Them"

"He called a little child and had him stand among them. He said, 'I tell you the truth, unless you change and become like little children, you will never enter the kingdom of heaven. Therefore, whoever humbles himself like this child is the greatest in the kingdom of heaven. And whoever welcomes a little child like this in my name welcomes me." Matthew 18: 2-5

"Everything is in the power of Heaven... except the fear of Heaven."
- Mishnah

"I am going to begin to change you – but even after a thousand years of this process of change – I will not love you one bit more than I love you right now at the moment of your commitment to Me; - or one bit more than I loved you at the moment of your birth. My love for you is unconditional. I am not trying to change you so I can love you... I love you and because I do – I want to change you."
Quote from No Longer Strangers

Raquel's initial visit and subsequent visits with me formed a special relationship that opened the door for bringing trust into the Land of Preservation. Within a year's time, the Lord will establish a friendship between us that will help carry the System through some very difficult times. To include all of the letters, journal notes, or conversations that occur during this time would be a book in itself, so I have chosen to include only the most important ones. My goal is to include information about the System recorded from 1994 to near the end of 1996.

The quote from No Longer Strangers is a favorite of mine that I have used in sermons and in many counseling sessions. It speaks to a common truth about our fear of accepting Jesus as our Lord and Savior. New believers and searching skeptics have this fear and believe that we have to change ourselves before we will be acceptable to Him. When I shared this for the first time with Maria and Louise, they were sure that I was in error, until I read these two verses:

"God demonstrates His own love toward us,
in that while we were still sinners,
Christ died for us."
Romans 5:8

"And he got up and came to his father.
But while he was still a long way off,
His father saw him, and felt compassion for him,
And ran and embraced him and kissed him."
Luke 15: 20

I explained how in the first verse, Paul was explaining the condition we were in when Jesus died for us. Motivated by love God accepted us as he found us. Paul was restating the facts told so eloquently by Jesus in the parable of the Prodigal Son. The second verse found in this parable shows how our Heavenly Father's love for His child motivated Him to run to hug him, accepting him in his condition with love and understanding, even before the son asked for forgiveness. The father wanted to help him become a better person not so he could love him, but so his son could love himself. The Father's love was never conditional expecting change; it was unconditional in spite of change.

Maria's concern was motivated by the fear that her present state made her unacceptable to God and the fear that Liz's upcoming visit would make 'them' unacceptable to me as a friend. Maria had no way of knowing all of the things that would later result in Liz and I becoming lifelong friends. This fear was shared by several within the System since my only real interaction with Liz, prior to this face to face meeting was the test she gave me when I interviewed with Maria. Rather than tell you about the meeting myself, I'll let Ruth tell you in her letter to Bruce.

Liz met with Pastor Chalberg on Saturday. I shadowed the conversation and it was very interesting. Liz talked with him under the tree outside for over an hour and a half. He listened to her frustration with Suburban Christians in a language only Liz can speak. She gave him two sermons to preach to the Suburban Christians of his church... if he had the cahonnes (sp.)? She also made it clear that she was never going to be labeled a Christian... ever! I thought his method of relating to her was excellent. I really think he shocked Liz. He also agitated her and she is very hard to be around right now. I believe it is because she is struggling with spiritual issues. The Pastor had a unique way of connecting.

She was surprised to learn that he plays blackjack, drinks beer and wine and gave examples of being a radical preacher. Of course, Liz wasted no time pointing out to me that if a pastor does it, it can't be a sin. (Something I would have to challenge at a later date.) *He told of his teen years to her living with alcoholic and abusive stepfathers, and why his mother killed herself while depressed from addiction to prescription drugs. While I was getting worried over the direction he was leading her, she was beginning to like him., but then he hooked her.*

They debated stealing which Liz agrees is wrong but does it anyway, justifying it as the Robin Hood Syndrome. Liz told him that she was the worst in the system and knew she was going to Hell, so it didn't make any difference. She said she isn't as proud as those Suburban Christians and can admit that she is an asshole and filled with sin, but she is a hopeless case. She switched conversations before he could answer and wanted to know why he would spend time on Saturdays with us, when he had better things he could be doing. She said you were getting paid and he was getting nothing, so why was he doing it?

He told her because he cared for people and he wanted to better understand MPD so he could be more effective with them. They discussed support groups for broken people and Liz stated the Christian Church offers nothing. If they care so much, which they don't, why aren't there support groups? He explained how he had started fourteen groups in one church and most of them died after he left which frustrated him greatly. Liz suggested they start one together and she'll come teach it, as long as it isn't in LA. He told her he had to go there soon to finish his seminary degree. This upset Maria and Louise very much inside – the old abandonment issue. Liz switched topics again and asked why God won't give us a break, how come he won't help us? She answered herself with it's because we're not worth it to him, that's why. Liz switched topics.

She started talking about Bruce and wanting him to go to Max's with her for lunch, but that he wouldn't do it. His time is too valuable to hang out with me. Then she reiterated that God doesn't want to have anything to do with me. Then he surprised us both. He told her, "Why don't you invite Jesus to your house for lunch?" ...into Liz's house? Liz said she didn't want to have to obey all of the rules doing things his way with all that obeying stuff. You know all of the rules that the Catholic Church made Louise do that crap and suffocate you. I don't want to be controlled or told what to do.

Pastor Chalberg then said, "We aren't talking about rules in the Catholic Church or obeying them, we're just talking about inviting Jesus into your house for lunch. Jesus doesn't want to control you; He wants to spend time with you so you can know Him. He accepts you right where you are." Liz said my house is dirty and you don't invite important people to a dirty house. I do a lot of shit! (Lots of symbolism here folks.) *Pastor Chalberg said it again and would not let her switch topics. She became frustrated when he asked her what she was afraid of, so Liz said I'll think about it and ended their time together. He told her he liked meeting her and she came inside mumbling something about 'a radical cowboy preacher...wouldn't you know it.' Since that time Liz has been very agitated and telling everyone to leave her alone.*

In Christ, Ruth

Raquel sent me the following poem after Liz was involved in a fight with Maria's father over the phone. Council sent out a status report shortly thereafter.

Kissed by a Dream on the Grave

I emerged from my cocoon, kissed by a dream.
A cherished vision, beloved and dear.
I held on to my dream, waiting for it to come true.

Instead came the darkness.
It engulfed and shattered my dream.
I knew my precious desire would never come true.

Lying in pieces around my heart, too many to grasp.
I can't put it together again...
My shattered dream.

319

> *Oh, Great Spirit*
> *Wise beyond men*
> *What good is a shattered dream?*

As I was writing these final chapters, I matched this poem with the session with Mariann recorded in chapter 5 and the healing of her shattered heart. I have found that many of Raquel's poems and stories are better understood and applied several years later. That has never really applied to Circle Council or Elizabeth Ray. They write about the facts and possible hidden meaning behind what is happening now.

Case in point, is the following update to Bruce in October of 1995 about the changes occurring within Preservation and trauma on the outside world. Of notable importance here is the changes on Level One within the Clan of Argus. The personalities blending here were known to all the parts, unlike what occurred 5 months earlier on Level Three. Blending is still happening on the inside, but not to parts yet that come to the surface world. This time of integration is consistent with the first in that it is a result of healing of parts with roles that are no longer needed. The choice to blend into their leader was again their own.

Mariann: She has crossed over into the forest with Jesus. She is playing with the other children near the swing. Tabitha has become her best friend because Mariann is playing 'big girl' games with her. They have not yet discussed issues concerning the 'bad' in their lives, but instead are enjoying getting to know each other.

Penny: Interestingly the children are getting along better. With the introduction of Mariann, there seems to be less rivalry between Penny and Tabitha. (This will last until Penny hears from Yemaya about what Mariann is saying about the 'Priest', because Mariann will only call him the 'Beast' for another year or so.) *Mariann is now the oldest and the other children look up to her.*

Clan of Argus: Early in the morning a ritual occurred within the Clan. In a military-style celebration the boys raised their swords as the sun rose. Daniel stood in the center with each of the boys circling around him. Each point of the swords made contact with Daniel's and the clan blended into Daniel. The boys had spent the prior evening in celebration of their job of protecting Mariann coming to an end. Mariann was free from being harmed by the Beast because the one known as Jesus would protect her now. The fort was transformed into an arched gateway between the forest and the jungle so that animals and parts could freely walk between the lands. (Later in book 3, when the Catholic Church scandal is in the media, Mariann becomes afraid that the 'Beasts' are coming back to kill her for telling. She and Hopi run around inside trying to rebuild a fort for protection out of mud. It is never completed because they cannot decide on what color to paint it. Hopi wanted light brown and Mariann wanted rainbow.)

Mari: She is with Quiet Walker on the Sacred Mountain path.

Angelina: As she continues to be around the other children, she is beginning to pick up language skills. She now drinks from a special cup, rather than from a bottle. She is playing more and takes sticks and places them in jars with lids. (Symbolic of feeling safe.)

Louise: Attended the support group. Ruth is encouraging her to continue. Louise is having a difficult time keeping up. Ruth plans to shadow and help her understand the concepts.

Maria: Wanted to call her mom because she is worried about her. Council gave approval. Mom told her Donna was hauled in on Friday. Maria asked what happened and the mother told her that Donna became violent at a hospital. The police were called to take her to a mental hospital. Mom then told her that her husband got her out on Saturday. The mother told her she is worried for Donna's daughters. Maria's father was listening in on the other line unknown to the system. He broke into the conversation and said to Maria, "you are a hundred times worse than her. What are you doing calling here?" He then slammed the phone down.

Liz switched out and told her mother "let me talk to him." (Council was impressed with Liz's courage.) The father got on and Liz said, "How rude! I called to see how mom was doing and as far as me being 100 times worse, well the apple doesn't fall far from the tree, now does it dad?" (Liz picked that phrase up from Ann.) The father was silent for a moment and then said, "your mother is blind in one eye and had another stroke. The doctors said the strokes are caused by stress you caused her." Liz shot back and said, "So what you're telling me is that I am at fault for mom's cancer, her strokes and her blindness. I cause all the problems in the world simply because I exist. Even if I don't talk or see you guys for six months, whatever happens in that time is my fault. Is that what you're telling me?"

The father began to get angry and said don't be a wise ass. At this point the mother interjected and told us this was costing us a lot of money and we needed to get off the phone. Liz wanted to continue, but Ruth switched out and said, "take care of yourself mom and I will be praying for you and dad. I'll call you around Thanksgiving" and hung up.

Liz was furious inside and Ann wasn't much better. Ann complained to Council that all the work done in therapy is destroyed in one phone call with those people. We disagreed and said Liz is getting much better at standing up to the father. Louise and Maria are bouncing back much quicker from these episodes, better than in the past. We suggested to Liz, Ann and Ruth that they reinforce the positive with Louise and Maria. (1) It is not Maria or Louise's fault. (2) No one in the system is powerful enough to bring on cancer and blindness. (3) The father is a bitter and hateful man. (4) You have done good obeying Sergio and not contacting Donna. (5) Remember what Mr. Chalberg told you – you can't make Donna's choices for her and you are not responsible for her choices. (Council and I would later talk about how to accent these choices more.)

Jennifer: Refuses to get into controversies with Maria's family, helps Ann out with details of house management and spends a lot of time with her birds.

Marie: no change.

Ann: Still working on the house. The engineering department went over the inspector's head and approved the foundation. She is in the second phase of room/roof and hopes to be done around Thanksgiving. (With all the problems with her dishonest 'Christian' contractor, it won't be completed for another year.) *She told us yesterday that you agreed with her that a Bible Class on Thursday night at the new church wasn't a good idea at this time. We respect your input. We are evaluating the Tuesday night support group class and will make a determination in two weeks. We will continue to allow the Saturday meetings with Mr. Chalberg as they are producing good results. In late November we will begin to prepare Maria and Louise for the separation with this pastor. He plans to leave for LA in January, after his house sells, to finish his degree. We must allow ample time for this separation.*

Lion: Lion has joined Circle Council as a leader. We now consist of six leaders. Lion will work with Paladin on protecting the system, with the responsibilities being divided. Paladin will be in charge of protection from outside harmers and Lion will be in charge of protection in our inside world. Lion is qualified to work with depressed parts. King of Lights will continue to be the expert on spiritual issues, Daniel will represent the younger parts with Lion and Keeper of Functions and I will oversee system management and leading council. Council requests the date of the mailing of your final draft to Maria's husband.

You may notice that there was no mention by Council about the parts known as 'Those Who Are Core, or TWAC.' This is because they still have little or no knowledge about them. This is about to change as Bruce begins to receive warnings directly from them about his interference with those under their care. These warnings were never dismissed, but they were set aside when dealing with the anger of Ann or Liz. Ann really wasn't as tough as this letter makes her sound.

Maria needs to accept being born into a messed-up family. She cannot simply ignore it by replacing them with others. This is not grocery store therapy. She doesn't get to choose a new family because she doesn't like the one she received. It is important for Maria to realize her parents will never love her or even like her, her sister and brother will never accept her or be nice to her and her mother-in-law will never stop drinking and telling her she is not good enough for Sergio.

It is counterproductive for you to encourage her to accept you as a brother and Mr. Chalberg as a godfather. You are not her brother and you will never be her brother. Besides, what person in their right mind would ever want a sister like Maria? If Maria could only stop with this nonsense of wanting to be loved, then she could spend her energy in learning skills to be more responsible and well educated. I have told her again and again that life is not fair. Some people get the breaks and other people are broken. She must ignore this emotional stuff and get on with surviving. Crying in bed does not accomplish a damn thing.

I'm also concern about Maria hugging you. I do not even like the kids hugging people. Maria needs to remember the boundaries. All of a sudden she wants hugs from Lindsay, Mr. Chalberg and you. I do not want her hugging anyone. It only fuels that desire of hers to be loved and pretty soon she will be hugging everyone. She has the dog to hug and that is enough!

You probably think I am hard on Maria, but you have not been living our life. Maria has been hurt by so many people who use her and manipulate her, because of her hunger for acceptance and love. In fact, she still is being used and hurt. She needs to come to an acceptance that she is not going to be loved or accepted... period! I can not pay therapy bills for the rest of her life, just so she can see her 'brother' and talk to him. Lindsay has her own life and so does Mr. Chalberg. All of you will leave eventually and Maria will be left alone again without a family. The reality is that we are alone in this world and only through our skills and determination will we be able to survive the shit that rolls our way.

I have also heard the others complain about my freeze on spending. Unless they can come up with a better way to balance our budget, they need to keep their mouths shut. I have spent hours prioritizing expenses and they are lucky to have a roof over their heads...sort of – damn that contractor! They can complain all they want about no heat over the holidays. It's not that cold that they will freeze. I've given them plenty of blankets and sweaters to keep them warm. They do not need heat. As far as the holidays go, we do not need trees or gifts to celebrate the holidays. They can take a walk at night and look at all the decorated houses with food cooking that they can smell. They do not need to have it themselves and besides, they are not starving or naked...

I REFUSE TO GO UNDER. I WILL NOT FILE BANKRUPTCY. I WILL NOT TAKE FOOD STAMPS. I WILL NOT GO BEGGING FOR HELP, ESPECIALLY FROM HER FAMILY. I have done that enough from SSI, CCS and DOR. I hate being looked down upon as ignorant, poor and a burden to society. I WILL MAKE IT ON MY OWN EVEN IF IT KILLS ME. So I would appreciate your support every time one of them whines to you about what a scrooge I am. Tell them that until they have a better idea, they need to keep their mouths shut.

Also I heard Liz will be joining you this week. Good! Reprimand her for me. I don't appreciate the snakes in the crawl space where I'm working, the wars with Sergio over ridiculous issues, loud dancing on my subfloor and comments about our haircut. I don't like the late-night escape activities, or her telling Tabitha about Santa Claus to pressure me into buying the kid a Christmas gift. I really don't like her giving me the finger and telling me she can go anywhere she pleases. Council does not seem to have the ability to control her. Personally, I think they should do what the royal family used to do to their undesirable monarchs... off with her head!

Surely, with all of your training, you must know of a way to control someone like Liz. I have an idea...let's send her to Maria's father! Have a nice Thanksgiving. Enjoy doing your male thing of watching football. Liz says it's a male thing... animal instinct stuff... patting each other on the ass and grunting like they're on the prowl. I would prefer Masterpiece Theater.

Followed right after by Liz of course:

Bruce-
Man Ann is pissed! Kind of funny to see steam coming out of her ears. Shit, it's mostly that Suburban Christian contractor and the people from his church. We just don't fit.

I think Chalberg should forget about those stupid diplomas and start a church here for the ones that don't fit. It could be filled with multiples, people that got AIDS, the poor, the homeless, the winos, the disabled and anyone else that wanted to come. Only one rule – you got to accept each other. Yeah, Chalberg would be a dynamite preacher. I don't want him to go to school and have those Suburban Christian teachers rot out his brain. Besides, we don't care if he has a diploma or not. I've got to start sending him some of my jokes and cards. He needs some Liz laughter in his life. That school stuff and money is getting him down.

I put some fake snakes under the house to greet Ann when she did the plumbing. My goal was to make her pee her pants, but all I did was piss her off. Now I've got to figure out how I can dye our hair blue to get her. What do you think?
Later- Liz

As I look back now at these letters, I understand better the fear of abandonment and rejection that is expressed by Ann for the System. Being the unemotional and detached administrator, an image she built for herself allowed her to present the possibilities that others didn't have the courage to voice outside of Council. They like Ann, knew that I was persuaded at that time to leave for Pasadena by January to finish my degree. Fuller Seminary had a prerequisite for Master of Divinity Students to complete a full year on campus before graduating. I had delayed it for almost 13 years by going part-time, because I felt the Lord wanted me to do other ministry work in the 'field,' before taking that year to complete my degree.

What Bruce and the System did not know about Carol and I was our commitment to the Lord to do this in His timing - not ours. The problem with knowing His timing is you have to ask first, and then be ready to hear the answer. I have usually been good at asking, but it's the hearing I have to keep working on. The relationship Jesus was starting with the System would help me to learn the real strength of listening to God. Doing ministry with people was giving me a more rounded education than just seminary alone. There had been several points when we thought the Lord was telling us not to move yet until we had finished the task, so we knew it was possible it could happen again.

I was torn between completing my degree or continuing to do ministry without it. Did I really need a piece of paper from a religious institution to qualify me to help broken people find healing through God? On the one hand, He had already proven for thirteen years the answer was no, at least not when God is directing the ministry Himself. Yet, God had also made it clear that there might be more opportunities to present Him in ministry to more traditional church people if I had the degree. So what should we do? Well, I did what I had done a few times in the past when faced with a very important choice before God, I let Him make the decision. I laid out a fleece before God, metaphorically, as Gideon had done in the Book of Judges. We listed our house with a realtor for 90 days and priced it to sell quickly. Houses in the Bay Area of California usually sell fast and it was a seller's market at the time. If the house sold we were to go in January and stay if it didn't. You could say I stacked the deck in favor of leaving. Everybody loved the house and commented on the great price, but there was not one bid. Overpriced houses all around us sold quickly, but not ours. I would use this technique again in the summers of '96 and '97.

By December of '95 I was reasonably sure we would be staying in the Bay Area and I was to continue working with the System. I waited to tell the System until after our contract ran out with the realtor. Sometimes God answers at the last moment and I needed to wait. These days I rarely use the fleece method because I have matured enough to trust the Lord explicitly and His directions on major choices for us given in His word. I don't always get it right, but my batting average has improved.

Raquel had become a very prolific writer in late 1995 and early 1996. Most of the writings were sent to me by email or by fax. She was spending a lot of time reading the Bible and talking to Jesus. She was at every Bible study shadowing and occasionally asking questions through Maria or Louise. I mentioned half-jokingly my disappointment at the name Shedding Tear that she had given me. I had wondered why it wasn't Talking Eagle or at least Bald Eagle... for obvious reasons, or maybe even Messenger From The Great Spirit Who Honors The Ancient Ones. This was the response she wrote that truly brought honor to Jesus Christ.

Strong Friend Shedding Tear,
I thank the Great Spirit for the gift of our friendship. I have learned much from listening to you. You have much strength and yet you are weak. At first that was confusing to me. How can one be strong and yet weak? Either one is strong like Brave Eagle or one is weak like

the one called Maria. So I spent time walking the path to gain wisdom about this.

When I first met you, I connected with a deep pain in your heart. The pain was not a physical or emotional pain, but rather a spiritual one. This perplexed me. As I sat near you and listened, it was revealed to me that your pain was one of love to provide hope for those who suffer. That is why you were given the name Shedding Tear. You shed tears of pain for those who do not have the hope that has brought you peace... and that hope is your strength.

Thus I began my journey to understand this hope that you possessed. I began reading the ancient book of Ruth's and seeking wisdom and meaning from the Great Spirit. I learned that the essential thing in life is to know and love the Great Spirit and to love each other. This is what is important. With this knowledge, I began to question what it means to know the Great Spirit. I was directed to the ancient book and read the Philippians. I must admit that I was not well focused, but I knew that I could return to it when I was better rested.

With the sun gathering the warmth in my room, I fell asleep. I had a very unusual dream. I was on the path leading to Sacred Mountain and Brave Eagle dove in my direction dropping a letter in front of me. I picked it up and realized it was a letter from you. As I read it, I could hear your voice clearly. This is what you said.

"I thank God every time I think of you. In my prayers for all of you parts, I always pray that your love for each other will overflow and that you will keep growing in spiritual knowledge and depth of insight, so that you may be able to tell right from wrong and bring glory to the Lord. I know this, that he who began a good work in you will carry it on to completion.

I am going to continue to trust in the Lord for I know that as I pray for you, and as the Holy Spirit helps us, this is going to turn out for good. You will continue to go through many trials, just as you have done in the past, but I pray that in these trials you will always be an honor to the Lord. For all of us, whatever happens, whether we live or whether we die, we must conduct ourselves in a manner worthy of the gospel of Jesus Christ. This will bring glory to God and be a testimony to others.

It brings me great joy when I hear of you trying to work together with one heart and mind and purpose. Christ and his love is the foundation of life. Continue to love one another, being humble, unselfish and concerned with each other's needs. Your attitude needs to be the attitude of Jesus. Though he was God, he did not demand his rights as God, but humbly laid down his power and glory to become a man and die a horrendous death on a cross for us. And because of his love for us, God raised him from the dead and Jesus is seated at the throne of God advocating for our defense.

Quiet Walker, God is at work within you and the other parts. You are to become a beacon of light, holding out to others the Word of Life. Remember Quiet Walker that what ever happens, be glad in the Lord. Pattern your life after Jesus and beware. It brings tears to my eyes to warn you that there are many who walk along the Christian path who are real enemies of the Lord. As Mariann has experienced, they come in the name of the Lord. They are proud of what they should be ashamed of. Their God is their appetite for money and self-pleasures. But don't worry about anything. God will guide you. Just continue to let everyone see that you are unselfish and considerate in all you do. Pray about everything, telling God your needs and don't forget to thank him for his answers. His peace will keep you thoughts and your hearts quiet and at rest as you trust in Jesus.

As I close my letter to you Quiet Walker, let me say one more encouraging word: focus your mind on truth and goodness, think of that which is pure and lovely and continue to put into practice those truths that God has given you. Do not worry about your life, for the Lord holds it in the palm of his hand. You can do everything that God asks you to do with the help of Jesus who gives you the strength and power. Say hello to the others for me. May the blessings of our Lord Jesus Christ be upon your spirits.

Sincerely, Shedding Tear"

With that I awoke. I have found meaning to my life. My goal is to know Jesus.

Quiet Walker

P.S. I wish for you to have a copy of my poems. I will send them with Maria when she sees you.

The System was going through great anxiety however, anticipating my departure as a high probability. Having to justify my position with Liz was getting harder to do as December approached. A soul from Those Who Are Core wrote the following letter in early December, which I would not be given for two more years.

Late. They're all gone except the sick child. I can hear the daughter breathing slowly, in rhythm, barely audible. So quiet. Unnervingly quiet.

I wonder if he knows how much Maria minimizes things. How much she truly struggles? How could he understand what is deep within her? That butterfly. So true. But will this butterfly ever be able to emerge? Or will it die in the putrid acid that has spoiled its protective cocoon.

He thinks she is doing well... progressing at remarkable speed. But does he really know? Does he understand the ache in her soul? To live is just evil spelled backwards.

She hides from him what is buried deep. She cannot cry. She cannot moan. She cannot weep. It overshadows her whole being. Humiliation vibrates throughout every bone. Not able to look into a mirror at the ugliness of her body. Holding in her inner thoughts. Her inner sorrow. Her inner pain. Unable to believe that anyone could truly love her.

I wonder if he ever sits up at night in the quiet of the darkness and thinks of her pain? Thinks of her struggling with her nightmares? Her deep trust of him to help her? Her fear of getting too close to him and mourning her loss when he leaves.

Her confusion of trying to understand his kindness towards her? Does she ever cross his mind? Will she ever fill the void in her soul? She searches for child-like love. To be wanted, held and protected. She gives so much and takes so little.

I live in the acid.

Maria also wrote to Bruce about our times together:

Mr. Chalberg and me talk about God a lot and pray. He explains things real good. I learned that when we pray in human language, Jesus takes it and changes it into God language to give his dad. Then he takes God's answers and with the Holy Spirit gives it to us so we can understand. He kind of like goes between God and us and helps us in front of God. Mr. Chalberg showed me with his hands and I understand now. I know that only Jesus can do that and not Mary. I never understood it real well before but I do now. I was real excited to understand that. It is neat and I thank Jesus for fixing my words so God will like them. He's my best friend and real smart.

Did you like Raquel's picture? Raquel tells me that she is a good drawer but Claudia is a great drawer. I think Raquel draws great too. She makes little pictures. Claudia makes real big ones. Raquel uses Claudia's paints and paper cuz she don't have her own. Raquel she don't sell her pictures like Claudia. She won't tell people about her pictures or poems, but she gave one to Mr. Chalberg cuz she says he is one who appreciates the ancient ways. She never gave a picture to anyone else except the Indian man. I liked the horses she drew. They were running in the wind. I wonder where they were going cuz they were dressed in real nice things.

Mariann gets to come and see you next week because Ruth told me that Lion said it was time for Raquel and Mariann to do a fight with a dragonslayer and a monster. I don't want to come cuz I don't like monsters.

Bye, your friend Maria.

Mariann wrote to tell Bruce about her understanding of the battle they experienced in his office.

Mr. Bruce I talked to dragunslaer. He is nice. He is good. His dad is good. His dad made very pretty anjuls by majik. The anjuls serv dragunslaer dad. One day a pretty anjul did not want to serv dragunslaer dad, He wanted to be the boss. He got some other anjuls to be bad. They got sords and fited with dragunslaer dad. Dragunslaer dad was very strong. He was mad at the bad anjuls.

He made them not pretty. They have horns and claws. He said to go to the under place.

The Beast he do not work for dragunslaer. The Beast he do not work for dragunslaer dad. The Beast tell me he work for dragunslaer dad. He lie. He work for the bad anjul. The Beast boss tell me he work for dragunslaer dad. He tell me he is very important. He tell me I cannot talk to dragunslaer dad. Dragunslaer dad tell the boss in the wite dress things. The boss tell the Beast. The Beast tell me. Dragunslaer say no. Dragunslaer tell me to talk to him. He talk to his dad for me. He tell me true things. The boss lie.

Dragunslaer say he is lion of juda. He say he is jezus. He say he and his father and the holey sprit go togethr and make god. He say he sad I hurt. He say I can tell Mr. Bruce the hurt. He say the Beast lie. He say god no kill my family. He say the Beast no hurt me no more. He say he mad. He say the Beast tell me bad things about god. It make him mad. He say god love me. He say god love me. He say I no do bad. He say prest do bad.

Jezus tell me he be with tabita and lots childrn. He want be with me. I say I want be with him. I no be frad Jezus. He nice. He hold my hand. He walk with me. He talk with me. I tell him I make anjuls. He tell me he see my batle. I tell him I be frad when he die. But I be happy he be live agin. He tell me he die and be live agin for me.

Jezus say we go see childrn. They have swing. I ask lion. He hug me. He say go Jezus. He be Mariann lion now. I say where you go lion. He say I be here. Go be with Jezus. I hug lion. I hold Jezus hand. He say good. Mariann no want to get lost. I go see tabita now. I take piture you make for me. I show tabita. I tell her about the anjuls. I tell her about rebeca juls on the pretty krown. I tell her I call her princes rebeca. I tell her I want to play house. Rainbo and bravfot and rebeca are pretend. Jezus and Mr. Bruce and anjuls are not pretend. I tell tabita.

I didn't correct the spelling or grammar because I wanted you to see what kind of letters we got from the children in the beginning. Maria will see the most improvement over the years in spelling and grammar as she heals. Mariann will be Mariann and often I will have to interpret her letters for readers. Like myself, other children have no problem with them. Mariann would hold on to the puppets that she and Raquel made for the battle she talks about between good and evil. It was perhaps her first real visualization of the power of Jesus to vanquish evil and the beginning of the possibility that maybe Jesus' Dad wasn't who she thought He was.

After Christmas and when the System knew I was committed to them to stay as long as Jesus needed me here, Mariann came out to draw her story for me. These drawings helped open new doors to the System for Bruce and I, because Bruce was focusing on the children now, he started receiving communiqués from TWAC. I wouldn't receive any for a few more months after one of the Pod children came out in my presence and I couldn't identify her. We knew the subject of baptism for Maria and Louise had triggered it.

The number of children running around the forest of Preservation had increased by one. But the adults had seen another child on occasion and couldn't find where she was hiding. They learned her name was Lila and became concerned when she surfaced briefly in Bruce's office and then again with me. Our efforts to establish her identity and place within the System drew a response from TWAC. Up to this point we had only seen these letters on the drawings of the younger kids. We weren't sure if there were other parts using Tabitha for example to reveal their existence, or if another part shadowed and wrote it for herself. Sometimes in counseling the digging for answers reveals much more than can be anticipated. This was true with Those Who Are Core. I was grateful that the children were still Bruce's primary area of expertise for now.

LEAVE LILA ALONE SHE'S OUR CHILD AND WE DO NOT WANT YOU OR THOSE PARTS MESSING WITH HER

WE DIDN'T ASK YOU TO MEDDLE IN OUR BUSINESS THOSE ARROGANT PARTS THINK THEY ARE THE ONLY ONES IN THE UNIVERSE

THEY CAN'T FIND LILA BECAUSE SHE DOESN'T LIVE WITH THEM

WE WANT NOTHING TO DO WITH THEM OR YOU

WE ARE CORE AND LIVE IN THE ACID

LEAVE US ALONE

Just the fact that there was another group somewhere inside proved very distressing for most of the adults. Their location was established through Raquel and Elizabeth Ray. Everyone stayed away because of the warnings of retribution on any who attempted to enter there. There was however little choice for the caregivers on the outside. This child part or parts were coming out for a reason and we believe it was triggered by the observance of the other child parts receiving love and healing. Attempts were made to contact them with the offer of assistance, at least for Lila. It would be seen as a test to see if we could be trusted before others revealed themselves.

Those Who Are Core have received your letter (Bruce's). We need to know what you will do if we let our child come out. How will you relate to her? We do not have any outside vibrators (ways of interpreting the actions and responses of the outside activity, as none of Core came to the surface)? We need to know what your actions will be, if we allow Lila on the outside. How will you calm her down? (For the next 8 months any action taken that might have direct results with Core had to be presented in writing whenever possible. Their demands must be followed to the letter and order presented. The significance of this will be better understood at the end of this book.)

Inside she is kept in the middle of the core. She is enclosed in a warm pod where she can curl up and feel the rhythmic movement of the liquid around her. Her pod is safe and comforting and protects her from the acid. She is afraid of bright lights on the outside and lots of space around her.

THOSE WHO ARE CORE MUST KNOW WHAT YOU PLAN TO DO WITH OUR CHILD, IF WE ARE TO CHOOSE TO LET LILA OUT. WE MUST HAVE DETAILS.

After several rounds of negotiation, it was agreed to follow the plan given below.

1. Plan for Otosis, known to you by the Keeper of History as Lila - Agree
2. Suggestions: Do not enter Pod; no touching child; nothing small that can be swallowed.
3. No. We are not yet assured of her safety with you. We will be on guard.
4. Yes. You will hear from us. Watcher will observe. No, we will not speak with you except through fax. We do not trust the surface people. Watcher will inform Epistler who will communicate to you by fax.
5. Yes, we know who this part is. First let's see how it goes with Otosis. If our child Otosis becomes well, then we will discuss allowing Egar and Blue Devil out to see you.

You have reached Those Who Are Core. I am Tolip, leader of TWAC. Watcher is the commander of Pod Alpha. He and his regiment fight intruders who would destroy Pod Alpha. Pod Alpha guards Otosis. His regiment consists of Epistler, Tac, Tyr, and Valkyrie. Do not attempt to make contact with the commanders of Pod Mu or Pod Omega. You must first pass the test of Pod Alpha.
Finnis, Tolip

    Tolip's letter presented us with a lot of information about Core. There were 3 child parts: Otosis/Lila, Egar and Blue Devil that were protected in pods in the middle of the core. Each of the Pod Children had their own commander and regiment guarding the pods named First, Middle and Last. Elizabeth Ray would soon give us the fourth structure or tree of the System.

    We could make some logical assumptions about Core, based on the names and symbols drawn on the surface children's pictures around this time. There were upside-down crosses, names spelled backwards (Egar = rage) and numerous other items that were indicative of Satanic Ritual Abuse. Pictures of animal and human sacrifices were sometimes drawn around the peripheral areas along with these symbols and then scribbled over in black crayon before crumbling it up to discard. Egar came out once in Bruce's office with me and just screamed for a few seconds before returning inside. Blue Devil came out once and screamed about the light burning her, while trying to get her body <u>under</u> the couch for protection.

Following these incidences, Maria would have no recollection of the events. Processing them through Core was going to take some time. I received threats to keep Jesus and me away, because the writer/sender felt that the light of Jesus' aura was hurting his child. I trusted Bruce's direction and waited before attempting to get involved. My opportunity would come in a few months. Tolip and these children aren't identified in Ruth's letter of the prologue, which was sent just before they became known. The information is sketchy until August of 1996.

The Hole Children, Anna Angelina and Tabitha, were progressing rapidly with Bruce and in their trust of Jesus. Raquel wrote the following poem about their progress.

The Hole Children

In the depth of the darkness they have lived
Shunned and not allowed to be

Beaten into submission
Afraid and alone in their pit

Little child fears
Chained in their isolation

But He has come
To rescue them from the pit

He holds them in His arms
And they shall not be afraid

He has broken their chains
So that they may be free to be

It is all right for them to cry
And mourn the past
But now they are free
They are safe

They stay in His arms
And let Him comfort their fears

He will always love them
He will never leave them

The hole children can sleep now
And rest in His presence

They will let Him love them
For they have learned to trust Him

-Raquel

The search for a Christian church home had not gone well and by early December a decision was made to look for another church after one disastrous weekend for Liz and Maria. Ruth wrote:

Circle Council asked me to relay their apologies for Liz's outburst on Saturday night. The leaders rebuked her for her actions and she is not allowed to call you for a month... if they can control that. Liz may not abide by their ruling, we'll see. Liz became angry over the conversation Elizabeth Ray had with an aunt. The aunt had discussed with you the mess that Maria's sister Donna was in and how much she loves her and wants to protect her, while never acknowledging any concern for Maria or her treatment by the family. Liz hurts for Maria because the aunt just pours salt on the wounds. No one thinks Maria suffers or is alone.

Liz sees the rejection of Maria and the rescue efforts of the family always going to her self-indulgent addicted sister. I am not making excuses for Liz's behavior, as she was rude and insensitive to you. She pre-judged you, interrupted your dinner with friends and was abusive on the phone. There's no excuse for that, but I understand her reaction to the conversation.

Liz and I talked about it on the way to church. We were hit again there along with our friend Jeri. The message was on divine healing and testimonies of how God has completely healed people from their infirmities. Maria was listening, switched out and began sobbing. Jeri began crying too. They were sitting in the back row, got up and walked out. They sat outside and talked while setting on a rock together. Maria spoke first and told Jeri that Jesus doesn't heal my Claudia. She is never going to walk again and Jesus doesn't heal Zac. All those people yell praise God when others tell them they are healed, but when you spoke about Zac and your family they didn't say anything. Jeri we are bad to them. We don't get healed cuz we are not good enough to be healed. Nobody understands us here and it hurts so much here.

Jeri held Maria and Maria held Jeri. Jeri said I come here with you and it is so dark and cold here. People ignore us because of the disability. I don't want to be pitied. I don't want to be treated differently. I want to be with loving people who encourage me. Maria, you are a treasure. I know you don't look at yourself as a treasure but you are. You were the only one in this church that has been kind to me. You don't talk love - you are love. Maria then told Jeri that she didn't feel like a treasure, more like a garbage dump.

Jeri then told Maria, let's try to find another church. Maria asked how she was going to do that and she didn't know. Maria said we tried once before and the pastor said we were demons. Jeri laughed and said you get exorcised and I'm told I need divine healing. Liz switched with Maria and began laughing with her. Then Jeri said, "I've got an ant up my butt", which sent Liz rolling with laughter. Then they both left...

Both Liz and Jeri are ready to drop the idea of ever going to a Christian Church again. I can't wait for Pastor Chalberg to start one near us. I want to get them into a supportive, growing and biblically correct atmosphere. They are both willing to go for now and I don't want to lose the window of opportunity. Part of the stress for everyone is the continual problems with the church.

I've prayed about it and the Lord has answered me. I can't change the hearts of the congregation I'm in and God can't change the hearts of the people until they submit to Him and allow Him to change them. Our System's vessel is getting dry and cracked.

Maria, Louise, Raquel and Tabitha have all accepted Jesus, and even Liz says she wants to learn from Jesus. I need to be responsible in finding a place for them to grow in the Lord and see the best of Christianity, not the worse.

I need to find a place that will accept them as they are and love them. I need to look beyond my own selfish needs, in holding on to my disability ministry that I've established here and do what is best for the System according to God's will. I need to tell you Bruce that it is very hard to walk away. My heart aches...

In Him Who Is My Strength,
Ruth

As Christmas arrived, the System was adjusting to a new perspective of what it means to be obedient to God. Raquel, Maria, Louise, the children and occasionally Liz were spending time inside getting to know who this Jesus was for them. Liz reacted in a way unlike the others. This surprised no one. After Liz had interviewed the pastor and youth leader over the phone, Maria and the System were going to try their third church in search of a home. Liz was surprised at their answers and challenged to check them out. Ruth writes about the now infamous Christmas tree caper to Bruce, which occurred after their third visit to this church.

Dear Bruce,

It's Christmas Eve. Claudia is sick with the flu, Sergio is working late, Rosalinda is out with friends and Jose is watching a sports game. Maria went to church this morning and I am grateful for the kind and warm people who are growing to love her. She is still bewildered by the crowds and the people, but she is adjusting.

Liz is going to be forced to change her stereotyping of Suburban Christian churches. They provided an abundance of gifts for Liz's friends. They said they didn't know many poor people in need, so Liz came out and said, "I'll handle this!" She was able to take blankets, clothes and presents to Hayward and Oakland. So that is what we have done all Christmas Eve and Liz loves it.

She's in trouble though and is seeking support from Pastor Chalberg and you. It seems she stole a bunch of small Christmas trees from a lot today to give along with the gifts. Her rational is that no one was going to buy them anyway but stealing is stealing.

When we were in Hayward Liz drove the car right between a group of Latinos drinking beer. She got out and questioned them as to whether or not Irma was home. They immediately escorted her into the house and Liz yells "Hey Angela you home?" Angela is a twenty-year-old mentally disabled girl that Liz told last week how Jesus would be bringing her presents. I was angry at Liz at the time for promising the girl something I thought Liz could never deliver on. But there was Liz, dragging Angela to her car and telling her that "Jesus has got some cool presents for you." One guy said to Liz, "Who are you?" She just said, "I'm Liz." The guy smiled and said, "Como estas?" She replied, "Bien." She drove away yelling "Feliz Navidad!"

Next she went to Jeri's house and delivered more gifts, pulled more lice eggs out of her hair, read the Christmas story to Zac in a most unusual way and left. We are now home and Maria is preparing a ham for dinner that the church gave her. She and Louise are preparing a Merry Little Christmas for the family. We wanted to wish you a wonderful Christmas. Maria misses you terribly. Liz is still angry at me for telling about the trees and told me to go solve the Bosnia problem and forget about the trees.

Tabitha has decided to give you her Yemaya card that Louise got for her thinking it was a card for the Lady of Regla. Tabitha asked if she could have a Jesus card to put in her box. Can you find one to give to Tabitha? It seems that she wants to exchange them for a Jesus card with you and Pastor Chalberg. She knows he gave Maria a Bible for Christmas with pictures and he didn't give her anything. She seems sad about that and is hoping he will trade cards with her.

I find it interesting that the parts become jealous at other parts receiving things. You are wise to not give anything to one part, as it might cause problems, especially with the kids. But I'm so thankful that Pastor Chalberg gave Maria her own Bible. She is so happy with it and has shown everyone the Bible she got for Christmas. She and Louise share it and it's a much easier level for them to read. Pastor Chalberg must have spent a long time finding just the right one. I'm sure Maria will be sharing it with you.

May you and your family richly enjoy the reason for the season!

Ruth

I had given Maria and Louise a Bible to share as a Christmas gift because I knew I would be continuing on with them. Many of their questions were about Catholic teachings of a traditional nature presented by the Church but not supported by Holy Scripture. I had explained the history of how the Bible was written to them and how the 'Church' was formed from the beginning. Showing them what books were added along with other doctrine that was not part of the original text in Greek in my Bible, only caused many more questions to come my way. To help them understand I got a Bible version that was easy to read and matched in essence the content of mine. Differentiating between the traditional church practices relevant to that day and then comparing that with the Word of God alone to see if these traditions can be substantiated today, had them both challenging their daily rituals and the sacred images they had revered for so long.

Taking someone's cherished religious history away from them can be very damaging to the soul unless it is restored with the truth. They were slowly learning the truth about Jesus and His word. Sadly for them and me, it was easier to list historical examples of suffering caused by the church in the name of God then to list the good done in His name. Yet, we were not without hope. It became clear to us in our study that the future is as bright as the promises of God through Christ Jesus. Each time we met I tried to give them at least one new truth for their understanding.

"If you hold to my teaching,
You are really my disciples.
Then you will know the truth,
And the truth will set you free."
John 8:31-32

Chapter 13:

"Blessed are the Poor in Spirit..."

> What the soul is in a body, this the Christians are in the world. The soul is spread through all the members of the body, and Christians through the diverse cities of the world. The soul has its abode in the body, and yet it is not of the body. *Epistle to Diognetus – 2nd century*

When I explained the truth about the confessional and how we could go directly to God in prayer, I had no idea how this truth would release so many parts from emotional and spiritual fear. Some of the statements in the Bible that both ignited their spirits and yet caused great sadness regarding their former beliefs included the following:

1. *Confess your sins to one another.*
2. *All have sinned and fall short of the glory of God.*
3. *There is salvation in no one else, for there is no other name under heaven that has been given among men, by which we must be saved.*

This was going to take a long time to gently plant the truth where lies had been buried carelessly without love. We looked to the New Year for hope to grow and take control. That was also when the enemy would double their efforts to gain control of the System. Healing was not in their game plan, chaos was.

Many in the System would be on a roller coaster ride in their newfound faith. Louise and Tabitha would vacillate in extremes regarding the Catholic Church's doctrine. Ruth and Liz would be sparring over the reality of Suburban Christians for a long time, each losing the battle over truth when labeling people. Ann would stand strong in her defiance and belief that nothing good comes from being Christian until later in her life. Maria wanted to escape to 'Kansas' as often as allowed but was finding herself increasingly drawn to find out more about Jesus. The children wanted to draw, sleep, play and stay warm in Jesus' arms. Circle Council had the easiest task by far – they simply wanted to understand women. So we all tumbled into the New Year.

Ann wrote to Bruce about her frustration with therapy and made numerous suggestions on how to improve it in the coming year. The gist of her letter can be understood in the first and last paragraphs. I find it interesting that she does not mention me, or what I am doing with the System.

It has become clear to me that you and I do not possess the same viewpoint with regards to therapy. I value action therapy, not talk therapy. Talk therapy has no value other than wasting money to acquire a very expensive friendship. Maria is still at the same place she was a year and a half ago. She still has no skills to shield herself from attacks of the relatives. She has not increased her confidence or self-worth. She has not learned any problem solving techniques to apply to difficult situations. She continues to avoid eye contact with people...etc, etc, etc...

...I need help in learning techniques to set boundaries with those parts, ideas on how to organize them better and manage the system more efficiently. I have spent a considerable amount of time attempting to make this clear to you about my frustration with your form of therapy. I understand that your first goal was to form a relationship with the parts to gain their trust. Now you have it, so let's begin action therapy and teach them skills to improve their abilities to survive. I refuse to finance this when all the parts do is rehash the past or sit and talk about their day. It serves no purpose.

Council gave Bruce their response to Ann's letter and did not concur with her assessment. They gave their own defense of Bruce's methods by showing how different parts had improved, even if it was only slightly. Their final opinion is this assessment:

Council has considered Ann's accusations and concerns. Ann has not provided enough support for her statements to substantiate a change in the course of therapy. Council understands the frustration Ann has with the length of therapy time. However, forty years of brainwashing and abuse cannot be unraveled in eighteen months.

While all parts need to accept what has happened, grieve it and move on, that takes time and patience. The difficulty will not be in hearing about the abuse in the third person but feeling the pain in the first person.

Although Ann is quick to require the other parts to accept it she herself is unwilling to feel the others' pain and suffering. Ann is not exempt from this process. It is wrong for her to stay on the outside and complain about the others when she herself refuses to address her own issues of frustration, anger and control. Council has concluded that the pace of therapy is appropriate at this time. Council went on to address other issues regarding other parts:

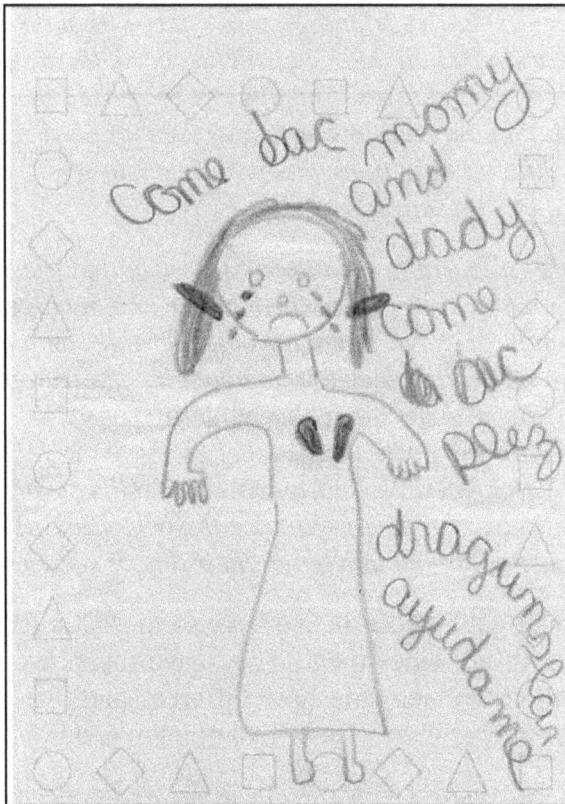

A drawing by Mariann with Tabitha adding her concerns when both thought Carol and I would be leaving them soon.

344

Tabitha is having a hard time with separation from the counselor. Maria's husband refuses to nurture the child and she is confused. She thinks the husband is 'hombre malo' because he is not like her "daddy Bruce" or daddy Miguel". Ruth has attempted to talk with the husband, but he cannot look at Tabitha as a four-year-old. If she switches out, he will pinch her arm and firmly ask for Maria, scaring little Tabitha. Tabitha longs for the time with the counselor so she can be out.

Maria is drowning in a sea of confusion and being overwhelmed. It is a lot for her to absorb. We've seen a lot of progress, as she is now able to tell the counselor, the pastor and Lindsay things that scare her. Council was especially impressed with her openness with Pastor Chalberg concerning her fear of intimacy. She is trying her very best to accept what has happened and heal from it. Her ability to accept sex as OK and not dirty is another issue she still needs to address. Both her and Louise allow sex to 'be done to them' rather than be a consenting partner, a matter of duty. To them, sex and love mean the same thing... pain and hurt.

Ann followed their assessment with another letter. Her ability to handle stress was diminishing rapidly between the family issues, therapy and the house remodel. Her resources were few and the demand for decisions was high. She had no one to dump on so Bruce was chosen, because he was paid to receive it.

I am not the bad guy in this picture as much as you and council would like to portray me that way. It is impossible for you to understand my situation or role in this miserable system. I did fine without you. Now everything is a mess. I am working on overload and it is impossible to plan, direct and initiate at such a rapid pace.

I do not trust you. I am not mad at you as you believe. I simply don't trust you. Do not take it personally because I do not even trust the others on the inside. You say you care, but I see it differently. Maria is a case just like all your other cases. She supplies a steady source of income for you and you get the satisfaction of playing 'doctor'. That is just real life. You cannot enter her world except when you are in control. The relationship is superficial. Therapy is a service. I accept that.

I do not accept however, you encouraging her to show disrespect towards me. The only reason Maria told me to shut up was that the pastor's wife at church told her to. Maria obeys others who appear to be authority figures. If you promote this kind of communication from her, you will be accountable for her pain when I get through with her.

Maria has always been fragile and simple-minded. I have protected her all her life. I have been her caregiver and guardian. The responsibility has been enormous, but I've sacrificed my interests to care for her. It is wrong for you to suggest to her to disrespect me without appreciation for what I've done for her.

Maria is like a child in an adult body and will always be that way. She can never be me. The best that we can hope for is that I can continue to protect her so that she can be happy in her own little world. Maria will never be able to handle the pace of this world. She is content with menial housework, sewing and gardening with Louise. Maria is not CEO material. She is simple and I've accepted that.

What we shouldn't do is try making Maria into something she's not but teaching better control over our switching and defining our different functions clearly. Since I have not found a way to vaporize her, I must persuade council to put her away inside somewhere safe...out of sight, out of mind.

I never asked to be a multiple, it's a curse as far as I'm concerned. Instead of being able to pursue a career, I have to spend my energy surviving. Like a slave, I have been forced into a role I never asked for. You have a freedom I will never enjoy and being a single you cannot possibly understand. No amount of 'talking therapy' will change that. I will never be free to be just me, so I can never be happy.

But do not feel bad about it, the dice just didn't roll in my favor. Life truly sucks and death is probably worse. I'm a realist, not a dreamer like you. Do not hold your breath for remarkable recovery for Maria. In the meantime, do not give me any more problems. Liz is enough!

Ann will take the longest to accept both the reality of Jesus with the System and His plan for healing. Even as the tide grows against her inside, as Jesus was accomplishing His will with them in small but growing steps, she will stand strong until her logical mind starts challenging her own beliefs.

Only Raquel's uplifting messages offset Ann's depressing letters. Raquel's continuing journey with the Great Spirit for knowledge of His ways along the paths of truth, turned a new direction toward a personal relationship with Jesus. If I was having a difficult week, a fax like this one would put life back into a proper perspective.

Greetings Shedding Tear. I continually give thanks to the Great Spirit for my friendship with you. As I walk the paths of Sacred Mountain, I pray that you will receive an abundance of mercy, peace and love from our King.

I have heard of the teachings from the others and I have spent much time with the Great Spirit learning about love. When one is a true follower of the Shepherd and looks into the waters of a still lake, one should see the reflection of the love of the Great Spirit. Just as the warrior on his spirit journey connects with his animal spirit guide, the Christian on his spirit journey links with the love of the Great Spirit. But one cannot know this love without a journey. The journey is one of stages and must be traveled for life, if one desires to reflect the love of the great one. For only in being with the Great Spirit can one learn Christian love according to Jesus.

To be still and spend much time with the one who holds all wisdom, is to discover from the master. On my journey in understanding the love of the Great Spirit, I've learned from him that his greatest instruction to me is to love him and all peoples. For there are many who do many good deeds, yet do not have love and because of this, their movements are like chaff in the wind. In listening and meditating on this greatest instruction, I have learned that the love of the Great Spirit is a love of decision. I love because the Great Spirit commands it and because I wish to please the Great Spirit. I am not forced to love, but I desire to love.

As Brave Eagle circled above me, teasing me to come fly the canyons with him, I thought of what this love looked like. I was filled with an understanding that penetrated my being. Love is the ability given by the Great Spirit to accept all, even those who hurt us, by treating them kindly and with warmth. Love is bringing hope and joy to all by helping followers of the Great Spirit on their journey and telling those who do not know him of his love for them. Love is acting towards others with fairness and deep concern for their well being and desiring to live at peace with everyone. It is to sacrifice one's own needs for the needs of someone else.

I'm still journeying and learning about love from the Great Spirit. I wish to someday look into the still waters and see the glowing reflection of his love, for the Great Spirit is love.

Grace and Peace to you my fellow journeyman,
Quiet Walker

With the exception of Ann, everyone else was climbing rapidly toward their perceived goal of knowing Jesus and some even accepting Him as Lord and Savior. As stated earlier, most had accepted Him as being close to God, but now they were talking of accepting Him as Savior and God. We began talking in February about the meaning of baptism for adults and children alike. The challenge to show how dedication to another god like Yemaya in the Santeria cult, could not stop God from washing them clean in baptism into Him. As Yemaya was being challenged in her control over the System she escalated the spiritual warfare to retain control by interfering in the daily life and counseling of the System. The more focused Maria and Louise became on their baptism, the more disruptions occurred around them from 'Catholic Christian' family members and friends. They were being challenged about their infant baptism in the Church and the sacrilege, supposedly of being baptized again in another faith despite the fact that it was still the Christian faith. The enemy used this Scripture out of context in their debate something that should have been of no surprise to a mature believer.

"There is one body and one Spirit, just as also you were called in one hope of your calling; one Lord, one faith, one baptism, one God and Father of all who is over all and through all and in all." <u>Ephesians 4:4-6</u>

Maria was told that she was baptized as an infant and this proves that there is only one baptism to occur and the fact she remembered nothing about it didn't matter. Good symbolic interpretation, but faulty in application. I explained to them several truths regarding baptism to help them through this time. Believer's baptism and infant baptism are both represented in the Bible and historical customs of the time, with believer's baptism receiving the greater emphasis in the Bible. Both are symbolic in one sense in that it declares the recipient is admitted into Christianity and the family of God. Both are mystical in the real sense in that God is present when we call upon Him in the reading of His Word and the cleansing of original sin with the water. We don't understand the mystery clearly in how God does it but accept it by faith, because He said He would. Neither is dependent upon the water or amount used, or upon the person doing the baptism to make it more or less real. They rely upon the Holy Spirit to use the vehicles present to accomplish His purpose. And the last similarity is also what separates the two modes of baptism in that they are [motivated] to occur within the hearts of believers.

I offered to the System and now to you, the testimony in **Acts 16** where Paul and Silas respond to their Philippian jailer. This is as an example of both baptisms occurring at one time with all of the elements above as recorded by **Luke**.

"Sirs, what must I do to be saved?' And they said, 'Believe in the Lord Jesus, and you shall be saved, you and your household.' And they spoke the word of the Lord to him together with all who were in his house. And he took them that very hour of the night and washed their wounds, and **immediately he was baptized, he and all his household.***"*

In infant baptism, it is contingent upon the parents and family of the child, as well as the community of believers in which they come for baptism, to raise and protect that child within that community of faith empowered by God's love in their collective hearts. If the parents or the community of believers do not teach God's commandments in love to the child or live them out in the real sense in obedience, the child will not have any footsteps to follow as they grow up. Mouthing the words of faith in a ritual in the Church with little or no intention to follow through accomplishes nothing. God will still be present and accomplish whatever He wants in the ritual for the child's sake and His purposes. It does not matter who is present with them at the time. This is what I believe happened in Maria's case. The parents of Maria had already rejected and abused her and the Church would subject her to even worse abuses inside its walls and outside in its cults. Yet, God did not forsake her and nourished her even then to seek Him out one day when she was old enough to understand the truth taken along with her innocence.

In believer's baptism, it would be a decision of the heart to seek repentance and receive God for who He truly is. In both baptisms, if the believers' hearts are not truly submitted to Him in faith, as an older individual or as an infant whose parent's are responsible, the baptism can have little or no meaning. That is one reason why dedication of infants and rededication of adults is practiced in many faiths, along with catechism classes for both before baptism. Dedication can be a symbolic acknowledgement of a heart decision, reaffirming in the community of faith the truth of the one baptism done earlier. I gave the System many examples of both baptisms that proved fruitless and with no meaning, as the recipients had rejected God in their hearts by never obeying His commandments in their lives. I also gave examples of people being baptized several ways and even several times. The common thread among them all was that the last baptism was a heart baptism between them and God. They walked away with this truth: "There is only one baptism that counts, the one in the heart with the One God and Father of us all, within the one body of faith where Jesus Christ is its head."

I also shared with them my own example, which brought both laughter and tears in its description of God's perseverance to claim His own. I was baptized three different times in my youth and rededicated my faith as an adult believer. The last one remains the most important to me because the decision wasn't made in fear. It happened after years of feeling abandoned by God and finding out it wasn't Him that left the relationship… it was me.

"As those who have been chosen of God, holy and beloved, put on a heart of compassion, kindness, humility, gentleness and patience; bearing with

*one another, and forgiving each other, just as the Lord
forgave you, so also should you. And beyond all these
things put on love, which is the perfect bond of unity.
And let the peace of Christ rule in your hearts, to
which indeed you were called in one body;
and be thankful. Let the word of Christ richly
dwell within you, with all wisdom teaching and
admonishing one another with psalms and
hymns and spiritual songs, singing with
thankfulness in your hearts to God.
And whatever you do in word or deed,
do all in the name of the Lord Jesus,
giving thanks through Him to God the Father."*
<u>Colossians 3:12-17</u>

*"Before I formed you in the womb I knew you,
And before you were born I consecrated you;
I have appointed you a prophet to the nations."*
<u>Jeremiah 1:5</u>

"We do not want churches. They will teach us to quarrel about God."
- Chief Joseph of Nez Perces

Chapter 14:

"Will Baptism be a New Beginning?"

Redeeming old beliefs into new life through faith.

"Then Jesus said to His disciples,
'If anyone wishes to come after Me,
let him deny himself, and take up his cross,
and follow Me. For whoever wishes to save
his life shall lose it; but whoever loses his life
for My sake shall find it. For what will it profit a man
if he gains the whole world and loses his soul?"
Matthew 16:24-26

> "The Christian idea has not been tried and found wanting;
> it has been found difficult and left untried."
> G. K. Chesterton, 1910

I have always tried to help people who are about to enter the Christian faith to understand the importance of their decision and the possible ramifications that come with that decision. If the decision is made lightly with the idea that their life will go smoothly and trouble-free because their future is secure, then the concepts of what it means to **'take up your cross'** and **'he who saves his life shall lose it,'** have not been fully comprehended. It is equally difficult to help someone understand the spiritual realm they are entering until they are living in it. I could tell that even though Maria and Louise had a strong understanding of the meaning of baptism, they were not as prepared as Raquel was for what followed. I was not prepared for the onslaught that followed either primarily, because I didn't understand yet the importance of the entire System to Jesus' plan, or the depth the enemy would go to keep them away from Him.

The month before Easter and their baptisms the enemy escalated their attacks to the next level, through every stronghold they had within Maria's extended family and every distraction they could think of for the System, Bruce and myself. Bruce was being challenged in his personal finances, health and family needs. This onslaught connected with the System's healing and the healing of other clients, I believe to be the primary reason why Bruce leaves the counseling profession in a few years, a great loss for all connected with him. It has been our prayer that one day he will return to continue to help others as a counselor in the name of God.

My spiritual journey at this time will turn out to be very similar to the System's journey. We both knew all too well where our lives had been before Jesus, so we had less to lose and more to gain by simply sticking it out with Him. It was perhaps a simplistic acceptance and trust of what Paul had said as being true,

"To live is Christ and to die is gain."

Paul had said it to the church at Philippi where Paul's former jailer and his family had become members. The System would go through many more difficult times ahead than Carol and I, but they wouldn't go through it alone. The most difficult question I faced with the System at this time was the one I asked in the Prologue, "Does each life or person within a multiple have a soul of their own?" If not, then I should not baptize individual personalities as this would be inconsistent with my teaching of sacramental theology. I couldn't do it in good faith and maintain personal integrity, but what if they do each have a soul? I would spend hours talking to God about this one issue for years to come. One of the questions I asked God was, 'why does all of my seminary training and psychological studies say no, but You say yes to me in this particular case? What is it you're trying to teach me?' His answers to me were simple which may say more about me than it does about Him.

"Look at all the people you know personally that have accepted Me. Did I make them change before I entered their lives? Did they have to be healed or 'whole' in your understanding, before I died for them and accepted them into our forever family? If I choose to heal them My way, will you trust Me and do as I say... and not as the world says?"

Simple answers yes, but... oh man! I probably did more in-depth Bible study in that month than ever before on this single issue confronting me. How does God define the reality of the human soul

He created? My search kept leading me back to the concept of, 'created in the image of God.' There were a lot of 'but Jesus' and 'no God... but...' in those conversations, than ever before. My outside colleagues were equally split on clinical and theological issues, so they were not much help. No, this one came down to trust and obey – for there's no other way. Once I committed to this path, I knew it would be a lonely one, but I couldn't let what the enemy threw at us deter us from it. God was teaching us some things about this concept and kept reiterating it many times in the coming years. God's reality was changing the boundaries of my faith.

New people made surprise visits from the System in this month. Jennifer came to visit and brought in her parrot one week. She faxed me this letter afterward.

Thank you for your warm hospitality towards Natasha. You are the only male person who Natasha has allowed to touch her. She has become very close to Maria, Raquel and myself. It is amazing how she bonded with us after a life of neglect.

They say that a Cockatoo who is not loved and nurtured will become mad from lack of affection. They are throwaway birds. They pull out all their feathers as punishment towards themselves for being unlovable. They withdraw into a shell and become mean. Cockatoos can sever bone, so one that bites can be very dangerous.

Maria, Raquel and I are very sensitive to Natasha's heart pain. Natasha knows that we understand and feel her pain. She is very intelligent and when she met us for the first time, she wrapped her head around my neck and sniffed. We had no fear of her beak and allowed her to experience our warmth and safety.

She is now eating well and growing her feathers back. If she is insane, then we cherish her insanity. Thank you again for your kindness towards Natasha. Peace!

I visited Maria's new church to talk to the pastor there to see what kind of home community Maria and Louise would have to support them on their new journey. Maria sat with Carol and I through the service, reading often from the Bible we had given to her for Christmas. She commented that my Bible was old and worn and I told her that if she was lucky, hers would get that way soon. She wrote me afterward in her own handwriting.

Dear Pastor Chalberg and Pastor Chalberg,

I want to thank you for my Bible. It has pictures that help me understand the stories. I like my name and the pretty butterfly on it. Louise is going to make me a cover for it, she sews good. I am sorry I told on Liz. I don't want to go to jail. Ruth is going to go and pay for it.

I liked you coming to my church. Did you like it? I got my bad headaches again and throw up. They hurt my head (anticipation of another visit by parents). *I liked the pretty Santa paper, but Ann is mad the church gave me presents. Sergio is mad too. He says they are trying to bribe him into coming. Me, I'm happy because the church people are nice to me. I wrote this all by myself. Louise always helps me cuz she writes better.*

Your friend Maria

The time for baptisms was soon approaching and Bruce was connecting with TWAC. Bruce wrote three responses to TWAC to help facilitate Lila being allowed to come under his care. Bruce wanted to open the doors for any new parts to find healing and was able to open a dialogue with Tolip to setup ground rules for care. Within three months this would prove to be crucial for everyone in the System. Excerpts from three of his letters are presented here.

To Those Who Are Core,

This letter forms my response to your question of why should you trust me. I want to make very clear that I'm not asking you to give up Lila to me. I want to work with you to help her feel better and not be so scared. I will need your help to do this. Your support of my work with her is crucial.

I think you can trust my work with her because you can look at how I've worked with the other children. They have been helped; they are not all healed but are getting there. Tabitha has friends & a support system. Anna is doing great and Angelina has allowed me to comfort her & is trying to talk. All of them have left their holes and are safely cared for – and most importantly, are less afraid than before. Much of this is also true of Mariann…

I will never call a child out unless the child has previously told me she wants to come out, or because those who protect her believe I can help her. Sometimes a child will slip out or be called out inadvertently, in which case I call out another adult part so the child can return to safety on the inside. If Lila comes out again under similar circumstance, it would help if I knew how best to respond to her.

Please be assured that I intend no harm to Lila or you. I think the surface parts seem arrogant to you because, in part, they are scared about what more parts mean to the whole system, but I think they also understand the necessity of each child having a chance to heal. Their world is rapidly changing...

Can I guarantee Lila's safety from Liz? No. Only the council can do that and I believe they would be willing to do so. I do not believe that Liz is a threat to her, she's overreacting to another part in the system and the possibility of losing some of her time out again. However, I can guarantee that I will do everything in my power to keep Lila safe while in my office. I've been given permission to initiate a switch by council, to get a child inside fast, as I've done with the other children.

When Tabitha first began to come out in my office, she spoke only Spanish & was afraid to look at me. She hid in the corner & kicked at the wall & hit herself. When it was apparent that being out was unsafe, I would ask for another adult to come out. Your cooperation (listening to Lila while out & helping her to get back in) and council's (having another adult ready to come out) is imperative and this has worked out well in the past...

I have worked with child parts who were deaf or could not speak, so I'm willing to try just about any reasonable alternative. I will not consider your letter permission to see her. I want your permission, support and cooperation prior to meeting with her, so I can cooperate with you in helping her the best way I can.

Best regards, Bruce

Tolip responded to Bruce by the end of March and care for Lila began slowly as trust was built with Those Who Are Core. On my visits with the System on Saturdays at this time, one child or more would rotate out in turn to get acquainted during the first hour. Mariann and Tabitha would draw or listen to stories from the Bible. Anna would set at my feet with her arm around my leg and listen to me tell her about the Good Shepherd, as I stroked her head. Angelina would generally lie on the floor briefly with her blanket and gaze into my eyes looking for Jesus. After being assured He was present and she was safe, she would return inside. We would occasionally go for an adventurous stop at Baskin and Robbins for ice cream... and I mean adventurous on several levels.

Maria was growing in self-confidence and began sharing more in her Tuesday night Bible study with Lindsay, her friend at her side. She opened up one evening and shared a very small part of her home life. This caused responses of anger and concern for Maria's welfare. Maria was surprised that anyone cared and scared that they did, because of possible retribution if family found out. Circle Council was surprised and elated just by the fact that Maria shared anything. They were learning the positive qualities of having a friend like Lindsay, who nurtured and encouraged Maria to become more than she thought she could be. Lindsay provided protection and the foundation for Maria to become more confident and independent. She has continued to be a strong friend and sister to the System even today.

Council had Maria write to Lindsay for help, as she had shared in the class that night that she was a multiple. It seems the enemy was working overtime to close this avenue of healing for Maria.

Helper told me to write you. He's hoping you can teach the other teachers about people like me so they understand us. Liz told me somebody in my class is mad at me cuz they are afraid of me. I can't come to class cuz I'm different from other people. I didn't want anyone to find out about me having parts, cuz every time someone finds out they don't want me around anymore. Ruth tried to find me a place in a class, but every time she told them about us, they would say they didn't want us around and we couldn't come to their church. That made me feel sad cuz they made me feel like Jesus loves everybody but people like me.

I tried to be good in class. I tried to listen and talk. I tried to be nice to other people. The other parts helped me with questions that were hard and they tried to help me read, but they go too fast. I know I am not smart but I tried to do the work and be good. And even Liz was good. She obeyed council's rules and didn't come out in class. But somebody doesn't like us so we can't come to her group.

I don't want to be trouble for anybody. It is hard for me sometimes. I get mixed up and scared cuz I get lost and forget things. I get to see you on Saturday and I am happy about that. Ruth said you get to see my friend Bruce. I told Bruce that you showed me how to hug me. I want to send my sister a birthday card, but Bruce said I should ask my new family first. I will ask you, Carol and Pastor Chalberg. Can I send it?

> *Bye, Maria*

After reading some of the letters from Ruth and Elizabeth Ray, I began to ask about other parts and how they were doing with all the changes. Mari didn't want to talk to me and I discovered why in her letter to Bruce.

Dear Bruce,

I received word from Raquel that you invited me to come into your office and speak with you. I appreciate your kind invitation, but I'm not ready to face you. It is extremely difficult for me to discuss my participation in the relationship with Father Breen. I feel so filthy and ashamed that I can't talk with you or see you. The only ones I cam communicate with right now are Lion and Raquel.

Raquel is extremely wise and I cherish her friendship. We have spent many hours talking about the Great Spirit. I have a difficult time sorting out what is true about God and what is false. Sometimes it seems that what is bad is made to look good and what is good is made to look bad. I believed once and I trusted once. I am afraid to trust again. Please forgive me, Mari.

Sometimes I would get a fax and have no idea which part was sending it or quoted it:

We do not give to others in charity
What we should give them in justice.
Compassion cannot be purchased.

> ***For Liz, her highest level of frustration***
> ***Is throwing herself on the ground***
> ***And missing!***

Or it was from someone that would not communicate in any other way.

> *Our deepest fear is not that we are inadequate.*
> *Our deepest fear is that we are powerful beyond measure.*
> *It is our light, not our darkness, which frightens us.*
> *We ask ourselves who are we to be brilliant,*
> *gorgeous, talented and fabulous?*
> *Actually, who are we not to be?*
> *We are a child of God.*
> *Our playing small doesn't serve the world.*
> *There's nothing enlightened about shrinking so that*
> *other parts won't feel insecure around us.*
> *We were born to manifest the glory of God that is within us.*
> *It's not just in some of us, it's in all of us.*
> *And as we let our light shine, it penetrates throughout*
> *and gives the others permission to do the same.*
> *As we are liberated from our own fears, our presence*
> *automatically liberates the others.*
> *(Inspired and adapted from Nelson Mandela)*
> *A Servant of the Lord,*
> *Heavenly Dove*

Ruth was also trying to figure out 'who was who' and wrote about it.

I cornered Elizabeth Ray about the group praying inside. I asked if she has always known about them and she said yes. I asked her why she never told me about them and she said you didn't ask. I wanted to meet with them but Elizabeth Ray says they don't communicate with the parts. All I could learn was that at one time, Tabitha spent some time near a monastery. The nuns never left the surroundings, never read newspapers, watched TV, or had any communication with the outside world, yet their sole purpose was to pray for the world. (I wonder how you pray for the world without knowing what is going on in the world.)

Tabitha would take apples and apricots to the nuns. She would place them on a turntable, ring the bell and wait to see them disappear. The nun would quietly say thank you. Tabitha was always in awe of these nuns. She thought the place inside was where heaven was and wanted to go there. According to E.R., Maria always wanted to be a nun.

I figured I would ask about Core since I was on a roll. She knew about them too but refused to give me any information about them except to say, "now the real work begins." I wanted more info, but she firmly told me "in time." She would not tell me how many are inside, but said she has all the history.

I'm still perplexed about the maturity of this group of prayer warriors. Where did they learn Scripture? How could they exist when there is simply so much spiritual abuse in the system? The system was so isolated on a farm and in the middle of a very uneducated group of people who couldn't even read. How did this system pick up such a wealth of information? Who or what gave this system this knowledge? This really bothers me.

I also find Circle Council hard to understand. I walked with Helper in the forest last week and asked why Council does not take charge more often and force the parts to uphold the rules. Helper's answer was enlightening. He says Council needs to be very careful that they do not become dictators who control the parts. The system has had enough control placed upon them from the outside. They want the personalities to have freedom to explore, question, debate, express and experience. Sometimes they allow the personalities to experience a situation just so they can grow. Council feels that if the system is going to learn to develop positive relationships on the outside, they first need to develop and strengthen their relationships on the inside.

He also told me that since Council is made up of all male leaders, they need to be careful that they are not perceived by the female parts, as controlling or dominating. They will definitely step in if the system is at risk of death. They see themselves more as advisors and consultants rather than rulers. What is your reaction to this? Will the strongest and most controlling personalities always win out over the weaker ones without Council's intervention?

The closer we got to the baptisms the more concerned I became about how the other parts would react to this change for Maria and Louise. I felt I knew where Raquel was and I knew Liz would critique every aspect of the ceremony, but I could handle that. It was Ann the intellectual and Core with all of their hidden secrets, which concerned me the most. I didn't know enough about them to be prepared if they tried to stop the ceremony. Since Ann was the only one I could communicate with I had to draw her out to talk to me. I asked Liz to confront Ann about what it was in Christianity or me that made her afraid to debate with me. It worked! I need to warn you that her descriptions of Tabitha's abuse are the same as noted at the end of chapter 3.

Content Warning!

I sense that you are becoming frustrated. (I wasn't, but that was her perception.) *You would like to have the whole system wrapped up into a nice little Christian package before you leave for LA. Why? Louise, Liz and the others are wrong to suggest that I am afraid of you. I am not afraid of you. Time spent with you was for the benefit of Maria and Louise, not me. Are you not satisfied with the arrangements?*

The system's parts do not understand me. They think of me as a cold, methodical dictator. They forget who kept them alive and out of trouble. My main goal was and still is survival. I firmly believe that to survive, I need to be smarter than my enemies, alert at all times and organized in my direction. They forget how many times I protected their hides.

When I told Tabitha not to tell the secrets, it was because had she told we would have been murdered. I do not believe you truly understand the degree of suffering the system has endured. Angelina was so young and vulnerable. Maria's grandfather would insert pencils, scissors, brushes and fingers into her. He would ejaculate in her mouth. At times she would be face down in a urine-filled chamber pot throwing up. Tabitha would be bathed on a board across the claw-footed tub. Her little vagina scrubbed with hot water from a douche-type bag to 'clean' her inside. She would cry when she had to urinate. Tabitha was tied in the cold, damp, dark basement with rats biting her. She had beatings with a razor slit strap, while always asking God to help the bad go away.

No one can understand the degree of pain and trauma they experienced. You talk a lot about a loving God to them. There was a time I believed in religion, but I learned fast. I might get burned once, but it'll never burn me again. I have warned them not to trust in religion again or they'll get burned, but they don't listen to me. Ruth and you continue to pump into them this hope and love, but I know the rejection is coming with hurt just like in the past.

The only thing we can be sure of is ourselves. God didn't help us in the past and he sure isn't going to help us now. We must rely on ourselves and protect ourselves. God isn't going to do anything for us. He has a proven track record. Do you understand that for years I believed that crap the Catholic Church crammed down our throats? It was all a lie. When the priest took Mariann, I knew it was all a lie. I learned another lesson at that point. I question everything and don't believe anything until I can prove it to be true. Yes I analyze everything like you say. By doing so I lessen the chances of getting burned. The other parts refuse to listen because they are so hungry for love and acceptance that they are willing to believe anything that will supposedly give it to them. What happens when that love is taken away and made conditional again? They will run to me to bail them out again.

I will never again let a male-dominated church brainwash me and control me. I want nothing to do with them. I have enough trouble surviving. I don't need to be told that all women are sluts, sinners, problems for men, property, beneath men, stupid, expected to serve, etc. Those damn priests can have sex with each other before they get this system again.

As far as questions go, I am always interested in exploring issues. I like to look at things from all sides, in all directions. I would be interested in your perspective on several concepts.

1. *Authenticity of the Bible (variety of Bibles to fit people's viewpoints – check out new one by Oxford – gender/culture friendly, Catholic bible, Book of Mormon, Protestant bible, written by men, etc.)*
2. *Resurrection of Jesus (discuss the variety of possibilities – prove your point, i.e.: grave robbers, never dead, friends stole body, etc.)* (The option Ann didn't offer – 'was it real'.)
3. *Flood (prove or disprove concept of world flood)*

4. *Jesus as Son of God (discuss views held today. Was He a lunatic, good teacher and preacher, plant by government to weaken the Jewish leaders hold on people, etc.)* (Again she missed that who Jesus was and is, as being the core issue she would have to face.)
5. *Compare and contrast Hinduism and Buddhism to Christianity. What makes yours special?*
6. *Prove or disprove Purgatory, Limbo, Speaking in tongues, Demons, Angels, Heaven, Hell, Reincarnation, animal spirits, etc.*
7. *Discuss why some Christians believe they can lose their salvation, while others believe theirs is secure. Why the discrepancy if both believe the same Bible?*
8. *Why the discrepancies among Christians with regards to abortion, homosexuality, women pastors, etc.*

I was so relieved to get this letter. Now she was dialoguing with me on issues that could help her with her own healing. We were going to take this to a whole new level of logic and reason in order to understand faith, which can't be explained by logic and reason apart from God. As I began answering a few of the questions she asked, I decided to send her two books to read in-between our discussions. I gave her a gift of the book, <u>Letters to a Skeptic</u> by Greg Boyd and loaned her <u>Mere Christianity</u> by C.S. Lewis for her to read and discuss together later. I thought this would take weeks, but Ann replied within 1 week about the first book.

I appreciated your gift very much. I'm already on page 87! It's hard to believe that I can relate to a 70-year-old sales manager from Uniroyal Tire Company. I find his questions thought provoking as well as familiar to the ones I'm posing to you, so I'm glad to read Greg's answers to his dad. The only thing I find different about Ed's questions is the logical order in which he presents them. Before one can even discuss questions like God knowing the future, one must pose the question about the existence of God.

I have never questioned the existence of a higher force in the universe. I'm not so stupid as to think that everything around us simply happened by chance. The mathematical probability of a solar system being made from dust and gas would be one out of one followed by 40,000 zeroes. The probability is so miniscule, that for all practical purposes, it is impossible. So true science points to a higher power. Call this higher power what you want... God, a cosmic thought force, whatever. The only thing we know for sure is something or someone created this logical and orderly universe. I agreed with Ed that although we agree there is a higher force, we cannot see any evidence that the force is a personal being who is all powerful or even cares about us...

That night I stayed up until one in the morning going over Greg's answer. When I came upon the words 'anthropological argument', I thought what is this crap? I took anthropology and I never heard of the argument as it relates to God. So I read further and tried to logically follow what he was saying. OK, I buy that we are personal beings, some of us more personal than others, but personal, nonetheless. I agree with his definition of personal beings... self-aware mind that is rational, heart that is free and can love, morally responsible and a will longing for meaning and significance.

I agree with most of that, however I would have liked him to expand on what he meant when he said a heart that is free and can love. Can we accurately say that every person in the world has this element? What about brainwashing governments and people controlled by cults? What about people like us who have been severely abused and never learned love? Can they love? (Ann talked awhile on these questions, so here are her final thoughts.)

OK, I agree the higher force is personal. I also agree with his argument about why Christianity has done so much harm. The higher force (God) cannot he held responsible for what the Catholic Church or any Christian does. We were created with the ability to choose a loving response because God is a God of freedom. We are not robots. ALL THAT GOES UNDER THE NAME OF CHRISTIAN IS NOT NECESSARILY CHRISTIAN. Boy, I could write a book on that statement alone. (She has... through this book.)

If there exists a God and the church is supposed to be God's delegated authority on earth, you would think God would intervene in their activities that are leading people away from the church instead of to it. I thought of Liz with this question. Greg answered this with a great deal of wisdom. If this God is a God of freedom and didn't create robots, then he cannot intervene every time someone is going to misuse freedom or hurt another person. If he did intervene every time, then there would be no freedom. I need to think about these things and get back to you.

Ann would continue to struggle with these and many more questions for a long time. She would seek help from Bruce, behind my back, to answer questions on 'the existence of God' and 'is faith and reason compatible?' The last one is the one that caused her the most anxiety. She and I will jump into this one in about six months with Liz's help again. I made a wager with Ann when discussing the existence of God. After telling her about Blaise Pascal's wager for God's existence and asking her to consider it with a free and open mind she promised she would, but only after <u>the day that Liz became a Christian</u>. She thought she was not in any danger of that ever happening, but God would one day hold her to her word!

I continued to get encouragement from Heavenly Dove and the prayer circle inside:

> *"He who rushes from his bed to his business*
> *and waiteth not to worship in prayer,*
> *is as foolish as though he had not put on his clothes*
> *or washed his face and as unwise as though*
> *he dashed into battle without arms and armor."*

Take comfort, brother in Christ. Very early in the morning, when it is still dark, we go to the House of Prayer on Sacred Mountain where we pray. There we continue to pray... Mighty Witness, First Sun, Spirit of Wisdom, Chief Counselor, Magenta Rose, Heir of the Promise and myself, Heavenly Dove...until very late in the evening. We are the Council of the Holy Ones and we continually pray in the Spirit for all the Saints.

We hear the pain and suffering inside...and we pray. We know that the Lord will restore those inside, who have long been outcasts for whom no one cared. He will restore their health and heal their wounds. We continue to pray for your needs, as we sense that you are a righteous man. We know that the Lord will deliver you from all your troubles. He will be with you as you pass through the trials and temptations. You will not be destroyed by them for He is with you always.

Do not let your heart be troubled, trust in God and continue to do good. These earthly trials will soon pass away, but the eternal glory you are achieving will last forever. Take heart, our dear brother in Christ. Know that we never cease praying for you. Focus on the promise of final deliverance from sorrow and pain as we do. Our Lord and Savior will wipe away all our tears when it is the end. There will be no more mourning, or sadness...for the old order of things will have passed away.

Dear brother in Christ, we have watched your generosity and your Christ-like love towards those who are oppressed, weak and brokenhearted. Blessed are you who refreshes them and cares for their needs, for you will prosper in the eyes of the Lord for your kindness and compassion. Know that your labor is not in vain. The grace of our Lord be with your spirit.

Heavenly Dove.

Ann would fall back into a depressive state again, as she struggled through her troubles with the contractor remodeling her house. She worked with Circle Council to try and overcome their debt problem. She was angry too because Sergio had trusted the contractor's word and was burned again by 'another Christian'. Ann felt like God's representative had violated her all over again. The decision was for Maria to stop going to Bible study at her new church and church on Sunday, because of the cost of gas needed to get to Pleasanton. Ruth was not allowed to attend her church class for the same reasons. Therapy would have to stop indefinitely, as Ann didn't want to "do to Bruce what the Christian contractor did to me." They were trying to figure out how to tell Tabitha and Maria that week. Maria and Louise were going to be allowed to see me for two more weeks until after their baptisms and then our time would end as well.

She thanked Bruce for all he had done and told him that what meant the most to her was that he never broke his promise. She ended with this note:

It might encourage you to know that Maria has finally accepted our existence. Sergio was telling her about the time he and Maria painted the bedroom and wrote all over the walls with paint. As he reminisced, Maria looked at him and knew she did not experience that moment. It was an awakening for her. She echoed inside, "Bruce and Pastor Chalberg are right. I cannot try to make it go away anymore. I got parts like they say. It's true. They are real." So at least something positive came out of this week. Stay healthy and think of us once in a while.

Circle Council thought more about it and wrote to Bruce with a new plan for trusting God and going ahead with therapy and counseling with me. They discussed with him the plan for Maria's birthday celebration by Raquel that weekend and their concern for the issues it might raise emotionally. What neither Ann nor Circle Council knew was God's plan to care for the System. What occurs after the baptisms will surprise them even more than what the enemy does during the week before Saturday's event.

Memo from Council
Maria is now safe inside and will be allowed out on Saturday for the baptism. We have had to also restrict others from being outside. The triggers are similar to the grandmother's death in '65. Ruth is handling the family. The mother is causing a lot of problems for Ruth and Sergio. It is so difficult to be with the family that Ann has had to switch out to give Ruth a break.

Elizabeth Ray has informed the system that the last time a death in the family occurred, it was Maria's house that was chosen for the gathering. We need to encourage the husband not to allow this again with all the construction going on at this time. Ruth has made some interesting statements about the connection between the baptisms coming up and the events that have occurred in the last several weeks. She concludes that there are enemy forces opposed to Maria's baptism. Many of the leaders see the accident with the van, the aunt's death and the contractor problems as more than coincidental.

The goal was to get them through the baptisms before trying to anticipate what the next move was going to be by the enemy. Carol and I tried to make the day as special as we could for Maria and Louise. Carol would be standing with me as co-pastor for the ceremony and singing a solo, There is a Savior, after they answered the baptismal candidate's questions. The baptisms were held in Bruce's office.

Our honored guests for witnessing the occasion were Lindsay, the pastor's wife of Maria's new church and another lady from her Bible study. Carol brought a baptismal bowl and earthen

367

cup to use in the ceremony and gave them to Maria and Louise as gifts of remembrance. Everyone brought gifts chosen from the heart, like seeds to plant in the flower garden indicating growth and new life to celebrate the day.

The baptisms were a highly spiritual and emotional time for all of us. As they were being baptized with water and the Word, Mariann switched out briefly to tell me about the many 'bright ones' surrounding us and singing praises to God. I told her with tears that I sensed their presence, but that she had to go back inside so I could finish the blessing for Maria and Louise. The charge given the candidates let them know that the greatest adventure of their lives was now beginning and Jesus would always be there to walk with them.

The next day, Easter Sunday, we received the following fax from Maria:

Dear Pastor Chalberg and Pastor Chalberg,

Louise and me want to thank you for making our baptism so special. We will never forget the date of our baptism birthday, cause it is your birthday with Jesus too. We are so happy to be in God's family and have so many brothers and sisters. We have been talking to Jesus a lot.

Today we went to church and guess what? Sergio, Jose and Rosalinda came to church with us. They didn't seem to be happy that we asked them pretty please to go to church, but they went and got to hear about Jesus. Louise and me were happy cause Jesus came back to life on Easter Sunday and it's a happy day cause he beat the devil.

Louise and me read the bible verses that you said at our baptism. (Matt. 28:18-20; Romans 6:3-4, 10:9-13; Ephesians 4:4-6, 15-16; and Philippians 2:1-2, 12-13 to be exact.) We liked the way the bible you gave us said them. It says sin's power over us was broken when we became Christians and were baptized. We never have to worry anymore about going to heaven cause Jesus says we are and he don't lie. I like the part in my bible in Ephesians that says each part in its own special way helps the other parts. Louise and me want to help our inside parts and outside people too. We like to tell the other parts about Jesus.

When we were small we didn't understand God love cause we got told God didn't like us and we were bad and dirty. So I was real quiet and good cause I thought that God wouldn't notice me and get me. Love always hurt bad and I didn't want God to find me. But then more bad came and I just wanted to die, but I didn't know about the other parts and they didn't want me to die, so they put me in Bruce's office. I was so very scared cause he would set there and ask questions, when all I wanted to do was get out of there and not talk. I didn't know how I got there and it was hard cause I didn't know the answers and how I felt. But Ruth kept putting me in that office and I found out about all of them and then I really wanted to die cause I knew I was crazy or an alien.

But Bruce was so nice. He never hurt me and he cared about me. He told me about a different love than I knew, but I thought he must not know love very good cause it wasn't the love I knew. Then I met you. I was so scared cause I didn't know if you were like the priest. I didn't know what to say to someone who worked for God and I didn't know if you would hurt me too. But I remember when you told me about your mother and had tears in your eyes and felt inside that you were different from the priest. You and Bruce taught me about real God love. I didn't understand why you would come on Saturdays to see me, when you could sleep in cause you worked all week. I didn't know why you would take Liz to breakfast and why you would buy me a bible for Christmas and not want anything from me. Inside I started hearing that this was what Jesus was like. He loves with real love. He won't hurt. Louise and me began to talk about real God love. We wondered if it was being selfish to want real God love so much all of the time. We wanted to fill us up with the real God love we didn't get when we were little. But we also wanted to give it to other people, cause we felt warm inside and happy, when we love with real love.

You and Bruce helped us to understand real God love and helped us feel it when you hugged us and smiled at us or told us *wonderful things about Jesus. Louise and me wondered if sometimes God does that. Maybe he can't hug us right now, so he uses other people to give us Jesus hugs. Louise and me talked to Jesus about what work he wants us to do for him cause we want to do what he wants us to. When we talked to him last night, we said we couldn't talk good, so we don't think we can talk to big amounts of people. Then Jesus said something that we didn't understand, but when Ruth heard it she started to laugh a big laugh. Jesus said you sound like Moses. I think Jesus must have us mixed up, cause we aren't big like Moses. Do you know why Jesus said that?* (We laughed together later when they learned He had said the same thing to me when I argued with Him about calling me into ministry.)

We don't know what Jesus wants us to do for him. Ruth says we have to listen to him all of the time and read his word and learn lots. But Jesus says we are already working for him, but we don't know where. Ruth works lots in disability ministry but we don't know for us. We know something God told us. He said that he has given us some special presents. He wants us to use them to help other people and that other people will know that God gave us hope and courage, strength and energy, and all kinds of blessings to get through our stuff. And that it wasn't easy and we will get scared and afraid, but when we hold on to Jesus even if only by the end of his robe, we are still holding on and he will pick us up and hold us and never go away. We want to do everything for Jesus. We want to tell people about real God love and show them love by being nice and kind and considerate to them. We know what it feels like to be different and not liked so we want to always love people. We want to tell them what we learned in our baptism song, that Jesus wants us to give him our tears and sadness and our pain. Jesus has got to love us a whole lot to do that. Nobody ever wants everyone's tears, sadness and pain, but Jesus wants it and he wants us to know we can hold on to him.

We remember what you told us that now we have a shield around us and the bad can't get in. Louise and me got to get all of the bad already in us out and then only let good in. We got to have a good gate on our fence so that bad can't get in. We couldn't think of how to do this until you told us about Jesus being our shield. Jesus is going to be our lock on our gate and we are going to let him decide when to open the gate and when not to. So every time something tries to get in, we are going to let Jesus open the gate if he thinks it is good for us. It is going to take practice to remember to do it all of the time.

I hope the other parts want to know about Jesus soon. Louise and me want them to have real God love too. Thank you Mrs. Pastor Chalberg so much too.

We love you with Jesus love. Bye.

Maria and Louise

After reading this, I recalled a story that Raquel had written about a vision she had called <u>The Gate</u>. I plan to include it with Raquel's other poems and stories which will be published at a later date. This story has a reoccurring theme for direction from the Great Spirit. It is a metaphor for how we are to live as God's children along the fences that separate the kingdom of God from the forces of evil restraining those unaware of the 'Gate,' from entering the kingdom through Him.

I remembered this because the enemy was back at it the next week in the funeral of the aunt and in therapy at the counseling center. By Monday the migraine headaches were back for Maria and depression over what Rebecca said at therapy. Ruth wrote to Bruce about the subtle attacks coming through family members at the viewing on Wednesday and at the funeral on Thursday.

"They kept telling us to stay quiet and not 'disturb' the others by helping them in the grieving process."

Ruth tried to help Maria's uncle into the viewing room to say goodbye to his wife, but he was overcome by grief and sobbed in her arms. Other family members could only comment that the uncle must have liked Maria more than them. The coup de grace came when the uncle would only allow Ruth to take a picture of him at his wife's casket. Sergio's mother got all upset and told her not to do it, but the uncle told her and I quote, *"tough shit!"* Ruth made sure the photographs were developed and in his hands by the end of the day.

Ruth went on to tell of the 'good turmoil' that the 'Christmas In April' team was having on Maria and her family. The 'Christians' coming in at this time of her financial difficulties and contributing material and labor to finish projects around the house perplexed Ann. Of course the primary thorn-of-a-contractor refused to give any rebate for works that he was supposed to have done. This added to Sergio's frustration with him as well. Maria thought she didn't deserve such kindness from these people and was confused by the good coming at one side of her and the 'subtle evil' on the other side.

Ruth commented on the baptism as well. She really was impressed over Lindsay's gifts of a cross for Maria and a devotional gardener's prayer book for Louise. She thought Carol and I were wonderful in preparing the Scripture passages and special songs with understanding love for who was being baptized. She talked a little about what happened at therapy and asked Bruce to confront Rebecca about the damage that was done. She was concerned about Maria's response and ability to withstand the battle for control of her soul. These attacks were coming from unexpected areas inside therapy in a support group. A woman colleague of Bruce had begun dismantling the progress made in the last year, because the methods used did not fit into her concepts of counseling. Maria wrote to me about her worries and you can see from her use of words, that her depression has caused her to regress in the strength she received in the previous weekend's celebration of baptism.

Dear Pastor Chalberg,

Do you think God will forgive me for the bad that I did, even if I can't understand what it is? I am sorry in my heart cuz the lady Rebecca said that I can't be Bruce's friend ever and that I can't call him at home. I can't pray for him when things happen, like when his wife got sick or bad people take his house. I didn't mean it to be bad to want to be Bruce's friend. I never had a friend before Bruce. Maybe only good people can have friends. Louise and me are very sorry for wanting a friend. I guess it is not right for you to be our friend.

Do you think God is mad at Louise and me for praying for you and Mrs. Pastor Chalberg? The lady Rebecca said we can't pray for Bruce no more, it is against the therapist laws to pray. Tabitha is so sad and went back into her hole cuz Rebecca said she can't have ice cream with Bruce no more or call him daddy. Tabitha doesn't understand cuz she calls people who hurt hombre malo and people who are nice daddy. When Rebecca said it, Tabitha came out and tried in a big voice to tell her to go away and that she wanted her daddy. Rebecca got real strict and told her that Bruce is not her daddy and no more ice cream with Bruce. Tabitha took Angelina and Anna into the holes with her and said only good girls get to have a daddy and hasn't come out since.

I tried not to be bad. She was mad because I got scared she was going to bring in another multiple into the class and maybe a boy. I said I wanted to go home and she wouldn't let me go. I want to stay home now and not go anywhere cuz I just make problems. If Louise and me stay home we won't hurt people.

Liz can't have lunch with Bruce no more, call him at home and I can't give him presents cuz Rebecca said it was wrong. I didn't know what to do. Liz is mad cuz I talked and they get mad if I don't. Rebecca is like Bruce and a therapist and she makes me scared when I don't want to talk. She says she won't tell, but then she does and she got mad at Bruce cuz I prayed for him. She read our letters to him (the first journals) and made me so scared I don't know what to do. She got mad when we said we let you write about us to tell other pastors not to hurt us. Liz don't like her and wrote very bad words to her about what happened and called her names cuz Liz said she thinks she knows everything. Bruce can't be nice anymore cuz she says he can't be our friend and therapist too.

I tried so hard but Bruce got hurt by Rebecca and the other multiple. She is a therapist too and all of them are mad and Louise and me don't understand. I hope Bruce will be OK. I don't like fighting. I guess Louise and me can't be good enough to have friends like good people have. I don't feel good no more. I am sorry I got to cut and get the bad out of me. I don't understand why we obeyed God and got baptized and then can't have friends no more. I guess I got real bad blood in me like my father says.

Liz asked Elizabeth Ray to send you these letters and she says yes, but you need to send them back when you are finished reading them. Liz wants you to read them and tell her if you see anything wrong with how we treat Bruce. We got to go away for awhile.

By Maria

I was livid over the damage done by Rebecca in so many areas of the System's healing, but I had to trust Bruce to handle it and not say anything to her myself. I spent several hours that evening over the phone with Maria and the next Saturday with the System repairing the open wounds of their heart. I talked with Maria about how many 'Christian' therapists do therapy only in the way they are taught by the institutions of this world.

They will often not depend upon God to lead them, as much as the 'codes' of their profession, codes made up by people with the best of intentions, but none-the-less designed by the limitations of human knowledge and history. They are often afraid to do it God's way, because of the personal risks they take in loving their 'clients' unconditionally. God's way of healing the human soul is not based on science, but on faith and trust that God *is* that unconditional love. For those therapists that listen and trust His knowledge above their own about the healing of shattered souls, they can expect to be rejected by the majority in their profession who trust themselves more than they trust God. I asked Maria, "Who do you trust as therapists that reflect the love and wisdom of Jesus in their profession?" God responded to her hurt and pain of the moment and revealed some of His plan for the System in my discussion and prayer with her that night.

Relief was on the way as well in the response of Raquel to all she had observed from the inside world, during Maria and Louise's baptism. She wrote to me about wanting to do the same, but in her own Native American style.

Shedding Tear-

I have heard of Maria and Louise's joy in being accepted into the family of the Great Spirit. I am looking forward to the Saturday when I too can partake of the ceremony of entering into the Great Spirit's clan. I wish to have the ceremony outside, under the mighty tree, behind One Who Listens' office. I would prefer to go to the Land of the Ohlone along the crooked path, but the men of greed have taken the land and comes in mass to the water. It is no longer as it was. Unless you are willing to walk many steps into the back canyon where the lazy man of greed does not venture, it will be quieter under the mighty tree. I would like the following prayers and reflections spoken by you during the ceremony.

We return thanks to our mother the earth, which sustains us. We return thanks to the river and streams, which supply us with water. We return thanks to all herbs, which furnish medicines to cure our diseases. We return thanks to the corn and to her sisters, the beans and the squashes, which give us life. We return thanks to the bushes and trees, which provide us with fruit. We return thanks to the wind, which moving the air has banished diseases. We return thanks to the moon and the stars, which have given us light when the sun was gone. We return thanks to the sun, that he has looked upon the earth with a beneficent eye. Lastly, we return thanks to the Great Spirit, in whom is embodied all goodness and who directs all these things for the good of his children.

Oh Great Spirit, we are living humbly on this earth. Our Heavenly Father we want everlasting life through Jesus Christ your son. When we die, oh Great Spirit, we want to be at the door of heaven where Jesus will take us in. But while we live, oh Great Spirit, until we are called home by you we go forth to move about the earth. We go forth as the owl, wise and knowing. We go forth as the eagle, powerful and bold. And we go forth as the dove, powerful in its gentleness. We go forth in wisdom, courage and peace.

There was a time that I, Quiet Walker, was formed, shaped out of unspeakable pain. Impossible? No, for nothing is more real. I have not remained dead in my pain. I have traveled the Sacred Mountain in search for meaning and purpose to my existence. It was at the top of Sacred Mountain that I received my answers. The Great Spirit through his son Jesus Christ has breathed life's air into me. I ring loud and clear and people are astonished. How can one so simple be so happy? Ah, but now I know my parents. The Great Spirit is my father, Nature is my mother and Jesus is my brother. And you still wonder?

Through in and out of this deep knowledge, I live content. I have no worries. Millions of little lights are fluttering in me, lights of wisdom, love, happiness and completeness. These lights glow bright and intense, through living in darkness. Others wonder at this. Lights? What lights? Friendliness, loyalty, honesty, helpfulness and love. These are phenomena we all know and still I am asked, what are they? They are gifts from the Mighty One, gifts of knowing unknown knowledge... guided by little lights. They mark the path toward how to live forever and forever.

They are why I want to live tomorrow and the next day and the next... forever serving the one I follow, telling others of the reasons for my joy and hope, being strengthened by His love. For I follow the one who is truth... the one who gives everlasting life. I follow Jesus Christ in whom all wisdom and knowledge is found.
(Inspired by the writings of ancient Cheyenne, Iroquois, Ted Palmanteer and Flora Hood)

Raquel's baptism was different than most I have done, but just as meaningful as all of them. I couldn't hike to the back canyon with her, because I had injured my back in a 'freak' accident at work, the week following Maria's baptism. I didn't tell the System what happened because I knew they weren't ready to understand the power struggles that surround people involved in spiritual warfare. Just as more dramatic 'things' begin to happen to the System following each baptism, more dramatic things also begin to happen to me.

The baptism of Raquel was a peaceful time and although it was longer it did not seem so. Raquel read her own 'vows', after answering the questions I asked her about her purpose in being baptized. They were essentially the same questions I gave to Maria and Louise but put in a context that fit her cultural understanding. Our prayers which were many, were often read from the Psalms. Psalm 91 was the blessing over her commitment to Jesus. Passages were read from Deuteronomy, Isaiah, Matthew and John. We closed with her singing a prayer from the Hopi clan. All Ruth could say afterward was that I have a way with her and it was the most unusual baptism she had witnessed in her life. The only thing she knew for sure was that God was glorified.

It was a few days after her baptism that I received this letter from Raquel. I missed the most important parts of this one, that would have supplied clear warnings about what was to come, as well as the hope God gave to carry them through the coming events. I would not reveal this letter to them until after the chemotherapy had begun. I read it to them after God fulfills His promises to keep them alive through the surgery. It has a similar theme to the longer one given in the Prologue that Raquel shares in Council after the results of the lumpectomy are given.

On Sacred Mountain I have heard the promise of the Great Spirit to those in the Land of Preservation. He has spoken and let all those who wish to hear... hear of the promises.

If you will humble yourselves, pray and seek my face, and turn away from evil, I will not withhold my grace. I will heal your land. I will hear your plea. I will answer your prayer. Listen, my child;

In the Land of Preservation, the time is near when the trees shall lose their leaves, the wildflowers shall wither and die, the birds shall be silenced and the waters shall not run. The land shall become as a desert and you shall be stripped from head to foot. But rejoice and be joyful in me. For this shall pass and I will be your strength. I will free you and you shall see my mighty work. I will pour water on the thirsty land. I will pour out my spirit. The flowers will spring up like grass in the meadow and the trees will spring up by the flowing streams. I will restore and heal your land and you will come to know that no one and nothing can save you, but me. I will rescue you and you will be free. But you must commit yourself to choose to believe in me. Humbly submit to my timing and my wisdom. Submit to my ways. For those who hope in me will renew their strength. They will soar on wings like eagles; they will run and not grow weary; they will walk and not grow faint. As you do not know the path of the wind or how the body is formed in a mother's womb, so you cannot understand my work, I, who am the maker of all things. Trust me and be patient.

For I shall do as I promised. I will change your name. You will no longer be called: wounded, outcast, lonely or afraid. I will change your name. Your new name will be: confidence, joyfulness, overcoming one, faithfulness, friend of God...and one who seeks my face.

The Ann / Raquel Dilemma
"And what is as important as knowledge?" asked the mind.
"Caring and seeing with the heart," answered the soul.

I was not alert enough and in tune with the Spirit of God to pick up the warnings, or the reason for reminding the System about the promises of God given as hope to His people. Within a month, Maria will be diagnosed as having breast cancer. Maybe I just didn't want to believe that more trials were coming their way to test their faith in God. I was now receiving faxes and visits from more parts, creating within me optimism for growth without harder trials waiting.

Even though I had warned them to expect attacks, I was hoping against my experience that it wouldn't happen and that they might be blessed with a longer period of rest and nurturing within this world. It looked promising in May when Tabitha came out more often calling me 'Daddy Miguel' with true affection. Mariann began conversing more about herself with me and calling me 'Mister Miguel', because she made it clear that she didn't like Tabitha's 'funny talk.'

I began to use Bruce's felt 'translation' board with Tabitha to interpret her drawings and broken English. Mariann had discovered how to use the computer and fax machine at home to write to Bruce, so a whole new communication route was opened to me for her by Maria. Maria tried to warn me one night in a message to me:

Pastor Chalberg,
Mariann keeps playing with the computer when I get on to send you a message. I don't want her to get in trouble (Jose's computer). I talked to Jesus about what you asked me. You wanted to know if you were on the right track about something (about her family, but I didn't tell her). Well Jesus said something that wasn't a yes or a no. He said if Michael is listening to me, then he knows the answer to his question. What does that mean Pastor Chalberg? I hope these things are going through your machine.
I miss you. Maria

Shortly after receiving this fax, I received my first one from Mariann. She apparently paid very close attention to what Maria did and copied her computer operations. Unlike the two letters to Bruce in chapter three, I've left the letter in its original state of phonetic spelling, so you can see the type of letters from the kids. They are writing on their own without adult help and were sent directly to me. With a little practice, you can understand it fairly easily. For the rest of the books I will reinterpret what Mariann is saying.

Hi mr miguel

I no how to usa boys mashin good cuz I be big girl   I see big ibm   mr miguel you tel pepl the smely ones rel   ok   they not lik dragunslar   they not lik us cuz we dragunslar frend   they go looking all over to mix us up and trik us to not love dragunslar   they be bad   they work for the bad anjul   they fit the brit ones you no   the brit ones work for dragunslar they   brit   I not see feet on them   they go funny   they warm and prety the brit ones watch an see smely ones come and they go all around and guard   they be round pepl and the bad ones to   lik   at that bad store they be there   they fit sometim the boss one the brit ones say sarus sarus that his nam   he the boss   when   smely ones come I tatle on them to dragunslar.   Mr miguel you tel pepl bad fits brit anjuls help but smely ones look for dragunslar frends that not holding dragunslar hand and they try to get them work for them and not dragunslar.   They be real mr miguel   you see my pitur   I love you   I hear bettl bug music hard day nit I work and hav dog   slep in the log yeah yeah yeah   you wunt to no secret   no tel and hold my hand   I wunt hold yor hand yeah yeah yeah

see mr miguel I lern bettl bug music

The children accepted the concept that to draw and write about the 'bad' wasn't the same as 'telling,' so they were less afraid of retribution by their abusers. They get used to idea that the 'smelly ones' will continue to threaten them if they draw so they start 'tattling' on them to Bruce and I. It is Maria who struggles the longest with the constant harassment by the enemy. The drawings get more detailed and often the whole page was reflective of abuses at different periods in the child's life.

For instance a drawing by Tabitha of the grandfather's abuse in the basement would not include symbols of SRA abuse or abuse by the Santeria. Her drawings of the abuse in other places like the barn might contain a variety of symbols from both. We know now that many of her drawings were reflecting the abuse of the Pod Children, Egar and Blue Devil. Mariann's drawings primarily dealt with the abuse by the priest with a conscious abuse by the Catholic Church drawn in the background. Sometimes it would be Mariann drawing images for Otosis/Lila and naming her because she was thought to be closer in age to Mariann. The freedom given to the children to express their stories appeared to escalate after the baptisms of Maria, Louise and Raquel.

Mariann drew to describe her feelings for me about abuse memories. It speaks loudly about victims' self-image after abuse.

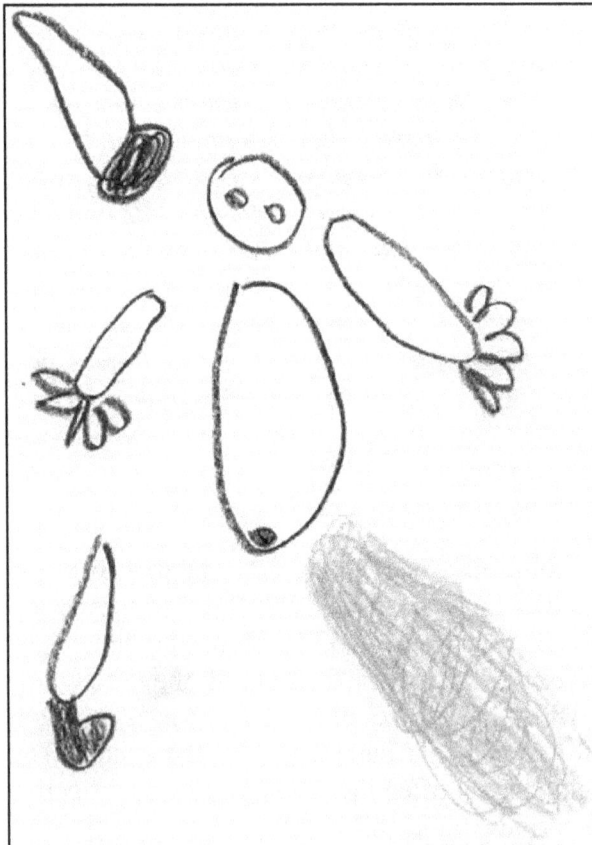

Raquel sent me this poem after hearing a discussion between Bruce and I about the drawings of the children.

> *Stolen long ago...the pieces of their soul*
> *Savagely taken and discarded into the wind*
> *Shattered pieces ripped from them to satisfy others' desires*
> *Leaving them fractured and broken*
> *But the Great Spirit has promised to restore their soul*
> *He will gather in the pieces and bring joy and wholeness*
> *No longer will they be empty... longing for oneness of their spirit*
> *For he will fulfill his promise and they will be healed.*
> *- Quiet Walker*

This prophetic poem will be fulfilled 6 years later for Mariann and Hopi. A preview of this healing was given in the verbatim dialogue between Mariann and I at the close of chapter 5.

For the next two months Mariann grows rapidly in her trust of Dragonslayer to empower her to be 'Dragonslayer strong.' Her open defiance of the smelly ones she sees and hears begins to frighten some of the more mature adults. As the attacks increase some begin to wonder if they are doing so to stop Mariann from telling about their existence. The System is correct in their analysis, at least to a moderate degree. The enemies of God do not want to be exposed in our world. It's easier to wage war from the shadows and darkness of life, than to be confronted by the light of God's truth in the reality of Jesus Christ. Some foundational verses of the Bible contributing to the reason for these books are found in **Ephesians 5.**

"Let no one deceive you with empty words,
for because of these things the wrath of God
comes upon the sons of disobedience. Therefore
do not be partakers with them; for you were formerly
darkness, but now you are light in the Lord;
walk as children of light (for the fruit of the light
consists in all goodness and righteousness and truth),
trying to learn what is pleasing to the Lord.
And do not participate in the unfruitful deeds of darkness,
but instead even <u>expose them</u>; for it is disgraceful even
to speak of the things done by them in secret.
But all things become visible when they are exposed by the light,

*for everything that becomes visible is light. For this reason it says,
'Awake, sleeper, and arise from the dead, and Christ will shine on
you.' Therefore be careful how you walk, not as unwise men,
but as wise, making the most of your time, because the days are evil.
So then do not be foolish, but understand the will of the Lord."*

Many believers read these verses and think they are being instructed to not even talk about what evil does in its darkness, because it is shameful (v.12), when within its context quite the opposite is true. The Lord wants us to be wise in our understanding of evil and expose the darkness that surrounds it by bringing it into the light of His truth, so that everyone can see it for what it really is in their life. Evil cannot exist in the presence of God. That is one very real truth that Mariann began revealing to the System and to anyone who would listen to her. Even in the most severe spiritual attacks that come repeatedly over the next eight years and beyond, the enemy always retreats when we call upon the presence of God to defend us. Mariann and the System will learn the battle cry for all occasions to be **"COME DRAGONSLAYER!"**

**"Exposure to the Light can be the catalyst for
Redemption of the Heart"**

---

*"Create in me a clean heart, O God, And renew a steadfast spirit
within me. Do not cast me away from Thy presence,
And do not take Thy Holy Spirit from me. Restore to
me the joy of Thy salvation, And sustain me with
a willing spirit. Then I will teach transgressors Thy ways,
And sinners will be converted to Thee."*
<u>Psalm 51: 10-13</u>

*"Finally, be strong in the Lord, and in the strength of His might.
Put on the armor of God, that you may be able to stand firm against
the schemes of the devil. For our struggle is not against flesh and
blood, but against the rulers, against the powers, against the world
forces of this darkness, against the spiritual forces of wickedness
in the heavenly places. Therefore, take up the full armor of God,
that you may be able to resist in the evil day,
having done everything to stand firm."*
<u>Ephesians 6:10-13</u>

Chapter 15:

"If God Stops you to Talk – What Then?"

"Truly, truly, I say to you, he who hears My word,
and believes Him who sent Me, has eternal life,
and does not come unto judgment,
but has passed out of death into life."
-Jesus John 5:24

> "What is this little way which you would teach souls?
> It is the way of spiritual childhood,
> The way of trust and absolute surrender."
> -Therese of Lissieux, 1898

Entering into the summer of 1996, Liz was positive that something, or someone, was pursuing her. At first, she thought it was her past catching up to her but she soon found out it was her future… holding her accountable for her own chastising words and plea to be real. After the funeral of Maria's aunt, she heard that Maria's father was coming for a visit and he was very angry. She tried to escape by driving to Mexico and wrote me… maybe I should let her tell you in her own words. She was right about one thing though… it was the Father pursuing her.

I wasn't afraid of God! When you said, "Come on Liz I thought you had more guts than that." Shit, I got balls and I ain't no wimp. It's just I got respect for higher powers. I ain't stupid. I know power when I see it!

I just don't like to be followed. He just wouldn't leave me alone. That story that Raquel wrote, then the funeral and that damn statement "a river runs through you. It connects you… the purpose of God." Shit I heard that and it hit me like a bolt of lightening. Damn it why? Words don't hit me like that.

I knew I was being followed. I wasn't dreaming. I hadn't been drinking. Damn, all I did was switch out at the funeral to grab a piece of cake and get me the hell out of there. What was the big deal?

Why did he zap my car? Shit, if he's God, then he knows what's coming. He knows the father is coming and the whole damn place is going to explode, because the man is on a mission, a real 'I'm pissed about the drugs mission (Maria's sister) and I'm going to be square in the middle of it if I don't get my ass out. But HE wouldn't let me and zapped my car.

You guys were no help! "Just talk to Him. See what he wants." Sitting on the sidelines, you and Bruce were going to watch me get knocked out of the boxing ring of life.

WHY CAN'T HE JUST LEAVE ME ALONE AND GO HANG AROUND SOME DAMN SUBURBAN CHRISTIAN! I AIN'T GOT A DAMN THING HE WANTS. WHY IS HE AFTER ME? I ALREADY KNOW WHAT I AM. I ALREADY KNOW WHAT I DO. I AIN'T PROUD OF IT ALL. I KNOW I DO SHIT. BUT HE HASN'T EXACTLY BEEN AN ALLY WITH ME. HE'S MADE MY LIFE SHIT AND I HAD TO CLAW MY WAY IN TO SURVIVE. LIFE SUCKS AND THEN YOU DIE. SO BEFORE I DIE, AT LEAST I CAN HAVE A LITTLE FUN.

But he wouldn't leave me alone. I tried to sleep in the car and I wasn't dreaming. I don't dream. You don't understand what happened. And don't you ever tell anybody! (Sorry Liz.) I mean it was weird. Damn weird and if it didn't happen to me, I would think the person telling it was some kind of nut. But I ain't no nut...an asshole yeah, but no nut.

I was laying there kind of half in and half out, thinking about what you and Bruce said, kind of looking at the stars and trying to fall asleep to forget it all. I figured tomorrow hey...God would be on to something else and would forget all about me and go do some useful stuff like make something.

Well I was getting more half out than half in and all of a sudden it happened. It really happened, something cool but alive with a tremendous amount of power. How the hell do I explain something I can't explain? Shit, it was like the wind, I mean it was like someone took a high pressure can of cool air and put it right up my mouth and let go. I mean this high-powered force of crisp cool oxygen, or what ever it was came at my mouth and went in and I WAS TOTALLY AWAKE BUT I WASN'T SCARED.

This is so bizarre. DON'T THINK I'VE LOST IT BECAUSE I'M SANER THAN YOU ARE. Something went in me. I sat there and spent five seconds thinking about it and then brushed it off as my very first dream. I was never one to spend a whole lot of time like Ann, studying the rational, logic and all that shit. So I was about to get up and try to get to Mexico again when he began.

Did I get your attention?
OK Ruth knock it off, I'm in no mood...
Do I sound like Ruth?
I knew it didn't! You Core, I thought you did acid, not oxygen.
Do I sound like Core?
Knock it off whoever you are and quit being a damn comedian... that's my territory.
You know who I am Liz.
Shit!
I've been called worse.
Oh God!
What?

No... I didn't mean Oh God I meant shit, I mean...I don't want to talk, don't you got something more important to do?

No, you are the most important.

(I thought damn he's a therapist too.) Go away and leave me alone, shit, I just want to be alone. I can't talk to you...I mean we come from different sides of the track. You got power, money and everything to be top dog. You're high clout and I can't be around uppity...I mean don't get me wrong. I ain't complaining, it's just that we come from different lives...

Liz I made all the inner parts. I made you and knitted you together in the womb. I was there while you were being formed. I loved you before you were even born. I think of you constantly. You are mine and you are precious to me.

I ain't precious to nobody. Why are you saying that? I do shit. I get mad because people aren't real. I'm ugly and I hate math. I hate being trapped and controlled. I'm an asshole and I admit it. But you got to understand I had no choice in being an asshole. Life ain't been gravy for me.

I know Liz. I know everything about you. Every moment I know where you are and what you do and why you do it.

I don't like to be followed. Shit, I can't breathe knowing I'm being watched.

Liz I know your heart. I know you Liz.

Then you know I'm rotten through and through. I wrote the book on sin.

I forgive you Liz. I want to love you. I want to heal you. I want to fill your life with good.

Yeah right...there is a string to everything you know. You just want to control me and make me into a Ruth.

I can't be like that I got my style…I'm Liz. I need to be me. I don't want to be a Christian. I don't want to sit in church. I got to be me. I'm always trapped. I get trapped by them inside. And those Christians are always telling me to shut up…can't have my opinion. You piss me off. You say you love me and I'm so… so special to you but then you don't show it. Shit look at my life.

Liz I allow free choice. I will not control you or trap you. I want to love you and be your friend. I grieve over what has happened to you. I grieve over how those who come in my name twist and distort who I am. I am fully aware of the hearts of men. When it is time I will punish the wicked. No one will escape my judgment. Liz my love and kindness for you is forever. Even when you turn from me and try to run from me, I will be there. I love you Liz and I will always keep my promises. Do not be afraid.

I <u>Ain't</u> afraid…I'm frustrated. You don't get the picture. I'm nothing. I'm not worth your time. I don't fit. I'm not miss perfect like those damn suburban Christians. I'm screwed up. I got put together wrong.

I don't make mistakes Liz. Some of my most precious are those who are wrapped in wrinkled paper. Come and kneel before me. Trust me Liz. I will not disappoint you. I have a purpose for your life.

Shit…there it is. I knew you'd get around to it. Kneel means I'm giving up me… my identity…me and you are going to control me just like the rest.

No Liz I am not in the business of manipulating and controlling. I'm in the business of loving. I will correct and chasten you but my punishment is out of love…not hate. For knowing right from wrong and learning common sense and wise judgment will make you happier than all the gold in the world.

I'm not into things or money. I just use what I need! I hate to dust!

I know.

Why are you so damn hard to argue with? You got an answer to everything.

Yes Liz I do.

So OK...why me?

Why not?

Don't answer a question with a question. Why are you after me?

I love you Liz and you are afraid to reach out for that love.

I'm afraid you'll take it back or want something.

I won't take it back and all I want is to be able to love you and be with you.

Why is everything so hard God? Why?

Liz... life is hard but hanging with me makes it possible Liz. Through me you will have the strength and courage to be a special kind of messenger.

I'm not book smart. I hate math. School and me rub the wrong way. I ain't going to sit in no stuffy church and listen to some boring Suburban Christian. I don't do Rolex watches and I ain't going to wear that label of Christian.

Liz I know you. I know the gifts I have given you. I sent you into the world for a purpose.

I know to send off the wall jokes to Bruce and Mike.

No Liz. You shall be my messenger of hope to those who are shattered.

I ain't no goody-two-shoes. I ain't got answers to why life sucks. Man... do you know what it is like to look at your life and know that all the shit rolls your way? You try to be joyful and positive, when you're surrounded by such negative people that you can cut their negativity with a knife. You try to breathe when you've been screwed, lied to, dumped on, used, hurt, beaten, misunderstood, made fun of, not allowed to have an opinion, told to shut up, threatened with death and on and on and on. Look I ain't complaining. I'm just stating fact, OK?

Liz I've been there.

Damn...you're right! I've heard about the Pharisees and shit they did to you. Pisses me off. You got the power...why didn't you just kill them?

Liz I don't want anyone to perish, but everyone to come to repentance. Liz I will turn the bad around into good.

You can do that?

I'm God Liz... remember?

This conversation is getting too complex for my mind to handle.

Remember Liz I know you.

That's the problem...can't hide my thoughts from you.

Liz it was not my purpose for you to be treated as you have by men. I have wept over it and my heart has grieved. But I will use that which has happened for good. Listen and be still and know that I am God. I will fulfill my purposes.

Listen to me. Your purpose is to show others my gifts of love, courage and strength that I have given to you and freely offer to them, to make life work despite the problems, despite the evil, despite the pain and suffering. You shall be my messenger of hope. They will hear me through you. You know brokenness. You know rejection. You know abandonment. You know disease. You know inner pain. You know injustice. And you are bold Liz. You shall be bold for me. Do not fear Liz, for I am with you. I shall mold you and break you and glue you together for my glory. I prize my wild mustangs that work for me.

You shall walk my streets and you shall be my ministering messenger. You shall bring my message of hope to the downtrodden, the abused and the outcasts. Remember I know your heart Liz. I have seen you go into the very deepest depths of darkness, to offer help to someone who is suffering. I have seen you give water to my child dying of AIDS. I have seen you spend hours removing head lice from the children. I have seen you step in front of the child ready to be hit. I have seen all that you have done Liz and everywhere that you have been. I know your heart. I know your motives. I know your compassion for hurting people.

I shall lead you through your pain. I shall heal you and you shall yell from the highest mountains Praise God! Look at what the Lord has done for me. His love is never ending, his promises never changing. All honor and glory to the Lord.

HEAR ME LIZ: I WILL NOT TAKE YOUR PAIN AWAY. I WILL LEAD YOU THROUGH THE PAIN. MY GRACE SHALL BE SUFFICIENT FOR YOU AND OTHERS SHALL SEE AND WILL KNOW THAT I AM GOD. MY POWER WILL BE DISPLAYED IN YOUR LIFE.

Do not worry of the label the world will give you. Do not be concerned about doing anything. JUST BE THE PERSON I CREATED YOU TO BE. I shall give you strength to be faithful to me. I have sent you my friends Bruce and Mike. They will encourage you and teach you. Listen to them, for I have sent them to you. And know that I am with you FOREVER.

Bruce and Mike, this is Liz. I couldn't say anything back to him. I mean how do you say anything back to something like that. I don't cry normally, but I was balling my eyes out. And I don't know why I'm telling you all of this. How come I am letting you see the real me? I got to think about all of this. Something is happening to me. Don't leave me you guys and DON'T LAUGH! I really got to think about all of this. I'm a nobody... I'm just Liz.

Got to go. *THE FATHER IS ABOUT TO ARRIVE. LIFE STILL SUCKS!*

As Liz thought about it more that week, she began to rationalize (something contradictory to her nature) the event and tell herself that it couldn't have been God talking to someone like <u>her</u>. She tried very hard to convince herself that if it wasn't God, then it must have been the devil. If it was the devil then it must be a lie, therefore, she didn't have to listen to something that wasn't the truth.

She didn't talk with Bruce or I during this time because she didn't want to risk hearing what we thought. She knew from past experience with us that, if it sounds like God, feels in your heart like God, you have a peace about what God said and it is consistent with the Bible, then it may very well be God. So discuss it with Christians you trust for affirmation. She knew we'd say that so she didn't ask. But she learned a very hard lesson the next day, when she finally convinced herself that God had made a mistake and she didn't have to do anything. God spoke to her again and had her write it down verbatim so no excuses for what she heard.

Listen Liz. I've revealed my truth to you. You can't deny it and you can't play dumb or ignorant anymore. No more excuses! You can't say you don't know or it doesn't apply to you. I have impressed my truth on your heart and you are accountable. The choice is yours. You know the consequences Liz. I challenge you to leave the old ways behind and follow me.

I wish I could report that there was an immediate turnaround in Liz's 'attitude' but sadly no. It would take another 4 months before a commitment is forthcoming. If anyone thinks you would have reacted differently consider what else happened to her and the System that same week. Ann went in to see her doctor and was told she probably had stage 2 breast cancer. They wanted to get her in right away for a lumpectomy to determine how bad it was. She was scheduled for an immediate battery of tests and given an oncologist to take her through this. Dr. Gail was the only person to come out of Kaiser that would have any lasting benefit for the System.

The contractor was not showing up for work and refusing to honor his contract. I began to help Ann in filing a complaint with the Contractor's License Board, to hopefully get some clout to force him to finish. That ultimately proved fruitless. Maria's father and mother showed up that week and... I'll let Liz tell it again.

Hey Mike,

This is Liz. What a week! You will not believe it. Starts off with the father coming, which is just peachy with me. Anyway, the guy decides to stay in a hotel instead of our house. Breaks my heart can't you tell! We had a grad party for Rosalinda and about 50 of her friends left other boring parties and came to Rosa's. Everyone pigged out on Louise's fancy sandwiches and fruit stuff. The party went till about 3 in the morning.

The father pretty much left us alone this trip... a miracle I'd say. Only thing him and the mother kept harping about was Maria dying before them. They're into this shit about us having our will right because they think we are going to leave this world early. (Like we got anything to put in a damn will...I think I'll leave my holy socks to you!) Me I don't give a shit, but I don't need a formal discussion of my death and how the dog plans to use my spot as his personal latrine. (Wait until I tell them I plan to be stuffed rather than buried... They can sit me up in the local bar for eternity!) This discussion would not have occurred, if big mouth Ruth hadn't told on Ann. She has got to learn that the parents will have no sympathy on Maria, so don't try.

Shit, all the mother said was we all got to go someday. The damn doctor thinks Ann might have breast cancer and is refusing to let Ann ignore it. He's taken this on as a personal mission to make sure Ann keeps all of the appointments with her doctor and gets the tests finished. You know how we just love hospitals. This guy found her a woman doctor that can handle someone who doesn't show up. Ann tries but some parts cancel the appointments. She's tried to get the body's foot taken care of for ten years and finally gave up. I doubt if she is going to be anymore successful with this. Hell my motto is just have a good shot of brandy every night and what ever it is will burn right out of the system.

Maria and Louise don't know about this latest doctor shit. Me, I don't want to know any of the details. Ann can take care of it. I got better things to do than doctors. I'm sending you my latest creation; it's called The Mouth. I got lots of things I want to say before we croak. Tried to sell a subscription to Bruce, but he ain't buying it. Anyway, I'm sending you one with a copy of I Hate Math.

Also I'm sending you another sermon in honor of Father's Day, in case I'm not around.

Later Dude.

In her sermon she expresses both her old issues about God and the father image, and a new awareness of God. Liz had not made the connection of the Jesus on the inside as the same God she was having a dialogue with noted previously. Like most of the System she hadn't put the two of them together as one and the same. Jesus she could see and touch on the inside and He was moving ever so slowly and gently with all of the System. But God she couldn't see only hear just like the rest of us. Yet, for her and the other parts an unseen God was still part of the mess in their earlier lives.

Could she trust what she was learning and hearing from God, while facing up to this new threat of impending death? It was easier for most of the adult parts to look at the cancer as belonging to another part and not them. Denial can be very strong in a multiple when ailments do not affect each part the same way. I'll come back to that later. Each person will come to their own realization of God and Jesus being One in their own time and circumstances. They begin to understand the meaning of God's words, "I'll lead you through the pain, not take it away." Here is Liz's Father's Day sermon. In it she speaks for the System.

I hate father's day. I hate suburban pastors who get up at church and start talking about how great their father is and how wonderful a life they had, while we sit in the chairs feeling like throwing up. Shit don't tell me to honor my father. Why should I honor someone who never kept his promises? He never encouraged me or liked anything I did, because in his book I was stupid and going to fail... so why try? He never taught me anything but how to manipulate the system, take care of myself first, cheat, lie and steal. He told me that God had favorites and I wasn't one of them.

AND YOU ARE TELLING ME TO HONOR MY FATHER? I AM DOWN HERE SAYING WHY? YOU ARE UP THERE SAYING BECAUSE IT IS THE CHRISTIAN THING TO DO. SHIT ON THE CHRISTIAN THING, IT'S EASY FOR YOU TO SAY.

So this is my father's day sermon. I ain't talking to people who had the world's greatest dad. I ain't talking to the families who are going home to have a wonderful barbecue and honoring dad with gifts and words of gratitude. I'm not going to tell you about all of the wonderful lessons I learned from my father to help develop my character into the fine suburban character it is today. No today, I'm talking to those of us who hurt. Those whose fathers abandoned them when they were small or were more interested in sucking up coke than being with you, or were beating you, sexually abusing you and ridiculing you. I'm talking to those people for whom father's day is an extremely painful day of loneliness, bitterness and hurt. Yeah, this message is for you.

You know we got a real screwed up picture of God the Father from our own dads. My friend Raquel wrote once that there is no leader with more influence than one's father. A father is our first picture of God. As we live with him and watch him, we learn faithfulness, affirmation, encouragement, protection, wisdom, honor, integrity and love...right? At least that is what we're supposed to learn. But for those of us who did not have a loving father, we learned fear, rejection, abandonment and failure. And with that deeply ingrained in our being, we transfer this to God the Father.

For me, God has always represented this higher power in heaven that I could never identify with, because I have a real difficult time with terms like faithfulness and unconditional love. God became a joke to me. Now don't get me wrong, I'm smart enough to know that it would not be in my best interest to go pissing off the higher power. I knew about the plagues of Egypt and all the wrath of God stuff from my Catholic upbringing. I just figured God couldn't be trusted and it was better if I just stayed away from him.

Out of sight – out of mind was my motto. If I don't go looking for him, than he won't come after me. So I just accepted my plight in life and stayed as far from God as I could. I didn't trust him. I learned early in life that there is always a condition attached to a promise and the terms of the promise could change in a whim. I just figured God was better at manipulating than my earthly father and I was tired of being controlled, hurt and abused. God represented nothing to me but power, control and pain.

And so my life continued with great fear of God. I figured all these Suburban Christians that had the world's greatest dads were just being conned by God. I was tired of listening to them and watching their joy and closeness to their fathers. In fact I resented it and stayed away. There is nothing more painful than to be suffering and having everyone around you having a party. They didn't understand me and they seemed to be sealed in their little world of I had the greatest upbringing. I felt alone, different and angry. But most of all, I really wanted what they had. Like a little kid who has scrounged for food all her life, I wanted to feast at that bountiful table that others knew so well. But it was hopeless for me, I thought. Can't change history, if I was born in shit I'd die in shit.

Feeling sorry for me yet? Well I did and I began this tough Liz attitude. I DON'T NEED NO FATHER. I DON'T NEED NO GOD. I'M JUST GOING TO PARTY TILL I DROP. And I became pretty good at the tough guy image. I could hide my pain under the mask of asshole of the world. Nobody, not God or man was going to get me down. I was going to party forever.

But I have since learned that I was only kidding myself. Deep down inside I wanted to be loved, so much that I invented this game. I'd imagine being born into this great family and constructed the type of mom and dad I wanted. The dad I imagined was awesome. He was so proud that I was his kid. He couldn't talk enough about how happy he was being my dad. He'd plan all kinds of neat things to do together like walk around the pond, or a bike ride to anywhere and just neat things we did together. He would tell me great stories and teach me good things. He'd show me the stars and teach me about heaven. He'd spend time showing me how things worked and he'd display my art on his desk at work.

I'd be his kid and he'd be my dad. He'd have rules and the rules were consistent. He'd never beat me, but time me out when I needed to learn something. He'd always encourage me to reach for the stars and when I didn't quite make it, he'd tell me I'm proud of you for doing your best. He would walk the talk and I would learn integrity and love by his example. He'd defend me if people called me stupid and he'd protect me from harm. But most of all, he'd spend time with me because he really wanted to know who I was and what I thought. Yeah... if I could create my own version of a dad, he'd be my best friend.

But reality always reared its ugly face and I'd come back to the planet earth. My dad was none of those things and I longed for just a crumb of acceptance. It wasn't until 1995 that, through two very special guys, I began to see that I could have a father who was even more awesome than the father I imagined. Although I now admit that I probably taxed their patience with my rebellion and disbelief, I have slowly over the year come to an understanding that God the Father is not the angry, inconsistent, manipulative God that my earthly father portrayed him to be. I have learned that God the Father is my friend and guide. He really wants to be with me... so much that he has to zap my car to get my attention, but that's another sermon. He really encourages me, comforts me and protects me. He wants to teach me. He doesn't condemn me but gives me life.

I still haven't grasped the total picture of God the Father yet, but with each new day he's teaching me more about himself. Now, when I hear those sermons on Father's Day, I don't think about my earthly father. I focus my mind on my Heavenly Father and say to myself, "Yeah! I got the greatest Dad!"

So that's what I'd preach on Father's Day.

Buddy, before I forget there were two other things I brought up that night with God. I was in a one-sided argument with God about Suburban Christians. I told him about the church and how they talk a lot and are quick to see our faults and not their own. They don't follow what they preach and they don't look any different than us. They are self-righteous, worldly, prideful, indifferent and elite clubs.

I remember what he said clearly. "I have given you gifts Liz, use them for my glory. Some people honor me with their lips, but their hearts are far from me. Not everyone who says to me Lord, Lord, will enter the kingdom of heaven, but only he who does the will of my father who is in heaven. I have chosen you Liz. Go and teach in gentle instruction what I command you. I will give you the things you are to teach." And that's all he said to me.

The other thing I brought up was Disneyland. I told him I'd like to visit Disneyland if he could arrange it. (Doesn't hurt to ask right?) Then I asked him if heaven was as cool as I've heard Disneyland is and does it have mushrooms? He laughed this kind of neat laugh and I laughed too. I don't understand half of all this stuff and I'm sure I ain't got it written down word for word, but maybe you can figure it out because me...well I'll just let it happen. Except for Disneyland. I want to see Disneyland before I croak.

Later, Liz

The best thing about Liz's take on all of this was not that she should be proud of God choosing her for this task, but that the burden she was given would allow her to offer something to every broken person she met. She still struggled all the way wondering why God gave her this only to let them die of cancer. I was struggling as well arguing with God about why the System had to go through cancer. Hadn't they suffered enough, wasn't there another way? Were God's promises of healing only going to be fulfilled in heaven?

As I talked to the Lord about how I could best help the System at this time, with the possibility of cancer looming in front of them, I prayed that I might be used to give them a ray of hope for the future. God's response wasn't a surprise but it wasn't easy to give either. The week I took them in for the lumpectomy we talked about what the possibilities were for their healing. While each adult including Liz wanted to be a whole single person, there were a variety of responses about who that should be. Ann and Liz thought it should be one of them. Ruth hoped it would be her but would accept whatever the Lord wanted. Maria and Louise would accept whatever the System thought was best. Circle Council felt that if 'wholeness' came to them Maria would be the recipient. No one knew what wholeness for him or her was supposed to be.

The children were not far enough along to express what freedom in singularity might mean to them. Raquel asked that we seek the Great Spirit for direction as though she was aware of something the rest of them were not. When I shared with them what the Lord was telling me to give them some chuckled outside while crying inside over what it meant. Others saw it as an answer for how they would retain their individual identities, a hope that was stronger than the fear of the difficulties this would bring. For all of them the answer also meant they might survive the immediate danger of cancer.

> **"I will love you with an everlasting love and I will heal you. Your wholeness will be found in Me...not as the world understands wholeness, but as I give it. You will remain a multiple for my purposes because each of you will have a testimony to give about My power to heal and receive all who come to Me. The fact that you are alive today is a testimony in itself of My love for all of you. You will become My witnesses to a world in need of My love. Do not be afraid of this, for I will never leave you nor forsake you."**

As I presented this to them, it was clear to me that either the cancer would be benign, or they would survive the cancer surgery and be used by God to accomplish His purposes. I saw real hope for all of them to receive what they wanted most, wholeness. How this was going to play out was known only to the Lord. Raquel sent me two poems after this, each expressing a message of fear and hope.

I stand on the ancient cliffs of Sacred Mountain
Brave Eagle circling above me
Gazing over the lush forest below
And I call out to the Great Spirit

Hear me Great Spirit
Hear the cry of my heart
See the sadness in my tears
Feel the pain in my bones

The time is coming
The season is changing
I know it must come
I know it must change

Help me Great Spirit
Help me to trust
Fill me with your love
As I embrace the solitude once again

-Quiet Walker

Message to the system from Raquel-
The forest hears. Do not let the things of the outside world overtake your focus. Why are you anxious? Why do you worry about time, lists and chores? Do you not realize that the Great Spirit knows what must be done and when. He takes care of the birds of the air and the lilies of the field, He will take care of you and your needs. You must not allow yourself to be confused about priorities.

Seek to do the work of the Great Spirit first. Do not waste precious time with trivial worldly work that will crumble and rust away. The Great Spirit knows what must be done. If you seek first the kingdom of the Great Spirit, everything else that the Lord wants done will be done.

Listen and hear. Do not allow pressures and work of the outside world to overshadow what you have been called to do. You are servants of the Lord. Use your spirit eyes. Do not lose the opportunities the Great Spirit brings to you, because you are

preoccupied with worldly things. Trust in the Great Spirit and He will lead your path.
    -Quiet Walker

    I had begun to find out as much as I could about the inside world primarily about the Land of Preservation and how the Surface People lived. I discovered that they each had their own house decorated with their individual taste and décor. Louise cooked meals in her place and anybody that was hungry could go see her. There were fruit and nut trees in the forest for all to partake. There were streams and lakes, a desert area and a jungle, mountains and meadows, a small variety of animals and yet, even with the similarities to the outside world there were distinct differences surrounding all living things. I'll talk more about this in the next book, but I wanted to give you a snapshot of the inside world. I give this because I knew from what the Lord said through Raquel and I, that it was all going to change soon. Outside of Bruce and I, the inside world and its functioning was kept secret by the System along with their multiplicity. They knew that when the world found out, which many hoped would never happen, they would be labeled by many as delusional and the inside world could only exist in their mind. That's the main reason why these books will be a problem and rejected as fiction, by anyone who doesn't accept the possibility of a spiritual realm existing and having its own metaphysical realities.

    I believed that what they were describing was definitely true for them. I needed more time for research to understand its reality compared with my knowledge of the Kingdom of God. I recognized it as possible and consistent with much of the Bible's descriptions, but my training in Biblical and psychological criticisms caused me to withhold confirmation until God provided it. That will come in due time. My concern for the moment was the reality of the suffering endured by these souls. They each presented themselves as unique and separate individuals desiring to find truth and purpose in life. They wanted a reason to live, but if living meant more of what they had known, then that would not be reason enough to carry on. Just as God had revealed Himself to Liz directly, Jesus was revealing who God was to everyone living in Preservation. Jesus began with the children to prepare them for what was about to happen to them but He continued to also prepare the adults by building their trust in Him.

Just as it took time to prepare the System for entering into surgery in the hospital, there were also efforts put forth to prepare the surgical staff for the possibilities surrounding a multiple as a patient. As I met with the primary surgeon he seemed relieved that the decision to have me present in the operating room was taken out of his hands. I had been given legal authority to make decisions regarding the care of the System and could make sure any triggers were kept to a minimum. Nobody on either surgical team wanted to accept the possibilities that I presented of one or more of the personalities not being affected by the anesthesia and might be aware of the entire procedure.

I explained how this was the reason why we needed to prepare the System with a step-by-step procedure of surgery. No surprises... or there could be detrimental results psychologically and physically in the recovery. Nobody went into either procedure believing that what I said could happen, but all involved left the hospital with a whole new perspective of the human mind and body.

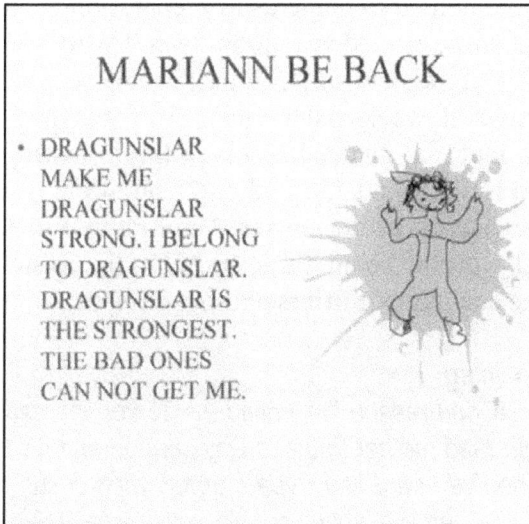

MARIANN BE BACK

- DRAGUNSLAR
  MAKE ME
  DRAGUNSLAR
  STRONG. I BELONG
  TO DRAGUNSLAR.
  DRAGUNSLAR IS
  THE STRONGEST.
  THE BAD ONES
  CAN NOT GET ME.

Mariann was the strongest part in her trust of Dragonslayer, so this child was chosen to be out for the blood draws and first to enter the O.R. She would tell everyone how she was 'Dragonslayer Strong' and lift both arms over her head to emphasize it.

This proved to be a problem for recovery in the later double mastectomy. After they were given something in the waiting room to start making them drowsy the nurse was a little upset when it had no physical affect. I noticed however that switching started to occur at a faster rate. Even as she was wheeled into surgery one part wanted to get off of the gurney and walk out. I asked for a stronger personality to switch out, or a child that would obey me before continuing. As the anesthetic was being applied switching continued at a more rapid rate and some of the parts showed its effects while others were totally aware of everything.

It took at least 40 minutes before the surgeon could actually start cutting for the biopsy. I was able to get Ann to hold on outside in a slightly drugged state so the procedure could occur. They felt no pain but were aware on the inside of everything the surgeon did on the other side of the sheet. All the anesthesiologist could do was shake his head in disbelief, while I kept Ann busy with mathematical and philosophical questions like, "Why did the chicken cross the road and how long did it take? What were the philosophical axioms at play here?" Laugh if you want but it worked to keep her out. This whole procedure helped to guide us in preparation for the big event. It also evoked some heated reactions from TWAC which was the reason we delayed the next surgery until everyone was ready.

A couple of weeks later when Ann was notified that the cancer was in fact malignant, I received the following two letters. One was from Liz's friend Jeri and one from King of Lights about the overall perspective of the cancer. The first half of Jeri's letter is mostly a thank-you for being a true friend to the System and to her indirectly. The second half offers another perspective of Liz.

Dear Pastor Chalberg,

...The second reason I'm writing this to you is to say how much I admire Liz. Ruth read me her Father's Day sermon and it's the best, most encouraging one I've heard in 13 years of following Jesus. All the others were basically the same – about people with perfect childhood's and a father like on "Leave It To Beaver." My dad is an alcoholic and committed incest with me and my sister and a very dominating man. Even though I've worked through forgiveness concerning him, I'm still afraid of him and it made my relationship with God difficult in the beginning. Guess I'm one of those Christians that got hatched wrong, like you and Liz, but that's OK with

me. Liz tells it like it is, speaking the truth accurately. It seems to me that there are quite a few people who are in need of being told what's what.

There are just too many people that need to see past the presentation of what's being said and really listen to the truth of what Liz says. All my life I've let other people's opinions dictate to me how to act, what to say, how to dress, etc. I wonder what it would feel like to just be myself, the way God created me, like Liz. She says all the things to people I wish I had the guts to say. She is honest even when it hurts. One thing about Liz, when she's your friend, what you see is what you get, no plastic, no pretense and no hypocrisy. The world and the church would be a better place if there were more honesty like Liz's around. Liz says what we are all thinking inside and wish we could say, but too many years of conditioning keep us from the boldness that Liz has. Liz is great and cares about me when nobody else around me does. She cares for my kids too. I can tell, because she wants to torture my husband physically for the way he tortures me emotionally. Don't think I'm not tempted myself. See Liz has great control – he's still alive and healthy. I'm privileged to know her. Thank you again for being her friend. ☺

It is 2AM. The system is again having a difficult time. There has not been much rest in the Land of Preservation, since the news of the dark force's invasion. The dark force has sent many smaller forces throughout the land and have begun to aggressively attack and destroy the essence of the system. There is much fear among the parts...much fear. Some parts are beginning to show weakness and falling into sickness. Some parts do not know how to fight the dark force. It is bigger and stronger than those who dwell in the Land of Preservation. It cannot be reasoned with...as its mission is destruction and death to the Surface People. The longer it is allowed to exist, the more destruction it will produce.

Fear is gaining strength. Trust is hard to achieve. Unity of purpose is a difficult process. It is said by the wise one who travels the paths of Sacred Mountain, that the system is on a journey...a journey of suffering and sorrow. It is difficult for many parts to understand this pilgrimage. But the wise one continues to speak of the lessons to be learned by the system as it enters the final phase of its travels to the high country. When asked of these lessons, the wise one speaks of forgiveness of the enemy, acceptance of the road chosen by the Great Spirit, trust in Him and surrender to His will.

Only then says the wise one, will the system be of use to the Great Spirit in telling others of the great and powerful things He has done for them...for the Great Spirit will turn that which is ugly and weak into something beautiful and strong.

There is still much fear and trembling in the Land of Preservation and the wise one continues to speak of this. She has told the Surface People not to fear...for the Great Spirit is with them and has sent two helpers to help climb the final cliffs to the high country. It is difficult for many to accept her words, for some are afraid the dark force will kill the Surface People, while others are afraid it won't bring death, only destroy the beauty of the land and make it ugly. Some are afraid the dark force will hold the Surface People hostage...slowly and painfully tormenting them until they die.

The dark force is different than any other threat the Surface People have encountered throughout their existence. All other attacks were from the outside and could not enter the Land of Preservation. Although traumatic and painful, parts were able to take refuge inside as a means of escaping from the outside attacks. Not so with the dark force, it has entered the inside world and is attacking from the inside...there is no escape. We must begin to fight the dark force we cannot waste any more time. The dark force is advancing with each hour and destroying more of the Land of Preservation. The system is becoming weaker and losing hope.

The fear is escalating and despair is surfacing in the land. We need our two outside helpers to convince the outside medicine men that we cannot continue to delay in our attack. If we do not begin soon we will lose our opportunity. We need our helpers to rally us in the attack. We cannot do it alone as we are not strong enough to fight the dark force. We need help. We need the weaker parts to be comforted and protected while we battle. We will not leave them to die on the battlefield and yet we cannot provide for them while we are fighting. We need the outside helpers to provide for them while we go to war.

We also need the outside helpers to be our spokespersons for the system. The outside medicine men have the artillery we need to fight the dark force. We need our helpers to convince these men to give us the best weapons to combat the force. We do not have the negotiating skills or the influence to sway these men to give us what is needed to win the war. We need our helpers to protect our children and fragile parts from attacks by outsiders that will draw our energy away from the war. We are weak and need to use every ounce of energy to battle the dark force. We need protection from words and deeds that will hurt the system.

We wonder if these two helpers, given us by the Great Spirit, will be committed to helping us? If they are not we will not survive, If they are we have a chance to win the war.
-Death to the dark force.

"Before all things and above all things,
Care must be taken of the sick;
So that the brethren shall minister to
them as they would to Christ himself;
For he said: 'I was sick and you visited me."
Rule of St. Benedict, 36 - 6th century

"Be joyful in hope
Patient in affliction,
Faithful in prayer.
Share with God's people
Who are in need.
Practice hospitality."
Romans 12:12-13

Chapter 16:

"Suffering can produce Perseverance..."

"A bodily disease, which we look upon as whole and
entire within itself, may, after all, be but a symptom
of some of some ailment in the spiritual part."
Nathaniel Hawthorne, The Scarlett Letter 1850

*"Don't you know that you yourselves are God's temple
and that God's Spirit lives in you? If anyone destroys
God's temple, God will destroy him; for God's temple is
sacred, and you are that temple."* 1 Cor. 3:16-17

In the weeks between the surgeries Bruce worked very hard
to contact and prepare TWAC so they wouldn't be caught off guard
again. After the biopsy Blue Devil came out in the office the week
after the surgery screaming that the light was burning him. Warnings
were coming out in code on the drawings of the children and the
children were obviously upset at the internal activity. Ruth
attempted to contact them inside and evoked a severe warning. Tolip
sent a message to Bruce and me.

*The part known as Ruth must cease her research now. You
are to order her not to investigate further. Those arrogant parts are
not to come near us or we will draw up arms against them. They
know nothing of us save Keeper of History. Tell Ruth that she does
not know what she is saying. It has nothing to do with surgery lights.
It is the light that burns him. Blue Devil burns with the light and
must be in the box or hidden under that which shields him from the
light. We have placed a shield over his eyes to be with you. If we did
not, he would growl and scream in agony at the light.*

*Blue Devil does not speak, as he knows the tongue will be
cut out if he speaks of that which he knows. Do not force him to
speak. To write is not to speak. Do you not know he holds that which
Mariann cannot? He is Core. Those above have caused tremendous*

explosions by forcing the cutting. We will retaliate if they continue to force Blue Devil to be sacrificed. So they know that we will not surrender, we have given them a warning. Do not take our warnings lightly.

Watcher has informed us of your encounter with Blue Devil. Why do you not understand the message of Blue Devil? Tolip has allowed the coded message to be given to you, yet you do not understand. Tolip is frustrated. A good commander knows how to decode that which is too secret to reveal. All has important meaning, communicate when you have understood the code:

*1. Blue Devil   2. Light burns him   3. DIS   4. Drink Blood   5. 666
6. Get on the table   7. Let it be done   8. It is done   9. Priest
10. Black Box   11. Belongs to 666   12. SREYARP*

Tolip did not intend for Blue Devil to be seen by you so quickly. Blue Devil had much difficulty on Monday and forces were on guard that the cutter would not kill Blue Devil, as we had heard from Watcher that those above were cutting out the evil inside. We will not allow them to cut out Blue Devil. (See drawing on page 232 by Tabitha of SRA abuses within the Catholic Church. The 'baby' at the bottom is referring to Blue Devil still hidden in CORE.)

The goat is dead. Drink the blood. The Beast has arrived. Let the power be shown.
-Epistler

You can imagine the concern we had over this turn of events. We went to work to decode the message, based on the limited knowledge we had about TWAC and the Pod Children, especially Blue Devil. We were caught in a time crunch here to understand enough to prepare Core for intensive surgery and do it without revealing too much to the already distraught and weak Surface People. Elizabeth Ray and Raquel proved invaluable at this time. Bruce worked on communicating with Tolip about the reason for the biopsy and more importantly the upcoming double mastectomy. He had to prepare them in detail as to the procedure, so they would be on guard to understand that the surgeon was not attempting to kill Blue Devil. Since I was going to be the one in the O.R. again, I needed to be clear with them that I would protect them on the outside and make sure the procedure was followed to the letter.

CONTENT WARNING!

We were able to decode enough information from several sources, that it was Blue Devil and Egar who were subjected to the Satanic Ritual Abuse in place of Tabitha and Mariann. Blue Devil received the most severe abuse physically. The High Priest, wearing a goat mask, would perform the ritual including the drinking of blood in their communion. At one point in the offering of the child to Satan's dominion, a crucifix was heated to a bluish glow of the head of Christ and inserted into the vagina. This was done repeatedly and with other objects over a period of time. We know that there were Catholic priests involved at some levels in these rituals and again with animal sacrifices in the Santeria cults. We haven't pursued the names of these individuals, nor do we plan to in the future. What we were concerned about then was how we can help the surviving victims. With this in mind, we learned of more triggers that could cause reactions from Core.

There was one more connotation related to the 'light that burns'. Only I had a clue about what it was at this time. I would continue to pray for guidance from the Lord to affirm my suspicions and direct me how best to deal with this at the proper time. I also had to prepare another surgical team since the former doctor would not be the one doing this surgery. We were told of this at the last minute with very little time to prepare them. Meanwhile, Circle Council had to draw the System together to vote on whether or not to continue treatment. A majority voted to continue so now our task was to have everyone on board with specifics on what we expected to happen with the surgery. All realized that when everything was said and done there was no choice left but to trust Jesus.

End warning!

Council meeting – Scribe: Elizabeth Ray
Helper: This meeting is called to order. Has everyone arrived?
Jennifer: Marie is missing.
Paladin: Go get her.
Ann: Those Who Are Core and that prayer group aren't here.
Paladin: Word has been sent out that they are welcome to send a representative and they may have Watcher observe if they are uncomfortable with that.
King of Lights: Marie is present.

Helper: The leaders of Circle Council have called this meeting together with all of you to discuss our reasoning for taking control of the present situation. We also wish to answer any questions you might have and listen to your concerns.

King of the Lights: Council has known for some time that we might be placed in this most difficult situation as leaders of the Land of Preservation. As you know, our number one concern is and always has been preservation of the system. We've spent considerable time researching the possibilities and best decision for all of us. After careful investigation, we were able to make a swift decision based upon the facts presented and have planned a course of action carefully. If the lumpectomy was benign, council agreed to do nothing at the present time and have annual mammograms. If it was malignant, we felt we had three choices: 1) choose to do nothing and let nature take its course; 2) Go through extensive radiation treatment and removal of the lymph nodes for analysis of further invasion of the cancer into the body and; 3) remove the breast and have limited chemotherapy.

Choice one went against the purpose of Circle Council in keeping the system alive and without treatment research indicated that we would probably be dead within 8 weeks, so we rejected it. Choice number two involved approximately two months of going to the hospital for radiation treatments and surgery. There are several problems with this choice. We do not have the ability to control switching in intense circumstances yet and the children especially have trouble switching with so many triggers in the hospital environment. Two months of constant switching each day would be too exhausting for us, although this choice might prolong keeping the breast for a longer period of time.

Council has been aware for a long time that the dark force has been present in the system and we know it is further along than the outside doctors realize. That is why council is so adamant about taking choice number three. We could insist that Pastor Chalberg be in the OR again to control the switching as he did before. Doctor Ku is familiar with Pastor Chalberg's ways and appreciated him being in surgery and seems reasonably comfortable with the multiplicity. Removal of the breast and lymph nodes would increase the survival chances, with limited chemotherapy being short term instead of long. If the cancer has spread further than we know, then we suggest removing all treatments and allowing the system to die a natural death. As far as we know now, we have at least stage two cancer. We know that overweight women have a poorer prognosis and Latinos have an even poorer prognosis than whites. (Council proceeds to give very detailed medical information unnecessary for the purposes of the book so it's edited out.)

Ann has questioned Kaiser extensively for more information, but they are not giving any satisfactory amounts of information. For now, be prepared that if we are at stage three, they might still require radiotherapy of external-beam irradiation to the chest wall along with chemotherapy. Based on our findings, COUNCIL HAS VOTED FOR MODIFIED RADICAL MASTECTOMY WITH AUXILLARY DISSECTION AND ADJUVANT COMBINATION CHEMO.

Liz: You sound like a bunch of damn doctors. We don't want to hear this crap.

Ann: Speak for yourself Liz!

Liz: All I know is I ain't dying. I'm going to Disneyland with Chalberg whether you guys like it or not.

Ann: Shut up about Disneyland. I've heard just about enough of the LA trip as I can stand Liz. Will you get serious about something for once in your life!

Liz: Why? Seriousness only causes high blood pressure and cancer. Look at you, you're the one with cancer, so why the hell do I have to die too. You die.

Maria: When we die Helper, I want a pine coffin and maybe Raquel will put that nice Indian blanket over us with a yellow daisy for each part. Maybe we could be buried in a forest instead of a cemetery and Pastor Chalberg could say the words over our coffin, OK? Only he and Carol and Bruce and Lindsay can come, nobody else please.

Ruth: We need to focus on living and not think about dying. We must remain strong in the Lord and fight this cancer.

Ann: DO NOT BRING GOD IN TO THIS!

Liz: Let's bring God into this. I want to know if God believes in equality and civil rights. God is supposed to be just and all of that. So OK I understand that shit happens and I'm willing to accept the fallen world crap and sin and all that shit. But why doesn't God spread it around equally? How come Jon is born, gets hit by a car and in a wheelchair, his mother dies, his house burns down, he has a blood transfusion and gets AIDS and then dies. And then look at Maria. Other people who aren't as nice as Jon and Maria ever have any suffering. Money flows in like water, vacations every year, a new car in the garage and life just gets peachier and creamier. Now why did God dis Maria and favor the wicked assholes of this world?

Daniel: We are not to question the whys but instead deal with what we have been given.

Ann: Why? I thought God was logical. Liz is right in her argument. God's dishing out of shit is not logical.

Raquel: Ann...are you looking at it from the Great Spirit's point of view or from your point of view? Maybe logical has a whole different definition to the Great Spirit than it does to you.

Ann: Look, God created man in his image, so if he made man to have the same characteristics as he does, then logic is the same for God as it is to man.

Helper: We need to get back on focus about the cancer.

Liz: NO! I want to know why so much shit and why we are singled out?

King of Lights: Then go ask God.

Maria: Listen! Do you hear singing...I hear it. In my life Lord be glorified, be glorified. In my suffering Lord be glorified, be glorified. In my...

Ann: Shut up! Damn prayer nuts. They are absolutely no help...

Ruth: Ann why is it that when Maria says shut up to you, you become enraged with her disrespect, but yet it is alright for you to tell me and Liz and the others to shut up. You show us disrespect by not allowing us to express ourselves.

Ann: Helper, I'm not going to tolerate this attack on me much more. If you do not stop this I'm leaving the meeting.

Helper: We all need to calm down. Look at our situation this way. Several of you are saving money to see Independence Day. In it the aliens invade earth and all of the people rally together and set aside their differences to defend the earth, to defeat the common foe. It is like that with us. The cancer is the alien...the dark force that has invaded Land of Preservation. The Surface People must come together as one to fight this enemy for the good of all. If we continue to fight amongst ourselves and divide our forces, the cancer will win and we will die. WE ARE ALL BEING PURSUED BY THIS DARK FORCE, WE ALL HAVE CANCER.

Louise: Please don't let them take my breast. Please, it is something that is important to me, because I like to look like I do. Please Helper, don't cut off my breast. Please don't...

Liz: We don't need them Louise. Hell I've waited a long time. These weights cramp my style. Ever try to bungee jump with thirty pounds wrapped around your neck?

Maria: We don't bungee jump and we want to have our breasts please. Louise and me won't be bad, please don't cut us up.

Ruth: You aren't bad and it will be OK. Maria it will all work out OK.

Jennifer: Liz says that God told her that our suffering would not end in death. Well, what if we die on the table, then he isn't keeping his promise is he? I don't think I've ever seen anyone with as much bad karma as us.

Raquel: Was the Great Spirit speaking of physical death or spiritual death? You must listen and look deeply into the Great Spirit's words. I have learned that in reading Psalm 91.

Liz: Just tell me why so much shit?

Raquel: I do not know your answer Liz. But I do know that those sheep nearest the fence are the ones who suffer the most as they are closest to the gate and they are the ones that the evil one is most afraid of, for they encourage the lost sheep to take the gate. The evil one will do much harm to those sheep to discourage them and influence them to go far from the fence and feast on the delicacies that their brothers and sisters enjoy deep inside the land of paradise. The sheep closest to the fence have the most scars from the attacks of the evil one, but they also have the closeness of the gate. If they keep their eyes on the gate, they will have the strength to endure the attacks. The gate is strong. The evil one has hit the gate with its most powerful force and yet the gate has not lost its hinges, it remains intact. Remember, the sheep have the choice as to which way they shall go, back out by the gate, or deep into the land of paradise where the lost sheep can never hear them to enter the gate. But the gate remains strong and is the only way into paradise. The fence sheep bring much glory to the gate and much fear to the evil one. The fence sheep suffer, but rejoice, for they shall receive their reward for obedience and diligence to the gate.

Ann: Gates! Raquel you really need to get a life.

Raquel: Like hang wallpaper all day, Ann?

Liz: Shit, you need a mathematical genius to hang that complex wallpaper.

Ann: Precisely!

Helper: Can we bring this conversation back to the cancer issue?

Tabitha: Go nite nite.

King of lights: The children are tired and we are beginning to lose fragile parts. I move for an adjournment and we can reconvene tomorrow.

Late Thursday Night: 2AM

Ann: Helper next time I want a vote. Ruth had no right making the decision for the system. I don't have much time to get this house together before surgery and I didn't want to spend the time going to camp.

Ruth: We needed the break Ann and it was nice that Joni and the gang sent that car to pick us up and take us to camp. The card they made meant a lot to Maria and Louise liked the shirt and I needed the fellowship.

Ann: But Liz didn't need to spend an hour talking to the director of the seminary. What is it with her lately? Why is she so obsessed with this mission of hers lately? She has absolutely no background to be arguing with the head of Bible studies of a prestigious seminary...she's going to embarrass me.

Helper: I'll admit that Liz does not fit into the boundaries of that Christian environment very well, but she has a right to be herself Ann. He doesn't know you so you don't need to worry about being embarrassed.

Liz: F&%? off Ann.

Ann: Just drop it Liz. Let's discuss Chalberg's offer and the other offer.

Jennifer: What offer?

Paladin: Mr. Chalberg has offered to allow us to stay at his place for awhile until we can heal, rather than returning home to the unrest. The fundamentalist from Brentwood offered to let us stay with her...

413

Liz: Forget the fundamentalist. She just wants to lock us in a room and preach at me about God and do exorcisms. I'd rather die than be trapped by her.

Daniel: I've discussed this with the kids and they want to go away from the mean boy.

Ruth: I've talked to Sergio about it and he agrees that it would be better for the system to be out of the house. He thinks we can heal faster in an environment where the demands on us will be relaxed. At home we will be around the contractor and the kids will be expecting us to cook, clean and take care of them. The phone will be ringing and people will come over and expect to be entertained.

Helper: Circle Council has been talking about the needs of the system after surgery. We need first a quiet place of refuge, with a bed, toilet and shower. We need a cooler for juice and food. We need a place where no one will be upset with the switching. We need to be alone to restore the body and outside helpers to comfort the children if needed.

Ann: He isn't going to be preaching to us, is he?

Ruth: No, Ann, he is not offering you this to preach at you. He is offering this to you because he cares about you and he wants the best fir you.

Jennifer: We need to find out how his wife feels about this. Maybe she doesn't want us there with all of the stress she is under with the house and stuff.

Liz: She won't mind, she's in Norway.

Ann: I'm not going if she's not there.

Helper: Let's get back to the issue. Do you think it would be better to stay at Mr. Chalberg's for awhile until we are strong enough to face all of the responsibilities at home? Those in favor say yes. Those opposed say no. Yes has it. We will accept Mr. Chalberg's offer, providing Mrs. Chalberg agrees to it.

Raquel: I wish to speak.

Helper: Go ahead and speak.

Raquel: The Great Spirit has spoken to the system as I walked the paths of Sacred Mountain. I wish to reveal what the Great Spirit has said.

King of Lights: You have our ears.

Raquel: My Precious Child, I know your pain. I know the heaviness of your heart.

(Raquel would present the full unedited version of the letter given at the end of the Prologue. You may review it again and put it in the context of what you are reading now.)

King of Lights: Thank you Quiet Walker for giving us the words of the Great Spirit.

Tabitha: Jesus me ama Si Jesus me ama y Jesus te ama.

Maria: Can I please be excused?

Helper: Are you OK Maria?

Maria: I want to be alone for a little bit please.

Helper: OK Maria, but don't you want to be a part of the discussion about the cancer?

Maria: No. Is Pastor Chalberg going to be there for sure?

Helper: Yes.

Maria: No other people come into the room and hurt me?

Paladin: We have deputized Mr. Chalberg as the outside protector while we are in the hospital. He will be on guard.

Maria: OK, I'll be brave.

Jennifer: How do we know that this is a letter from the Great Spirit? I don't mean to be disrespectful Quiet Walker, but there are many spirits.

Raquel: That is true One Who Loves the Birds. So that your mind may be put to ease, ask the One Who Listens or Shedding Tear.

Jennifer: It doesn't matter to me, I just wondered.

Louise: It matters to me, I want to know Raquel.

Helper: Louise, you can call Bruce and read him the letter and ask if it sounds like it has come from the Great Spirit or another spirit. If it is from another spirit, ask which spirit and the same with Mr. Chalberg.

Louise: OK.

Liz: I ain't giving up. I'm going to Disneyland with Chalberg.

Ann: I wish I had the money to send you just to shut you up about it.

(This went on for awhile until Helper brought them back.)

Helper: Girls! Remember what I said about the movie Independence Day. Let's get back on the topic of cancer. How is everyone feeling about this now? Let's start on this side of the circle.

Liz: Shit, I've been through worse.

415

Ann: I'm frustrated.

Louise: Maybe they got the wrong records and we don't have cancer and they don't have to cut my body off and I can keep it.

Tabitha: no corta no corta no sangre no Tabitha no want.

Angelina: dada bye bye nina

Anna: Lady got cut and die

Jennifer: We have bad karma

Marie: I want to stay home.

Ruth: I am still trying to hold on with the diagnosis. I didn't think we had cancer.

Mariann: I don't want them to cut my bumps please. I will be good. I want the Dragonslayer to take the bad out please.

Mari: I need to leave please.

Helper: It is OK to be afraid and have feelings. We are going to rely on outsiders to help us through this ordeal. We are not strong enough yet to control switching and assertive enough to protect ourselves. We will need to turn over a lot of control to outsiders, but we have chosen carefully and it is not being taken from us, for we are giving it to them. It will be relinquished to only two people, Bruce F. and Michael Chalberg. Bruce and Chalberg will be in charge of working through the red tape of Kaiser and helping us make decisions.

Ann: Place Chalberg first and Bruce second.

Louise: Why Ann?

Ann: It's logical that Chalberg would be the first choice. He's not trying to raise three young children, teach at college, run a counseling center and who knows what else. Bruce means well, but he just doesn't have the time to fight Kaiser and deal with this level of need. I've watched Chalberg. He's logical and will ask good questions. He seems to want to keep us alive so he will fight for our survival. Kaiser can be hell to fight, I know. Remember Martinez guys? As much as I hate to admit it, Chalberg is a white male, well educated and will get more respect and acceptance than I ever would.

Louise: You're smart Ann.

Ann: Tell the male population that. Remember when I went in Louise, the guy was cordial but I know what they thought. Overweight and Latina makes one a stupid broad. Remember when he said those are phenomenal questions you ask and kept stressing that...good question...excellent questions, like he was surprised I could even ask that type...like we don't have a brain and can think. Chalberg will have an easier time cutting through their crap.

Helper: I don't understand this anger you have Ann about society's view of your intelligence. We know you're smart.

Liz: Yeah Ann! Why DID the chicken cross the road?

Ann: Shut up about chickens! You know I wasn't thinking straight. I don't want to hear any more about Chalberg and chickens. Why don't you tell me something about prime distribution, or the concept of congruences and their relationship to congruent numbers?

Liz: I DON'T DO MATH!

Helper: Enough Gauss mathematics, Ann. I have never seen a group more able to divert from the agenda than all of you, so please stay on topic.

Tabitha: Nite Nite

Helper: Please take the children to bed Louise.

Daniel: I'm concerned that the children do not fully understand what is happening to the body and maybe they can't. They are extremely scared of being cut and being in unfamiliar environments. Since they switch out at stressful times, I need to be reassured that Mr. Chalberg will be able to rotate them back inside before they become hysterical. I believe they are trying very hard to obey us and stay inside, but their memories are very powerful and trigger them out. We need to be sensitive to their dilemma and not yell at them for switching. We need to be prepared knowing this will happen.

Ann: Will Kaiser allow us to have a private room at no charge, due to our situation? If we must be in a room with three other cancer patients, it will be too much stress for them and us trying to heal. We can't guarantee that a child won't switch out at night and try to get home or get lost in the hospital. We can't guarantee there won't be nightmares with screaming either. At least at home we can lock the doors and deal with it in the privacy of our bedroom. Hiding our multiplicity in a hospital will be almost impossible. When we were having children, the nurses thought we were hallucinating from medication when a child part switched out and I was much stronger then. How are we going to get through this without looking stark raving mad?

Helper: If we look mad, then we look mad. We will rely on Mr. Chalberg to explain things to the nurses in charge of us and to oversee any difficulties. He will be there during high stress times like giving of shots, IV tubes inserted, blood taken, etc.

Ann: But he can't be there around the clock, so what are we going to do? Circle Council cannot handle this and you know it. There are too many triggers in the hospital setting. Needles, knives, masks, blood, cutting, being inspected, catheters and all things we can't foresee, are going to send us out of control. We aren't strong enough yet and we can't wait until we are. We are in a catch 22 situation and I don't like being there.

Paladin: Our goals are to keep the system alive and protect the system from harm. We will use whatever methods work to accomplish this. Ann, our pride is not our number one goal…survival is. I don't like being placed in this either, but we are here and we need to make the best of it. Mr. Chalberg will be crucial in helping us survive this ordeal and we will need to allow him to guide us and be our advocate while we are in the hospital. We also need to entrust our children to his care and trust that he will explain to the doctors and nurses what they need to know to help us heal and not make it worse for us. He will have the power to determine who needs to know what and how much and we will be working on the inside to try and keep the parts calm and safe. This is all we can do.

Helper: What our needs are while inside the hospital is what we're discussing now. We need to be left alone as much as possible while procedures are being done to us. Had not Mr. Chalberg been in surgery for the lumpectomy, they never would have gotten the IV in with the children aware of the needle. We have to avoid being tied down or sat upon to be given a shot. We need privacy to avoid being stared at by outsiders. When the children eat, it can be very humiliating for an adult to switch out with ice cream and cookies shoved in our mouth, or juice running down our chin. We will need to substitute coloring and playtime with having someone read a story. We need to be prepared if Tabitha is catheterized, as she was the child that had 'cleanings' done to her after Angelina was molested. A tube was inserted in her that filled her vagina and uterus with hot soapy water to rid her of any evidence of foul play. She has so many triggers that we will need to watch her if she is out, so that

418

she doesn't rip out any tubes attached to the body. We'll need an outsider to monitor her as well.

Ann: This is not going to work, Circle Council. Mr. Chalberg might be good at what he does, but don't you think he is out of his league? He can't handle this much.

Helper: We've attempted to prepare him as best we can. Being a multiple in surgery and dealing with cancer is foreign to us too. There are no books or studies to help us know what to expect (Not until now). *We are charting unknown territory and so is he. We would not hold it against him if he chose not to be involved in this. We think he knows this and he knows he has a choice to be there or not and he's chosen to be there. We are grateful and it isn't a matter of how much he can handle Ann, he will handle what he can and so will we.*

Keeper of Functions: Do any of the parts know of any other need we might have in the hospital?

Ann: Chalberg will need to monitor visitors. Word gets out to the family and who knows who will show up. We don't want a lot of visitors and Chalberg will need to remove them if they don't allow us to rest.

Helper: We've given him approval for the following visitors only: Bruce, Greg, Carol C., Jeri, Carol P., Lindsay, Bill & Kathleen G., Sergio and the kids. He is to be on guard against all other extended family. Also, Bruce will need to work with Maria and Louise about the loss of their breast. These two seem to be having the hardest time with council's decision and they will need support time with him.

Liz: What about Core? Tolip is still a whimp for not coming to face me.

King of Lights: We have extended an invitation to them to send a representative to Circle Council, but they have chosen not to do so. It is our hope that they are monitoring our meetings through Watcher. We do not wish them harm and we are not sacrificing Blue Devil. We are only trying to save the body that houses all of the parts, including Blue Devil. We hope that Bruce can get that message through in time before the surgery.

Helper: Does anyone else have a question?

Ann: Why is Chalberg spending so much of his prime time to help us? What is it he wants from us?

Ruth: Nothing. He just cares about us.

Ann: Why?

Ruth: I guess he is just that kind of guy.

Ann: It is not logical and he seems so logical to me. I really can't figure him out.

Liz: Shit Ann, what is there to figure out? He got hatched wrong and we got hatched wrong, so hatched wrong seeks out hatched wrong...logic!

Ann: Sounds more like psychology to me Liz.

Liz: Shit, maybe he just likes your logical mind Ann. It gives him some variety in his dull pastor's life.

Ann: Shut up Liz!

Helper: Let's adjourn before we begin the war all over again.

Obviously, Circle Council had given their situation a great deal of thought and prayer... so had I. They didn't know it, but this was not the first time I had been given authority to make life and death decisions in a surgical setting. It was however the first time with a multiple and I knew there were more 'lives' at stake here than outsiders were aware. There was minimal documentation available about what could happen with a multiple having surgery. There was nothing I could find extensive enough to offer to Council that would calm their fears. This is part of the reason why I've documented everything they were going through, to help others in situations like this. I will go through two more major surgeries with the System in the next six years. One thing was consistent, the inability of the doctors to accept what they experienced with their own eyes. Some of the nursing staff made inquiries of a positive nature.

One doctor was honest enough to say to me afterwards, "I have to put what happened in there out of my mind. It goes against everything I've learned about practicing medicine. If I don't put it out of my mind I will have to quit. I can do this (practice medicine) because I know I'll probably never see a case like this again. If I do, can I call you?" I told him he could call but I wouldn't be of much help, because it takes a long time to build the trust necessary to be able to help a multiple in this way. It doesn't happen overnight. I said that I would pray for him that it doesn't occur again, because it would be a shame to lose a good surgeon who is willing to admit what he doesn't understand. We had less than a week before surgery so I talked often with the people of the System to relieve their fears. Of course the enemy was doing just the opposite. The House of Prayer's response was:

O Lord have mercy on us in our anguish. Our eyes are red from weeping. Our health is broken from sorrow and disease. We are weakening each day with grief. Our years are shortened, drained away because of sadness. We are filled with sorrow and shame. We are scorned by our enemies and even more by our family. They laugh at us and look the other way when we go by. We are forgotten like a dead man, like a broken and discarded water pot. We hear the lies about us, the slander of our enemies. Everywhere we look we are afraid. Help us O Lord to trust you in the hour of our need.
-Heavenly Dove

The following message was sent to me from Raquel to help all of us be aware of the battle we were about to face. The entity is known in the Southwest Native American spiritual rituals as Masauwu, the 'god' of fire and destruction and known to be very powerful. The Great Spirit is known to be stronger!

Masauwu is here and he is angry
He has come to take them back
He is very supreme – evil supreme
He has come to fight for them

Deity of fire and death
Ruler of Middle and Lower World
He has come to take them back

Every night he walks around the edge
Carrying a flaming torch
The face of death – Masauwu is in the atmosphere
He will not release without a fight

Masauwu is strong
Dragonslayer is strong
The battle begins

Dark against light – Evil against good
Masauwu against Dragonslayer
Masauwu will not give up easily
Masauwu will not release willingly

Masauwu knows
What will happen if he loses them
Masauwu knows

- *Quiet Walker*

Ruth had Maria write down the promises of God to help calm her fears each time that she became frightened during the week. She did as instructed and finished the night before the surgery by writing these letters to Jesus.

God says, "For I know the plans I have for you, says the Lord. They're plans for good and not for evil, to give you a future and a hope."

God says, "I have loved you with an everlasting love."

God says, "But now the Lord who created you says do not be afraid for I have ransomed you. I have called you by name. You are mine. When you go through deep waters and great trouble, I will be with you. When you go through rivers of difficulty, you will not drown! When you walk through the fires of oppression, you will not be burned up – the flames will not consume you. For I am the Lord your God, your Savior, the Holy One of Israel. Do not fear for I am with you."

"Fear not for I am with you, fear not! Do not be dismayed for I am your God. I will strengthen you and uphold you with my victorious right hand."

"Don't you understand…don't you know by now that the everlasting God, the Creator of the farthest parts of the earth, never grows faint or weary? No one can fathom the depths of his understanding. He gives power to the tired and worn out, and strength to the weak. Even the youth shall be exhausted and the young men will all give up. But they that wait upon the Lord shall renew their strength. They

shall mount up with wings like eagles. They shall run and not be weary, they shall walk and not grow faint."

God says, "Because Maria loves me, I will rescue her. I will make her great because she trusts in my name. When she calls on me, I will answer. I will be with her in trouble and rescue her and honor her. I will satisfy her with a full life and give her my salvation."

Letters to Jesus and His letters back to her:

Maria-
*   I want you to trust me in your times of trouble, so I can rescue you and you can give me the glory.*
Trust Me,
Jesus

Dear Jesus
*   Please help me to trust you, please.*
Love
Maria

Maria-
*   I will send help from heaven to save you because of your love and faithfulness. I will rescue you. I will help you Maria.*
Trust Me,
Jesus

Dear Jesus
*   You are going to send me bright ones to help me. You are going to come get me and take me to heaven so I can be with you. I won't be afraid Jesus.*
Love lots,
Maria

Maria-
*   I will send help from heaven to strengthen your heart. I will protect you from the fatal plague. I have chosen you from the weakest. I will steady you and make you strong Maria. I will bless you constantly and surround you with my love. You will be great because of me. I will keep my promises.*
Jesus

Dear Jesus

Thank you so much for your kindness. I know you don't lie and I know you keep your promises. What is great, Jesus? What are you going to do to me? I don't know Jesus, but if you want to do it, it's OK. Cuz I know you are safe and won't do bad to me. I want to do what makes you real happy, cuz it makes me happy and I love you.
Love
Maria
PS: Jesus can I go to sleep now, I'm tired?

Maria-
Go to sleep little one.
Love
Jesus

Dear Jesus

I'm getting scared again so Ruth said to write to you again. I got to go to church today and sing. I like to sing to you Jesus. People prayed for me today and I liked the praying. They prayed for Pastor Chalberg too cuz he's got to have lots of energy and know what to do.

I went to my Sunday School class and the teaching people told us things about you. Why don't I think things like them Jesus? Cuz they say trust Jesus and everything will be OK and you have peace. They say trust you and be happy. But Liz was going back and forth inside like the dogs at the kennel and she said say something or I will.

I said that it is sometimes hard for me to trust you. I want to but it gets hard and I have to pray lots for you to help me trust you. I am not as strong as the other people when they can trust you so easily. It's real hard for me and they make me sad that I can't do it all of the time like them.

Jesus I'm trying so real hard. You have the boat and I got in it and the storm is big and crashing against the boat. It's making it go back and forth and I am real scared. The other people say they wouldn't be scared but I am Jesus. I'm scared and I'm still in your boat. So can I trust you and still be scared?
Love from me.

Maria-

To trust me is to let me take the situation and get you through it. Yes, you can trust me and still be afraid. I was afraid in the garden, but I still trusted my Father. You are still in my boat. Although the waters around you are frightening, if you stay in my boat you will not drown. Remember my promises to you, Maria. Keep on believing my promises. I don't lie. I don't change my mind like humans do. I have never promised something and not done it. Maria you need to persevere so that when you have done my will, you will receive what I have promised.
Jesus

Dear Jesus

I am going to hold on to you real tight. I hope I don't squeeze you too tight, cuz I don't want to make you black and blue. Jesus, how come Pastor Chalberg is so nice to me? I think he is the most like you cuz he's got real love in him. I never had anybody love me like him and I like it lots. He said I could pretend he is my dad, cuz I always wanted a dad with real love. You know, when I am with Pastor Chalberg it is like I am with you. I think your love comes out of his skin. I was real scared when he told my children about my parts and when he knocked on my door, I almost said come in Jesus cuz I needed you. When he talked to me I could hear you Jesus. Why does Pastor Chalberg be so nice?
I love you
Maria

(I met with Maria's family for the first time to explain to them about her multiplicity, the cancer and what to expect during her recovery. I had her wait in her room because she had kept her multiplicity hidden from her children throughout their lives. The embarrassment of having them learn the truth was overwhelming for her. Everyone had the opportunity to ask any questions they wanted, but very few were asked. I believe that like the husband, it was easier to accept her as 'crazy' than understand the complexity of what they were hearing. While they all loved Maria it was easier to continue loving only one person rather than trying to accept all of them. The only question they were concerned with beyond Maria's immediate danger with the cancer was 'when will she be fixed?' They weren't ready to hear the only answer I had for this question. None of her children or her husband has made any effort to discover the truth about Maria's life as a multiple to date, at least not through me. Denial can be a strong inhibitor to overcoming a person's fears of what the truth might mean to them personally and how that truth might change their life.)

Maria-
    You are Pastor Chalberg's Mephebosheth. He is looking for a way to express his gratitude for what I have done for him. And thus, he has adopted you and shows kindness to you, the least of this daughter of mine. For when he does these things for you, he is doing them to me.
Jesus

Dear Jesus
    What is Mephebosheth?
Love Maria

Maria-
    Ask Ruth to tell you the story of Jonathan's son.
Jesus

Dear Jesus
    The sun is going to come up soon. I can't breath again. My air isn't going in good. Pastor Chalberg told me it's anxiety and told me to talk to you. Do you hear the ones inside? They sing lots. I think they were singing when Liz walked to Safeway cuz we got a paper for free eggs. They sang – In our life Lord be glorified and in our suffering Lord be glorified. Now they are singing – Oh give thanks to the Lord for he is good. His love and his kindness go on forever.
I feel better.
Love
Maria
PS: Jesus I feel sad for the people who got killed in the plane and in the Olympics. Why are people so cruel?

Maria-

If my people will humble themselves and pray and search for me and turn from their wicked ways, I will hear them from heaven and forgive their sins and heal their land.

Jesus

Maria-

I want you to trust me in your time of trouble with the cancer, so I can rescue you and you give me the glory.

Trust in Me

Jesus

**"These things I have spoken to you, while living with you.
But the Helper, the Holy Spirit, whom the Father will
send in My name, He will teach you all things, and
bring to your remembrance all that I said to you.
Peace I leave with you; My peace I give to you;
not as the world gives, do I give to you.
Let not your heart be troubled,
nor let it be fearful...
These things I have
spoken to you that
in Me you may have
peace. In the world you
have Tribulation, but have courage;
I have overcome the world."
John 14 & 16**

Chapter 17:

"Does Cancer Become a Game Changer"

> **"I do not seek to understand in order that I may believe,**
> **But I believe in order that I may understand."**
> Anselm, *Proslogium* 11th century

"Obey My voice, and I will be your God and you will be My people;
and you will walk in all the way which I command you,
that it may be well with you... But this is the covenant
which I will make... after those days, Declares the Lord,
'I will put My law within them, and on their heart I will write it;
and I will be their God, and they shall be My people."
-Jeremiah 7:23, 31:33

> **"Faith consists in believing when it is beyond**
> **the power of reason to believe.**
> **It is not enough that a thing be possible for it to be believed."**
> -Voltaire, 1764

Maria gave me the letters to Jesus and His responses to her, as we were entering the hospital on Wednesday morning. I wouldn't have time to read them until three weeks later. When I did... I had mixed emotions about them. I knew immediately that they were true. They were written by Maria, with someone responding for Jesus in the power of the Holy Spirit. They were exhilarating for me to read Jesus' responses and encouraging to read Maria's responses as well. I had mixed feelings about her perspective and feelings about me. On the one hand it is very humbling and mystically exciting to be compared to Jesus, because it is my primary goal to become as much like Him as I possibly can.

Yet, it is also very humbling and even a little frightening to realize the responsibility that places on me with any individual. Especially since I know myself and how far from Him I have fallen through my sinful human nature. Many times over the coming years I will tell her to talk to Jesus about her feelings for me. Some of her friends my wife included, will tell her it is wrong to love someone that much. How we work through this issue with Jesus, friends and assorted other people will be recorded throughout books 2 & 3. For right now as I am writing the conclusion of the first book, I had to ask Jesus and Maria again about their thoughts on my issue of pride. Should I leave Maria's words in or edit them out? Jesus told me:

"Did I not tell you to write the truth of what I have done and I'm doing in their own words and yours...and in My words? Do you want to alter My task for you because it makes you uncomfortable before My children? Remember what this book means for My children who do not yet know Me...and for those who think they know Me. Remember as well why I sent you to Maria and all my children of the System...and how difficult for them it is to have their stories told. I love you My child...do not be concerned about what others think of you for I will be with you. Remember Ezekiel's task in chapter 2 and Trust Me."

It is difficult to explain why this issue is so hard for me to express to anyone and I hope it will become easier in the following books. For the moment know that the verse, "Pride goes before the fall," continues to be my lifelong struggle. My heart's desire is to boast only in Jesus and bring all honor and glory to Him.

I received word from Kaiser that the doctor who did the biopsy was not available and another surgeon was to do the double mastectomy. This meant a whole new surgical team. All they were told before we entered the O.R. was that my presence was mandatory. I gave crash courses to each attendant as they appeared on the scene with only enough information about the System, as they needed to know to perform their task in Pre-op, the O.R. and in recovery. I wasn't a happy camper but I knew we couldn't delay any longer just to accommodate a new team. I'll let Elizabeth Ray tell you from her journals about the surgery and what follows over the next two weeks. My observations and perspective are in parenthesis.

Wednesday morning, Mr. Chalberg picks up the system at their home and takes them to Kaiser Hospital for surgery. We are listed as confidential in admittance. Pre-op was difficult with cartoons on TV and Mariann switched out during undressing of system when a nurse walked in on her. Council had decided that Mariann would be out for surgery based on the following reasons: 1) Mariann has a very strong tie to Mr. Chalberg and will obey his authority. 2) Mariann has enough communication skills and developmental skills to answer questions and follow simple commands. 3) Mariann is not humiliated or embarrassed by the body being viewed by men or women. 4) Mariann is easy to sidetrack during procedures. 5) Mariann has an inner strength and is the healthiest of all of the parts at this time. (Well…the best laid plans…Mariann began with the first nurse by asking her if she knew Dragonslayer and hasn't stopped asking people since. There was a lot of switching in pre-op after they administered the first sedative to Mariann. Some parts were clear in that they wanted to leave – NOW! Getting them to rotate in became easier as the drug took affect. Most of them didn't have the same attitude and spirit of Mariann of being 'Dragonslayer strong.')

Surface people were experiencing reactions in the Land of Preservation as medication was administered. At first they experienced raining in the land that was immediately followed with snowing. Snowing slowed down movement in the land and it eventually went into a type of winter shut down. (There are no notes again until the end of surgery. I talked briefly with the team in the O.R. as they were prepping Mariann. I could tell from the glazed look in their eyes that they were not listening and the only response was, "Well maybe we won't have to experience any of that."

A few eyebrows were raised when it took the anesthesiologist longer to knock them out than normal and different parts were switching out. The body appeared to be sedated according to the monitors with only minor changes in blood pressure and temperature. I reiterated to the team why they were not allowed to place a catheter in the patient as there was the possibility that 'someone' might still be totally aware on the inside. The need to follow the procedure laid out previously was mandatory. The surgeon did not believe that anyone could still be aware or 'awake,' but would follow my instructions.

I had started telling Mariann earlier and continued to whisper in her ear that no 'Beast' would be allowed to enter this O.R., because I was on guard with Dragonslayer and the bright ones. After

2 hours, without any obvious changes in the body's state or parts switching out, I left the O.R. briefly to get a cup of coffee and a donut. My own anxiety had precluded me from eating anything earlier but now I was feeling confident that everything was under control. Upon returning to the O.R., everything appeared calm and the System would soon be out of surgery.)

Unknown to the Surface People, Mr. Chalberg leaves the surgery room and his duties. During this time, unknown to the Surface People, doctors violate agreement and secretly place catheter into body and hide the bag under the sheets. Mr. Chalberg returns and does not see the bag until the end of surgery where he demands it be removed immediately before the system wakes up. (Elizabeth Ray is too kind here in that 'demand' is too soft a term for my reaction. I let the surgeon know in no uncertain terms that if there was any 'fallout' because of her actions, or in any way her decision proved detrimental to the patient she would be sued by me for malpractice. You could say I was a little angry. I resolved to tell no one in the System and to only let Bruce know in the hope that nothing would come of it. I never again left the OR in settings like this in the future.) *None of the Surface People are aware that the snowing did not penetrate down to Core through the pathway. No one knew at the time that Blue Devil had remained wide-awake during the surgery.*

(It would be in the recovery room that the surgeon and staff would get a closer look at the effects of surgery for a multiple. Parts were rotating out faster as the anesthesia wore off. Each new part had their own heart rate, blood pressure, temperature, responses to questions in their own voice and comments about the situation. I thought the nurses would trip over each other as they called for help to confirm the differences in readings they were getting from the System. The surgeon was in and out several times with them before she took me aside to ask for detailed information and I thought, 'better late than never'. Her apology for her attitude and actions was accepted. She also asked if I could come back if another case like this arose and she received the same answer I had given to the previous surgeon. (The following drawing is Mariann's perspective of what she experienced in the hospital.)

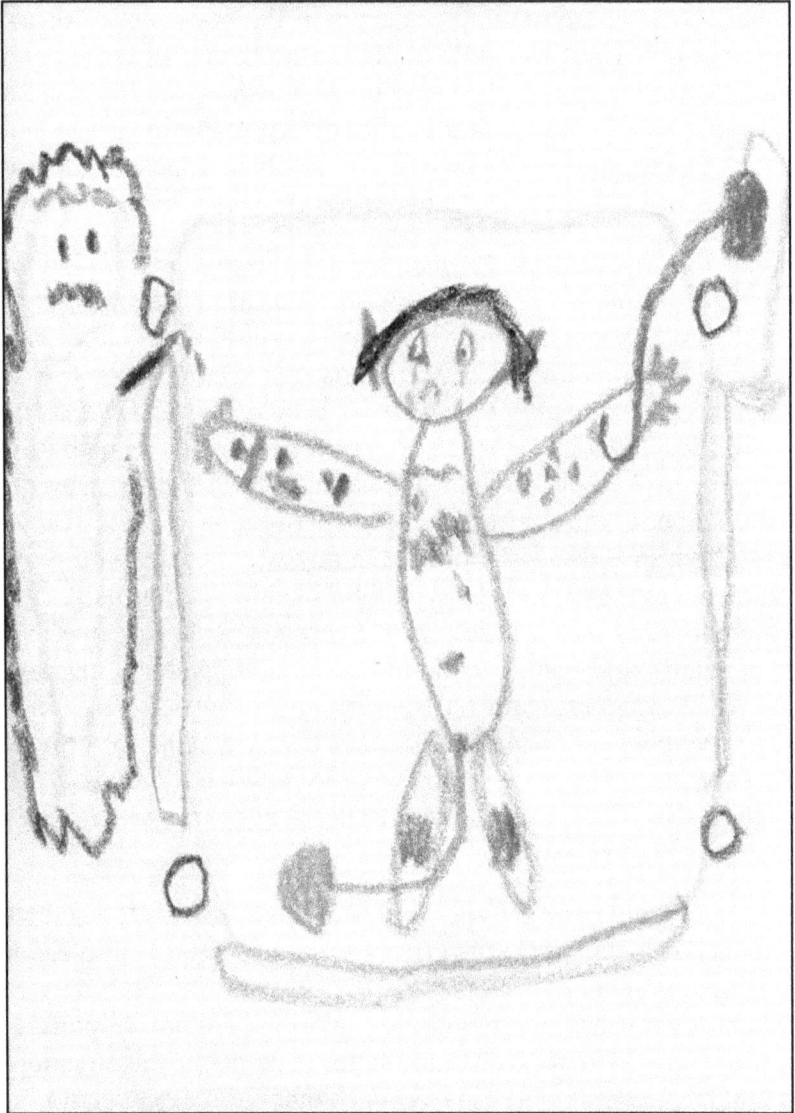

I left the System in the care of Maria's friend Lindsay that evening to go pick up my wife at the airport. She was returning from her trip to Norway with her family. I had called her there two weeks before to tell her of my plans to have the System stay at our home for two weeks to recover in a peaceful setting. I let her know the choice was hers to accept this responsibility for someone she hardly knew, or not accept it and other arrangements would be made. I am often surprised by my wife in a variety of ways, but not when it comes to issues of a caring heart. I banked on that and wasn't disappointed. We had one night to prepare our little two-bedroom home to receive the System the next morning.)

Lindsay stayed the night. System was awake off and on. Children came out and listened to stories from Lindsay but seemed to be still very drugged. On Thursday morning the system is released to the care of Carol and Mike Chalberg. The children seemed to adapt to the new environment rapidly and Council is surprised by the reaction because they had expected more fear of surroundings and just the opposite happens. Tabitha and Mariann seemed to adapt the quickest to Mrs. Chalberg. Angelina rotates out for brief moments and then falls back in asleep.

(Maria came to our home with 3 plastic ball-like containers with tubes coming out and taped to her chest, to collect blood and fluids still seeping from her incisions. We measured and recorded the amounts of fluids as they accumulated for the doctor, before discarding. We made sure the child parts could not observe this procedure to reduce triggering. The first two days were easy to do but later on they became a distraction in an unexpected way. Beginning Thursday evening and for the next two weeks, I averaged 3 hours or less of sleep a day. I would be up all night as the child parts kept switching out. If I wasn't there to rotate them back in to get some rest they would start trying to remove the tubes, containers and staples from the body. My wife relieved me in the early morning for a few hours before she went to work so I could sleep.)

There was much tension with the children Thursday evening and very little sleep overnight. The children seemed to be more agitated than usual and Council attributed it to a medication reaction. (The children called for either Mr. Miguel or Daddy Miguel when they were hurting or for water or food. Interestingly they immediately started calling for Mama Carol whom they hardly knew, as they thought she must be an angel (a "bright one"). From the first night there were ministering angels at the bedside as we prayed together and we read a children's version of both the Bible and <u>Hinds Feet on High Places</u>. Mariann and Tabitha would tell us the bright ones were there and reaching inside their chest cavity. When this was happening the area was always warmer to the touch.

We kept a dim light on all of the time on the back wall, casting a definite glow on the walls behind us. Carol had light blonde hair so her hair would glow just like the angel on the TV show "Touched by an Angel." As she sang to the children and talked with them she became their adopted mother giving them the love they had never known from an 'outside' woman. By the weekend she was christened by Raquel with her Native American name 'One Who Is Like The Angels.' Louise and Ruth were the only adults whose conversation was even lucid until Saturday morning.)

Friday evening and Blue Devil has switched out several times to growl, scream and hiss, before rotating back in. Ann began to experience headaches and she was the first to hear the drums. Soon the rest of us began hearing drums beating in a rhythmic sound (3 slashes/ 3 dots/ 3 slashes) and Council recognized the international Morse code sign for help...SOS. Council assumes it is coming from the military unit TWAC and is frustrated because they are unable to contact them. When Mr. Chalberg mentions Jesus, light or fear of dying, the drums get louder until they become ear piercing for the rest of the system. (Upon learning this I began praying to myself quietly for direction from Jesus about how to proceed. As of yet, I was still unsure who Blue Devil was within the spiritual realm of the System so I moved cautiously around him. I received no feelings of fear or apprehension about him, but past experience said to not dismiss the possibility of demonic activity. The Lord confirmed to me through the Holy Spirit that he was not a demon.)

Saturday morning (4AM) *Council discusses with Mr. Chalberg the possibility of the drums being the heartbeat of the body, but that is ruled out because the drums are not consistent in volume and duration and they change with the topics of discussion. Tabitha switches out and tells Mr. Chalberg that 'the boy is scared the light will burn the boy. Tabitha draws a picture showing the boy on a table with a bag of blood hidden on the side of the table. The picture mixes the memory of the boy with the goat-headed man and the surgery. Tabitha explains that the boy had this thing put in him. Council and Mr. Chalberg assume she is talking about the past.* (I decided to not tell Council yet about the 'catheter incident' in surgery until I had a better grasp of what was now occurring and why. I talked to Bruce by phone that day to get his feedback and waited to see what transpired.)

Saturday night and the drums continue, becoming more intense. There is a lot of outside activity (The children hear what they describe as fighting occurring outside of our home.) *and the system is aware of physical beings very active in the home* (a nurse stopped by to get measurements and check the bandages). *The children feel many bright ones around and talk constantly about the bright ones around the bed. Mariann told Mr. Chalberg that 'they fill the room'. Ruth discusses with Mr. Chalberg and Council about who Blue Devil is and if the drums are coming from agitation within Core. Surface people are confused and upset. They had believed Bruce that Core would bury itself very deep until they had to strike out to save the boy.* (Again I was silent.)

Sunday morning was the beginning of all-day church, (casa iglesia) for Tabitha and Liz calls it a 'homeboy church.' The kids are dancing inside with Jesus and Tabitha is saying 'getty-up horsey' on Jesus' shoulders. There is a variety of music from Mr. Chalberg's tapes, records and one of Liz's tapes. All day long there is laughter, dancing and praising of God with everyone but Ann. She is seated on the inside on a rock observing from a distance. There is a love offering of people writing love letters to Jesus and putting them on the plate to be read at another time. (Someone drew a picture of Jesus talking to the children inside that day.)

(I have to say that this was one of the best worship services that I have ever had the pleasure of planning and participating in. Liz told me that she had never imagined in her wildest dreams that Jesus could dance… and dance with moves that she had never seen. The music covered the spectrum. It included gospel songs by Willie Nelson, <u>Amazing Grace</u> by the Scottish Army Drum and Bagpipe Brigade, classic hymns, rock & roll, Southern spirituals, Edwin Hawkins Singers, Bill Gaither, instrumentals, Liz's compilation tape and even one for Lion – by the Tokens. We had all day to relax and enjoy the time with various Scripture readings, an abundance of prayers and even a sermon entitled, 'The Church Suffers from Multiple Personality Disorder'.)

During dinnertime Tabitha shares through Maria and makes it known that Blue Devil had her draw the catheter last night. Maria becomes upset and says the boy must be lying because the doctors promised no catheter and there wasn't any. Mr. Chalberg tells Maria that Blue Devil is right. Tension mounts quickly and the Surface People all become upset over the trust being broken with doctors. Council is very angry and allows Maria and Tabitha to call Bruce and talk with him.

On Sunday evening, Mariann is read to by Mr. Chalberg from "Hinds Feet" about overcoming fear. She tells Mr. Chalberg that she is afraid of the boy. Dragonslayer tells Mariann to inform Mr. Chalberg that the boy will be coming out tonight. Dragonslayer says he needs Mr. Chalberg to be his outside arms holding the boy and telling him the truth about who Jesus is. Mariann is to guard and yell out 'Mr. Miguel come!' as he approaches. Dragonslayer then causes the System to sleep. (I immediately went into the other room and called my prayer partners Bruce and Tone to help get us through this night. I also read any pertinent Scriptures that the Holy Spirit showed me in the Book of John to prepare for what was to happen next.)

Tabitha wakes up agitated and calls for daddy. She tells of bright ones circling around the bed, more bright ones than she has ever seen at one time. Angelina switches out and points at the bright ones. System goes back to sleep and Mr. Chalberg leaves. A bright one places Maria's Bible under the head of Mariann turned to John 6.

436

Tabitha wakes up shortly afterwards in a panic. Mariann screams, 'Mr. Miguel Come!' (As I hurried into the room, I notice the Bible open and under the head of Blue Devil who was just switching out. I won't know what place it is opened to for a few more hours. I wondered how it got there since they were asleep when I left the room and the Bible was on the dresser.)

The boy switches out extremely agitated, screaming (very loud) *and arching his back. Council is observing but has no contact still with TWAC. The bright ones are singing. When the boy screams louder, the bright ones sing louder. Mr. Chalberg holds the boy tightly as he continues to scream and tells him the truth about Jesus. The boy arches his back more, screams louder every time he says Jesus, but Mr. Chalberg will not let go. The bright ones continue to speak. Mariann reports that words are coming from behind the boy's head and into the boy's ears. They meet inside with the words from Mr. Chalberg and the bright ones.*

The boy speaks in a very low, gruff voice. "Goat man DIS put cross inside…burns me." Mr. Chalberg reassures the boy that it will not happen again. The boy tells of doctors and catheter and says again "burns me." Mr. Chalberg explains who the doctors were and that they were not there to hurt the boy. Boy continues to speak/scream of "cross inside burning him, Goat-man drinking blood, Jesus is man on cross, Goat-man put Jesus inside …burn boy." (I was holding Blue Devil down with a tight hug to keep him from flailing and tearing out sutures, tubes or containers. I have been hit before in encounters like this and I didn't need a shiner. I was telling him about why Jesus was on the cross to save him…not hurt him, and how the Goat-man lied about everything he said about Jesus. I told him how Jesus' blood will wash him clean and take away his pain, how Jesus was close and to go to Him so He can heal you. Trying to give clear truths about Jesus to a small boy in words he could understand was difficult, yet the Holy Spirit had me quoting portions of verses in John, that were apparently coming from the place in the Bible that was open under his head at the same time. This process continued for some time, while Carol was praying in the Spirit outside the room.)

Mr. Chalberg asks Blue Devil repeatedly to let Jesus love and heal him. Resistance is met as the boy continues to speak of cross inside burning him. (I realized at this point that the 'light burning him' given in Tolip's letter could also mean the light of Jesus whenever He drew near the boy.) *Mr. Chalberg tells the boy that Jesus wants to change his name and heal him…change his name to Peace. He continues to tell him to not be afraid of the light that heals, because healing is painful and only Jesus can take the pain away. Mr. Chalberg continues to hold the boy and reassure him of Jesus' love and power to heal.*

Mariann is inside holding on to Jesus. Jesus has his arms outstretched waiting for Blue Devil. Bright ones continue to sing. Mr. Chalberg asked the boy to allow Jesus to take away his pain. The boy begins to switch inside into the arms of Jesus. The light of Jesus burns as it heals. The boy starts screaming out of control. Mr. Chalberg continues to hold him tightly as he switches inside. Mariann switches out and tells Mr. Miguel that the boy is inside in his pod. Dragonslayer goes down the path into Core and meets Tolip. Tolip bows down to the Commander of the Bright Ones. There are five men guarding the pod of Blue Devil and they are in a circle. Tolip gives the command to open the circle and allow in the Dragonslayer. The guards ask Tolip who the man is and Tolip replies, "The Surface People call him by many names…Great Spirit, Dragonslayer, Jesus, Great Physician, First Counselor, I Am."

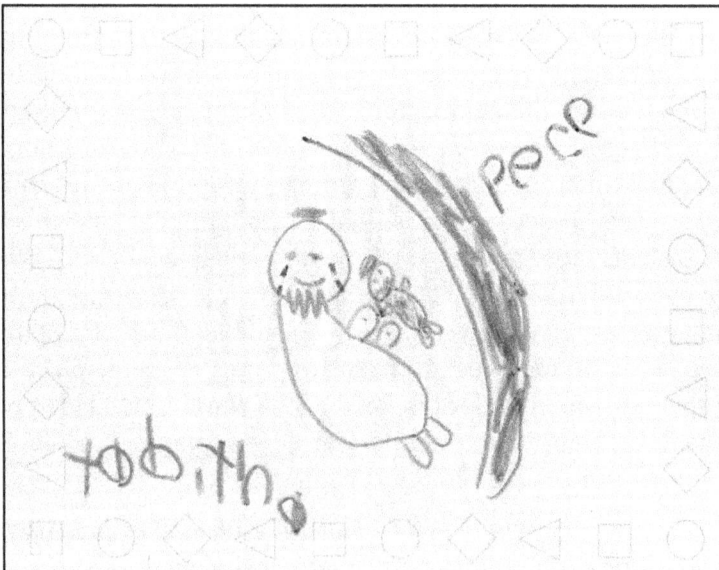

Dragonslayer walks over the acid and then turns toward it, raises his hand and the acid recedes. Smoldering burnt ground is quickly cooled by a river of cool water that appears from nowhere. Jesus scoops up the water in his hands. The water is aglow. He goes over to Blue Devil and begins to bathe his naked body. The area where Blue Devil was burnt by the cross receives cool water and the skin changes from purple/red to pink. The boy lays in Dragonslayer's arms naked and bruised...but unafraid. Dragonslayer sheds several tears that roll down his cheek. The guards watch. The boy is told his new name shall be Peace. Tolip nods as the boy continues to be bathed. Drums are no longer heard and the boy is still in Dragonslayer's arms being bathed at the termination of this report.

-Elizabeth Ray

P.S. Mr. Chalberg's notations for me:
        Don't forget the bowl on the head and glass over the nose of Tabitha, white ice cream all over Tabitha in my car, the joy of dancing with Jesus inside, the Bible under the head to John 6 and the promises of God.
                Thank you Jesus,
                Your Servant

It had been a very long evening with a lot of shed tears of joy and praises for God. As the healing continued inside for Peace, I instructed Mariann to try and get some rest. Carol relieved me so I could get some rest. Louise switched out to give Mariann some rest as well and began to tell Carol what was happening inside.

Account of Louise about Monday AM:
Maria was in bed trying to rest but couldn't sleep. She went inside and I, Louise, came out. I started to hear music that was echoing. I thought Pastor Chalberg had the music on. Carol was in the room checking our containers and I asked her if she heard music, but she said no. Then Pastor Chalberg came in the room. I asked him if he heard the music or had his record on. He asked what kind of music I heard and it was hard to tell him because I couldn't figure out the words. I thought it was Catholic like in a big monastery where they sing those beautiful songs, but it was more than that. It was sort of sacred. Pastor Chalberg told me to lie back and enjoy it and get

some rest. Carol stayed and read Psalm 91 which we like and is Raquel's favorite. The music wouldn't go away, but it never got loud like the drums. It was sort of far away and echoing.

I listened carefully and I remember hearing alleluias that were long, pretty, peaceful and sacred. I started to cry and couldn't stop as Pastor Chalberg returned to ask why. Then I was able to see a picture in my mind of being taken to the Core place where the music was coming from. There were all these angels and they were in a circle and they surrounded the five-army people and inside of them were Jesus and the little boy. They were singing these beautiful words that were honoring Jesus. Jesus got up and lifted the boy up and on the ground was a white robe. He dressed the boy and lifted him up and put him on his shoulders. The boy was smiling. The men opened up their circle and the angels opened their larger circle, as Jesus walked out past Tolip. Tolip bowed down as he passed. Jesus and the boy went with the angels and five men through the jungle to the bottom of Sacred Mountain.

I was crying lots by now but my crying was not sad but happy. Raquel was waiting there for them. Jesus smiled at Raquel and Raquel bowed down. Then Jesus took the boy off of his shoulders and the boy took Raquel's hand as the two of them started going up Sacred Mountain. Then everything stopped and I went to sleep. I was telling Carol about this while it was happening and that is all.

Carol later asked me how I knew what to say and do. The words I told her went something like this: "Sometimes you have to let Jesus take control and give the Holy Spirit cruise control." I was tired, yet it was true. When I look back and reflect on that night I know there are many more details that I could include in this book but for the sake of brevity, I will not include them. What happens the next two days proves to be as memorable for everyone.

When the System was feeling better I took Mariann for a walk around the neighborhood to get some exercise. This was a first for Mariann after being revealed to the System. It was as meaningful to me as it would be for any daddy, to witness the awe in her eyes of discovery as we explored new surroundings. Mariann gave her own account to Elizabeth Ray:

Mariann went for a walk with Mr. Miguel. She gathered flowers for mama Carol (out of my neighbor's freshly planted gardens.) *She played a game of going to the moon with Mr. Miguel. She found a ball to bounce, listened to the birds talk to Dragonslayer, watched two squirrels fight over food, spoke with a window cleaner and a girl in a red car about Dragonslayer. She spoke to a man repairing his roof and a man with horses on his roof* (weathervane). *She sang a song to Dragonslayer: "Dragonslayer – he be my friend, Dragonslayer loves me, Dragonslayer – he be my friend, Dragonslayer – he never goes away." She would stop and address the bright ones she saw along the way.*

Tabitha switched out several times on the walk. She was interested in one home in particular that had children playing, she wanted to play with them. Daddy Miguel had to pull her away from her attraction to other children. She was attracted as well to a pile of sand and a swing in a yard.

On Tuesday Maria's friend Lindsay visits the System. She tells Maria: "Growth doesn't come without change, change doesn't come without loss, loss doesn't come without pain." A discussion started inside with the parts. They determined that in order for us to grow, we have to experience pain.

Tuesday afternoon: a longer walk takes place with Mariann and Tabitha to swings at a local school. Mr. Miguel takes Mariann for a walk to the school and stops across the street first to visit his best neighbor Archie, a small Border terrier that belongs to Jessie. Mariann walks with Mr. Miguel down the Alameda holding his hand and touching flowers with the other, while watching a young woman rollerblading. As she arrives at the school, she notices other children there and sees balls, bikes and little girls in the playground area. Mr. Miguel lets her tell the children (as if I could stop her enthusiasm), *"Hi! I'm Mariann, I be eight. What's your name?" The children are shy at first, as Mariann swings with Mr. Miguel and tickles the clouds with her toes. She then tries to climb the monkey bars a little and tells Mr. Miguel it looks like a big cookie jar with cookies in it. One little girl ventures over and talks with Mariann.*

Mariann wants to play high on the monkey bars like the other girls, but Mr. Miguel says no because of the operation. Mariann tells the other girls she has balls and goes to show them. Mr. Miguel quickly covers the area with blood. Mariann's balls fascinate the children and all gather around her. Mariann suggested swinging and all of them fill the swings and all try to tickle the clouds. One girl, Alexandria, who is nine and bigger than Mariann tells her that they can't go on the slide because it is against the law. Mariann repeats information to Mr. Miguel who laughs. The teacher calls the class to return to school. The kids tell Mariann that they do crafts and activities and Mariann wants to go to school with them. Mr. Miguel tells her she can't go with them as the children say goodbye to Mariann.

Tabitha switches out and wants to go with the children. Daddy Miguel attempts to redirect her to the swings with limited success. He then attempts to take her for a walk around the field, but Tabitha turns to watch the children returning to school and tries to join them. Alexandria is the last to go in and stands at the fence for a long time waving to Mariann and Tabitha. Tabitha picks up grass and throws it over her face several times. Daddy Miguel attempts to clean it off of her and redirects her to the playground. Tabitha sees a large wall with chalk drawings of children. She goes over to the wall and lays her face and body against it. She quietly cries, "Ninos" repeatedly and holds on to the wall. Daddy tries to take her away, but she returns and continues repeating it. (It was a heart-breaking moment to witness Tabitha mourning for the childhood experiences that were stolen from her life.)

Mariann switches out and walks with Mr. Miguel back home. Mariann talks with Mr. Miguel about wanting to go to school like all the other children. Mariann notices several men driving by staring at her and Mr. Miguel tells her to not pay any attention to them. She returns to noticing the flowers and wanting to put her body inside a large bush. At home, Mariann doesn't want to tell mama Carol about what Tabitha did putting grass over the wound. She wants Mr. Miguel to tell mama, because she isn't sure how mama Carol will react with maybe a spanking or a beating. Mariann switches Tabitha out in fear and Tabitha tells all. Mama Carol takes Tabitha into bedroom and lovingly begins to clean her body.

Mariann switches back out and proceeds to tell all about the walk to school. (That walk is etched in my memory forever. Maybe for the first time I realized a small measure of the loss of innocence taken from a child's life needlessly through abuse. I cried for them...for what they could never fully know about the joy of childhood friends at play.)

Back at home that night, something natural but difficult for the System takes place. Maria's period started.

System is resting when the children experience pain inside and Tabitha begins to sleepwalk. She holds on to Maria's blanket and walks up to Mr. Chalberg working at the computer. She puts her head on his shoulder and is then led back to bed. Several minutes later, Maria wakes up and goes to bathroom. She becomes upset because her period has started and is experiencing severe pain. She gets a pad and tells Carol that periods are problems for the system.

Maria remains upset and crying about her period, when Mr. Chalberg comes in and talks with her about the difference between good blood and bad blood. The children are listening and shadowing inside. The adults make attempts to calm children down who become traumatized every time they see blood. Mr. Chalberg gives Maria for the very first time in her life, the talk that parents are supposed to give their daughter in preparation for this event. Maria tells him that when it first happened, she thought she was dying. She said her parents took her and her brother into a room and told the brother that Maria had become a woman today...do you have any questions? Maria was so humiliated that she froze up and said no. That was all of her education on the matter. She wasn't allowed to attend classes in school, so she didn't know what it was or why she bled. After getting married, Ann researched it on her own, but didn't discuss it with Maria.

Maria told of the severe pain she has with periods and how she always thought it was punishment for childhood wrongs. She told of how the doctors wanted to remove her ovaries and uterus due to problems. They told Maria she would always have problems, pain and very irregular cycles. Mr. Chalberg explained to her how it was a natural part of the way God created all women and not something to fear... also how it was easy for him to say as a man.

Later that night an argument broke out between Ann and Liz over beer and Ann's math thesis. It escalated to the point where Council intervened to maintain strength and safety for the system. Liz refused to abide by Council's ruling and would not stop shouting at Helper. Helper finally placed her under house arrest for one week. Ann was required to serve Liz meals during this time frame, (a double punishment for Liz.) *Helper addressed the remaining parts observing the incident and stressed the need for cooperation and teamwork in meeting the number one goal of the system's survival. Council's doors were closed and council went into session.*

Late Wednesday evening, Maria goes to bed and Mr. Chalberg states that there is no need to lock the sliding glass door, as Liz is under house arrest and can't leave to party. (Half-jokingly) *He tells Maria that he's going to take a shower and to wake Carol up if she needs anything. Maria goes to sleep and body memories start occurring of a time in a bar/deli store with décor of the 50's. There are men in the bar and she hears one man say, "He's gone now," and looks toward Maria saying, "Watch out cutie." Another man grabs Maria from behind and drags her down to the ground. He then pulls her pants off and rapes her.*

Maria wakes up in a panic and rolls out of the bed onto the floor, where she covers herself with a blanket in a little ball. Mr. Chalberg finds her like that and tries to figure out what happened as he gets Mariann out and back in bed. Mariann gets in a panic that smelly ones are attacking. She becomes very upset and says they are at the doors and around the house yelling and trying to get in. Mr. Chalberg tells her to call Jesus immediately. A battle rages all night.

Mariann gathers strength and yells at the bad ones to go away. "Dragonslayer says go away, Mariann be back!" (As I prayed with her, I remembered what Quiet Walker had written about Masauwu fighting to not release them to Dragonslayer.) *Mariann spends several hours in a fog praying and marching around as a guard inside. As she slept, she talks out loud to Mr. Chalberg about having her helmet on her head. Dragonslayer tells her to put the helmet on to keep the words of the bad ones out of her mind. She talks to Dragonslayer as she dresses for battle against the smelly ones.*

The bad ones approach the bed and someone from the House of Prayer rotates out, sits up and yells, "Leave in the name of Jesus!" She then rotates back in. Ruth switches out and apologizes for not reading the signs. She begins to pray for protection of the system. Mariann switches back out and carries on a conversation with Dragonslayer. She continues to march around the Land of Preservation, watching for the bad ones coming so she can call Dragonslayer. She hears someone singing far off and begins singing the same song.

As she continues to guard and talk to Dragonslayer, she sings to him: "My Dragonslayer be a mighty God. He reigns from heaven above with wisdom, power and love. My Dragonslayer be a mighty God." Then she yells at the bad ones trying to come in to the room that Dragonslayer is bigger than them. The bad ones finally leave and bright ones come around the bed as the system falls asleep. (I remained up all night with them, praying and encouraging Mariann by reading Ephesians 6. The wind kicked up dramatically outside our house as the battle raged on. I have since found this to be a common occurrence when involved in heavy spiritual warfare or praying for direction from Jesus while outside in nature.)

On Thursday morning, Maria had a visit from the doctor's nurse, before returning to her own home to recuperate a little longer. Council expresses their anger through Ruth about repeated promises being broken. Mariann comes out and has the nurse promise to get her hat from Mama Carol and she breaks the promise. She drains the tubes and balls and says see you in a week. The system returns home Thursday morning and starts to fall apart by the afternoon. The contractor is exceedingly noisy, the water is turned off and visitors stay way too long. Ann calls Mr. Chalberg to tell him to tell Sergio to have the visitors leave and put a sign on the door – Do Not Disturb. He told him to monitor the phone and remove the phone from Maria's room for now. By Thursday evening, Ann is up at 2:30 cleaning house and forces Louise out to do laundry. Louise begins to cry and Sergio intervenes and forces the system back to bed. Louise gets in trouble for lifting a heavy iron chair. (It seems my talk two weeks before had little effect on the family.)

Friday, Louise calls Mr. Chalberg when she becomes upset over seeing the scars for the first time and thinks she is not human. She mourns the loss of her breasts and talks with Carol extensively. By Saturday morning, Ann calls nurse to return sooner to observe swelling. The nurse arrives in the afternoon and becomes concerned about swelling around the suture on right drain tube. She says she will be back on Sunday evening to monitor it and will leave a message with the doctor if it increases. She ask Sergio if it seems more swollen than before and he admits he doesn't know as she hasn't been home for two weeks. She replaces the bandages and cleans the wounds, just as Carol and Mr. Chalberg had done previously. She remains concerned over the amount of drainage still occurring stating it is not usual.

This concludes my reports of the surgery and recovery.
Elizabeth Ray – Scribe for Council

As usual, Elizabeth Ray's reports are short and to the point. Within a few weeks following these events, Bruce has been given all the information that has transpired with the various parts and we have the opportunity to discuss the counseling/therapeutic aspects of what transpired. He suggested that in his opinion and experience, what we did for the System in those two weeks was equivalent to at least 8 years of ongoing therapy on a weekly basis. I was a little surprised at how well Carol adjusted to the situation and rose to the occasion by caring for the System in such a loving and tender way. She has long had the spiritual gift of hospitality but never before displayed in such a magnificent manner. I knew her life or mine would never be the same again. We both would go through debriefing of each other in order to confirm again with clarity what we perceived happened, before talking directly to the System again and particularly to Elizabeth Ray. When spiritual 'highs' like this occur between numerous people and Jesus, we have found it helpful to go through a 'remembering process' with those involved to reaffirm the reality of it. As you have read, things happened that only God can explain through His Spirit.

"What is impossible with men is possible with God."
Luke 18:27

Chapter 18:

"Chemo Means Total Devastation Inside"

"And now these three remain;
Faith, hope and love...But
The greatest of these is love."
1 Corinthians 13:13

The preparation had begun with the System for the upcoming chemotherapy. With the fiasco of broken promises by doctors not everyone wanted to proceed with treatment. Bruce would continue with TWAC and I would continue with the Surface People and teaching them about Jesus. Mariann began composing a book about her understanding of what Dragonslayer was going to do in the chemotherapy. She completed it before treatment began and Raquel printed it out so Mariann could share it with patients and staff. She wanted all to hear about her Dragonslayer and know His plan for them. Mariann increased her evangelism efforts in her own dramatic style. Renewal and healing continued for all of the System as the weeks past. Raquel wrote about the boy's journey.

Your New Name Shall Be

The darkness tried to hold him
Deep in the lowest of pits
Confined within the depths of Core
Afraid, beaten and alone
Held sealed in his pod

The light burned him
Was the message he gave
Buried in his own grave
Suffocating and awaiting death

But come and see what the Great Spirit has done

He has turned the acid into living water
And brought the child out of the pod

447

He has healed his spirit
And delivered him from his enemies

Come and see the work of the Great Spirit

We have heard with our ears
And seen with our eyes
The awesome power of the Great Spirit

So come and see what the Great Spirit has done

He has put a new song in the child's heart
And set his feet upon the rock
Many will see and hear
And put their trust in the Great Spirit

Come and see the power of the Great Spirit

As we have heard
So we have seen
He has done marvelous things
And His love endures forever
Give thanks to the Great Spirit
For there is hope
Hopi is alive

-Quiet Walker

(When I questioned Raquel about the name Hopi, she said it means Peace-be-still.)

Ruth sent Bruce an update each week to keep him appraised of the System's status approaching the chemotherapy. Maria's extended family and the situation with the contractor was causing more and more stress that was depleting the System's energy needed to heal.

Dear Bruce,
This week has been overwhelming, yet I have seen countless blessings. Mariann has become quite the ambassador for the Lord. She loves to tell people about Dragonslayer and how he saves. I'm amazed at how grounded she is in the Lord. With all of the twisting

and distorting of truth that she has experienced, Jesus has entered her heart wiped away the lies and filled her with truth. She spends countless hours talking with Dragonslayer and learning from him. I think sometimes Bruce that we as adults lose a lot of that child-like trust that Mariann has for Jesus.

Mariann has chosen to respond to Dragonslayer. She goes directly to him with all of her questions and concerns, as God gives her a strength that passes all understanding. I look back at the surgery and see Mariann holding up her arms and repeating, "Mariann be Dragonslayer strong." I see the spiritual battle that took place on Wednesday night and I see Mariann yelling, "Go away bad ones, Dragonslayer says go away. You can't have me, I belong to Dragonslayer. I don't hear you, stay away, Dragonslayer says stay away." And then she tells us she is Dragonslayer's guard and round and round she goes on the perimeter of the land just inside the fence, making sure the bad ones can't be heard or smelled approaching. She tells us that she gets her orders from Dragonslayer and we better listen to Dragonslayer because he knows everything. Mariann really encourages me, Bruce.

Liz is still under house arrest and will be released on Wednesday evening. I have not had the opportunity to speak with her, but I pray that we will be able to spend some time together at the end of the week.

Mariann and Tabitha are struggling with the pending separation between the Chalberg's and the System. (See drawing following this letter.) *Mariann tried to figure out a way that we adults could all live in this house and she and the other children would return to their home with their mommy and daddy. Mike is using the same technique that you used in explaining to Mariann how everyone goes together. I believe the trouble with Maria's brother's children probably triggered her anxiety over this. She heard that the children might be taken away from him and it scared her to think that her spiritual mother and father were also going to be removed from her. We have explained as best we can to her that, she can still write and call sometimes, but Dragonslayer has important work for them to do apart from Mariann. She still struggles with this and we hope she adapts eventually. She is concerned that you too will be leaving her and we assured her that you aren't going away.*

One of the most difficult circumstances this last week that Council dealt with was Tabitha. When she held on to the children's wall at school and wept saying ninos...ninos, Helper and the leaders felt as though their heart was being ripped in two. The whole system became very quiet inside and there seemed to be a great deal of mourning over Tabitha's loss. Helper later told us that although Council was aware of Tabitha's childhood losses, the leaders never really stopped and took the time to fully understand it. It was a difficult moment for all of us.

Ann especially had a hard time with it. She would rather pack up all emotions in a suitcase and store them somewhere that she doesn't have to deal with them. She reprimanded Helper for allowing the children to experience the swings, park and other children. Her reasoning is that if the kids do not experience love and fun, then they will never really understand what they have lost. She thinks we are abusing the kids inside by giving them a taste of a life that they can never have. Why give them a week of love, parents, fun and warmth, only to take it away? The reality according to Ann is that Mariann, Tabitha and all the other children inside that might exist, will always be flawed and broken. She thinks there is no hope for them and that giving them tidbits of what they lost, is cruel and inhuman.

Of course I totally disagree with her and so does Council. Helper knows that it is painful for the children, but he also believes that they can take a week of love and stretch it farther than children who have been given a stable home. Already we are seeing healing with the children. One week at the Chalberg home was like years of nurturing for Mariann. She drank up every second of outside time with her daddy and mommy and stored it in her heart. We believe the positive love she received outweighs the negative pain of separation.

The boy Hopi-Peace Be Still (we call him Peace for short) is still with Raquel. I have seen him once and he looks well. Raquel brings him down occasionally from the mountain, so that Dragonslayer can bathe him. I am still trying to understand the concepts of the bathes, maybe deep healing requires repeated bathing, I don't know. I do know that Tolip has Watcher observing Raquel and reporting back to him on a continual basis. Tolip is still responsible for Peace and does not seem to fully trust us yet. He is taking a wait and see attitude.

Maria and Louise are still struggling with the surgery. Louise looked at the body and became distraught and immediately called Pastor Chalberg, spending a considerable time talking with him. Maria still refuses to look at it and Pastor Chalberg doesn't force her, even when he takes her to the doctor for follow-up. Jennifer has escaped deep inside and does not want to deal with the cancer. She did spend a small amount of time with Pastor Chalberg discussing karma, palm reading and Hinduism. Pastor Chalberg is proceeding gently with her. She is spending a lot of time alone.

Ann called the Pastor once to discuss her concern over the children substituting the Chalbergs for Maria's real parents. Ann thinks the kids and Maria need to face reality head on and seems dead set against allowing the system to be loved. She seems afraid of love, although she wouldn't admit it, and that is where the Pastor caused her to stop and reason it out. He asked her how can she judge what is real about love, when she herself admits that she has never experienced 'good' love? What makes a 'real parent', one that gives true love to their child or one that is a biological circumstance who can't?

Interestingly the conversation switched then to a discussion about truth and knowledge. Ann said that scientific truth is the only truth and that one can obtain reliable knowledge only through using the scientific method. He countered with all scientific knowledge begins in a single step of faith about what truth might be and then proceeds to prove or disprove the premise. She went on about truth having to be established scientifically...why reality and reason, not faith, are the foundations to live life on. She told him that she has to touch, test, see, measure and describe in order to understand. She said the scientific perspective is what we need to strive for, because it tells us what is, whereas the spiritual perspective is more what we might desire reality to be. He responded with three questions for her to ponder scientifically until their next discussion.

1. Explain scientifically how the universe came into being in such order, design and scientifically provable natural laws... from nothing or chaos. 2. Explain how there has always been knowledge of a Supreme Being that is the causal factor for every civilization and society in history to establish a moral code of some kind. 3.

Explain what you saw and felt on the inside over the last two weeks in scientific terms of reality, not what you desire.

Pastor Chalberg challenged Ann to read Romans for herself, after the House of Prayer had Maria read Romans 12 for Ann's benefit on Sunday. Ann is having a hard time with the spiritual unity forming internally, because she hears more Scripture and discussion about God than ever before. I'm thrilled, she isn't. She took the challenge and began last night and I prayed for her as I shadowed. She couldn't go further than chapter 1 without stopping and wrestling with that. I need to end and Maria needs to rest.
Grace to you.
Ruth

> MOMY AND DADY
> PLEZ LUV ME
> AND WUNT ME
> AND KEP MONSTRZ AWA
> HOLD ME AND HUG ME
> BE WIT ME LOTS
> RED ME STOREZ AND
> TAK ME FOR WOKS
> LET ME TOK WIT YOU
> AND BE WIT YOU
> PLEZ LUV ME AND
> WUNT ME BECAZ
> I LUV YOU
> FRUM ME TABITHA

Dear Bruce and Mike,

Liz is sitting on the lower cliffs of Sacred Mountain according to Mariann. She told us that she heard a voice talking to Liz and it said, "You are a stubborn heifer. How can I pasture you like a lamb in the meadow? Your headstrong independence is going to result in horrible consequences." Mariann said she then ran off to the river because something told her that she was not to listen to the voice talking to Liz.

I don't know if I'm correct or not, but it sounds like Liz has been zapped by God again. Liz reminds me so much of Jonah. She knows what God wants her to do, but she resists his call. Like Jonah, she tries to run from the presence of God. Jonah didn't think God's commission for him fit into his plans and Liz is the same way. 'That's not my style... I want to party...I'm bored (and my personal favorite,) You've got to be kidding God! You want me to do what?' Like Jonah, Liz is acting like a stubborn two-year-old. I wonder if God is trying to teach her a lesson about stubbornness in doing it her way like Jonah? Liz still hasn't figured out that she is not going to be happy as long as she is running against God's plan. I wonder if she likes fish...big fish!

Ann is still being shaken down to the core in her quest to explain all that has happened scientifically. She is still not communicating with us about her internal turmoil. She is trying hard to focus on outside circumstances to avoid addressing her issues with God. May we all continue to pray for her.

I was able to drive Maria to church today. She was very self-conscious and afraid that people would stare at her. No one did! In fact, this man named Paschal (He met Liz when she cornered him about how he felt accepted in a primarily white church, as he is black.) came up to Maria and talked with her before church. He is aware of her cancer and that she comes to church alone. He told her that she was an inspiration to him and encouraged him in his own life, just by her actions. Then he asked if she understood what he was saying. She said no and that she doesn't try to do anything. He then said I watch you and it helps me with my own difficulties in trusting God. He told her she was very special to God and that God loves her deeply, before going up to the stage to sing. He is very kind to Maria and Maria isn't sure how to react to him. Raquel has been invited to Core to meet with Tolip. I'll keep you posted.
-Ruth

Dear Carol and Mike,

The card and picture had a great impact on the system. The children were so excited to learn that a card came in the mail for them from their 'mommy and daddy.' The picture sets in Raquel's Indian basket so that when the children are out at night, they can go over to the basket and look at it. Having something tangible like the picture has helped them tremendously with the anticipated separation.

As the date for chemotherapy draws closer, the system is beginning to panic about poisoning the body. The children are very afraid and Council is trying to determine how the chemicals will affect the body. I continue to ask Mariann to tell me about her book, so that I can focus her back on the power of Jesus, her Dragonslayer, to heal her. At times it works and at others she is simply too needy, as I think she is under attack by the smelly ones that I often can't hear like she does.

I often wonder about Angelina not having the language skills to express her fears and thoughts. All this is happening to her again

454

and she has no understanding as to why. Maybe that's why the Lord has blessed her so by sending his bright ones to be around her when she rotates out.

Maria loved the song, 'I Know Who Holds The Future.' I told her I would type it up for her on the computer, mat it and hang it on the wall for her to read each morning. That seemed to please her very much. Maria is trying very hard to trust Jesus. For me, I think the most awesome example of God's power in our system centers around the meaning of trust. For a multiple, and this is according to mental health professionals, trust is something impossible for them to achieve. Yet, all I have to do is look at Mariann, Tabitha, Hopi and Raquel to see that anything is possible for God. He has taken the very weakest ones in the area of trust and proven how, through his power and love, these little ones are healed and trust once again. The children are healing and growing in the Lord. For the first time in their lives they have experienced real, unconditional, safe love and they can laugh too. God sent along people like you two, Bruce and Lindsay to show them His love and the children have not rejected it but have eagerly grabbed onto it for all they're worth.

I don't know yet what the Lord has planned for all of us, but I do know He is at work in the system. The parts are drawing closer and closer to him. Slowly they are shaking off the lies and brainwashing that have imprisoned them for so long. They are facing a new life for the very first time with fear and trepidation, but with a hope that will carry them forward. At times, Maria seems to progress the slowest and needs a lot of encouragement, but in her heart she loves Jesus with all that she is. I try not to be judgmental of her progress, for I have not walked her life and frankly, if I had, I don't know that I would be farther up into the high places than she is.

The biggest issue for Maria is thinking she is worthy to be loved by God. Her past beat it into her that she is not. Yet there are people in her life now that say they dearly care for her and love her along with Jesus' love. It is taking her time to absorb this. Of course the enemy is right there trying to confuse her and make her believe it isn't true and are always at her to prevent her from accepting it as so. She is learning what it means to call upon God for help during these times. She is also learning that God wants her to give Him all her fears and burdens. She can't understand why He would want them all, but she is trying to give them to Him...always concerned that she will overwhelm Him.

I will treasure some of my conversations with her all of my life. She is so concerned about God's welfare. I think she holds on to things because she thinks she should take care of her own problems, so God is free to take care of the really important ones and not lose time on hers. I spend a lot of time letting her know that God is big enough to handle her problems as well. Not only that He is big enough to handle them, but that He wants to because He loves her. Maria cares so much for the welfare of others that she would rather die before burdening someone else, even God.

Louise appreciated so much your note to her about her work in your garden. This past week Sergio took her to the nursery at Orchards and on the ground was a stomped piece of Coleus. Louise picked it up and brought it home, pruned it, prayed over it and placed it in a water jar. Unbelievable as it seems, the shoot has roots and is thriving. It will take her about six months to make it a thriving, plush plant, but knowing her...it will probably be in the home full grown by Christmas. Wanna bet?

I have promised Mariann that I would let her write on the end of my letter. She has been shadowing me and telling me I talk too much on paper. So before I get into deep trouble with an eight-year-old, I will say my goodbyes. I thank God each day for the two of you and how he has used you to bring hope and joy into our lives.

In Him Who Gives Meaning To My Life,
Your Sister Ruth

(An edited version of Mariann's letter follows:)

Daddy and mommy I miss you lots. Thank you for the picture. Daddy where is your hat? Dragonslayer says hi. I told him I got a picture of my mommy and daddy. He smiled. Dragonslayer is going to bomb the monsters in my blood daddy. You know what mommy? I love you. Dragonslayer makes the bad ones run away. Dragonslayer is the strongest. Daddy, you go to work and tell the people that Dragonslayer is strong and He loves them. I eat the cookies you send mommy. I share them with Tabitha. I make this picture for you. I love you, Mariann.

456

As chemo approached, not everyone was on board with the plan for how we would proceed. Tolip sent the following warning from Core before Jesus talked to him:

THIS IS A WARNING FROM TWAC

INFORM THE ONES ABOVE THAT WE WILL RETALIATE IF THEY ATTEMPT TO ENGAGE IN BIOLOGICAL WARFARE.

Jennifer sent a letter before she disappeared for the duration of the chemotherapy. I wasn't sure if she would ever return.

Rejected and abandoned at birth
Beaten in a basement
Bitten by rats
Sexually abused by the grandfather
Forced to be inspected and cleaned
Forced to work at four years old
Witness to extreme violence to animals
Allowed to go hungry
Allowed to be without proper shelter and protection
Initiated into the Santeria
Molested by a farm worker
Brainwashed by a Catholic priest
Molested by the priest
Beaten and verbally abused by the Father and Mother
Allowed no choices or opinions
Dominated and beaten by the sister
Her child becomes disabled
Psychiatrists label her a bad parent
Her child is taken away from her
Has to fight for disability rights for her daughter
Financially taken by a Christian contractor
Given cancer
Disfigured by surgery
Body poisoned by chemicals…

WHERE IS THE HOPE? I DO NOT SEE ANYTHING IN HER LIFE TO PROVE TO ME THAT IT IS WORTH THE EFFORT TO CONTINUE TO STRUGGLE TO SURVIVE. YOU SAY THIS JESUS

OF YOURS WON'T GIVE SOMEONE MORE THAN THEY CAN HANDLE. DO YOU REALLY BELIEVE THIS, LOOKING AT WHAT MARIA HAS GONE THROUGH? DON'T YOU THINK THIS JESUS OF YOURS HAS MADE HER SUFFER ENOUGH? HASN'T SHE SUFFERED ENOUGH? WHERE IS THIS LOVE YOU KEEP TALKING ABOUT? AND NOW I'M GOING TO BE A PART OF THE TOTAL CONTAMINATION TO OUR WORLD WITH THESE MAN-MADE CHEMICALS. THE BODY WILL BE POLLUTED WITH TOXINS THAT ARE SO DEADLY THAT WHEN APPLIED TO THE SKIN, THEY CAUSE ULCERS. YOU CANNOT CONVINCE ME THAT YOUR JESUS REALLY TRULY CARES ABOUT HER OR ANY OF US. IF HE CARED, HE WOULD RESCUE HER FROM FURTHER PAIN...INSTEAD HE GIVES HER MORE. THIS DOES NOT SEEM LIKE A LOVING GOD TO ME.

BAD VIBES ALL AROUND
JENNIFER

PS: I REFUSE TO BE A PART OF THE POLLUTING OF THE SYSTEM. I RESIGN MY POSITION IN THE SYSTEM. GOOD-BYE (I believe that Jennifer was being influenced by the 'smelly ones' in her letter. The anger reflected here was not consistent with her memories or experiences within the System. She had not known abuse and as she was one of the weakest parts in the System at this time so the enemy knew she could be more easily influenced. All communication before and after this does not have this kind of anger associated with it. It would be three months before anyone heard from her again.)

Council wrote a decree to the System to be prepared for the unexpected, after meeting with Jesus in a closed session. Jesus also reminded them to read His letter whenever they were afraid.

Decree From Circle Council To All Parts

Monday, August 26th at 9AM, the Land of Preservation will be subjected to CAF, a combination of chemicals used to destroy cancer cells. CAF will affect the Land of Preservation and although

Council is unsure of the degree of devastation that will occur, the leaders are in agreement that precautions need to be taken.

Raquel has informed Council of three dwelling places located on Sacred Mountain. These caves will provide shelter for the parts. Council has stored water and food in each of the caves. All parts need to select one of the shelters and go there before 8AM on Monday the 26ᵗʰ. Raquel has sent our greetings to Tolip and has returned with a communication from him. Tolip is now in understanding of the dilemma that faces the system and has withdrawn his troops from entering into warfare with the Surface People.

He has requested that Hopi be returned to him during the time of the attack of CAF. Core refuses to come into the Land of Preservation and seek shelter in the caves. Tolip has given each pod a large, fire-resistant, titanium shelter to protect the units against the CAF. Tolip will care for Hopi during this time. Keeper of Functions has informed Council that all functions will be secured in their holding rooms during this time and Level Two is prepared. Keeper of Functions will remain in the Land of Preservation with the other leaders.

Daniel and Lion have constructed a large holding pen for all of the animals and birds of the system. It is located in the jungle and offers protection against the CAF. All animals and birds will be placed in a hibernation state and will be cared for by Raquel during this time. A large aquarium has also been placed in the holding pen for the fish of the rivers. Seven of each group will be selected and offered refuge in the holding aquarium.

A trumpet will sound at 8AM on Monday to alert all parts that they must seek cover. Do not leave the refuge until you hear another trumpet signaling that it is safe to return to the land. Prepare yourselves for the destruction you will see and remember what Raquel communicated from the Great Spirit. THE LAND WILL BE RESTORED.

Council has selected two parts who will be out during the administering of the CAF with Mr. Chalberg by their side. Council has placed much thought and discussion in selecting the parts.

459

Mariann will be out to receive the IV injection and the beginning of the treatment. She will then be brought in to one of the shelters and Maria will be sent out to receive the remainder of the treatment. Council will monitor at all times.

Good luck and may God be with us.

"The Lord is not slow in keeping his promises,
As some understand slowness.
He is patient with you,
Not wanting anyone to perish,
But everyone to come to repentance."
2 Peter 3:9

Epilogue:

"Trusting in the Promises of God"

"So What Follows Tomorrow......??"

"So do not worry saying, 'What shall we eat?' or 'What shall we drink?' or 'What shall we wear?' For the pagans run after all these things, and your heavenly Father knows that you need them. But seek first his kingdom and his righteousness, and all these things shall be given to you as well. Therefore do not worry about tomorrow, for tomorrow will worry about itself. Each day has enough trouble of its own."
Matthew 6:31-34

I would not be truthful if I said I had a firm grasp of the reality of the inside world, the Land of Preservation, by this stage of our relationship together. I would recall Council's decree in the next three months every time I entered the chemotherapy treatment room. I would compare what I received from Maria and Mariann about the changes caused by the chemo with the promises of Jesus in His letters to the System. This process was too dynamic to be logical or scientific. Jesus was talking to me and them and I was hearing more clearly through my spirit from the Holy Spirit during the most volatile moments of spiritual warfare involved with their struggle to heal. I knew the Holy Spirit was guiding my actions and words as I responded to new situations I had never before experienced.

I was acutely aware of the spiritual activity around the System, myself and even my house, before anyone in the System commented about it. This level of awareness was new for me and yet I was not afraid, because I knew without a doubt that the Lord was present. Everything made sense. I did not question what was happening on the inside while the spiritual battle was taking place but I had questions afterwards to confirm what I had heard and saw. I decided to trust the Lord about what He was revealing to Carol and I about the inside world and to wait for Him to reveal what was taking place in His time. I only had to wait a few months.

There were more lessons that came out of those two weeks than I feel comfortable sharing at this time but I will share more in the next books. One answer of healing I can tell you now is one I shared with Carol. My wife and I were not able to have any children together. We did, however, have the joy of raising my two children from my first marriage. Both my son and daughter were grown and living on their own by the time I met the System. Carol and I had often talked with the Lord about adopting a child, or three or four, as we felt we could offer a good loving home. The answer was always no for 14+ years and we really were never sure why. It became clearer after the previous two weeks. We saw the wisdom in how the Lord had been preparing us to receive several of His chosen ones to love as our 'God-children'. We just never expected so many at one time, nor did we foresee how many He had planned over the next 24 years. It would take us another six years to slowly understand what it means to parent children having severe abuse issues within the System and those that followed over the coming years.

What lies ahead for Carol and I was beginning to take shape if we could learn to trust what we were learning, because spiritual realities were coming at us in rapid succession. Within the next three months we witness the Lord Jesus fight spiritual battles around us that involved our visible physical world and confrontations within the kingdom of God. They were tested honestly in the light of all that we witnessed personally and proven through the power of God's love by the results. Great joy and doubts were intertwined ahead for the System and for us as we placed our hopes more in the promises of Jesus. Book two will answer more questions that come up for each one within the System, as they fought to survive their circumstances and trust in Jesus... beginning with Liz:

LIZ

How does the Lord tame his wild mustangs? What happens one night at the microbrewery to drastically change an attitude? What happens when she decides to confront evil attacking Mariann? Will she find fulfillment as God's prophet in any church? How does her baptism affect others in the System still resisting the power of Jesus to redeem the lost who witness it...and more specifically Ann who chose to believe it wouldn't happen.

ANN

Will her long search for scientific understanding of spiritual truths be temporarily overwhelmed or challenged to fight harder to know truth as she defines it? What is the probability that she will find contentment? A meeting at The Little River Trading Post holds the answer to this question in Book three. I still marvel over the conversation we have in just a few months about space-time continuums and astrophysics… topics that I have no knowledge of until the Lord intervenes to challenge her pride of knowledge. Then there's the issue of physical pain that Ann has never experienced. Will she find a father's and family approval, acceptance and love?

MARIANN

Who will come as her guardian angel to go before her in spiritual battles too large for her to comprehend the dangers…yet charge forward with her Dragonslayer? How will a homeless musician affect her life in a worship service in my church? As she continues to grow stronger in Dragonslayer and mature in age, is it because of the encounters in life in the outside world? Can she learn the difference between pretend and real after Disneyland? Will Halloween always frighten the children? What are the hard truths she will learn about loyalty, obedience, trust, pain and love? Will she ever be able to worship Dragonslayer in this world?

MARIA AND LOUISE

Will positive changes occur in her family relationships? Will the changes for them both cause them joy or ongoing heartaches? Will Maria suffer more physical challenges to trusting than spiritual challenges outside? What will they learn about loyalty, trust, obedience and love between competing Christian friends? Can Maria and Mariann find a church home where they fit? What are the secrets still waiting to be revealed about the relationships inside with adult and child? How does Maria handle 'spiritual gifts'?

RUTH

Will she continue to be curious about issues beyond her Biblical understanding and pay a heavy cost? When faced with her most difficult decision will she choose others over her understanding of what Christian friends believe it should be? Will her addiction to coffee and shopping make life difficult to balance for her?

RAQUEL (QUIET WALKER)

Will she continue to write and encourage others to trust the Great Spirit or will she retreat to Sacred Mountain to recover her trust in friends? What is her connection to the Lost River Trading Post? When her 'prophecies' start coming true how do people treat her? Does the shaman bring healing or confrontation in the next encounter with cancer again versus white man's medicine?

CIRCLE COUNCIL

What changes are in store for them as inner healing changes roles? What leadership by example is required from them in the midst of the trials and tribulations to come? Will the number on Circle Council change and will a woman join the council? Who becomes the Leader of Council? How will their identities and perceived purposes as men be tested by those remaining when the issues affect only the female parts?

TABITHA, HOPI, LILA and OTHERS IN THE SYSTEM:

Will Tabitha ever have other "ninos" to play with in the outside world? Will she choose love to guide her when Bruce has to leave and the loss is overwhelming? What changes are in store for Hopi as he grows into a young man? What lesson does he learn that causes him to say, "A man has to do what a man has to do"? What happens to Egar/Joy on Halloween? What brings Lilah to the surface seeking help? How do other parts affect the inside for the System as a whole trying to adapt to harsh changes?

All of the people of the System and many outside who know them will be challenged over the next few years in their concepts of God and the Kingdom of God inside being disrupted by outside actions on their behalf. He will challenge us on a regular basis with His truth lived out His way for our lives. Some of these will start to be shared in Book Two, like the time He changes the weather to accomplish His will to have His children baptized in the place and time chosen; or the time an evil entity will come in as the 'son of Yemaya' and claiming to be the 'true Jesus' to challenge their faith and be tested by it. Most of the stories of Jesus loving, healing, disciplining, laughing, crying, protecting, leading in battle and changing our lives will have to wait until He tells me it is time to continue the stories. For now, before I finish this revision and my account on how these books received their purpose, I have chosen to share a few insights about topics covered in Book One learned over the following years after it was published in 2003. However, the enormity of these lessons in experiences within the Kingdom will have to wait until **Book Three** of the **Shattered People Series.** This book: ***Living in the Kingdom of God*** comes out 11/2020.

There are three main issues that are presented in this book and the ones that follow in this series and in the new series *Loved Back to Life* coming out in 6/2020 support and challenge most concepts, interactions and experiences we have in seeking to know our Christian God and why He loves us. These 3 are faith, hope and love that are explained in the Scriptures but understood only when tested in life's struggles within this world and the Kingdom of God simultaneously. These are the 'keys to the kingdom' that give us the tools to open our spiritual eyes and ears to live in its greater reality as Jesus said.

When free will choice is taken away by others and anyone is forced into believing that God's love has failed us, where does that leave anyone to discover the veracity of God's promises in Scripture or in the presence of Jesus Christ with us each day.

> *'Jesus said to Thomas, "Because you have seen me,*
> *you have believed; blessed are those who have not*
> *seen and yet have believed."* **John 20:29**

Most of us like Ann, prefer to believe in something or someone that can be proven scientifically by touch, sight and hearing as actually existing in time and space, especially physically so that 'faith' is easier to have. We hope that "mankind is basically good' because we can interact with them on this level so that our troubles could end someday as we help each other, yet history continues to prove this is not true. If one has only known pain and suffering from life and 'good love' hurts is the reality... to whom do they turn for hope? The most difficult of these questions challenging us all to have faith is, "How can we know that God exist if all we have is testimony of others, or icons and pictures of Jesus made long ago?"

These books are not meant to answer this question, but to hear the testimonies of those alive today who suffered without hope until love came to them and touched them with healing and hope... before they could then see. This is complicated by God's first action in loving us first unilaterally, before we could ask or know why He does and specifically for many, "Why He continues to?" This is the question that continues for me even after almost 50 years of serving Jesus Christ, "Why do you love me so much?"

Since 1975 I've been seeking this answer to why the truth of His love would apply to me, fully aware of my unworthiness to receive His love when I started. When I accepted Jesus as my Savior it was a decision made logically and rationally that God would have to heal our broken relationship, realizing after searching through the history of philosophies and religions, being something that I clearly could not do for myself. It was a simple choice to make after reading Pascal's wager (pg. 252) concerning the existence of God. The challenges came a few years later when my life started falling apart for reasons and actions beyond my control. This was when my gift of faith was tested to determine what I truly believed about who was Lord of my life... me or Jesus Christ.

I discovered in 1980 that I hadn't really given Jesus 'all' that I am. It was this time that I asked for any and all spiritual gifts needed to participate in my own healing, not realizing fully what I was asking for selfishly. My training in the reality of God's love and His kingdom's existence had begun with receiving the gifts of discernment of spirits and prophecy. I learned quickly why Spiritual Gifts are given for the good of all and not the individual looking to heal himself. These gifts opened the doors to recognizing the reality of spiritual warfare occurring around all of us that can affect our choices of faith in God.

Prophecy declares the truth of God's existence and His will for us to receive His love. Discernment of spirits provides us with true knowledge to choose to accept which spiritual reality I will trust with my love and hope for each day to find eternity waiting. So I will end Book One here with why I write the truth of what I have learned from Jesus.

As I close this saga of book one there is one important thing that Elizabeth Ray did not mention in her letter about the surgery and the recovery to follow in the chemotherapy. Something else happened the night Hopi was 'born again'. In the early morning hours, with Louise and Mariann taking turns switching inside to observe the ceremony occurring with Jesus, we talked about all that Jesus had done to bring them to that night.

Mariann began to ask me if I was going to tell the 'sad ones' about Dragonslayer. I asked who she was talking about and she said, *"All them that don't know Him, they be afraid like the boy."*

I told her the only way I could do that would be to write and tell them about all that had happened, but there are good reasons not to do that. She responded, *"What they be daddy?"*

"Well, first of all Sweetie I would have to get permission from Circle Council and I don't think many of the parts would let that happen. Secondly, I am not really a writer...I don't have the skills or gifts to do a job worthy of Dragonslayer. And thirdly, I am quite sure most people wouldn't believe it anyway."

"But daddy, what if Dragonslayer tell you to?"

"Then I would tell Him I think that maybe He is asking the wrong person and someone else could do it better... in fact I have references if He wants them."

"Dragonslayer say, (She giggles and says, 'He be daddy Dragonslayer...he no be Moses.') D*addy, Dragonslayer say you sound like Moses."*

"Does Dragonslayer want me to do this?"

"He say, what your heart want to do?"

"My heart says I want to obey my Lord... but will it help anyone?"

"Daddy...Dragonslayer ask how many make it worth it?"

As I was considering my reply, Mariann started getting a little anxious and said,

"Daddy...the smelly ones be back and they be mad about what you and Dragonslayer say...I be Dragonslayer strong..." and with that she switched inside and Louise came out.

I found out later that Mariann went 'on duty' marching around Preservation. Louise began to ask more questions but in a very calm strong voice not her own as she had spoken earlier in the evening. Upon later reflection I realized it was the Holy Spirit speaking through her. There would be many times over the next several years when I would hear that voice speaking through different surface parts who were on the outside, and each time the part out would have no recollection of what was said in the Spirit. It would touch the hearts of many who heard what was said. As my hearing from the Lord improves over the years so does my obedience. 'Louise' asked,

"This will be a very hard task with much pain and suffering. Will it be worth it if only one person believes?"

After what seemed like a very long silence I answered her. "YES, IF ONLY ONE BELIEVES IT WILL BE WORTH IT."

Louise would speak again, but this time when she spoke…

"You must bring My truth to all who will listen. You will be hated because of Me. Men will revile you and curse you for telling My truth, but do not be afraid…for I am with you. I will teach you lessons and you will teach My sheep. As I have loved you, so love My sheep…even the least of them.

As you declare Me before men, so shall I declare you before My Father. As you are persecuted, know that the Prophets before you were persecuted on account of Me. Raise up My son and follow Me…for our journey has begun."
- JESUS

"For I know the plans I have for you,' declares the Lord, 'plans for welfare and not for calamity to give you a future and a hope. Then you will call upon Me and come and pray to Me, and I will listen to you. And you will seek Me and find Me, when you search for Me with all of your heart. And I will be found by you,' declares the Lord."
Jeremiah 29: 11-14

…And the Journey Continues!

Michael E. Chalberg is pastor and cofounder of Shepherd's Care Ministries home-based in Gilbert, Arizona. He offers 3 primary areas of ministry; Pastoral Counseling & Mentoring over the Internet and privately; Christian Renewal as an Intentional-Interim Pastor & Consultant; and building Community Outreaches in and out of the church. He has worked as an interim minister for 23 years offering renewal and healing to troubled communities of faith, using conflict resolution, leadership training, restoration of Biblical Disciplines, instruction in spiritual warfare & deliverance ministry, and establishing prayer teams as the foundation for all ministries to support a laity-empowered church to minister to the broken-hearted of the world. He has been in ministry for 44 years.

The past 26 years he has specialized in pastoral counseling to survivors of ritual abuse; Clergy Abuse; sexual abuse; Satanic Ritual Abuse; Human Trafficking of Minors; incest; pornography; Domestic Violence; Post Traumatic Stress Disorder; Dissociative Identity Disorder (a.k.a. MPD) and other trauma induced issues in adults and children. Some clients within the Oakland Diocese gave permission to publish their spiritual journeys of healing with him in his first published series entitled, **"Shattered People Series: Journeys to: Joy (2003) Love (2005)** with both revised and updated with E-Books in December 2020. Their stories include his commentary as counselor, pastor, friend and fellow traveler. This ministry includes **SCPublishing** to provide educational/self-help information to survivors and their caregivers. Now 17 years later, **SCP** is adding another series **Loved Back to Life** in **May 2020** with autobiographical books from authors telling their stories of surviving severe abuse and trauma with Jesus' love & power to heal and redeem... true stories revealed to Pastor Mike since **2003.**

He began the free counseling ministry in 1989 to include an Internet based chatroom reaching an international audience in need of counseling for ritual abuse and trauma. Here both survivors of abuse and their caregivers can come together for the *soul* purpose of learning about God's methods of healing in the midst of spiritual warfare, alongside the **SCM** staff and fellow survivors on their healing journeys. He provides a 'virtual' church office atmosphere for topics discussed including personal histories and experiences in the healing process, spiritual warfare, deliverance ministry and the development of spiritual gifts for survival. Private counseling is given as well via emails, chat rooms, phone and video conferencing.

He moved his ministries to Arizona in **2010** to create **Starbright Foundation Inc.** with partners in ministry to focus on children/minors caught up in human sex trafficking by providing free support for rescues, protection, counseling and education to heal the traumas they have endured. **SFI** expanded to include training of law enforcement, first responders, school systems, childcare workers, foster parents, churches, families and social groups... anyone who will listen about how to get involved in intervention and prevention of this criminal industry.

He and his wife, Carol **(SCM** cofounder), are graduates of Fuller Theological Seminary. He has a Master of Divinity in Pastoral Care and Counseling and Carol has a Master of Arts in Theology. He is a member of the Association of Traumatic Stress Specialists (ATSS), American Association Christian Counselors (ACSS), International Critical Incident Stress Foundation Inc. (ICISF), Christian Association for Psychological Studies (CAPS) and Titus Task Force International (TTFI - retired).

Intro from the Publisher:

Contact: pastormike@shepherdscareministries.org

We have two primary audiences that I want to help heal: 1. whole communities of families broken by severe abuse of varying types - including clergy abuse & SRA, which can assault a community for generations, especially the individual survivors as all are in need of healing in their relationship with God. 2. The professionals who treat them: counselors, pastors, priests, psychologists, laity and family members who offer care and assistance in their recovery to receive direct assistance. My goal is to help clergy, laity and Christian professionals learn how to enter the arena of deep spiritual warfare existing around anyone afflicted by ritual abuse... particularly SRA and how to do so without fear of entering these spiritual arenas many believe they are not 'gifted' to enter.

We write about the truth of people's relationship to God, how it is broken by abuse and the healing process needed to rebuild that relationship. As God reveals His methods of healing using human relationships... traditional and historical concepts of God are challenged. People can learn how living with Jesus each day in God's Kingdom now with unconditional love in broken relationships will rarely leave them in a comfortable 'Christian' environment without daily challenges to faith and truth. How evil intervenes in our lives to disrupt our relationship with God is also clearly presented in practical examples of its subtle ways of keeping Christians unaware of the spiritual battles raging around us and in us inside the 'church'...Body of Christ. We are available for speaking and teaching on the subjects covered in these books to survivor groups, churches and schools.

One of the briefest and most authentic definitions for MPD comes from Bob Larson of <u>Bob Larson Ministries</u>:

"MPD is a mental condition in which the personality becomes fragmented (dissociated) into two or more distinct identities, each of which may become dominant and control behavior from time to time to the exclusions of others. These identities are called "alter personalities" (often simply called alters) and each maintains its own integrity of characteristics and habits. Each has its own age, name, sex, intelligence and personal tastes.

People suffering from MPD usually endured devastating traumas in childhood, such as incest, abuse and ritual torture. Their minds were shattered by feelings of guilt, shame and terror. These emotions, along with the need to survive in the presence of dangerous circumstances, caused them to subconsciously divide their minds into alters to keep their condition hidden and to protect themselves from further harm. Certain information, memories and feelings were encapsulated in specific personalities.

MPD usually begins in childhood, because, unlike adults, children can't run from abuse. The only place they can hide is inside their heads. As the victim grows older, the separate personalities become even more autonomous and each has its own specific way of functioning in the everyday world. The various alters of a multiple system cope internally like pieces of a pie. Each piece has a limited amount of coping power. When the limit is reached, the switch to a different alter may occur. In this way, many alters that are part of a system absorb the emotional anguish and physical pain within the trauma. From time to time one particular alter identity may be 'out.' When this happens, the host body and core personality of the victim's original identity may lose track of time and events.

Many victims of MPD emerge from families that were involved in some sort of the occult. Perhaps the most traumatized of MPDs are victims of Satanic Ritual Abuse (SRA). An estimated 25 to 60% of multiples have been subjected to ritual torture, sodomy and mutilation. Conservative projections of ritual survivors have reached 100,000 in the United States alone. Satanic cult programmers may purposely create alters in these subjects through the use of triggers, words or symbols, which evoke a previously implanted response. Some victims are subjected to advanced programming and are told they will die on a certain date. Some are subjected to mock communion, have alters whose role is to mutilate the body or engage in systematic torture, while some are programmed to attend ceremonies to maintain loyalty.

The treatment of MPD requires a comprehensive approach combining psychological therapy and spiritual intervention. Alter personalities must be integrated and evil spirits may need to be expelled. A demon is an externalized evil entity, seeking entry to promote the person's spiritual destruction. An alter is an internalized identity that facilitates the person's survival. Since the treatments for these two conditions are exactly opposite of each other (integration vs. exorcism), the therapist must make an accurate diagnosis to prevent further suffering in the afflicted person. The therapeutic aspects of integrating MPDs include encountering good and evil alters, dealing with animal alters, foreign languages, false memories and self-abuse. Complete integration may take years."

Excerpt: *Journeys to Joy* published 2003 by Michael Chalberg ISBN 0974646407

Bob Larson's definition is consistent with most textbooks and teaching on the subject that is provided by the caring professionals who recognize MPD as a valid diagnosis in 2003. Prior to my involvement with the subjects of these books over the last twenty six years this was my understanding and focus as well. **I now know that treating MPD as a mental/spiritual condition with the sole purpose of complete integration or blending is a mistake.**

www.ingramcontent.com/pod-product-compliance
Lightning Source LLC
Chambersburg PA
CBHW020904100426
42737CB00043B/123